A Guide to Federal Taxation

The West Legal Studies Series

Your options keep growing with West Legal Studies

Each year our list continues to offer you more options for every area of the law to meet your course or on-the-job reference requirements. We now have over 140 titles from which to choose in the following areas:

Accounting and Financials for the Law Office	Family Law
Administrative Law	Intellectual Property
Alternative Dispute Resolution	Interviewing and Investigation
Bankruptcy	Introduction to Law
Business Organizations/Corporations	Introduction to Paralegalism
Careers and Employment	Law Office Management
Civil Litigation and Procedure	Law Office Procedures
CLA Exam Preparation	Legal Nurse Consulting
Computer Applications in the Law Office	Legal Research, Writing, and Analysis
Contract Law	Legal Terminology
Court Reporting	Paralegal Internships
Criminal Law and Procedure	Product Liability
Document Preparation	Real Estate Law
Elder Law	Reference Materials
Employment Law	Social Security
Environmental Law	Sports Law
Ethics	Torts and Personal Injury Law
Evidence Law	Wills, Trusts, and Estate Administration

You will find unparalleled, practical support

Each book is augmented by instructor and student supplements to ensure the best learning experience possible. We also offer custom publishing and other benefits such as West's Student Achievement Award. In addition, our sales representatives are ready to provide you with dependable service.

We want to hear from you

Our best contributions for improving the quality of our books and instructional materials is feedback from the people who use them. If you have a question, concern, or observation about any of our materials, or you have a product proposal or manuscript, we want to hear from you. Please contact your local representative or write us at the following address:

West Legal Studies, 5 Maxwell Drive, Clifton Park, NY 12065-2919

For additional information point your browser at
www.westlegalstudies.com

A Guide to Federal Taxation

Jeffrey A. Helewitz

THOMSON
DELMAR LEARNING

Australia Canada Mexico Singapore Spain United Kingdom United States

WEST LEGAL STUDIES

A Guide to Federal Taxation
Jeffrey A. Helewitz

Vice President, Career Education Strategic Business Unit:
Dawn Gerrain

Editorial Director:
Sherry Gomoll

Senior Developmental Editor:
Melissa Riveglia

Editorial Assistant:
Brian E. Banks

Production Director:
Wendy A. Troeger

Production Manager:
Carolyn Miller

Production Editor:
Matthew J. Williams

Marketing Director:
Wendy E. Mapstone

Cover Design:
Dutton & Sherman Design

COPYRIGHT © 2005 Thomson Delmar Learning, a part of The Thomson Corporation. Thomson, the Star Logo, and Delmar Learning are trademarks used herein under license.

Printed in Canada
1 2 3 4 5 XXX 08 07 06 05 04

For more information contact Delmar Learning,
5 Maxwell Drive, Clifton Park, NY 12065

Or find us on the World Wide Web at
www.thomsonlearning.com or
www.westlegalstudies.com

ALL RIGHTS RESERVED. No part of this work covered by the copyright hereon may be reproduced or used in any form or by any means—graphic, electronic, or mechanical, including photocopying, recording, taping, Web distribution or information storage and retrieval systems—without the written permission of the publisher.

For permission to use material from this text or product,
contact us by
Tel (800) 730-2214
Fax (800) 730-2215
www.thomsonrights.com

ISBN 1-4018-1039-X

NOTICE TO THE READER

Publisher does not warrant or guarantee any of the products described herein or perform any independent analysis in connection with any of the product information contained herein. Publisher does not assume, and expressly disclaims, any obligation to obtain and include information other than that provided to it by the manufacturer.

The reader is expressly warned to consider and adopt all safety precautions that might be indicated by the activities herein and to avoid all potential hazards. By following the instructions contained herein, the reader willingly assumes all risks in connection with such instructions.

The Publisher makes no representation or warranties of any kind, including but not limited to, the warranties of fitness for particular purpose or merchantability, nor are any such representations implied with respect to the material set forth herein, and the publisher takes no responsibility with respect to such material. The publisher shall not be liable for any special, consequential, or exemplary damages resulting, in whole or part, from the readers' use of, or reliance upon, this material.

CONTENTS

Preface   xi

Chapter 1   1

Sources of Tax Law   1

Introduction   1
Genesis of Tax Law   2
Sources of the Law and Tax Research   6
   Statutes   6
   Administrative Action   8
   Judicial Decisions   17
General Proceedings   20
Ethical Concerns   27

Chapter 2   30

Individual Income Taxation   30

Introduction   30
Sources of Income   38
   Wages and Salaries   41
   Interest and Dividends   45
   Rental Income   49
   Retirement Plans   50
   Other Income   52
   Income Not Subject to Federal Income Taxation   53
Allocation of Income   54
Gains and Losses   56
Adjustments to Income (Schedules A&B)   66
   Medical and Dental Expenses   67
   Taxes   67
   Interest   70
   Charitable Gifts   73
   Casualty and Theft Losses   73
   Job and Miscellaneous Expenses   74
   Moving Expenses   75
Credits   75
Ethical Concerns   93

CHAPTER 3 96

Income Taxation of the Sole Proprietorship 96

Introduction 96
Income 99
Expenses 109
   Advertising 112
   Bad Debts 112
   Car Expenses 114
   Commissions and Fees 114
   Depletion 114
   Depreciation 115
   Employee Benefit Programs 116
   Insurance 117
   Interest 117
   Legal and Professional Services 117
   Office Expenses 117
   Pension and Profit Sharing Plans 117
   Rent 117
   Repairs and Maintenance 122
   Supplies 126
   Taxes and Licenses 126
   Travel, Meals, and Entertainment 126
   Utilities 127
   Wages 127
   Other Expenses 142
Ethical Concerns 148

CHAPTER 4 150

Income Taxation of Partnerships 150

Introduction 150
Form 1065 164
Tax Accounting for Partnerships 169
   Exclusion from Partnership Accounting Rules 169
   Accounting Principles 170
Partnership Income or Loss 174
Partnership Distributions 178
   Allocation of Distributions 181
Termination of a Partnership 186
Ethical Concerns 186

CHAPTER 5   189

Income Taxation of Corporations   189

Introduction   189
The Balance Sheet and Income Statement   201
Dividends   208
Reorganizations   214
   "A" Reorganizations   216
   "B" Reorganizations   217
   "C" Reorganizations   217
   "D" Reorganizations   218
   "E" Reorganizations   219
   "F" Reorganizations   219
Form 1120   219
   Income   223
   Deductions   225
   Taxes and Payments   228
   Form 1120 Schedules   229
Subchapter S Corporations   236
Form 1120S   248
Ethical Concerns   250

CHAPTER 6   253

Estate and Gift Taxation   253

Introduction   253
Form 706: United States Estate and Generation-Skipping Transfer
   Tax Return   300
Assets   302
   Schedule A—Real Estate   302
   Schedule B—Stocks and Bonds   303
   Schedule C—Mortgages, Notes, and Cash   304
   Schedule D—Insurance on the Decedent's Life   305
   Schedule E—Jointly Owned Property   306
   Schedule F—Other Miscellaneous Property   307
   Schedule G—Transfers During Decedent's Life   308
   Schedule H—Powers of Appointment   309
   Schedule I—Annuities   310
Deductions   310
   Schedule J—Funeral and Administrative Expenses   311
   Schedule K—Debts of the Decedent   312
   Schedule L—Net Losses During Administration   312
   Schedule M—Bequests to Surviving Spouse   313
   Schedule N—Qualified ESOP Sales   313

Schedule O—Charitable, Public, and Similar Gifts and Bequests   314
Schedule T—Qualified Family Owned Business Interest Deduction   314
Schedule U—Qualified Conservation Easement Exclusion   315
Credits   315
Schedule P—Credit for Foreign Death taxes   315
Schedule Q—Credit for Tax on Prior Transfers   316
Schedule R—Generation-Skipping Transfer Tax   317
Schedule S—Increased Estate Tax Due to Excess Retirement Accumulations   318
Ethical Concerns   319

CHAPTER 7   322

Fiduciary Income Taxes   322

Introduction   322
Form 1041: Part I, Estate's Share of Alternative Minimum Taxable Income   331
General   331
Income   331
Deductions   341
Taxes and Payments   344
Schedules   344
Form 1041: Part II, Income Distribution Deduction on a Minimum Tax Basis   349
Form 1041: Part III, Alternative Minimum Tax   349
Form 1041: Part IV   350
Ethical Concerns   351

APPENDIX A   353

Tax-Related Web Sites   353

GLOSSARY   355

EXHIBITS

1–1	Form 872	22
1–2	Form 1040X	24
2–1	Form 1040	31
2–2	Form 1040EZ	38
2–3	Schedules A & B (Form 1040)	68
2–4	Form 1098	71
2–5	Schedule R (Form 1040)	82
2–6	Form 8812	84
2–7	Form 8863	90
3–1	Schedule C (Form 1040)	97
3–2	Form 8829	118
4–1	Schedule K-1 (Form 1065-B)	156
4–2	Form 1065	160
5–1	Form 1120	193
5–2	Form 1120S	197
5–3	Form 1120-A	218
6–1	Form 706	254
7–1	Form 1041	323

PREFACE

All persons involved in law or business are acutely aware of the necessity of having a decent working knowledge of federal income taxation. For the most part, however, the persons who generally have such knowledge are accountants and tax professionals who have specifically studied tax law and accounting. The legal professional is at a disadvantage in most areas of practice without some background in taxation. *A Guide to Federal Taxation* bridges the gap between law and taxation to provide the legal professional with the knowledge and skills necessary to represent clients effectively in all areas of practice.

The purpose of *A Guide to Federal Taxation* is to assist the small firm practitioner, legal assistant, and owner of a small business in understanding the federal income tax implications of working and operating a business. An understanding of federal income tax policy is important to protect and further the interests of the client in every aspect of law. Federal taxation forms an integral part of family law, estate and trust administration, small business and corporate law, general litigation, and personal injury. Despite the importance of the tax implications of almost every decision that has legal implications, few legal practitioners have an educational background in tax law. Without a basic understanding of federal taxation, the legal professional will be at a disadvantage, not only in representing clients but also in managing the law office itself.

A Guide to Federal Taxation was developed to integrate law and tax policy, thereby providing the legal professional with a basic theoretical understanding of federal taxation in the major areas that would arise in most small firm practices. To achieve this goal, *A Guide to Federal Taxation* not only provides the reader with a basic understanding of tax law and research, and the workings of the Internal Revenue Service, but also goes line by line through all of the federal tax forms that a law office will encounter in its daily practice. There is no other textbook available that meets this specific need. Current textbooks are either designed specifically for accountants or for specialized areas of tax law. *A Guide to Federal Taxation* is designed exclusively for the law student, legal assistant, and practicing legal professional to provide a complete yet simple to comprehend guide to the world of federal taxation. The textbook is a complement to legal texts on business, estate planning, and litigation, yet can stand on its own as a primer or primary textbook in a course designed to provide a basic overview of federal tax policies.

Organization of A Guide to Federal Taxation

The textbook is divided into seven chapters and is structured in a manner comparable with any school-established method of course instruction. Most importantly, the textbook is written in a manner that is comprehensible to law, paralegal, and undergraduate students; its goal is to demystify taxation for nontax professionals.

Each of the seven chapters is constructed in a similar format. Every chapter begins with an introduction that outlines the basic principles that will be covered in the body of the chapter. The chapters are arranged to take the student from basic tax law and policy, including the elements of tax law research, through individual taxation, the taxation of all the various business formats, and concluding with the taxation of trusts and estates. Each chapter provides numerous examples and practical tips to assist the legal professional in garnering a complete understanding of the tax principles involved. Every chapter includes, as exhibits, the federal tax forms that correspond to the area under examination, and the text follows the form to assist the student in understanding how the principles discussed are actually applied. The chapters conclude with a discussion on ethical concerns and a review to cement the material in the minds of the students.

Unlike most textbooks that merely provide lists of the terms used in the chapters, *A Guide to Federal Taxation* provides key terms and their definitions at the end of each chapter. The terms are redefined throughout the text to reinforce chapter terminology in the mind of the student. Each chapter also provides summaries of judicial decisions that are germane to the text material and highlight the importance of tax planning and policy in a legal practice. Exercise problems are sprinkled throughout each chapter to provide a direct hands-on approach to tax law.

Supplemental Learning Tools

An **Instructor's Manual** is available on-line at <http://www.westlegalstudies.com> in the Instructor's Corner. Written by the author of the textbook, the Instructor's Manual includes learning objectives, lecture notes, sample exams and answers, and supplemental judicial decisions.

Students, professionals, and instructors are invited to visit the **Online Companion** to *A Guide to Federal Taxation* at <http://www. westlegalstudies.com>. The Online Companion includes application exercises, Internet exercises, study tips, chapter notes, a quick review for each chapter, and the complete text of Circular 230, a document of regulations governing practice before the IRS.

Acknowledgments

The author and publisher would like to thank the following reviewers for their feedback and suggestions for improvement at each manuscript stage:

Sandra Augustine
Hilbert College

Meerabelle Dey
Private Practitioner

Dr. Robert N. Diotalevi
Florida Gulf Coast University

Brian Halsey
Peirce College

Cathy Neal
University of Cincinnati, Clermont College

Judith Streich
Minnesota State University Moorhead

Anne Stevens
Cuyahoga Community College

Linda Wimberly
Eastern Kentucky University

About the Author

Jeffrey A. Helewitz received his J.D. and LL.M. in International Business and Trade from Georgetown University Law Center and an M.B.A. in Finance from New York University. He has worked for the National Office of the Internal Revenue Service and was in private practice for several years. Currently, Mr. Helewitz is a Court Attorney for a Civil Court Judge in New York.

Mr. Helewitz is the author of 20 textbooks designed for paralegals and lawyers, as well as numerous articles. He has taught law at both C.U.N.Y. School of Law and Touro College Law Center, and is an active C.L.E. lecturer.

CHAPTER 1

Sources of Tax Law

Introduction

Regardless of the nature of the law practice, all legal professionals must be aware of the federal tax implications of the problems they encounter. There is no single area of law that does not have a direct or indirect tax consequence for the parties. For this reason, if for no other, the legal professional must become familiar with federal tax policy.

This textbook is designed as an overview of basic federal tax law for the paralegal and undergraduate student that can be used later on as a desk reference companion for the working legal professional. It is beyond the scope and purpose of this book to provide a detailed legal analysis of all fields of tax policy; however, this text will address major federal tax problems in a practical and focused manner. Throughout the textbook are references to the corresponding federal tax form that must be prepared and filed when dealing with a particular area of tax law. This allows the student to see how tax policy directly applies to the general legal problem being addressed.

One important caveat: The legal professional, unless otherwise qualified, is neither an accountant nor a tax preparer. The legal professional advises and determines whether certain transactions are reported as income, deductions from income, credits against taxes, or are nontaxable events. Legal tax practice involves application of tax principles to past events as well as planning to avoid negative tax consequences in future transactions. The actual mathematical computations are much better and more appropriately left to the financial professional unless the legal professional is qualified in that area by education or experience.

This textbook is divided into seven chapters, each dealing with a specific area of tax law. For the student or legal professional, these chapters will provide a general discussion of tax problems and relate those tax consequences to the appropriate federal tax return. Selected reference materials assist the professional in finding detailed information. Because tax implications are so pervasive, all persons involved with the law must be alert to potential negative or favorable tax consequences.

Genesis of Tax Law

The government's ability and power to tax is derived from various sections of the U.S. Constitution. Article 1, Section 8, Clause 1 confers on Congress the "power to lay and collect taxes, duties, imposts and excise. . . ." Section 2, Clause 3 and Section 4 of Article 1 mandates that "direct taxes be apportioned among the states," and Section 8, Clause 1 states that "all debts, imposts and excise shall be uniform throughout the United States." As early as 1866, the U.S. Supreme Court found that Congressional power to tax is extensive, and only limited by the Constitution so that direct taxes must be apportioned and indirect taxes must be uniform (*License Tax Case*, 72 U.S. 452 1866).

A **direct tax** is one that is levied directly against the person who is obligated to pay it, such as income taxes. An **indirect tax** is one that is levied against a person who may pass that burden on to another, such as a tax imposed on imports that is paid by the importer but passed on to the eventual purchaser.

The principle of apportionment means that, when Congress attempts to raise a specific amount of money, for instance, to cover the cost of a war, Congress is obligated to divide that total sum among all of the states according to each state's number of citizens. These direct taxes are divided in such a fashion that the burden falls equally on all citizens as reported by the states.

direct tax
A tax that is levied directly against a person who is obligated to pay it

indirect tax
A tax that is levied against a person who may pass that burden on to another

Exercise

Is the concept of apportionment fair? Do you believe that all citizens should pay for items that they do not approve or that they do not use?

Exercise

Locate a Supreme Court case that discusses the difference between an excise and a direct tax. What is the difference, according to the Court?

Although tax laws have been challenged periodically, the courts have never found Congress to lack the power to tax. However, the courts have found particular taxes to be unconstitutional. The reason behind these decisions lies not in the inherent power of the Congress but in the given tax law under scrutiny that violates some other constitutional prohibition, such as the division between church and state.

Exercise

Using the library or the Internet, locate a decision of the U.S. Supreme Court that found a tax unconstitutional because it infringed on a person's rights under the Bill of Rights to the Constitution.

In 1913, Congress passed the Sixteenth Amendment to the Constitution which granted it the power to levy and collect taxes on income, from whatever source derived, without apportionment among the several states. Note that until the passage of the Sixteenth Amendment, Congress lacked a statutory basis for imposing taxes on income, despite the fact that it could impose other types of taxes.

The Sixteenth Amendment forms the basis of the modern income tax policy of the United States. The federal government taxes income "on whatever source derived," making individuals subject to a direct tax responsible for reporting and paying taxes on all of their income. It must be noted that other countries impose taxes on income from specifically designated sources, as do certain states (primarily with respect to income resulting from the operation of a business). This difference is mentioned for the purpose of tax planning; although the federal government will tax income regardless of its source, total tax liability (federal plus state and local) may be reduced by careful geographic placement of assets.

The first federal tax imposed by Congress was enacted into law in 1791, taxing distilled spirits and stills. Over the years, Congress enacted various tax statutes, and in 1939, in an effort to provide uniformity and consistency among these laws, the first codification of the tax laws was created by Congress as the **Internal Revenue Code (IRC) of 1939**. A **codification** is the placement of all laws pertaining

Internal Revenue Code (IRC) of 1939
First codification of the U.S. tax laws

codification
Placement of laws in a sequential and logical order

4 Chapter One

enactment
Legislative process to create a law

sponsor
Person who proposes a new law

bill
Proposed legislation

Government Printing Office (GPO)
Agency that prints bills

House Ways and Means Committee
Congressional committee that deals with tax legislation

Senate Finance Committee
Congressional committee that deals with tax legislation

to a given topic in a sequential and logical order rather than in chronological order of enactment. Prior to its enactment, Congress published the Report of the Joint Committee on Internal Revenue Taxation, "Codification of Internal Revenue Law," p. IX (1939), reprinted at 26 U.S.C.A. XIXX–XX, analyzing the history of federal taxation in the United States up to that point. This report may be invaluable in researching the history of federal tax policy. Subsequently, the IRC has been completely revised twice, first in 1954 and then in 1986. Although the various provisions of the code have been amended or revised since 1986, there has not been a major overhaul of the entire code since that time. Therefore, for the tax practitioner and student, the official statutory basis of current federal tax law is the Internal Revenue Code of 1986 as amended, and it should be referenced as such.

Exercise

Using the Internet, locate the Report of the Joint Committee on Internal Revenue Taxation.

Tax laws, as with all other federal legislation, comes about by means of a formalized legislative process referred to as **enactment:**

A. The starting point for the introduction of any new federal statute is to have a member of the House of Representatives or the Senate propose an item of tax legislation, thereby becoming the **sponsor** of the proposal. Pursuant to the provisions of the Constitution, all revenue bills are required to originate in the House; however, on a practical basis, typically the executive, by means of the Treasury Department, proposes tax legislation which the president then has formally introduced in the House as a bill sponsored by one of the representatives.

B. The proposal, called a **bill,** is printed by the **Government Printing Office (GPO)** in a format known as a slip, a document that contains only the provision of the bill and the name(s) of its sponsor(s). The slip is then forwarded to the legislative committee that has authority over the area of law covered by the bill. Tax bills are referred either to the **House Ways and Means Committee** or the **Senate Finance Committee.**

Exercise

Using the GPO Web site, obtain a copy of a slip.

C. Once the bill has been referred to the appropriate committee, the committee holds hearings on the matter. Typically, officials from the Treasury Department present their comments, as do interested members of the public. Transcripts of these hearings are published and eventually may be used by the courts and/or legal professionals to understand or interpret what Congress intended in the writing of the enacted law. It is not unusual for the wording of the bill to be influenced by the submissions attendant on these hearings. Often these written submissions form a part of the prospective regulations that provide official interpretations of the law. Treasury regulations are discussed later in this chapter.

D. The committee produces a report on the bill, which is then debated by the chamber of Congress that introduced the legislation. These committee reports become part of the legislative history of the bill, and may be used to determine the intent of the eventual legislation.

Exercise

Obtain a copy of a committee report on a proposed item of tax legislation. How does the report vary the wording of the original bill?

E. If the bill is approved, it is sent to the opposite chamber of Congress for consideration. If the House and Senate versions of the proposed legislation differ, the matter is submitted to a **conference committee** to resolve such differences. Once the conference committee makes its report, the bill is sent back to the respective chamber of Congress for further hearings and debates. This conference committee report may also be used to discern how Congress intended the legislation to be interpreted and applied.

F. If the restructured bill is eventually approved, it is sent to the president for signature. The president may either sign the bill, at which point it becomes law, or veto the bill, by which means the president indicates disapproval of the legislation. Should the president veto the bill, it may still become law if the House and Senate override the presidential veto by a two-thirds vote of its members.

G. When the bill becomes a law it is published as a **Public Law.** Public Laws are numbered chronologically, with the first number representing the legislative session and the second number indicating the number of the law enacted during that legislative session. Example: PL 99-33 indicates the thirty-third law passed by the ninety-ninth Congress.

Once passed and published, the bill becomes a tax law.

conference committee
Congressional committee that resolves differences between the House and Senate versions of a bill

Public Law
Bills that are enacted into law

6 Chapter One

Sources of the Law and Tax Research

As indicated in the preceding section, the basic source of all federal tax law is a federal statute; however, that is only the starting point for the practitioner. Tax laws, like all other federal laws, must meet constitutional mandates and are subject to judicial review. Further, the substantive area of law to which the tax law is addressed is also subject to judicial scrutiny. Because these laws are administered by a federal agency, the **Internal Revenue Service (IRS),** that agency's administrative actions also have a legal impact. Therefore, the tax law researcher should be alert to the three sources of federal tax law:

> **Internal Revenue Service (IRS)**
> Agency that oversees taxes

1. Statutes
2. Administrative action
3. Judicial decisions

Statutes

As discussed, the primary sources of federal tax laws are the statutes enacted by Congress. These laws are available to the public in published form in the following chronological order of dissemination:

> **slip law**
> Published by the GPO when a bill becomes a law

- **Slip laws.** These laws are published by the GPO in the same manner as a bill is first published, only now it is a law rather than a proposal for a law.

> ***United States Law Weekly***
> Weekly publication that publishes laws it deems significant

- ***United States Law Weekly.*** This weekly magazine, first published by the Bureau of National Affairs, prints the laws it deems "significant" that have been passed during the preceding week. (It also publishes summaries of recent cases it considers noteworthy.)

> ***United States Code Congressional and Administrative News* (USCCAN)**
> Monthly publication that includes texts of laws

Exercise

Locate *United States Law Weekly* on the Internet.

- ***United States Code Congressional and Administrative News* (USCCAN).** This monthly publication includes the texts of all laws passed during the preceding month as well as presidential proclamations and executive orders. In addition to the actual text, USCCAN includes selective legislative history of the law, a subject index so that new laws may be researched by subject matter, a popular name index, and a conversion table to the U.S. Code.

> ***United States Code Service* (USCS), *Advance Pamphlet***
> Monthly publication of laws that were passed with a conversion table

- ***United States Code Service* (USCS), *Advance Pamphlet.*** This monthly publication includes the texts of laws passed during that month plus summaries of proposed legislation and a conversion table to the U.S. Code. A **conversion table** indicates how the numbering of a law in one publication corresponds to the numbering in a different publication.

- *United States Statutes at Large.* This bound hardback volume includes all of the slip laws enacted during a congressional session in the chronological order of their enactment. *Statutes at Large* represents the official text of all bills passed into positive law and it includes a subject index that is cross-referenced to these laws.

- *United States Code* (USC). This codification lists all laws that have been passed by Congress according to subject matter rather than by chronological order of enactment. USC is an official publication that began publishing in 1926 and is revised every six years. In addition to containing the official text of a law, USC organizes all statutes into 50 titles by topic and provides a subject index, a popular name index, and a conversion table to Statutes at Large. To update the information affecting each statute, USC maintains a **pocket part,** a stapled update that appears in a pocket at the back of each volume prior to the update being printed in an annual cumulative volume. The Internal Revenue Code appears in title 26 of the U.S. Code.

- *United States Code Annotated* (USCA). This annotated version of the U.S. Code contains statutes that are numbered exactly as they are numbered in USC (i.e., the Internal Revenue Code is 26 U.S.C. and also 26 U.S.C.A.). In addition to the full text of the statute, USCA provides the following supplemental information.

    A. Legislative history, including the date of publication in *Statutes at Large*
    B. Historical notes that explain any legislative history
    C. Cross-references to other selected materials, such as law review articles, form books, and jury instructions
    D. **Westlaw** cross-references (Westlaw is West's computer-assisted legal research program.)
    E. **Code of Federal Regulations (CFR),** as will be discussed, lists any published agency material and indicates any agency action affecting the statute under scrutiny
    F. **Notes of Decisions,** which follows each section or group of sections of the statute, includes a number of topics covered by those section(s) of the statute, followed by

conversion table
Method of indicating how laws that appear in one publication can be found in another publication

United States Statutes at Large
Bound publication containing all slip laws enacted during a congressional session

United States Code **(USC)**
Codification of all U.S. laws

pocket part
Stapled update to legal publications

United States Code Annotated **(USCA)**
Annotated version of the U.S. Code

Westlaw
Computer-assisted legal research program

Code of Federal Regulations (CFR)
Official publication of government agency rules

Notes of Decisions
Section of USCA containing synopses of judicial decisions

8 Chapter One

synopses of judicial decisions that have interpreted or discussed that section of the statute in recent decisions

G. Pocket parts to update material

United States Code Service (USCS)
Annotated version of the USC

- **United States Code Service (USCS),** which is another annotated version of USC that provides similar annotations to USCA, geared to other lawyers' co-op publications.

Exercise

Locate section 61 of the Internal Revenue Code in both USCA and USCS. What difference do you find in the annotations?

For the tax law researcher, the first source of research is always the tax statute, because federal tax law is statutorily based. The researcher, however, must be alert to the fact that tax laws change periodically, and must check the law in effect at the time the transaction under scrutiny occurred—not necessarily the current law or the interpretation of current law—to resolve the problem. In almost no other area of law is attention to date quite as important.

Note that the previous sources are available on-line for the researcher.

Administrative Action

regulations (Regs)
Agency interpretation of tax laws

Federal tax laws are administered under the auspices of the secretary of the treasury. Pursuant to this statutory mandate, the secretary of the treasury, through the Internal Revenue Service, a subdivision of the Treasury Department, promulgates **regulations,** or **Regs,** that provide the public with the agency's interpretation of the statute. Regulations for newly enacted tax statutes are published within one year of the law's passage, and proposed regulations are published for comments and hearings before they are finalized. Once completed, the Regs are published in the Code of Federal Regulations, the source of all federal administrative regulations.

TAX LAW & POLICY

Title 26—Internal Revenue
CHAPTER I—INTERNAL REVENUE SERVICE, DEPARTMENT OF THE TREASURY
SUBCHAPTER A—INCOME TAX
PART 1—INCOME TAXES
NORMAL TAXES AND SURTAXES

TAX BASED ON INCOME FROM SOURCES WITHIN OR WITHOUT THE UNITED STATES
DETERMINATION OF SOURCES OF INCOME
26 CFR 1.861-1

§ 1.861-1 Income from sources within the United States.

(a) Categories of income. Part I (section 861 and following), subchapter N, chapter 1 of the Code, and the regulations thereunder determine the sources of income for purposes of the income tax. These sections explicitly allocate certain important sources of income to the United States or to areas outside the United States, as the case may be; and, with respect to the remaining income (particularly that derived partly from sources within and partly from sources without the United States), authorize the Secretary or his delegate to determine the income derived from sources within the United States, either by rules of separate allocation or by processes or formulas of general apportionment. The statute provides for the following three categories of income:

(1) Within the United States. The gross income from sources within the United States, consisting of the items of gross income specified in section 861(a) plus the items of gross income allocated or apportioned to such sources in accordance with section 863(a). See §§ 1.861-2 to 1.861-7, inclusive, and § 1.863-1. The taxable income from sources within the United States, in the case of such income, shall be determined by deducting therefrom, in accordance with sections 861(b) and 863(a), the expenses, losses, and other deductions properly apportioned or allocated thereto and a ratable part of any other expenses, losses, or deductions which cannot definitely be allocated to some item or class of gross income. See §§ 1.861-8 and 1.863-1.

(2) Without the United States. The gross income from sources without the United States, consisting of the items of gross income specified in section 862(a) plus the items of gross income allocated or apportioned to such sources in accordance with section 863(a). See §§ 1.862-1 and 1.863-1. The taxable income from sources without the United States, in the case of such income, shall be determined by deducting therefrom, in accordance with sections 862(b) and 863(a), the expenses, losses, and other deductions properly apportioned or allocated thereto and a ratable part of any other expenses, losses, or deductions which cannot definitely be allocated to some item or class of gross income. See §§ 1.862-1 and 1.863-1.

(3) Partly within and partly without the United States. The gross income derived from sources partly within and partly without the United States, consisting of the items specified in section 863(b) (1), (2), and (3). The taxable income allocated or apportioned to sources within the United States, in the case of such income, shall be determined in accordance with section 863 (a) or (b). See §§ 1.863-2 to 1.863-5, inclusive.

(4) Exceptions. An owner of certain aircraft or vessels first leased on or before December 28, 1980, may elect to treat income in respect of these aircraft or vessels as income from sources within the United States for purposes of sections 861(a) and 862(a). See § 1.861-9. An owner of certain aircraft, vessels, or spacecraft first leased after December 28, 1980, must treat income in respect of these craft as income from sources within the United States for purposes of sections 861(a) and 862(a). See § 1.861-9A.

———(b) **Taxable income from sources within the United States.** The taxable income from sources within the United States shall consist of the taxable income described in paragraph (a)(1) of this section plus the taxable income allocated or apportioned to such sources, as indicated in paragraph (a)(3) of this section.

———(c) **Computation of income.** If a taxpayer has gross income from sources within or without the United States, together with gross income derived partly from sources within and partly from sources without the United States, the amounts thereof, together with the expenses and investment applicable thereto, shall be segregated; and the taxable income from sources within the United States shall be separately computed therefrom.

Regulations interpret the statute and are generally promulgated prior to the statute actually being tested by application. However, once the statute's provisions are applied to a given transaction, IRS provides three other administrative interpretations of the tax law: revenue rulings, revenue procedures, and acquiescence.

revenue ruling (Rev. Rul.)
IRS decision on a particular tax question

Revenue rulings (Rev. Ruls.) are administrative decisions of the IRS based on actual factual application of the statute. Revenue rulings are written in the same manner as a judicial decision and are required to be published. Rev. Ruls. are initially published in the ***Internal Revenue Bulletin,*** a weekly publication of the IRS, and eventually are compiled into a publication called the ***Cumulative Bulletin*** **(C.B.)** several times each year. A revenue ruling has the force of case law against the IRS.

TAX LAW & POLICY

Rev. Rul. 2002-73
2002 IRB LEXIS 463; 2002-45 I.R.B. 805; REV. RUL. 2002-73
November 12, 2002

Rev. Rul. 2002-46, 2002-29 I.R.B. 117, holds that grace period contributions to a qualified cash or deferred arrangement within the meaning of § 401(k) of the Internal Revenue Code or to a defined contribution plan as matching contributions within the meaning of § 401(m) are not deductible by the employer for a taxable year if the contributions are attributable to compensation earned by plan participants after the end of that taxable year.

Rev. Rul. 2002-46 modifies Rev. Proc. 2002-9, 2002-3 I.R.B. 327 (as modified and amplified by Rev. Proc. 2002-19, 2002-13 I.R.B. 696, modified and clarified by Announcement 2002-17, 2002-8 I.R.B. 561, and amplified, clarified, and modified by Rev. Proc. 2002-54, 2002-35 I.R.B. 432) to add to the Appendix of Rev. Proc. 2002-9 a change in method of accounting to conform to the holding of Rev. Rul. 2002-46. Thus, taxpayers wishing to change to a method consistent with Rev. Rul. 2002-46 must apply for automatic approval under Rev. Proc. 2002-9. Rev. Rul. 2002-46 provides that the scope limitations in section 4.02 of Rev. Proc. 2002-9 do not apply to a change to a method consistent with Rev. Rul. 2002-46, unless the taxpayer's method of accounting is an issue under consideration for a taxable year under examination within the meaning of section 3.09(1) of Rev. Proc. 2002-9 when the Form 3115, Application to Change a Method of Accounting, is filed with the national office.

Upon further consideration, the Internal Revenue Service has determined that it is appropriate to waive the scope limitations of section 4.02 for this change only for a limited period of time. Accordingly, the APPLICATION section of Rev. Rul. 2002-46 is modified to read as follows:

APPLICATION

A change in a taxpayer's treatment of contributions to a method consistent with this revenue ruling is a change in method of accounting to which §§ 446 and 481 apply. A taxpayer that wants to change its treatment of contributions to a method consistent with this revenue ruling must follow the automatic change in method of accounting provisions in Rev. Proc. 2002-9, 2002-3 I.R.B. 327 (as modified and amplified by Rev. Proc. 2002-19, 2002-13 I.R.B. 696, modified and clarified by Announcement 2002-17, 2002-8 I.R.B. 561, and amplified, clarified, and modified by Rev. Proc. 2002-54, 2002-35 I.R.B. 432), with the following modifications:

(1) The scope limitations in section 4.02 of Rev. Proc. 2002-9 do not apply to a taxpayer that wants to make the change for its first taxable year ending on or after October 16, 2002, provided the taxpayer's method of accounting for contributions addressed in this revenue ruling is not an issue under consideration for taxable years under examination, within the meaning of section 3.09(1) of Rev. Proc. 2002-9, at the time the Form 3115 is filed with the national office;

(2) To assist the Service in processing changes in method of accounting under this revenue ruling, and to ensure proper handling, section 6.02(4)(a) of Rev. Proc. 2002-9 is modified to require that a Form 3115 filed under this revenue ruling include the statement: "Automatic Change Filed Under Rev. Rul. 2002-46." This statement should be legibly printed or typed on the appropriate line on any Form 3115 filed under this revenue ruling.

revenue procedure (Rev. Proc.)
IRS dictate of procedural requirements

Revenue procedures (Rev. Procs.) are guidelines concerned with the administrative procedures for taking a matter through the IRS, and are printed in the same manner as revenue rulings. The tax practitioner should always determine appropriate procedures by researching the regulations and the revenue procedures.

TAX LAW & POLICY

Rev. Proc. 2002-75
26 CFR 601.201: RULINGS AND DETERMINATION LETTERS.
2002 IRB LEXIS 553; 2002-52 I.R.B. 1; REV. PROC. 2002-75

SECTION 1. PURPOSE AND NATURE OF CHANGE

The purpose of this revenue procedure is to modify Rev. Proc. 2002-3, 2002-1 I.R.B. 117, by deleting sections 4.01(11) and 4.01(41). Sections 4.01(11) and 4.01(41) provide that the Internal Revenue Service will not ordinarily rule on the application of §§ 162 and 816 of the Internal Revenue Code to certain insurance arrangements.

SECTION 2. BACKGROUND

.01 Rev. Proc. 2002-3 sets forth those provisions of the Internal Revenue Code under the jurisdiction of the Associate Chief Counsel (Corporate), the Associate Chief Counsel (Financial Institutions & Products), the Associate Chief Counsel (Income Tax & Accounting), the Associate Chief Counsel (Passthroughs & Special Industries), the Associate Chief Counsel (Procedure and Administration), and Division Counsel/Associate Chief Counsel (Tax Exempt and Governmental Entities) relating to issues on which the Internal Revenue Service will not issue letter rulings or determination letters.

.02 Section 4 of Rev. Proc. 2002-3 sets forth those areas in which rulings or determination letters will not ordinarily be issued.

Section 4.01(11) provides as follows:

Section 162.—Trade or Business Expenses.—Whether the requisite risk shifting and risk distribution necessary to constitute insurance are present for purposes of determining the deductibility under § 162 of amounts paid (premiums) by a taxpayer for insurance.

Section 4.01 (41) provides as follows:

Section 816.—Life Insurance Company Defined.—Whether the requisite risk shifting and risk distribution necessary to constitute insurance are present for purposes of determining if a company is an "insurance company" under § 1.801-3(a) of the Income Tax Regulations, unless the facts of the transaction are within the scope of Rev. Rul. 78-338, 1978-2 C.B. 107, or Rev. Rul. 77-316, 1977-2 C.B. 53.

.03 The Service has provided guidance regarding whether, for federal income tax purposes, an arrangement constitutes insurance and whether an entity that provides insurance to an insured that has an ownership interest in that entity will be treated as an insurance company. Rev. Rul. 77-316 involved an insurance subsidiary that assumed only the risks of its owners and/or affiliates and concluded that to the extent the assumed risks were not transferred outside of the economic family, the transaction would not be treated as insurance. Under the economic family theory, the amounts paid as premiums to the subsidiary would not be insurance premiums deductible under § 162 and the subsidiary would not be an insurance company. In Rev. Rul. 78-338, the Service distinguished the economic family theory advanced in Rev. Rul. 77-316 and concluded that premiums paid to an insurer owned by its 31 insureds-shareholders were deductible under § 162.

.04 Rev. Rul. 2001-31, 2001-1 C.B. 1348, announced that the economic family theory would no longer be followed, Rev. Rul. 77-316 was obsoleted, and Rev. Rul. 78-338 was modified. Rev. Rul. 2001-31 also stated that certain captive transactions may be challenged based upon the facts and circumstances of each case.

.05 Since publication of Rev. Rul. 2001-31, the Service has provided additional guidance on the tax treatment of certain captive insurance arrangements. Rev. Rul. 2002-89, 2002-52 I.R.B., addressed arrangements between a parent corporation and its wholly-owned captive insurance subsidiary that conducted varying amounts of insurance business with unrelated parties. In Rev. Rul. 2002-90, 2002-52 I.R.B., the Service concluded that the premiums paid by 12 operating subsidiaries to a captive insurance subsidiary owned by a common parent are deductible under § 162. Finally, in Rev. Rul. 2002-91, 2002-52 I.R.B., the Service concluded that a group captive, which was formed by fewer than 31 unrelated insureds, with each insured having no more that 15% of the total risk, was an insurance company.

.06 Consistently with the case-by-case approach announced in Rev. Rul. 2001-31, and the guidance provided in Rev. Rul. 2002-89, Rev. Rul. 2002-90, and Rev. Rul. 2002-91, this Revenue Procedure deletes sections 4.01(11) and 4.01(41) of Rev. Proc. 2002-3. The Service will now consider ruling requests regarding the proper tax treatment of a captive insurance company. However, some questions arising in the context of a captive ruling request are so inherently factual (within the meaning of section 4.02(1) of Rev. Proc. 2002-3) that contact should be made with the appropriate Service function prior to the preparation of such request to determine whether the Service will issue the requested ruling. In addition, for information concerning the Large and Mid-Size Business Division Pre-Filing Agreement Program, see Rev. Proc. 2001-22, 2001-1 C.B. 745.

SECTION 3. PROCEDURE

Rev. Proc. 2002-3 is modified by deleting section 4.01(11) and section 4.01(41).

SECTION 4. INQUIRIES

Inquiries regarding whether the Service considers a proposed captive transaction so inherently factual that it cannot rule, should be directed to Chief,

14 Chapter One

Branch 4, Office of the Associate Chief Counsel (Financial Institutions & Products) at (202) 622-3970 (not a toll-free call).
SECTION 5. EFFECT ON OTHER DOCUMENTS
Rev. Proc. 2002-3 is modified.

acquiescences or **nonacquiescences** Printed decisions of IRS as to whether it will follow or not follow a tax court ruling

Acquiescences, or **nonacquiescences,** are printed by the IRS to indicate its agreement or disagreement with the decisions of the tax court (see later in the chapter). These acquiescences do not apply to the taxpayer who has received the decision from the tax court, but indicates the IRS's policy with respect to how it will determine similar matters in the future.

TAX LAW & POLICY

CHIEF COUNSEL:
In re: Freedom Newspapers, Inc.
Venue: C.A. 9th
Docket No. 915-75 Dec.: Dec. 28, 1977
Opinion: T.C. Memo 1977-429

Tax, Years & Amounts			Deficiency	
		Determined		**Redetermined**
Income	1971	$48,000		0

ISSUE:
Whether the payment of $100,000 to petitioner by a broker negotiating the sale of a newspaper to petitioner, constitutes a reduction of petitioner's basis in the purchased newspaper or is ordinary income.

DISCUSSION:
Mr. Taylor was a broker, engaged by Perry Publications, Inc. to sell a group of newspaper properties. Taylor offered to sell four of the properties to petitioner. Petitioner was willing to buy three of the properties but was reluctant to purchase the fourth, the *Jackson County Floridan (Floridan).* Taylor would receive his commission from Perry only if all the newspapers were sold. It was anticipated that the commission would be in excess of one million dollars. In order to induce petitioner to purchase the *Floridan,* Taylor and petitioner entered into an agreement to the effect that Taylor would sell the *Floridan* or pay petitioner $100,000. Taylor could not sell the *Floridan* as agreed, and paid the $100,000. The Court found that even though the petitioner contracted with two different parties, the two agreements were, nevertheless, each a part of the same transaction. Therefore, the $100,000 received by petitioner from Taylor was merely a reduction of the cost of the newspaper.

The Tax Court made the factual determination that the agreement between petitioner and Taylor could not be separated from petitioner's purchase of the *Floridan*. This factual finding dictated the Court's legal conclusion that the $100,000 received from Taylor was merely a reduction of the cost of the newspaper. Respondent argued that the agreement between Taylor and petitioner should be viewed as separate and distinct from petitioner's purchase of the newspaper. This factual finding would have dictated a legal conclusion that the $100,000 represented nothing more than liquidated damages for Taylor's failure to sell the *Floridan* at the agreed price within the agreed time period. It thus appears that the Court's factual findings are determinative of its legal conclusion.

There is sufficient evidence in the record to support the Court's determination that the agreement between petitioner and Taylor could not be separated from petitioner's purchase of the *Floridan*. As Perry's broker, Taylor was intimately involved in the sale of the newspapers to petitioner. Taylor stood to make over one million dollars in commissions upon closing the sale of all four newspapers. Thus, had Taylor not been involved in the sale of the newspapers, he never would have entered into an agreement with petitioner. Taylor agreed that he would sell the *Floridan* for petitioner or else pay "liquidated damages" of $100,000. Although the agreement specified the $100,000 was payment for "liquidated damages", the Court looked at the entire transaction and concluded that the $100,000 represented a reduction in the purchase price. In effect, it appears that Taylor agreed to a reduction of his commission on the sale. This would have the effect of reducing petitioner's cost and hence its basis in the *Floridan*. Therefore, the facts and circumstances in the instant case suggest that the two agreements involved were entered into by parties intimately involved in the same transaction. Therefore, the Court's fact finding does not appear to be clearly erroneous.

The Commissioner's non-acquiesence in *Brown v. Commissioner,* 10 BTA 1036 (1928) does not mandate appeal of the instant case. The key factor in the commissioner's non-acquiesence in *Brown,* was that the third party payment was made by an independent party not involved in the transaction between the buyer and seller. The instant case is clearly distinguishable. Taylor, unlike Bache, was intimately involved in the sale of the newspapers by Perry to petitioner. Taylor, as the broker negotiating the sale, cannot be viewed as an independent third party to the transaction. The amount of commission Taylor received on the sale had a direct impact upon the cost to petitioner, hence on his basis in the property. It was Taylor's prerogative to reduce the amount of his Commission to insure that he in fact received a commission in this all or nothing sale. Therefore, since Taylor unlike Bache was a party to the transaction, the Commissioner's non-acquiesence in *Brown* does not mandate that the instant case be appealed.

The Court also relied on *Arrowsmith v. Commissioner,* 344 U.S. 6 (1952) as subsequently applied by the Court in *Federal Bulk Carriers, Inc. v. Commissioner,* 66 T.C. 283 (1976), aff'd on other grounds, 558 F.2d 128 (2nd Cir. 1977) to reach its holding that the $100,000 received by petitioner from Taylor was merely a reduction of the cost of the newspaper. As long as the Service accepts the Court's finding that the agreement between petitioner and Taylor cannot be separated from petitioner's purchase of the *Floridan,* it would appear that the *Arrowsmith* doctrine would be controlling. In the instant case, Taylor was a party intimately involved in the sale between petitioner and Perry. Therefore, it naturally follows that any payment received by petitioner from Taylor was merely a reduction of his Commission and thus a reduction in petitioner's basis in the *Floridan.* The *Arrowsmith* doctrine would not be applicable in a situation such as *Brown,* supra, where there was an independent third party involved in the transaction.

RECOMMENDATION:
Acquiesence
BERNARD B. KORNMEHL
Attorney
Approved: STUART E. SEIGEL
Chief Counsel
By: John C. Calhoun
Technical Assistant to Director
Tax Court Litigation Division

Tax Reform Act of 1976
Federal law that revised tax law and procedure

private ruling letters
IRS decisions that only affect specific taxpayers

In addition to the foregoing, pursuant to the **Tax Reform Act of 1976,** the IRS now provides access to **private ruling letters.** These rulings are determinations made by IRS with regard to individual taxpayers on matters the IRS feels are not sufficiently significant to warrant publication in the form of a revenue ruling. This is analogous to a "short-form" decision rendered from the bench by a trial judge. Congress, however, has mandated that these private rulings be made available upon request, so as to provide equal application of the tax laws. Private ruling letters have some persuasive impact, but they are not treated as legal authority as are the regulations, revenue rulings, and revenue procedures.

TAX LAW & POLICY

PRIVATE RULING 200227009
INTERNAL REVENUE SERVICE NATIONAL OFFICE TECHNICAL ADVICE MEMORANDUM

"This document may not be used or cited as precedent. Section 6110(j)(3) of the Internal Revenue Code."

Section 42—Low-Income Housing Credit

42.04-00, 167.14-11, 168.00-00, 263A.00-00, 7805.05-00

PRIVATE RULING 200227009; 2002 PRL LEXIS 471
DATE: March 11, 2002

REFER REPLY TO: CASE MIS No.: TAM-111584-02/CC:PSI:B5

Release Date: 7/5/2002

INTERNAL REVENUE SERVICE
NATIONAL OFFICE TECHNICAL ADVICE MEMORANDUM

Industry Director
Natural Resources & Construction (LM:NRC)

Taxpayer's Name: * * *
Taxpayer's Address: * * *
Taxpayer's Identification No: * * *
Tax Year Involved: * * *

[1] This technical advice memorandum (TAM) modifies TAM 200043016 (July 14, 2000) to make it consistent with Revenue Ruling 2002-9, 2002-10 I.R.B. 614, as it applies to the issue of impact fees.

[2] Further, this TAM lifts the suspension on consideration of the impact fee issue in TAM 200203013 (October 9, 2001), where the taxpayer requested, in part, that relief under 7805(b)(8) of the Internal Revenue Code as to the issue of impact fees, be extended to it and that TAM 200043016 be applied without retroactive effect. Based on the holding in Revenue Ruling 2002-9 and the modification of TAM 200043016 by this TAM, 7805(b)(8) is not applicable.

Judicial Decisions

As with all statutes, the tax laws are subject to judicial scrutiny. The federal taxpayer has two sources of judicial review: the tax court and the general federal courts.

If the IRS determines that a taxpayer has failed to pay the appropriate amount of tax, called a **tax deficiency,** then prior to paying such alleged deficiency the taxpayer may petition the **tax court** for a determination of liability. Historically, the tax court was an administrative court, but pursuant to the **Tax Reform Act of 1969** it became a court established under Article I of the Constitution and is now called the **United States Tax Court.**

tax deficiency
IRS determination that a taxpayer has failed to pay the correct tax

tax court
Federal court that hears tax matters

Tax Reform Act of 1969
Federal statute that made the tax court an Article I court

United States Tax Court
Official name of the tax court

Tax Court Reports
Publication for decisions of the tax court

memorandum decision
Tax court decision based merely on factual determinations

The three categories of tax court decisions are:

1. A decision reported in the official **Tax Court Reports** if, after initial determination by one of its 19 judges, it is reviewed by the chief judge

2. A decision based merely on factual determinations without any application of law; may be unofficially reported by Commerce Clearing House and the Research Institute of America as a **memorandum decision**

3. An officially reported decision reviewed by the entire court prior to final determination, if so required by the chief judge

---

TAX LAW & POLICY

KEENE V. COMMISSIONER OF INTERNAL REVENUE
T.C. Memo 2002-277; 2002 Tax Ct. Memo LEXIS 286; 84 T.C.M. (CCH) 514

Petitioner taxpayer claimed zero income on his 1997 and 1998 joint federal income tax returns despite earning income for both years. Respondent Commissioner of Internal Revenue determined a federal income tax deficiency. The taxpayer failed to challenge the deficiency. The Commissioner proceeded to *levy and moved for summary judgment pursuant to U.S. Tax Ct. R. 121.*

    The taxpayer challenged the assessment on the ground that the notice of deficiency was invalid allegedly because no section of the Internal Revenue Code made him "liable" for any tax. However, the taxpayer did not take advantage of the opportunity to file a petition for redetermination with the tax court. The taxpayer was thus barred from challenging the existence or amount of his underlying tax liability in the collection review proceeding. Even if the taxpayer could challenge the deficiency, the appeals officer complied with 26 U.S.C.S. § 6330(c)(2)(B). The appeals officer obtained and reviewed transcripts of account with regard to the taxable years at issue. The transcripts of account on which the appeals officer relied contained all the information prescribed in Treas. Reg. § 301.6203-1. The Commissioner sent the taxpayer a notice that he owed taxes and such notice constituted a notice and demand for payment within the meaning of 26 U.S.C.S. § 6303(a). The taxpayer failed to raise any defense to the collection action. The tax court, on its own motion, also imposed a penalty under 26 U.S.C.S. § 6673(a)(1) of $5,000 for filing a frivolous and groundless claim.

If the taxpayer pays the alleged deficiency, he or she may seek a refund by filing suit in a federal district court. In federal district court, the taxpayer is entitled to a trial by jury. As an alternative, the taxpayer may also file suit in the **court of federal claims** that sits only in the District of Columbia and which affords no jury trials. This court has jurisdiction over claims against the federal government. The decisions of both these courts are officially published in the *Federal Supplement.*

Decisions of the tax court and the federal district courts may be appealed as of right to the U.S. Court of Appeals sitting in the state in which the taxpayer resides. Decisions of the federal claims court are appealed to the Court of Appeals for the Federal Circuit in the District of Columbia. Decisions of these appellate courts are published in the *Federal Reporter.*

Federal Supplement
Official publication for federal district court decisions

Federal Reporter
Official publication for decisions of the U.S. Court of Appeals

Exercise

Locate and read the decision of *Fisher v. Commissioner,* 59 F.2d 192, that discusses the taxability of a transfer of property from an employer to an employee during the term of the employment.

petition for certiorari
Request to have supreme court review the matter

United States Reports
Official publications for decisions of the U.S. Supreme Court

As a last resort, the parties may petition to the U.S. Supreme Court for review. This request to be heard by the Supreme Court is called a **petition for certiorari** (review). If certiorari is granted, the decisions of the Supreme Court are published in *United States Reports, Supreme Court Reports,* and *Supreme Court Reports, Lawyers' Edition.*

In addition to the preceding, all federal judicial decisions, except those emanating from the tax court, are unofficially reported in *United States Tax Cases* (**USTC**) and *American Federal Tax Reports* (**AFTR**).

The federal tax law researcher has several other sources available for locating applicable tax law in addition to those discussed. The two most commonly used sources are the *Standard Federal Tax Reporter* and the *United States Tax Reporter.* These loose-leaf volumes provide an extensive and comprehensive annotation of the Internal Revenue Code, including the official text, legislative history, proposed legislation, judicial interpretations, and prose analyses prepared by the editors. These volumes are periodically updated by loose-leaf inserts.

Supreme Court Reports
Publication for decisions of the U.S. Supreme Court

Supreme Court Reports, Lawyers' Edition
Publication for decisions of the U.S. Supreme Court

United States Tax Cases (USTC)
Unofficial publication of tax court decisions

American Federal Tax Reports (AFTR)
Unofficial reporter for tax court decisions

Exercise

Locate in the library the Standard Federal Tax Reporter and the United States Tax Reporter. How would you use these sources as part of your tax law research? Do you find these volumes more or less helpful than other forms of research? Discuss.

Standard Federal Tax Reporter
Loose-leaf service

United States Tax Reporter
Loose-leaf service

Federal Tax Citator
Publication that updates tax cases

Tax Notes
Publication that updates tax decisions

Taxpayer Bill of Rights Acts of 1988 and 1996
Federal statutes that granted taxpayers certain rights vis-a-vis IRS

Internal Revenue Service Restructure and Reform Act of 1998
Federal statute designed to curb IRS abuses

audit
IRS examination of a taxpayer's return

examination
IRS audit

correspondence audit
Audit by exchange of letters

office audit
IRS examination in which the taxpayer

To update federal tax material, the practitioner can access both the **Federal Tax Citator** and **Tax Notes,** as well as Shepards and the computer-assisted legal research update services.

Exercise

Using a computer-assisted research program, update the *Fisher* case you located previously.

General Proceedings

All tax law problems begin with an IRS determination. Because of perceived abuse of IRS power during the last decades of the twentieth century, Congress enacted various statutes designed to protect taxpayers from overly intrusive IRS practices. The first of these, the **Taxpayer Bill of Rights Act of 1988,** PL 100-684, was soon followed by the **Taxpayer Bill of Rights Act of 1996,** PL 104-168, and the **Internal Revenue Service Restructure and Reform Act of 1998,** PL 105-206. The thrust of these enactments is to provide for a kinder, gentler Internal Revenue Service. Whether they have been effective depends on the person questioned, and is beyond the scope of this textbook.

The basis of U.S. federal tax policy is the voluntary self-assessment of the taxpayer, whereby the taxpayer files annual or quarterly tax returns, depending on the nature of the taxpayer, and pays the amount of tax indicated as owing based on such assessment. Returns so filed are audited by the IRS on a selective basis. Pursuant to the taxpayer bills of rights, IRS cannot continually audit specific taxpayers without a rational basis for such procedures.

If the IRS determines that there is an error in the amount of taxes paid or income reported, the so-called deficiency previously discussed, then the IRS may conduct an **audit,** generally referred to as an **examination,** with the taxpayer. The three types of examination audits conducted by IRS are:

1. A **correspondence audit** pursuant to Regs. section 601.105(b)(2) which involves an exchange of letters between the IRS and the taxpayer

2. An **office audit** pursuant to Regs. section 601.105(b)(2)(i) in which the taxpayer brings his or her records to an IRS office

3. A **field examination** pursuant to Regs. section 601.105(b)(3) in which an agent for the IRS visits the taxpayer at the taxpayer's home or office

The taxpayer is entitled to be represented at any of these examinations.

After the examination or audit is concluded, IRS may send a **no-change letter** indicating that it is accepting the return as originally filed, or may send a letter informing the taxpayer that a deficiency has been assessed. If the taxpayer disagrees with the result determined by the agent, the district director of the Internal Revenue Service will send the taxpayer a **30-day letter,** detailing the agent's findings and permitting the taxpayer to file for an administrative review within the 30-day period. It is important to note that an administrative review is not required to institute litigation. Further, any controversy may be settled by negotiation between the taxpayer or his or her representative and a member of the IRS Appeals Office.

If the initial review does not conclude satisfactorily, the taxpayer will receive a formal **90-day letter** that permits the taxpayer 90 days in which to file a petition with the tax court. No further action may be taken by the government during the 90-day period, and, if a petition is filed, until the conclusion of the tax court's deliberations plus 60 days. Taxpayers have a right to receive a 90-day letter; the 30-day letter is considered informal and no such right attaches to it.

When a deficiency is asserted by the government, the taxpayer is often asked to sign the following forms.

> **Form 879,** a waiver of the right to a 90-day letter
> **Form 872** (Exhibit 1.1), an authorization of an extension of the statutory period of limitations to assess a deficiency

Prior to enacting the taxpayer bills of rights, most taxpayers felt constrained into signing such releases; currently, the taxpayer's decision as to whether to give the release is more discretionary with the taxpayer because of the prohibition against IRS retribution.

It should be noted that the process herein discussed applies only to those deficiencies caused by an honest error or reasonable interpretation of the tax laws. Fraudulent claims are handled as a criminal matter and are beyond the scope of this textbook.

The administrative procedures involved if a taxpayer is seeking a refund based on an overpayment are slightly different from those involved if IRS asserts a deficiency. To request a refund, the taxpayer or his or her representative must file a **Form 1040X** (Exhibit 1.2) as an amendment to Form 1040. Such claim is required to be filed before the taxpayer can institute a lawsuit for a refund.

The filing of a refund claim requires the taxpayer to assert all of the grounds he or she is alleging as the basis of the claim. The failure

---

field examination
IRS audit in which an IRS agent goes to the taxpayer

no-change letter
IRS acceptance of original return

30-day letter
Document giving a taxpayer 30 days in which to challenge an IRS determination internally

90-day letter
Document giving a taxpayer 90 days in which to file suit in the tax court

Form 879
Document used to waive the 90-day letter

Form 872
Document used to grant IRS an extension of the statutory period to assess a deficiency

| Form **872** (Rev. January 2001) | Department of the Treasury–Internal Revenue Service
Consent to Extend the Time to Assess Tax | In reply refer to:
Taxpayer Identification Number |

_____
(Name(s))

taxpayer(s) of _____
(Number, Street, City or Town, State, ZIP Code)

and the Commissioner of Internal Revenue consent and agree to the following:

(1) The amount of any Federal _____ tax due on any return(s) made by or
(Kind of tax)

for the above taxpayer(s) for the period(s) ended _____

may be assessed at any time on or before _____ . However, if
(Expiration date)

a notice of deficiency in tax for any such period(s) is sent to the taxpayer(s) on or before that date, then the time for assessing the tax will be further extended by the number of days the assessment was previously prohibited, plus 60 days.

(2) The taxpayer(s) may file a claim for credit or refund and the Service may credit or refund the tax within 6 months after this agreement ends.

MAKING THIS CONSENT WILL NOT DEPRIVE THE TAXPAYER(S) OF ANY APPEAL RIGHTS TO WHICH THEY WOULD OTHERWISE BE ENTITLED.

YOUR SIGNATURE HERE ➤ _____ (Date signed)

SPOUSE'S SIGNATURE ➤ _____ (Date signed)

TAXPAYER'S REPRESENTATIVE
SIGN HERE ➤ _____ (Date signed)

CORPORATE NAME ➤ _____

CORPORATE OFFICER(S) SIGN HERE ➤ _____ (Title) _____ (Date signed)
_____ (Title) _____ (Date signed)

INTERNAL REVENUE SERVICE SIGNATURE AND TITLE

_____ (Division Executive Name - see instructions)   _____ (Division Executive Title - see instructions)

BY _____ (Date signed)
(Authorized Official Signature and Title - see instructions)

(Signature instructions are on the back of this form)   www.irs.gov   Catalog Number 20755I   Form **872** (Rev. 1-2001)

Exhibit 1.1 Form 872

Instructions

If this consent is for income tax, self-employment tax, or FICA tax on tips and is made for any year(s) for which a joint return was filed, both husband and wife must sign the original and copy of this form unless one, acting under a power of attorney, signs as agent for the other. The signatures must match the names as they appear on the front of this form.

If this consent is for gift tax and the donor and the donor's spouse elected to have gifts to third persons considered as made one-half by each, both husband and wife must sign the original and copy of this form unless one, acting under a power of attorney, signs as agent for the other. The signatures must match the names as they appear on the front of this form.

If this consent is for Chapter 41, 42, or 43 taxes involving a partnership or is for a partnership return, only one authorized partner need sign.

If this consent is for Chapter 42 taxes, a separate Form 872 should be completed for each potential disqualified person, entity, or foundation manager that may be involved in a taxable transaction during the related tax year. See Revenue Ruling 75-391, 1975-2 C.B. 446.

If you are an attorney or agent of the taxpayer(s), you may sign this consent provided the action is specifically authorized by a power of attorney. If the power of attorney was not previously filed, you must include it with this form.

If you are acting as a fiduciary (such as executor, administrator, trustee, etc.) and you sign this consent, attach Form 56, Notice Concerning Fiduciary Relationship, unless it was previously filed. If the taxpayer is a corporation, sign this consent with the corporate name followed by the signature and title of the officer(s) authorized to sign.

Instructions for Internal Revenue Service Employees

Complete the Division Executive's name and title depending upon your division.

If you are in the Small Business /Self-Employed Division, enter the name and title for the appropriate division executive for your business unit (e.g., Area Director for your area; Director, Compliance Policy; Director, Compliance Services).

If you are in the Wage and Investment Division, enter the name and title for the appropriate division executive for your business unit (e.g., Area Director for your area; Director, Field Compliance Services).

If you are in the Large and Mid-Size Business Division, enter the name and title of the Director, Field Operations for your industry.

If you are in the Tax Exempt and Government Entities Division, enter the name and title for the appropriate division executive for your business unit (e.g., Director, Exempt Organizations; Director, Employee Plans; Director, Federal, State and Local Governments; Director, Indian Tribal Governments; Director, Tax Exempt Bonds).

If you are in Appeals, enter the name and title of the appropriate Director, Appeals Operating Unit.

The signature and title line will be signed and dated by the appropriate authorized official within your division.

Catalog Number 20755I   Form **872** (Rev. 1-2001)

Exhibit 1.1 (Continued)

Form 1040X — Amended U.S. Individual Income Tax Return

Department of the Treasury—Internal Revenue Service
(Rev. November 2003)
OMB No. 1545-0091
► See separate instructions.

This return is for calendar year ► _____ , or fiscal year ended ► _____

Please print or type

- Your first name and initial | Last name | Your social security number
- If a joint return, spouse's first name and initial | Last name | Spouse's social security number
- Home address (no. and street) or P.O. box if mail is not delivered to your home | Apt. no. | Phone number ( )
- City, town or post office, state, and ZIP code. If you have a foreign address, see page 2 of the instructions. | For Paperwork Reduction Act Notice, see page 6.

A If the name or address shown above is different from that shown on the original return, check here . . . . . . ► ☐

B Has the original return been changed or audited by the IRS or have you been notified that it will be? . . ☐ Yes ☐ No

C Filing status. Be sure to complete this line. **Note.** You cannot change from joint to separate returns after the due date.

On original return ► ☐ Single ☐ Married filing jointly ☐ Married filing separately ☐ Head of household ☐ Qualifying widow(er)
On this return ► ☐ Single ☐ Married filing jointly ☐ Married filing separately ☐ Head of household* ☐ Qualifying widow(er)

* If the qualifying person is a child but not your dependent, see page 2.

Use Part II on the back to explain any changes

		A. Original amount or as previously adjusted (see page 2)	B. Net change— amount of increase or (decrease)— explain in Part II	C. Correct amount
	Income and Deductions (see pages 2–6)			
1	Adjusted gross income (see page 3)			
2	Itemized deductions or standard deduction (see page 3)			
3	Subtract line 2 from line 1			
4	Exemptions. If changing, fill in Parts I and II on the back			
5	Taxable income. Subtract line 4 from line 3			
Tax Liability				
6	Tax (see page 4). Method used in col. C			
7	Credits (see page 4)			
8	Subtract line 7 from line 6. Enter the result but not less than zero			
9	Other taxes (see page 4)			
10	Total tax. Add lines 8 and 9			
Payments				
11	Federal income tax withheld and excess social security and tier 1 RRTA tax withheld. If changing, see page 4			
12	Estimated tax payments, including amount applied from prior year's return			
13	Earned income credit (EIC)			
14	Additional child tax credit from Form 8812			
15	Credits from Form 2439, Form 4136, or Form 8885			
16	Amount paid with request for extension of time to file (see page 4)			
17	Amount of tax paid with original return plus additional tax paid after it was filed			
18	Total payments. Add lines 11 through 17 in column C			

Refund or Amount You Owe

19	Overpayment, if any, as shown on original return or as previously adjusted by the IRS	
20	Subtract line 19 from line 18 (see page 5)	
21	**Amount you owe.** If line 10, column C, is more than line 20, enter the difference and see page 5	
22	If line 10, column C, is less than line 20, enter the difference	
23	Amount of line 22 you want **refunded to you**	
24	Amount of line 22 you want **applied to your** estimated tax	24

Sign Here
Under penalties of perjury, I declare that I have filed an original return and that I have examined this amended return, including accompanying schedules and statements, and to the best of my knowledge and belief, this amended return is true, correct, and complete. Declaration of preparer (other than taxpayer) is based on all information of which the preparer has any knowledge.

Joint return? See page 2. Keep a copy for your records.

Your signature | Date | ► | Spouse's signature. If a joint return, **both** must sign. | Date

Paid Preparer's Use Only

Preparer's signature | Date | Check if self-employed ☐ | Preparer's SSN or PTIN
Firm's name (or yours if self-employed), address, and ZIP code | | EIN
 | | Phone no. ( )

Cat. No. 11360L
Form **1040X** (Rev. 11-2003)

Exhibit 1.2 Form 1040X

Form 1040X (Rev. 11-2003) Page **2**

Part I — Exemptions. See Form 1040 or 1040A instructions.

If you are **not changing your exemptions,** do not complete this part.
If claiming **more exemptions,** complete lines 25–31.
If claiming **fewer exemptions,** complete lines 25–30.

		A. Original number of exemptions reported or as previously adjusted	B. Net change	C. Correct number of exemptions
25	Yourself and spouse			
	Caution. If your parents (or someone else) can claim you as a dependent (even if they chose not to), you cannot claim an exemption for yourself.			
26	Your dependent children who lived with you			
27	Your dependent children who did not live with you due to divorce or separation			
28	Other dependents			
29	Total number of exemptions. Add lines 25 through 28			
30	Multiply the number of exemptions claimed on line 29 by the amount listed below for the tax year you are amending. Enter the result here and on line 4.			

Tax year	Exemption amount	But see the instructions for line 4 on page 3 if the amount on line 1 is over:
2003	$3,050	$104,625
2002	3,000	103,000
2001	2,900	99,725
2000	2,800	96,700

31 Dependents (children and other) not claimed on original (or adjusted) return:

(a) First name Last name	(b) Dependent's social security number	(c) Dependent's relationship to you	(d) ✓ if qualifying child for child tax credit (see page 5)
			☐
			☐
			☐
			☐
			☐

No. of your children on line 31 who:
- lived with you ▶ ☐
- did not live with you due to divorce or separation (see page 5) ▶ ☐

Dependents on line 31 not entered above ▶ ☐

Part II — Explanation of Changes to Income, Deductions, and Credits

Enter the line number from the front of the form for each item you are changing and give the reason for each change. Attach only the supporting forms and schedules for the items changed. If you do not attach the required information, your Form 1040X may be returned. Be sure to include your name and social security number on any attachments.

If the change relates to a net operating loss carryback or a general business credit carryback, attach the schedule or form that shows the year in which the loss or credit occurred. See page 2 of the instructions. Also, check here ▶ ☐

Part III — Presidential Election Campaign Fund. Checking below will not increase your tax or reduce your refund.

If you did not previously want $3 to go to the fund but now want to, check here ▶ ☐
If a joint return and your spouse did not previously want $3 to go to the fund but now wants to, check here ▶ ☐

Form **1040X** (Rev. 11-2003)

Exhibit 1.2 (Continued)

of the taxpayer to assert a legal basis for the claim may preclude the taxpayer from asserting such basis in any subsequent litigation.

As indicated, IRS has the ability to enter into agreements with taxpayers to settle disputes, and may negotiate not only on any additional tax liability, but also with respect to any interest and/or penalties charged. However, the IRS may only settle such disputes if there is a question with regard to either the actual tax liability or the ability of the IRS to collect the amount due.

After completing administrative procedures, a taxpayer may seek judicial review of the IRS decision. For a deficiency, after the 90-day letter has been issued, the taxpayer may petition the tax court for review. If the amount in controversy is less than $50,000, the taxpayer may request a special **small tax case procedure** pursuant to IRC sec. 7463(a), which is an expedited procedure presided over by a **special trial judge** appointed by the chief judge pursuant to IRC sec. 7443A.

For a refund, the taxpayer must seek judicial review either in the federal district court or the court of federal claims (see earlier in the chapter).

In the judicial proceeding, if the taxpayer is an individual or a small business, the government bears the burden of proof by a preponderance of the evidence with respect to factual issues. This burden lies with the government when the taxpayer:

A. Produces credible evidence with respect to any relevant fact
B. Substantiates any item questioned by the IRS
C. Maintains all requisite records
D. Cooperates with the government's reasonable requests pursuant to IRC sec. 7491

If the taxpayer is successful in the lawsuit, either initially or on appeal, the taxpayer may receive reasonable costs and attorney's fees. However, costs will only be awarded in instances in which the Service's position could not be substantially justified. Also, no such recovery is allowed if the taxpayer's net assets exceed $2 million for an individual or $7 million for a corporation.

Practical tip

The Internal Revenue Service is always open to negotiation to settle tax disputes. When representing a client, you can always attempt to reach a resolution of the problem prior to taking any judicial or administrative action. Such settlements may include a reduction of the total amount of tax due, forgiveness of interest and penalty payments, or additional time in which to pay any moneys due.

Form 1040X
Document used to request a refund

small tax case procedure
Expedited procedure for controversy involving less than $50,000

special trial judge
Person who presides over small tax cases

Circular 230
IRS rules with respect to the responsibilities of tax preparers

Ethical Concerns

Attorneys, certified public accountants, and other persons who qualify under IRS rules are permitted to represent taxpayers in all IRS proceedings. IRS has promulgated certain rules with respect to the responsibilities of such representatives in **Circular 230**, title 31, subtitle A, part 10 of the Code of Federal Regulations. Pursuant to these rules, attorneys and those who work under their supervision are required to provide IRS with all requested documents unless such documents are deemed to be privileged. Further, IRS mandates due diligence with respect to preparing, assisting in preparing, and filing tax returns and related documents; and determining the correctness of representations made to the government.

In advising a client, Circular 230 states that an attorney may not advise a client to take a deduction or exclude an item from income unless the attorney believes that there is a reasonable expectation of it being substantiated by the tax law and that it is not fraudulent. These same requirements apply to income tax preparers who may also be subject to a $250 fine for making assertions that are not reasonably capable of being substantiated in fact or law. The penalty may be increased to $1000 for a willful misstatement.

Any person representing a taxpayer on any tax matter should become acquainted with the provisions of Circular 230.

CHAPTER REVIEW

All legal professionals must become conversant with the tax implications of the legal problems they are solving. To this end, the professional must be able to research appropriate tax law and be familiar with Internal Revenue Service procedures.

The source of federal tax law is the Internal Revenue Code, which appears in title 26 of the U.S. Code. To research a tax problem, the legal professional should look not only at the law itself, but also to the annotations to the code and the loose-leaf services. These services provide not only the text of the law, but also references to other related materials, legislative history, judicial decisions, and editorial prose interpretations of the law.

In addition to federal legislation, tax law is created by administrative action and judicial decisions. The administrative agency that oversees tax law is the Internal Revenue Service, which publishes its own rulings and procedures in the Cumulative Bulletin and the Code of Federal Regulations. The administrative actions that interpret the tax law are called revenue rulings and revenue procedures.

Judicially, federal tax laws are interpreted by the U.S. Tax Court if the taxpayer petitions for review prior to paying any alleged deficiency, or the regular federal courts if the taxpayer first pays the alleged deficiency and then seeks a refund.

Prior to seeking judicial revue of a federal tax problem, the IRS provides for certain administrative procedures to resolve the problem, and the legal professional should remember that the IRS has the authority to settle all tax disputes on behalf of the government. As a general principle, it is better to attempt to settle a tax problem and keep judicial intervention as a last resort.

KEY TERMS

acquiescences or nonacquiescences

American Federal Tax Reports (AFTR)

audit

bill

Circular 230

Code of Federal Regulations (CFR)

codification

conference committee

conversion table

correspondence audit

direct tax

enactment

examination

Federal Reporter

Federal Supplement

Federal Tax Citator

field examination

Form 872

Form 879

Form 1040X

Government Printing Office (GPO)

House Ways and Means Committee

indirect tax

Internal Revenue Code (IRC) of 1939

Internal Revenue Service (IRS)

Internal Revenue Service Restructure and Reform Act of 1998

memorandum decision

90-day letter

no-change letter

Notes of Decisions

office audit

petition for certiorari

pocket part

private ruling letters

Public Law

regulations (Regs)

revenue procedure (Rev. Proc.)

revenue ruling (Rev. Rul.)

Senate Finance Committee
slip law
small tax case procedure
special trial judge
sponsor
Standard Federal Tax Reporter
Supreme Court Reports
Supreme Court Reports, Lawyers' Edition
tax court
Tax Court Reports
tax deficiency
Tax Notes
Tax Reform Act of 1969
Tax Reform Act of 1976
Taxpayer Bill of Rights Acts of 1988 and 1996

30-day letter
United States Code (USC)
United States Code Annotated (USCA)
United States Code Congressional and Administrative News (USCCAN)
United States Code Service (USCS)
United States Code Service (USCS), *Advance Pamphlet*
United States Law Weekly
United States Reports
United States Statutes at Large
United States Tax Cases (USTC)
United States Tax Court
United States Tax Reporter
Westlaw

CHAPTER 2

Individual Income Taxation

Introduction

An old adage states, "There is nothing more certain in life than death and taxes." To that saying the legal professional may add, "or that all legal problems have federal tax consequences." This does not necessarily mean that every transaction or occurrence has a negative tax implication (such as having to pay taxes); the consequence could be a reduction of income upon which a tax is imposed, or a reduction in the actual amount of the tax due and owing.

The starting point for any discussion of federal income taxation is section 61 of the Internal Revenue Code which defines "gross income," the figure upon which tax liability is calculated, as "income from whatever source derived. . . ." This section of the code then continues to provide a nonexclusive list of 15 separate items to exemplify the concept of gross income. Each of these items appears on **Form 1040,** the basic federal income tax return for individuals. Form 1040 is shown in Exhibit 2.1, and each of the items appearing on that form will be discussed separately in this chapter. The term **item** is used to denote any figure used on a tax return that represents income, a deduction from income, exclusion from income, or a credit against taxes owed.

Form 1040
Basic federal income tax return for individuals

item
Any figure used to express income, deduction, credit, or nontaxable event

Individual Income Taxation **31**

Form **1040**	Department of the Treasury—Internal Revenue Service **U.S. Individual Income Tax Return** 2003	(99)	IRS Use Only—Do not write or staple in this space.

Label (See instructions on page 19.) **Use the IRS label.** Otherwise, please print or type.	For the year Jan. 1–Dec. 31, 2003, or other tax year beginning , 2003, ending , 20	OMB No. 1545-0074
	Your first name and initial	Last name	Your social security number
	If a joint return, spouse's first name and initial	Last name	Spouse's social security number
	Home address (number and street). If you have a P.O. box, see page 19.	Apt. no.	▲ **Important!** ▲ You **must** enter your SSN(s) above.
	City, town or post office, state, and ZIP code. If you have a foreign address, see page 19.		

Presidential Election Campaign (See page 19.)
▶ **Note.** Checking "Yes" will not change your tax or reduce your refund.
Do you, or your spouse if filing a joint return, want $3 to go to this fund? ▶

You ☐ Yes ☐ No   Spouse ☐ Yes ☐ No

Filing Status
Check only one box.

1 ☐ Single
2 ☐ Married filing jointly (even if only one had income)
3 ☐ Married filing separately. Enter spouse's SSN above and full name here. ▶
4 ☐ Head of household (with qualifying person). (See page 20.) If the qualifying person is a child but not your dependent, enter this child's name here. ▶
5 ☐ Qualifying widow(er) with dependent child. (See page 20.)

Exemptions

6a ☐ **Yourself.** If your parent (or someone else) can claim you as a dependent on his or her tax return, **do not** check box 6a . . . .
b ☐ Spouse . . . .
c Dependents:
(1) First name   Last name | (2) Dependent's social security number | (3) Dependent's relationship to you | (4) ✓ if qualifying child for child tax credit (see page 21)

If more than five dependents, see page 21.

No. of boxes checked on 6a and 6b ____
No. of children on 6c who:
• lived with you ____
• did not live with you due to divorce or separation (see page 21) ____
Dependents on 6c not entered above ____
Add numbers on lines above ▶ ____

d Total number of exemptions claimed . . . .

Income

Attach Forms W-2 and W-2G here. Also attach Form(s) 1099-R if tax was withheld.

If you did not get a W-2, see page 22.

Enclose, but do not attach, any payment. Also, please use Form 1040-V.

7 Wages, salaries, tips, etc. Attach Form(s) W-2 7
8a Taxable interest. Attach Schedule B if required 8a
b Tax-exempt interest. **Do not** include on line 8a . . . 8b
9a Ordinary dividends. Attach Schedule B if required 9a
b Qualified dividends (see page 23) 9b
10 Taxable refunds, credits, or offsets of state and local income taxes (see page 23) . . 10
11 Alimony received 11
12 Business income or (loss). Attach Schedule C or C-EZ 12
13a Capital gain or (loss). Attach Schedule D if required. If not required, check here ▶ ☐ 13a
b If box on 13a is checked, enter post-May 5 capital gain distributions 13b
14 Other gains or (losses). Attach Form 4797 14
15a IRA distributions . . 15a b Taxable amount (see page 25) 15b
16a Pensions and annuities 16a b Taxable amount (see page 25) 16b
17 Rental real estate, royalties, partnerships, S corporations, trusts, etc. Attach Schedule E 17
18 Farm income or (loss). Attach Schedule F 18
19 Unemployment compensation 19
20a Social security benefits 20a b Taxable amount (see page 27) 20b
21 Other income. List type and amount (see page 27) 21
22 Add the amounts in the far right column for lines 7 through 21. This is your **total income** ▶ 22

Adjusted Gross Income

23 Educator expenses (see page 29) 23
24 IRA deduction (see page 29) 24
25 Student loan interest deduction (see page 31) . . . 25
26 Tuition and fees deduction (see page 32) 26
27 Moving expenses. Attach Form 3903 27
28 One-half of self-employment tax. Attach Schedule SE 28
29 Self-employed health insurance deduction (see page 33) 29
30 Self-employed SEP, SIMPLE, and qualified plans . . 30
31 Penalty on early withdrawal of savings 31
32a Alimony paid b Recipient's SSN ▶ _____ 32a
33 Add lines 23 through 32a 33
34 Subtract line 33 from line 22. This is your **adjusted gross income** . . . . . ▶ 34

For Disclosure, Privacy Act, and Paperwork Reduction Act Notice, see page 77.   Cat. No. 11320B   Form **1040** (2003)

Exhibit 2.1 Form 1040

32 Chapter Two

Form 1040 (2003)   Page **2**

Tax and Credits

Standard Deduction for—
- People who checked any box on line 36a or 36b **or** who can be claimed as a dependent, see page 34.
- All others:

Single or Married filing separately, $4,750

Married filing jointly or Qualifying widow(er), $9,500

Head of household, $7,000

35 Amount from line 34 (adjusted gross income) 35
36a Check if: ☐ **You** were born before January 2, 1939, ☐ Blind. } Total boxes
              ☐ **Spouse** was born before January 2, 1939, ☐ Blind. } checked ▶ 36a
  b If you are married filing separately and your spouse itemizes deductions, or you were a dual-status alien, see page 34 and check here . . . . . ▶ 36b ☐
37 **Itemized deductions** (from Schedule A) **or** your **standard deduction** (see left margin) . . 37
38 Subtract line 37 from line 35 38
39 If line 35 is $104,625 or less, multiply $3,050 by the total number of exemptions claimed on line 6d. If line 35 is over $104,625, see the worksheet on page 35 39
40 **Taxable income.** Subtract line 39 from line 38. If line 39 is more than line 38, enter -0- 40
41 **Tax** (see page 36). Check if any tax is from: **a** ☐ Form(s) 8814   **b** ☐ Form 4972 . . 41
42 **Alternative minimum tax** (see page 38). Attach Form 6251 42
43 Add lines 41 and 42 . . . . ▶ 43
44 Foreign tax credit. Attach Form 1116 if required 44
45 Credit for child and dependent care expenses. Attach Form 2441 . . 45
46 Credit for the elderly or the disabled. Attach Schedule R . . 46
47 Education credits. Attach Form 8863 47
48 Retirement savings contributions credit. Attach Form 8880 . . 48
49 Child tax credit (see page 40) 49
50 Adoption credit. Attach Form 8839 50
51 Credits from: **a** ☐ Form 8396   **b** ☐ Form 8859 . . 51
52 Other credits. Check applicable box(es): **a** ☐ Form 3800
   b ☐ Form 8801   **c** ☐ Specify _____ . . 52
53 Add lines 44 through 52. These are your **total credits** 53
54 Subtract line 53 from line 43. If line 53 is more than line 43, enter -0-. . . . . ▶ 54

Other Taxes

55 Self-employment tax. Attach Schedule SE 55
56 Social security and Medicare tax on tip income not reported to employer. Attach Form 4137 56
57 Tax on qualified plans, including IRAs, and other tax-favored accounts. Attach Form 5329 if required . 57
58 Advance earned income credit payments from Form(s) W-2 58
59 Household employment taxes. Attach Schedule H 59
60 Add lines 54 through 59. This is your **total tax** . . . . ▶ 60

Payments

If you have a qualifying child, attach Schedule EIC.

61 Federal income tax withheld from Forms W-2 and 1099 . . 61
62 2003 estimated tax payments and amount applied from 2002 return . 62
63 **Earned income credit (EIC)** 63
64 Excess social security and tier 1 RRTA tax withheld (see page 56) 64
65 Additional child tax credit. Attach Form 8812 65
66 Amount paid with request for extension to file (see page 56) 66
67 Other payments from: **a** ☐ Form 2439 **b** ☐ Form 4136 **c** ☐ Form 8885 67
68 Add lines 61 through 67. These are your **total payments** . . . . ▶ 68

Refund

Direct deposit? See page 56 and fill in 70b, 70c, and 70d.

69 If line 68 is more than line 60, subtract line 60 from line 68. This is the amount you **overpaid** 69
70a Amount of line 69 you want **refunded to you** . . . . ▶ 70a
  ▶ **b** Routing number [ ] ▶ **c** Type: ☐ Checking ☐ Savings
  ▶ **d** Account number [ ]
71 Amount of line 69 you want **applied to your 2004 estimated tax** ▶ 71

Amount You Owe

72 **Amount you owe.** Subtract line 68 from line 60. For details on how to pay, see page 57 ▶ 72
73 Estimated tax penalty (see page 58) 73

Third Party Designee

Do you want to allow another person to discuss this return with the IRS (see page 58)? ☐ **Yes.** Complete the following. ☐ **No**

Designee's name ▶   Phone no. ▶ ( )   Personal identification number (PIN) ▶

Sign Here

Joint return? See page 20.
Keep a copy for your records.

Under penalties of perjury, I declare that I have examined this return and accompanying schedules and statements, and to the best of my knowledge and belief, they are true, correct, and complete. Declaration of preparer (other than taxpayer) is based on all information of which preparer has any knowledge.

Your signature   Date   Your occupation   Daytime phone number ( )

Spouse's signature. If a joint return, **both** must sign.   Date   Spouse's occupation

Paid Preparer's Use Only

Preparer's signature ▶   Date   Check if self-employed ☐   Preparer's SSN or PTIN

Firm's name (or yours if self-employed), address, and ZIP code ▶   EIN   Phone no. ( )

Form **1040** (2003)

Exhibit 2.1 (Continued)

It is important to note that, for federal income tax purposes, the federal government taxes all income regardless of its source. This is not necessarily the case for all state income taxation. As most practitioners are aware, persons residing in the United States are subject to both federal and state income taxation (and many localities impose their own income tax as well), but not all items of income appearing on a federal income tax return necessarily appear on a state tax return. Each state's taxing procedures must be individually analyzed.

Practical tip

Always prepare the federal income tax return first—it helps in preparing any state return that may have to be filed.

The threshold question in any analysis of federal income taxation is the determination of which person is obligated to file federal income tax returns. Generally, all persons who are U.S. citizens or who reside in the United States or Puerto Rico must file. The filing requirement applies to individuals regardless of whether they are wage earners, dependents of other income producers, or self-employed. Remember, this is simply the requirement to file a federal income tax return—it is not determinative of whether any tax may ultimately be due. Further, if a person has had taxes withheld from any income received during the year and does not owe any taxes, he or she must file an income tax return to have this withheld income refunded.

Exercise

Does the federal taxing policy apply to aliens? Order a copy of Publications 518 and 519 to determine IRS rules relating to nonresident aliens and aliens who are residents in the United States for any portion of the tax year.

Once it is determined that the person is required to file a federal income tax return, it is necessary to ascertain the taxpayer's filing status. The United States imposes a **progressive income tax rate**, meaning that the percentage of income that must be paid as taxes increases as does the taxpayer's income level. However, there are different tax rates for each category of taxpayer, and so the determination of taxpayer status is crucial to the determination of the amount of tax that might be assessed. Currently, the IRS recognizes five categories of taxpayer:

1. **Single.** A person is considered single or unmarried if, on the last day of the tax year, he or she is legally considered

progressive income tax rate
Percentage of income taxed increases as the income increases

single
Filing status

unmarried. This means that if a person is married all year long but is divorced on December 31, he or she is deemed to be single for that entire tax year. Note that the determination of marital status is made pursuant to state law.

Example

A couple has been married for three years and the two are having marital difficulties. For the first three years of the marriage they filed "jointly" as a married couple (see the following entry). In the fourth tax year they separated on the last day of that tax year. In the fifth year they divorced. What is the couple's tax status for tax years four and five?

married filing jointly
Filing status permitted for persons who are legally married on the last day of the tax year

2. **Married filing jointly.** A couple may file under this status if they are married on the last day of the tax year. For federal income tax purposes, a couple is considered married if they have a ceremonial marriage or a common law marriage where such marriages are recognized. Such married couples may file a joint return if both parties agree to do so. An advantage to filing a joint return is the tax rates are less for persons in this category.

Practical tip

The tax law practitioner should always obtain evidence of a client's marital status if he or she has any inclination that this might cause a tax problem.

married filing separately
Filing status permitted for persons who are legally married but who wish to have each spouse's tax liability computed individually

3. **Married filing separately.** Even if a couple is married, the two may elect to file separate tax returns for certain financial reasons. It is conceivable that, because of disparate incomes, filing separately may produce a lesser overall tax liability than if the couple filed jointly. To determine the financial benefit, the tax professional should prepare the tax return under both categories to determine the amount of actual taxes due with each filing. Note that this status does not necessarily reflect *marital* status, meaning that a couple who has legally separated may still file a joint return or may elect to file separately.

head of household
Filing status

4. **Head of household.** A person may file under this status if he or she is considered unmarried at the close of the tax year, has provided more than half the cost of keeping up a house

during that year, and is responsible for the maintenance of a dependent child or parent. A married person may use this status if he or she is married to a nonresident alien or is legally separated pursuant to the person's state law.

5. **Qualified widow(er) with dependent child.** This category is permitted for surviving spouses for two years following the death of the other spouse. To qualify, the person must have been married to the decedent and eligible to file a joint return in the year of the decedent's death (eligibility is the requirement, not actually filing under that status), has not remarried, and claims as a dependent a child, stepchild, adopted child, or foster child.

qualified widow(er) with dependent child
Filing status

When assisting a client in the preparation of a tax return, the practitioner must first determine the appropriate filing status of the client because of the effect of such determination on the client's eventual tax rate.

The following judicial decision is appended to highlight the court's interpretation of "head of household" filing status.

TAX LAW & POLICY

PELAYO-ZABALZA V. COMMISSIONER OF INTERNAL REVENUE
T.C. Summary Opinion 2002-134

Respondent determined a deficiency in petitioner's Federal income tax for the taxable year 2000 in the amount of $4,679.

After a concession by respondent, the issues for decision by the Court are as follows:

(1) Whether petitioner is entitled to head of household filing status. We hold that he is not. . . .

An adjustment to the amount of petitioner's standard deduction is a purely mechanical matter, the resolution of which is dependent on our disposition of the disputed issue regarding petitioner's filing status.

BACKGROUND

This case was deemed to be submitted fully stipulated, and the facts stipulated are so found. Petitioner resided in Sacramento, California, at the time that his petition was filed with the Court.

Throughout the taxable year 2000, petitioner was married to Rita Pelayo and lived with her, together with the couple's two daughters, in Sacramento, California.

During 2000, petitioner was employed as a laborer and received wages in the amount of $11,767. Rita Pelayo was also employed in 2000 and received wages in the amount of $2,576.

Petitioner timely filed a Form 1040A, U.S. Individual Income Tax Return, for the taxable year 2000. On his return, petitioner designated his filing status as head of household and claimed the standard deduction in the amount corresponding to that filing status. Petitioner also claimed: (1) Deductions for dependency exemptions for his two minor daughters, Alejandra Anae and Araceli, and (2) the maximum earned income credit. Petitioner did not claim a child tax credit.

Petitioner reported on his income tax return for 2000 the wages that he received, and he attached to his return a Form W-2, Wage and Tax Statement, from each of his two employers. Petitioner did not report on his return the wages that his spouse received, nor did he attach to his return the Form W-2 from her employer.

Petitioner's income tax return for 2000 was prepared by Juan E. Hernandez of Zeta Enterprise in Sacramento, California. Petitioner sought the assistance of a return preparer because he was unable to prepare a return himself. Petitioner is a native speaker of Spanish, and his ability to speak and understand English is extremely limited.

The record does not disclose whether Rita Pelayo filed an income tax return for the taxable year 2000.

In the notice of deficiency, respondent determined that petitioner's filing status was "married filing separately" rather than "head of household." Respondent also determined that petitioner was not entitled to either (1) deductions for dependency exemptions or (2) an earned income credit. Respondent also adjusted the amount of petitioner's standard deduction to correspond with the determined filing status. Finally, respondent did not make any allowance for a child tax credit.

DISCUSSION

A. Filing Status

In order to qualify for "head of household" filing status, an individual must satisfy several requirements. One of those requirements relates to the individual's marital status. Thus, as relevant herein, section 2(b)(1) provides that "an individual shall be considered a head of a household if, and only if, such individual is not married at the close of his taxable year."

The parties stipulated that petitioner was married to Rita Pelayo and lived with her throughout the taxable year 2000. Under such circumstances, petitioner does not qualify for "head of household" filing status. Cf. secs. 2(c), 7703(b) (regarding certain married individuals living apart who are treated as not married).

In view of the foregoing, we sustain respondent's determination on this issue.

C. Conclusion

We are satisfied that petitioner is a conscientious taxpayer who tried to fulfill his Federal income tax obligations by securing the assistance of a professional tax return preparer. Unfortunately for petitioner, his preparer gave him erroneous advice. Although this fact might have insulated petitioner from liability for a penalty if respondent had determined one, a taxpayer's good-faith reliance on a professional tax preparer does not insulate the taxpayer from liability for the underlying tax itself.

Reviewed and adopted as the report of the Small Tax Case Division.

To give effect to respondent's concession and our disposition of the disputed issues, Decision will be entered under Rule 155.

Once filing status has been ascertained, the taxpayer is entitled to claim **exemptions** from income subject to taxation. Two types of such exemptions are **personal exemptions,** which the taxpayer takes for oneself, and **exemptions for dependents**. A **dependent** is any person for whom the taxpayer contributes more than half of the person's support, provided that the dependent person is a relation or a member of the household of the taxpayer in question. The taxpayer is entitled to this exemption even if the dependent died during the tax year, provided that the taxpayer meets the support requirement for the period during which the dependent was alive. The purpose of the exemption is to permit the taxpayer with a minimum amount of income to avoid being subject to income taxation.

Practical tip

All federal income tax forms are available on-line at <http://www.irs.org>.

An example of a dependent exemption appears in *Knight v. Commissioner,* 1994 U.S. App. LEXIS 17221, the petitioner appealed from order of the U.S. Tax Court, which granted summary judgment to the respondent commissioner of the Internal Revenue Service in petition challenging constitutionality of *26 U.S.C.S. § 152*(e) under which the respondent disallowed the petitioner's exemptions for his children for failure to obtain declaration that the custodial parent would not claim exemptions.

The petitioner paid child support to his ex-wife in an amount that constituted more than one-half of each child's support. He claimed income tax exemptions for his children. The respondent commissioner of the Internal Revenue Service disallowed these exemptions under *26 U.S.C.S. § 152*(e), which provided that a noncustodial

exemption
Reduction in gross income permitted for every taxpayer and for each of the taxpayer's dependents

personal exemption
Specified amount of income not subject to taxation

exemption for dependents
Rule permitted a taxpayer to exclude from income a specified amount for each of the taxpayer's dependents

dependent
A person for whom the taxpayer provides over half of his or her support

parent could claim exemptions for his dependent children only if he obtained the custodial parent's written declaration stating that the custodial parent would not claim the exemptions. The petitioner failed to obtain the required declaration. In his redetermination petition, the petitioner alleged that section 152(e) was unconstitutional. The tax court granted summary judgment to the respondent. The court affirmed. Section 152(e) did not create an unconstitutional irrebuttable presumption. A statutorily defined irrebuttable presumption was not unconstitutional in statutes that regulated economic matters. Section 152(e) did not determine guilt; nor did it inflict punishment. Thus, it was not a bill of attainder. Section 152(e) did not violate the petitioner's right to equal protection. The difference in treatment of alimony and child support was justified by their difference in nature.

The court affirmed the summary judgment for the respondent. The statute did not create an unconstitutional irrebuttable presumption because it regulated economic matters, it was not a bill of attainder because it did not inflict punishment, and it did not violate the petitioner's equal protection rights by treating alimony differently from child support.

The remainder of this chapter will analyze the provisions of Form 1040, the basic federal income tax return for individuals. Persons with simplified income sources and standard deductions can file a simplified version of this form, called the **Form 1040EZ** (see Exhibit 2.2). For our understanding of federal income tax law, however, the Form 1040 provides a greater breadth of analysis.

Sources of Income

As stated previously, IRS taxes a person on "all income from whatever source derived." This figure is the person's **gross income.** From gross income certain items may be subtracted to arrive at a figure called the **taxable income,** the amount on which the tax is assessed. These subtractions from gross income are called **deductions,** and will be discussed later in the chapter.

The term *income* as interpreted by the court and the Internal Revenue Service reflects not only cash received by a taxpayer but also goods, services, and any other financial benefits to the taxpayer that are capable of being quantified and are not considered to be *de minimus*. **Quantify** means to attribute a specific dollar amount to an item. The ***de minimus* rule** states that IRS will not tax certain benefits received by the taxpayer that have little or insignificant value.

Form 1040EZ
Simplified federal individual income tax return

gross income
All income from whatever source derived

taxable income
Income from whatever source derived

deduction
Item used to reduce amount of taxable income

quantify
Allocating a dollar value to an item

***de minimus* rule**
An item of little or inconsequential value will not be taxed by the IRS

Individual Income Taxation

Form 1040EZ — Department of the Treasury—Internal Revenue Service
Income Tax Return for Single and Joint Filers With No Dependents (99) **2003**

OMB No. 1545-0675

Label (See page 12.) Use the IRS label. Otherwise, please print or type.

- Your first name and initial | Last name | Your social security number
- If a joint return, spouse's first name and initial | Last name | Spouse's social security number
- Home address (number and street). If you have a P.O. box, see page 12. | Apt. no.
- City, town or post office, state, and ZIP code. If you have a foreign address, see page 12.

▲ **Important!** ▲
You **must** enter your SSN(s) above.

Presidential Election Campaign (page 12)
Note. Checking "Yes" will not change your tax or reduce your refund.
Do you, or your spouse if a joint return, want $3 to go to this fund? ▶
You: ☐ Yes ☐ No   Spouse: ☐ Yes ☐ No

Income
Attach Form(s) W-2 here.
Enclose, but do not attach, any payment.

1. Wages, salaries, and tips. This should be shown in box 1 of your Form(s) W-2. Attach your Form(s) W-2. 1
2. Taxable interest. If the total is over $1,500, you cannot use Form 1040EZ. 2
3. Unemployment compensation and Alaska Permanent Fund dividends (see page 14). 3
4. Add lines 1, 2, and 3. This is your **adjusted gross income**. 4

Note. You must check Yes or No.

5. Can your parents (or someone else) claim you on their return?
   ☐ Yes. Enter amount from worksheet on back.
   ☐ No. If **single**, enter $7,800.
   If **married filing jointly**, enter $15,600.
   See back for explanation. 5
6. Subtract line 5 from line 4. If line 5 is larger than line 4, enter -0-.
   This is your **taxable income**. ▶ 6

Payments and tax
7. Federal income tax withheld from box 2 of your Form(s) W-2. 7
8. Earned income credit (EIC). 8
9. Add lines 7 and 8. These are your **total payments**. ▶ 9
10. **Tax.** Use the amount on **line 6 above** to find your tax in the tax table on pages 24–28 of the booklet. Then, enter the tax from the table on this line. 10

Refund
Have it directly deposited! See page 19 and fill in 11b, 11c, and 11d.

11a. If line 9 is larger than line 10, subtract line 10 from line 9. This is your **refund**. ▶ 11a
  ▶ b. Routing number □□□□□□□□□   ▶ c. Type: ☐ Checking ☐ Savings
  ▶ d. Account number □□□□□□□□□□□□□□□□□

Amount you owe
12. If line 10 is larger than line 9, subtract line 9 from line 10. This is the **amount you owe**. For details on how to pay, see page 20. ▶ 12

Third party designee
Do you want to allow another person to discuss this return with the IRS (see page 20)? ☐ Yes. Complete the following. ☐ No
Designee's name ▶   Phone no. ▶ (   )   Personal identification number (PIN) ▶

Sign here
Under penalties of perjury, I declare that I have examined this return, and to the best of my knowledge and belief, it is true, correct, and accurately lists all amounts and sources of income I received during the tax year. Declaration of preparer (other than the taxpayer) is based on all information of which the preparer has any knowledge.
Joint return? See page 11. Keep a copy for your records.
Your signature | Date | Your occupation | Daytime phone number (   )
Spouse's signature. If a joint return, **both** must sign. | Date | Spouse's occupation

Paid preparer's use only
Preparer's signature ▶ | Date | Check if self-employed ☐ | Preparer's SSN or PTIN
Firm's name (or yours if self-employed), address, and ZIP code ▶ | EIN | Phone no. (   )

For Disclosure, Privacy Act, and Paperwork Reduction Act Notice, see page 23.   Cat. No. 11329W   Form **1040EZ** (2003)

Exhibit 2.2 Form 1040EZ

Form 1040EZ (2003) Page **2**

Use this form if	• Your filing status is single or married filing jointly. • You (and your spouse if married filing jointly) were under age 65 and not blind at the end of 2003. If you were born on January 1, 1939, you are considered to be age 65 at the end of 2003. • You do not claim any dependents. • Your taxable income (line 6) is less than $50,000. • You do not claim a deduction for educator expenses, the student loan interest deduction, or the tuition and fees deduction. • You do not claim an education credit, the retirement savings contributions credit, or the health coverage tax credit. • You had **only** wages, salaries, tips, taxable scholarship or fellowship grants, unemployment compensation, or Alaska Permanent Fund dividends, and your taxable interest was not over $1,500. **But** if you earned tips, including allocated tips, that are not included in box 5 and box 7 of your W-2, you may not be able to use Form 1040EZ (see page 13). If you are planning to use Form 1040EZ for a child who received Alaska Permanent Fund dividends, see page 14. • You did not receive any advance earned income credit payments. If you are not sure about your filing status, see page 11. If you have questions about dependents, use TeleTax topic 354 (see page 6). If you **cannot use this form,** use TeleTax topic 352 (see page 6).
Filling in your return For tips on how to avoid common mistakes, see page 21.	If you received a scholarship or fellowship grant or tax-exempt interest income, such as on municipal bonds, see the booklet before filling in the form. Also, see the booklet if you received a Form 1099-INT showing Federal income tax withheld or if Federal income tax was withheld from your unemployment compensation or Alaska Permanent Fund dividends. **Remember,** you must report all wages, salaries, and tips even if you do not get a Form W-2 from your employer. You must also report all your taxable interest, including interest from banks, savings and loans, credit unions, etc., even if you do not get a Form 1099-INT.

Worksheet for dependents who checked "Yes" on line 5
(keep a copy for your records)
	Use this worksheet to figure the amount to enter on line 5 if someone can claim you (or your spouse if married filing jointly) as a dependent, even if that person chooses not to do so. To find out if someone can claim you as a dependent, use TeleTax topic 354 (see page 6).
	
	A. Amount, if any, from line 1 on front + 250.00 Enter total ▶ A. _____
	B. Minimum standard deduction . . . . B. 750.00
	C. Enter the **larger** of line A or line B here . . . . C. _____
	D. Maximum standard deduction. If **single,** enter $4,750; if **married filing jointly,** enter $9,500 . . . . D. _____
	E. Enter the **smaller** of line C or line D here. This is your standard deduction . . . . E. _____
	F. Exemption amount.
	  • If single, enter -0-.
	  • If married filing jointly and—
	    —both you and your spouse can be claimed as dependents, enter -0-.
	    —only one of you can be claimed as a dependent, enter $3,050. F. _____
	G. Add lines E and F. Enter the total here and on line 5 on the front . . G. _____
	
	If you checked "No" on line 5 because no one can claim you (or your spouse if married filing jointly) as a dependent, enter on line 5 the amount shown below that applies to you.
	• Single, enter $7,800. This is the total of your standard deduction ($4,750) and your exemption ($3,050).
	• Married filing jointly, enter $15,600. This is the total of your standard deduction ($9,500), your exemption ($3,050), and your spouse's exemption ($3,050).

Mailing return	Mail your return by **April 15, 2004.** Use the envelope that came with your booklet. If you do not have that envelope or if you moved during the year, see the back cover for the address to use.

Form **1040EZ** (2003)

Exhibit 2.2 (Continued)

Example

A dentist agrees to fill a cavity for an accountant in return for the accountant preparing the dentist's income tax return. Although no money changes hands, each has received an item of taxable income. The fee the dentist typically charges for filling a cavity quantifies the income received by the accountant, and the accountant's typical fee for tax preparation quantifies the dentist's income. Each such quantified item must be reported on both income tax returns.

Example

Pursuant to state law, a landlord who retains a security deposit from a tenant must give the tenant interest on that amount. In a given year, because of reduced interest rates, the tenant's interest on her security deposit is $2.63. Although such an amount reflects income, if the tenant forgets to report that item it will probably be considered *de minimus* and not result in any negative tax consequences.

Form 1040 divides income into various categories, and each will be discussed sequentially.

Wages and Salaries

The concept of wages and salaries includes all compensation that an employee receives for services rendered. Typically, most employees receive money for the services they provide; however, many employees receive certain other items of a quantifiable nature which may have to be included as income under this category. When an employee receives free use of a company car for personal as well as business needs, free meals at the workplace, and other such items, these benefits are usually referred to as **fringe benefits.** The determination as to whether such fringe benefits must be included as income is statutorily determined, meaning that if an item is not specifically excluded from gross income then it must be included as wages to the taxpayer. The list of excluded benefits appears in section 1.61-21 of the Income Tax Regulations. Generally, if the benefit is offered to all employees regardless of level of compensation, such item is not considered to be part of the employee's wages. If the benefit is only provided to highly compensated personnel, however, those persons must include the fair market value of those benefits as part of their salaries and wages.

fringe benefits
Financial benefits in addition to wages and salaries afforded employees

Example

A large law firm provides free lunches to all of its employees. None of the employees must report the value of these meals as income. However, if free meals are provided only to the firm's senior partners, those partners must report the meals' fair market value as part of their wages and salaries.

In addition to the nondiscriminatory test (the benefit being provided to all employees), in order to be excluded from income the benefit must be of the type the business offers for sale to customers and clients, thereby accruing no additional cost in providing them to employees.

Example

An airline provides free travel tickets to its employees. Such benefit, if offered on the same basis to all airline personnel, would not be considered part of the employees' wages or salaries.

Once these two tests are met, nondiscriminatory treatment and no-additional-cost services, the following items have been statutorily determined to be excluded from an employee's wages.

qualified employee discount
Permitting an employee to purchase the employer's goods at a reduced price which may or may not be considered a taxable benefit

working condition fringe benefit
A financial benefit derived as an adjunct to wages for employees

A. **Qualified employee discounts.** These discounts are sales to employees at a reduced rate or with a rebate attached. However, certain limitations are imposed. For services, the discount cannot exceed 20% of the price of the service offered to the general public. For property, the discount cannot exceed the company's gross profit on the product.

B. **Working condition fringe benefit.** This exclusion relates to property the employee uses in furtherance of the employer's business, such as the use of a company car for salespeople.

C. *De minimus* benefit. As discussed, if the value of the benefit is nominal or minimal, such item does not form a part of the employee's wages.

Example

At the end of each year a company gives each of its employees a small token gift as well as a bonus based on a percentage of the employee's salary. The token gift would be considered *de minimus*, whereas the bonus, as a percentage of the employee's salary, is includable as part of the employee's wages.

D. **Qualified transportation.** This excludes such items as transit passes, fare cards, and tokens. This exclusion is limited to $100 per month.

E. **Qualified moving expenses.** Moving expenses will be discussed later in the chapter.

F. **Athletic facilities.** This exclusion from income exists for any athletic facility maintained on the employer's premises or operated by the employer for its employees and their families.

athletic facility
An employee fringe benefit if maintained for workers by the employer

Unless the item appears on this list, or appears in the following discussion of other exclusions, the item is regarded as part of the person's wages or salary. Each year the employer is required to provide the employee with a wage or salary form indicating the value of such benefits during the year, as well as any taxes that have already been withheld, and this figure is used to determine the taxpayer's gross wages or salary. Remember, however, that persons who also operate on a barter system will be able to substitute the value of the services or products they receive as a barter exchange.

Exercise

Blackhound Bus Lines offers its employees free travel on its buses. Would this be includable as part of the employees' wages? Would your answer be different if the bus company "bumps" paying passengers to accommodate employees? Explain.

In a private ruling, No. 9816007, 1997 PRL LEXIS 2260, the IRS was presented with the following facts:

X is a distributor of vehicles manufactured by Y, an affiliated company. X, for various business reasons, provides vehicles to certain X employees for their use for a specified period of time. During the years at issue, X included an amount in the recipient employees' incomes and wages based on the formula used by the Service in settling adjustments proposed for prior taxable years of X with regard to the same issue.

Specifically, during the years at issue, X determined the includable amount by applying the automobile lease valuation rule of sec. 1.61-21(d) of the regulations to the fair market value of the vehicles as determined under the safe harbor set forth in Notice 89-110: manufacturer's invoice price plus 4%. X determined the manufacturer's invoice price based on the invoice price of the vehicles sold by Y (the manufacturer) to X (the distributor), rather than on the invoice price to the dealer. X added to its invoice price the various costs of obtaining the vehicles from Y and an additional 4%. Neither sales tax nor title fees were added to the invoice price for purposes of calculating the fair market value under the safe harbor.

The value of the use of employer-provided vehicles is a fringe benefit that must be included in gross income under sec. 61(a)(1) of the U.S. Code, unless otherwise excluded. Furthermore, the fringe benefit is remuneration for employment and, thus, wages for purposes of the FICA tax and income tax withholding, unless an exception applies. The amount included in income and wages is generally based on the benefit's fair market value. At issue is whether X is entitled to use the automobile lease valuation rule of sec. 1.61-21(d), instead of the general valuation rule of sec. 1.61-21(b), for purposes of valuing the use of the vehicles provided to employees during the years at issue. Whether the special valuation rule is available for these vehicles depends on whether X improperly applied the valuation rule within the meaning of sec. 1.61-21(c)(5). Incident to that issue is whether X is entitled to use the safe harbor method of manufacturer's invoice price plus 4% for purposes of calculating the fair market value to be applied to the annual lease value table.

Because X owns, rather than leases, the vehicles provided to X employees, the safe harbor provided in Notice 89-110 of manufacturer's invoice price plus 4% is not available to X. Rather, sec. 1.61-21(d)(5)(ii)(B) of the regulations provides that the safe harbor value of automobiles OWNED by the employer is the employer's cost of purchasing the automobile, provided the purchase is made at arm's length. However, this safe harbor is not available for automobiles MANUFACTURED BY THE EMPLOYER (OR AN ENTITY WITH WHICH IT IS AGGREGATED UNDER SECTION 1.61-21(c)(4)). If an automobile owned by the employer is manufactured by an entity with which it is aggregated, such as the vehicles owned by X but manufactured by Y, section 1.61-21(d)(5)(ii)(B) specifically provides that the value of the automobile MUST BE DETERMINED UNDER SECTION 1.61-21(d)(5)(I) BASED ON THE AMOUNT THAT AN INDIVIDUAL WOULD HAVE TO PAY IN AN ARM'S-LENGTH TRANSACTION TO PURCHASE THE PARTICULAR AUTOMOBILE. (Emphasis added.)

Consequently, the safe harbor provided in Notice 89-110 is not available to X for valuing the vehicles at issue for purposes of applying the automobile lease valuation rule. The fair market value of the vehicles should have been determined under section 1.61-21(d)(5)(i) of the regulations based on the amount that an individual would have to pay in an arm's-length transaction to purchase each vehicle and that value should have been applied to the annual lease value table.

Since the fair market value of the vehicles at issue was not properly determined, the automobile lease valuation rule of sec. 1.61-21(d) was not properly applied and, under sec. 1.61-21(c)(5), X is no longer entitled to use the special valuation rules for valuing the use of such vehicles. Rather, X must value the use of the vehicles under the general valuation rules provided in sec. 1.61-21(b) of the regulations. Specifically, the value of the use of each vehicle provided to X employees equals the amount that an individual would have to pay in an arm's-length transaction to lease the same or comparable vehicle on the same or comparable conditions in the geographic area in which the vehicle is available for use.

Furthermore, the operation of sec. 1.61-21(c)(5) to make the special valuation rules unavailable to X for valuing the use of the vehicles during the years at issue is not affected by X's reliance on the method used to settle adjustments made in a prior audit cycle. The adjustment for the years at issue was based on the Service's statement of a rule in mediums of official pronouncement; see *Elkins,* supra, at 681, namely, section 1.61-21 of the regulations and Notice 89-110. By contrast, X's deficiency resulted from its reliance on the method considered appropriate by an individual agent in settling an adjustment for prior years although in apparent direct conflict with the plain language of section 1.61-21 of the regulations and Notice 89-110.

Neither is the proper application of the rules in section 1.61-21 of the regulations and Notice 89-110, as set forth herein, hindered by the existence of any settlements between the Service and other taxpayers in the industry on allegedly more favorable terms with respect to valuing employee use of company vehicles. See *Davis v. Commissioner,* 65 T.C. 1014, 1022 (1976); *Keel v. Commissioner,* T.C. Memo. 1997-278.

X is not entitled to use the additional safe harbor provided in Notice 89-110 (manufacturer's invoice price plus 4%) for determining the fair market value of the vehicles provided for the use of X employees for purposes of applying the automobile lease valuation rule.

X is no longer entitled to use the automobile lease valuation rule provided in section 1.61-21(d) of the regulations for purposes of valuing the use by X employees of the vehicles at issue.

X's reliance on an erroneous interpretation of Notice 89-110 that was nonetheless consistent with the method used by the Service in settling adjustments made during a prior audit cycle of X does not preclude the Service from retroactively collecting any underwithheld taxes attributable to the erroneous interpretation.

Interest and Dividends

Interest represents income a person receives from various types of passive investments. A **passive investment** is one in which the person merely provides money to someone else, the other person providing all of the work. Interest income can be derived from bank accounts, loans, money market accounts, and general obligations, and represents the cost to the borrower for using the investor's

interest
Income derived from persons who are using the taxpayer's money

passive investment
Income derived from investments for which the taxpayer does not perform services

money. Certain items called dividends are actually deemed to be interest, such as income from deposits in credit unions, building and loan associations, and credit savings banks. All such items appear on Form 1040 as interest income.

Example

A woman loans her brother-in-law $10,000 to start a business. This loan is documented by a promissory note in which the brother-in-law agrees to pay the woman 10% per year as interest on the loan until the entire sum is repaid. Each year that the loan is outstanding, the brother-in-law pays the woman $1000, and that amount is includable as interest income to the woman.

---

dividend
Investor's return on investment

Dividends represent an investor's profit resulting from an investment in which the investor holds an ownership interest. Typically, shareholders in a corporation or members of an LLC receive dividends on the business's profits reflective of their percentage ownership in the enterprise, and the amount of such dividends must be included as part of the investor's gross income. In many instances, however, the investor may receive property or stock distributions rather than cash, and the taxability of such items follows slightly different rules.

For property dividends, distributions in property of the enterprise rather than cash, the fair market value of the item must be reported as part of the investor's gross income. Note that the quantification is "fair market value," not the "book value" of the item—the value of the property as it appears on the enterprise's accounting books.

For share dividends, the taxpayer does not have to report any income in the year that the share dividend is received. Rather, the year of receipt determines the value of the share, such value being called the holder's **basis** in the stock. Only when that share is sold is the investor required to report any gain or loss on the item. The gain or loss is calculated as the difference between the item's basis and the selling price.

basis
Original value of property in the hands of a taxpayer, sometimes reflecting the original cost plus improvements to the property

Note also that if the dividend represents the return of the investor's investment rather than income generated from the operation of the business, then the taxpayer receives no income.

Example

A man has held stock in a corporation for many years. The corporation decides to dissolve, and returns to the shareholder $20,000. Of this $20,000, $2000 represents a dividend from the operation of the business, $15,000 represents the return of the investor's initial investment, and $3000 represents growth in the value of the investment. The shareholder must report $2000 as dividend income and $3000 as a capital gain (discussed later in the chapter). The $15,000 is not income to the shareholder.

In the following case the court had to determine whether the taxpayer was entitled, in addition to other tax matters, to a pension income exclusion and whether he had unreported dividend income.

TAX LAW & POLICY

SMITH V. COMMISSIONER OF INTERNAL REVENUE
T.C. MEMO 1987-613 (1987)

Respondent determined a deficiency of $5,075 in petitioner's 1982 Federal income tax and an addition to tax under section 6661 in the amount of [Text Deleted by Court Emendation] $508. Respondent also determined that petitioner was liable for additions to tax under section 6653(a)(1) in the amount of [Text Deleted by Court Emendation] $254 and section 6653(a)(2) in an amount equal to fifty percent of the interest due on the $5,075 underpayment. Further, at trial, respondent orally moved for damages pursuant to section 6673. The issues for decision are (1) whether petitioner was entitled to a pension income exclusion; (2) whether petitioner had unreported dividend income; (3) whether petitioner is liable for additions to tax under section 6653(a); (4) whether damages should be awarded under section 6673; and (5) whether this Court has jurisdiction to abate interest on the deficiency.

GENERAL FINDINGS OF FACT

Petitioner resided in Silver Spring, Maryland, when he filed his petition with this Court. He timely filed a 1982 Federal income tax return. On September 30, 1985, petitioner made an advance payment to respondent of $5,075 in order to stop the running of interest on the underpayment of tax. At trial, petitioner requested that this sum be returned to him. He also asked the Court to abate the already accrued interest and to return the filing fee he paid to petition this Court.

I. Excluded Pension Income [Omitted]

II. Unreported Dividend Income

Respondent contends that during 1982, petitioner received dividend income from Dow Chemical Company, Parker Pen Company, McCormick & Co., and Transamerica Corporation totaling $1,001 which he did not include in income. Respondent determined that petitioner had unreported dividend income by comparing Form 1099 information reported by payors of dividends, with petitioner's tax return. Yetta Fleishman, respondent's witness from his office in Philadelphia, Pennsylvania, testified how the "matching program" uses the taxpayer's social security number to compare this information. Ms. Fleishman further testified that through the matching program, respondent was able to establish that petitioner received $36,000 in dividend income, $1,001 of which was not reported on his 1982 Federal income tax return.

Petitioner did not deny receiving these dividends. Rather, he testified that he could not verify the amount of his dividend income because either he could not locate his records, or he had discarded them. Moreover, petitioner steadfastly maintained that he possibly reported the dividends, but that one of the Schedules B on which these dividends may have been reported was now missing from his return. Petitioner failed, however, to produce a "complete" copy of his tax return. On the return that was filed, petitioner's dividend income was reported on seven Forms Schedule B. On line 10 of the seventh Form B, petitioner totaled his dividend income for the taxable year as $36,024.52. Petitioner's handwritten note on line 10 indicates that this amount represents the total "from all sheets." Petitioner's net dividend income, after subtracting capital gains distributions, as carried over from line 15 on this Form B to Form 1040, line 9a, was $35,099.35. These facts negate petitioner's claim that a Schedule B form is missing from his return.

Respondent's determination as to the amount petitioner received in dividend income is presumed to be correct and petitioner bears the burden of proving otherwise. *Welch v. Helvering,* 290 U.S. 111 (1933); Rule 142(a). Petitioner failed to produce any evidence on the issue of the omitted dividend income and therefore has failed to carry his burden of proof. We hold for respondent on this issue.

   III. Section 6653(a)—Additions to Tax For Negligence
      Or Disregard Of Rules And Regulations

Respondent contends that petitioner is liable for additions to tax under sections 6653(a)(1) and (2) because he failed to ascertain the rules governing the inclusion of his disability pension in gross income, he failed to report $1,001 of dividend income, and he failed to maintain adequate books and records of his dividend income.

Section 6653(a) provides for an addition to tax if an underpayment is due to negligence or intentional disregard of rules and regulations. Respondent's determination is presumed correct and the burden is on petitioner to prove these additions are erroneous. *Enoch v. Commissioner,* 57 T.C. 781 (1972); *Leroy Jewelry Co. v. Commissioner,* 36 T.C. 443 (1961).

Generally, taxpayers are required to maintain permanent books of account or records sufficient to establish the amount of gross income, deductions, credits, and other matters required to be shown in their tax returns. Sec. 1.6001-1(a), Income Tax Regs.

In this case, petitioner has not shown that he maintained any records of his dividend income. His failure to keep the records necessary to establish the amount of his gross income indicates that petitioner was negligent. Petitioner's

> negligence is also apparent in his disregard of the rules which required him to include his disability pension in income. We think the facts recited above clearly show that petitioner was negligent. Petitioner has not carried his burden of proof on this issue and we, therefore, uphold respondent's determination.
> Decision will be entered for the respondent.

Rental Income

Rental income is any income that a taxpayer receives for permitting someone else to use or occupy the taxpayer's property. Rental income can be derived from real property, such as an apartment or a summer home, or from personal property, such as a snowblower. All financial benefits received from renting property must be reported by the lessor as part of his or her gross income. Additionally, if the lessor receives **advance rents,** rent paid for future use of the property, such amounts must be reported by the recipient in the year received, not in the year covered by the future payment. Also, any property received to cancel a lease is also considered rental payment. Note that **security deposits** paid by the tenant are not rental income because they will be returned to the tenant at the termination of the lease if the tenant fulfills all rental obligations. Further, any other items that the tenant provides as a financial benefit to the lessor are includable as rental income.

rental income
Money received from leasing property

advance rent
Rent paid for future use of the premises or property

security deposit
Funds left with a lessor by a lessee that must be returned to the lessee at the termination of the lease if the lessee has completely fulfilled his or her rental obligations

Example
A summer house that is being rented is in need of a paint job. The tenant agrees to paint the house. The value of that painting is considered rental income to the landlord.

Not all rental income, however, is subject to taxation. The lessor is entitled to reduce the amount of rental income by the value of any expenses incurred in maintaining the property so that it is in a rentable condition.

Example
A landlord may deduct from the amount of rent received for leasing the summer home the cost of repairing the home's chimney.

If a lessor uses the property for personal use as well as for producing income, expenses of maintaining the property must be apportioned between the personal and rental use.

Example

A woman owns three houses, but only uses one of them one month each year. The remaining months she rents the house to students. Any expenses she has in maintaining the premises must be allocated; only eleven-twelfths of such expenses may be used to reduce the amount of her rental income for this house.

Retirement Plans

As a general rule, if the taxpayer did not pay for any part of his or her retirement, annuity, or pension plan, all amounts received by the taxpayer are considered income. An **annuity** is generally an insurance contract whereby a premium is paid for a number of years and at a certain age the annuitant is guaranteed a set amount of yearly income for life. If the taxpayer contributed to the cost of the plan, any income received from such plan that represents the return of the taxpayer's contribution is not taxable; only the amount received above that contributed sum is subject to federal income taxation. Note that distributions from a **Keogh plan,** a retirement plan established by a sole proprietorship or partnership, are completely taxable.

There are two methods used to compute the percentage of income derived from such plans, depending on when the taxpayer starts to receive distributions. If the initial distribution occurred prior to November 18, 1996, the taxpayer may use the **general rule** or the **simplified rule.** If distributions started on or after November 18, 1996, the taxpayer must use the simplified rule to compute the taxable portion of the distributions if the plan is a qualified plan.

Under the general rule for nonqualified plans, the taxpayer first determines his or her cost (investment, contribution) to the plan and divides that by the expected total return on the plan. This division creates a percentage. For each payment received, the taxpayer excludes that percentage of the payment as a return on investment.

annuity
A form of insurance in which, for a premium paid, the insured is guaranteed certain payments for life starting at a specified age. These payments are income to the recipient for the amount over the return of the premium payments

Keogh plan
Retirement plan for self-employed individuals

general rule
Method of determining the nontaxable amount of annuity payments

simplified rule
Method of determining nontaxable portion of an annuity payment

Example

Jane contributes $30,000 to her annuity plan. Based on actuarial tables, Jane can expect to receive a total of $300,000 in payments over her lifetime. Her percentage of excludible income is computed as follows:

$$\frac{30{,}000}{300{,}000} = 0.10$$

Consequently, 10% of each payment Jane receives is considered a return of capital, and she only includes 90% of such payments as retirement income.

Under the simplified plan, the taxpayer, using tables provided by the IRS, determines the total number of payments he or she can expect to receive over a lifetime. Note these payments are calculated on the taxpayer's life expectancy at the time the first payment is made. The taxpayer divides his or her contribution to the plan by the number of expected payments to determine the dollar amount that is deemed to be a return of capital.

Example

Using the same cost of $30,000 from the previous example, assume, pursuant to the tables, that Jane can expect to receive a total of 210 lifetime payments. To compute the nontaxable amount, the cost is divided by this number:

$$\frac{30,000}{210} = 142.86$$

Therefore, from each payment Jane can deduct $142.86 from the amount of her taxable retirement plan income.

If the annuity provides for successor benefits, such as to a surviving spouse, the calculations must include the life expectancies of both parties.

The tax law professional should also be alert to the fact that a person's social security benefits may likewise be subject to federal income taxation. For each benefit category, the IRS provides what is termed a **base amount.** If all of a person's income less deductions plus one-half of his or her social security benefits exceed that amount, the federal government taxes that excess income (IRC section 86).

In *Montgomery v. United States,* 18 F. 3d 500 (7th Cir. 1994), the appellant, the United States, sought review of the judgment in favor of appellees, husband and wife taxpayers, in the United States District Court for the Southern District of Indiana, Indianapolis Division, in appellees' suit for a refund of federal income tax.

Appellant challenged an adverse judgment in a suit for refund of federal income tax by appellees, husband and wife taxpayers. Appellee husband made contributions from his after-tax income to a defined benefit pension plan established under Civil Service Retirement System, *5 U.S.C.S. § 8331* et seq. Later, pursuant a new amendment, *5 U.S.C.S. § 8343a,* appellee husband elected to receive an alternative form of annuity, which consisted of a lump sum, upfront payment equal to his investment and a periodic annuity payment. Appellee claimed that this lump sum payment added a defined contribution element to his defined benefit plan and that the return of

base amount
Amount of income above which IRS taxes social security benefits

his investment, as reflected in the lump sum payment, was not taxable under *26 U.S.C.S. § 72.* The appellate court reversed, holding the alternative form of annuity was a defined benefit plan with an acceleration feature arbitrarily tied to any employee contributions and not a defined contribution plan. The fact that the amount of acceleration was tied to the amount of the contributions did not create a defined contribution plan because there was no such plan that simply returned an employee's contributions to him.

The appellate court reversed the judgment in favor of appellees, husband and wife taxpayers, in their suit for a refund of federal income tax. A lump sum payment made under an annuity created by the Civil Service Retirement System was not a nontaxable return of an investment. The annuity in question was a defined benefit plan and the accelerated lump sum payment was not a defined contribution component of a hybrid plan.

Other Income

In addition to the foregoing, Form 1040 includes a category of "Other Income" to take into account other sources of revenue to the taxpayer. This category includes the following:

alimony or **maintenance payments**
Payments made to a former spouse deemed to be income to the recipient spouse and a deduction from income for the payor spouse

A. **Alimony** or **maintenance payments.** Such payments are income to the recipient spouse, and are deductions from income for the payor spouse.

Exercise

Is a lump sum property settlement deductible as alimony? Why or why not? Read Barrett v. U.S., 74 F.3d 661 (5th Cir. 1996).

B. **Court awards.** Any funds received either by means of a settlement of a legal dispute or resulting from a final judgment of the court may or may not be included as income to the recipient depending on the nature of what the award represents. For example, any money received that represents actual loss to the recipient is not includable because it is compensatory in nature, reimbursing the party for loss. Conversely, any amounts reflecting punitive damages are not compensatory in nature and are considered "other income" to the recipient.

Example

A litigant in a personal injury action is awarded $500,000. Of that amount, $65,000 represents medical bills he had to pay, $25,000 represents lost wages, and the remainder represents pain, suffering, and mental anguish. Of this total amount, only $25,000 is taxable because it represents compensation for taxable income lost due to the injury. The remainder of the award is compensatory for out-of-pocket expenses and damages for the loss of nonquantifiable well-being.

C. **Cancelled debts.** If the taxpayer owes money to someone who forgives the debt, the taxpayer has received a financial benefit in that these funds may be kept rather than returned. As such, the amount of the cancelled debt is included as income. Note, however, if the funds were originally given as a gift rather than a loan, the funds would not be taxable to the recipient even though he or she is not required to repay the gift. The forgiveness of a loan may be considered a gift, depending on the surrounding circumstances.

D. **Barter.** The fair market value of property received as a barter exchange must be reflected as income (see earlier discussion in the chapter).

E. **Royalties.** A royalty is a fee received by the holder of an intellectual property right from a person the property right holder permits to use the property. Intellectual property subject to royalty payments includes copyrights, patents and service, and trade marks.

cancelled debt
Forgiveness of a loan that is considered income to the debtor

barter
Exchange of goods or services with no money passing hands

royalty
Payment made for use of intellectual property

Income Not Subject to Federal Income Taxation

As a corollary to the preceding ideas, the tax law professional should be aware of the several categories of income that are not subject to federal income taxation. A comprehensive discussion of all such items is beyond the scope and intent of this text book, but some of the more frequently encountered items are:

Accident and health insurance benefits
Proceeds from a life insurance policy
Gifts, either inter vivos or testamentary

As an example, in *Diedrich v. Commissioner,* 457 U.S. 191 (1982), the petitioners sought review of a decision of the U.S. Court of Appeals for the Eighth Circuit that petitioners realized taxable income to the extent the gift taxes paid by donees exceeded petitioners' adjusted bases in the property transferred to the donees.

Petitioners made various gifts of stock and voting trust certificates to donees on the condition that the donees pay the resulting federal and state gift taxes. A decision that petitioners realized income to the extent that the amount of the gift tax exceeded the adjusted basis in the property transferred was affirmed. The "reality," not the form, of the transactions governed. An examination of the donor's intent did not change the character of the benefit. The fact that the gift tax obligation was discharged by way of a conditional gift rather than from funds derived from a pregift sale did not alter the underlying benefit to petitioners. A donor who made a gift of property on condition that the donee pay the resulting gift taxes realized taxable income to the extent that the gift taxes paid by the donee exceeded the donor's adjusted basis in the property.

The court affirmed because the form and the intent of the gifts did not matter and the fact the gift was conditional did not change the benefit to petitioners.

Additional items not subject to federal income taxation are:

- Government transfer payments, such as public assistance, welfare, and veterans' benefits
- Scholarships and fellowships that pay for tuition, fees, books, supplies, and equipment (not for room, board, or other living expenses)

Allocation of Income

The preceding section of this chapter discussed the various sources of income that must be reported on the federal Form 1040. However, that discussion has not addressed the threshold question, Who is deemed to be the recipient of such income? Over the years many court and administrative decisions have been handed down to clarify this matter of the income recipient.

The basic legal principle involved states that, for earned income, the person who actually performs the services for which the income was earned reports the revenue. Many attempts have been made to **income shift,** having the earned income be attributable to someone other than the income earner, typically a spouse or child who might fall into a lower tax bracket pursuant to the American progressive income tax rates. Some legal methods that have been employed to shift income include the creation of a corporate entity as the income producer, disbursing its revenue to employees and shareholders, or the creation of a trust to accomplish the same goal. In almost all circumstances such tactics have failed to pass legal muster.

For unearned income, income derived from interest, dividends, royalties, and so forth, it is generally easier to shift the tax burden. However, be aware of the fact that all unearned income of a minor is attributable to the parent. This is not the case of a minor's earned income which is attributable specifically to the minor.

The following judicial decision is the seminal case in the area of income shifting.

---

income shift
Attempt to have earned income attributed to someone other than the income earner

TAX LAW & POLICY

LUCAS V. EARL
281 U.S. 111 (1930)

This case presents the question whether the respondent, Earl, could be taxed for the whole of the salary and attorney's fees earned by him in the years 1920 and 1921, or should be taxed for only a half of them in view of a contract with his wife which we shall mention. The Commissioner of Internal Revenue and the Board of Tax Appeals imposed a tax upon the whole, but their decision was reversed by the *Circuit Court of Appeals, 30 F.2d 898.* A writ of certiorari was granted by this Court.

By the contract, made in 1901, Earl and his wife agreed "that any property either of us now has or may hereafter acquire . . . in any way, either by earnings (including salaries, fees, etc.), or any rights by contract or otherwise, during the existence of our marriage, or which we or either of us may receive by gift, bequest, devise, or inheritance, and all the proceeds, issues, and profits of any and all such property shall be treated and considered and hereby is declared to be received, held, taken, and owned by us as joint tenants, and not otherwise, with the right of survivorship." The validity of the contract is not questioned, and we assume it to be unquestionable under the law of the State of California, in which the parties lived. Nevertheless we are of opinion that the Commissioner and Board of Tax Appeals were right.

The Revenue Act of 1918 approved February 24, 1919, c. 18, §§ 210, 211, 212(a), 213 (a), 40 Stat. 1057, 1062, 1064, 1065, imposes a tax upon the net income of every individual including "income derived from salaries, wages, or compensation for personal service . . . of whatever kind and in whatever form paid," § 213 (a). The provisions of the Revenue Act of 1921, c. 136, 42 Stat. 227, in sections bearing the same numbers are similar to those of the above. A very forcible argument is presented to the effect that the statute seeks to tax only income beneficially received, and that taking the question more technically the salary and fees became the joint property of Earl and his wife on the very first instant on which they were received. We well might hesitate upon the latter proposition, because however the matter might stand between husband and wife he was the only party to the contracts by which the salary and fees were earned, and it is somewhat hard to say that the last step in the performance of those contracts could be taken by anyone but himself alone. But this case is not to be decided by attenuated subtleties. It turns on the import and reasonable construction of the taxing act. There is no doubt that the statute could tax salaries to those who earned them and provide that the tax could not be escaped by anticipatory arrangements and contracts however skilfully devised to prevent the salary when paid from vesting even for a second in the man who earned it. That seems to us the import of the statute before us and we think that no

distinction can be taken according to the motives leading to the arrangement by which the fruits are attributed to a different tree from that on which they grew.
Judgment reversed.

Gains and Losses

As part of the Income section of Form 1040, the taxpayer is required to report any gain or loss resulting from the sale or exchange of property the taxpayer owned. Any gain represents income to the taxpayer, whereas any loss may be used to reduce the amount of the taxpayer's taxable income.

To calculate whether a transfer of property resulted in a gain or loss, the taxpayer must first determine his or her basis, or cost, in the transferred property. The following guidelines may be used to assist in determining this value.

A. If the property was purchased, the taxpayer must include his or her cost as reflected in the bill of sale of the item itself or of any item that had been purchased that was traded as the purchase price of the property in question. This figure may be increased by sales tax, freight and storage charges, professional fees, and any other amount disbursed to acquire the property. The value may also be reduced if the property had been damaged by the loss in value occasioned by the damage.

B. If the property was acquired by inter vivos gift, the taxpayer's basis is the fair market value of the item on the day of receipt. If the item was acquired by testamentary transfer, the basis for the recipient is either the fair market value of the property on the day of receipt or the donor's basis in the property. To determine whether the subject taxpayer had a gain or loss on the transfer of the gifted property, for gain the IRS uses the donor's basis, for loss the fair market value on the date of the gift.

C. If the property was acquired as compensation for services rendered, its cost is the fair market value of such services.

D. If the acquisition qualified as a "like kind exchange" it is the basis of the property originally transferred. To be a **like kind exchange,** the property received must be similar to the property given, and the property must have been held for investment or business use. For example, if sole proprietors swap computers they use in their businesses, the transfer would be a like kind exchange. The transfer of the properties also must

like kind exchange
Transfer of similar items that does not result in a taxable event

be virtually simultaneous and interdependent. With such a transfer there is no tax due on the exchange date, only when the property is eventually sold. If one party receives cash as well as property, his or her basis is the basis of the property transferred plus the cash received.

Exercise

A woman agrees to sell a golf course that she holds for a selling price of $2 million. At the closing the purchaser says he does not have the cash but is willing to give her a restaurant, a store, and a small apartment building he owns in exchange for the golf course. Would this qualify as a like kind exchange? Explain.

The following judicial decision discusses the court's interpretation of like-kind exchanges.

TAX LAW & POLICY

MAXWELL V. UNITED STATES OF AMERICA
1988 U.S. Dist. LEXIS 16990 (S.D. Fla.)

The Plaintiffs in this case, Mark T. Maxwell, Gertrude Maxwell, and Nancy Bell, were beneficiaries of a certain land trust designated as "Trust No. 665" for which the Southeast Bank of Riviera Beach acted in the capacity of trustee. The Seminole Building in Palm Beach, Florida, was acquired by the trust in 1980, as investment property.

There came a point in time when a Mr. James Skeffington on behalf of Seminole Associates approached the Plaintiff, Mark Maxwell, and proposed that Seminole Associates buy the Seminole Building. The Plaintiff, Maxwell, referred Skeffington to his attorney, H. Gordon Brown. (Brown later became involved with the escrow agreement, which is the subject matter of this litigation.)

At the same time Maxwell was interested in acquiring two parcels of real property located in Fort Lauderdale and in Michigan. According to the deposition of Maxwell, H. Gordon Brown advised the parties that they should make a like kind exchange of the properties under *Section 1031 of the Internal Revenue Code* to avoid paying on the gain at that time.

In February of 1981, H. Gordon Brown, on behalf of the Beneficiaries and Trust No. 665, assisted in drafting the purchase and sale agreement for the Seminole Building. On February 21, 1981, Skeffington, on behalf of the purchasers, and John C. Patten, Jr., on behalf of Trust No. 665, for the sellers, executed a purchase and sale agreement for the acquisition of the Seminole Building. Both sides agreed that the agreement provided for a total purchase price of two million five hundred thousand ($2,500,000.00) dollars less assumed mortgages and a one hundred thousand ($100,000.00) dollar earnest money deposit.

The agreement provided in pertinent part:

Upon prior written request of Seller, less than fifteen (15) days prior to the Closing Date, Purchaser agrees to comply with the reasonable requests of Seller with respect to Seller's election to execute a *Section 1031 I.R.C.* exchange (referred to as a "Third Party" exchange) of the Premises for real estate to be acquired by the Purchaser, provided, however, that the Closing Date is not to be extended or delayed beyond April 2, 1981.

On April 8, 1981, an escrow agreement was entered into between the parties wherein they agreed to place the cash proceeds of the sale of the Seminole Building into an escrow fund for the purpose of facilitating a future contemplated purchase of real property. That real property was then to go to the Plaintiffs. The Escrow Agreement provided in pertinent part:

The Seller alone shall have the right to terminate this escrow prior to the use thereof for purchasing the contemplated real property, but in any event this escrow shall terminate one (1) year from date, and on termination, all assets on deposit shall be transferred to the Southeast Bank, Trustee of Land Trust Number 665, and the Buyer and Escrow Agent Shall thereafter be relived [sic] of this agreement.

The Government points out in its memorandum of law that there is no explicit mention in the Escrow Agreement of an intention to effectuate a Section 1031 like kind exchange.

On or about April 13, 1981, the parties "closed" on the Seminole Building and title to the property was transferred to Seminole Associates. From the proceeds of the sale one million nine hundred eighty three thousand ($1,983,000.00) dollars was transferred into the escrow account at Southeast Bank in accordance with the escrow agreement. At this point in time, no property had been identified by the seller or purchaser as property to be exchanged for the Seminole Building.

In June of 1981, H. Gordon Brown on behalf of the Trust offered to purchase the Grand Union Supermarket in Fort Lauderdale, from an Alvin B. Lowe. The real estate transaction closed on September 1, 1981. At the closing of the Grand Union property, Trust No. 665, paid one hundred thousand ($100,000.00) dollars in cash to Lowe and executed a purchase money mortgage for the remaining purchase price of nine hundred thousand ($900,000.00) dollars. (It was stipulated to at the hearing for the motion for summary judgment that the $900,000.00 cash which had been in escrow had been used to purchase money market certificates.)

In October of 1981, the Trust offered to buy and in November of 1981, did buy K-Mart Property in Kingsford, Michigan, for a price of one million one hundred ninety-two thousand ($1,192,000.00) dollars. The Southeast Bank disbursed fifty thousand ($50,000.00) dollars to assist in the purchase of that property. Beneficiaries to the Trust took title to the K-Mart Property on either December 31, 1981, or sometime prior to January 1, 1982.

Plaintiffs filed tax returns for the year 1981, and failed to report any gain realized on the sale of the Seminole Building and it is the Plaintiff's contention that the transfers of property qualified as like kind exchanges for which any tax on gain would be deferred until a later time. The Internal Revenue Service assessed deficiencies which were paid by the Plaintiffs in this case and the present litigation ensued.

STATEMENT OF THE LAW

Section 1031(a) of the Internal Revenue Code of 1954, states in pertinent part:

No gain or loss shall be recognized if property held for productive use in trade or business or for investment is exchanged solely for property of a like kind to be held either for productive use in trade or business or for investment.

As pointed out in the Government's memorandum of law, the reason for the deferment stems from the congressional recognition that in an exchange of like kind property, where the newly acquired property is used in a trade or business or is held for investment, the taxpayer has not received a gain or suffered a loss in an economic sense. Rather, the new property can be considered as substantially a continuation of the old investment which has never been liquidated.

With the facts as previously stated and with that statement of law, the question before the Court is whether or not an exchange took place within the meaning of Section 1031 or whether the transaction which occurred was actually a sale and not a like kind exchange. Various factors must be looked at by the Court to determine whether or not there was, in fact, a like kind exchange or in actuality a sale of property which would then subject the property owners to payment on taxable gains.

"The very essence of an exchange is the transfer of property between owners, while the mark of a sale is the receipt of cash for property." *Carlton v. United States,* 385 F.2d 238, 242 (5th Cir. 1967). The contemplated receipt of cash, however, is not dispositive of the issue of the distinction between sale or exchange of property. While there can be receipt of cash as a contingency in a like kind exchange, there cannot be a sale with receipted cash and then a future purchase of property unless there is an integrated plan for purchase involving what has been termed as a "bullet-proof escrow agreement." See *Carlton,* Id.; *Briggs v. Commissioner,* 632 F.2d 1171 (5th Cir. 1980); *Swain v. United States,* 651 F.2d 1066 (5th Cir. 1981).

The wording of Section 1031 seems also to require simultaneity of the transfer of property. This, however, is also not the case. Courts have granted leeway to the parties to a like kind exchange for the transfer of those properties to take place and in *Starker v. United States,* 602 F.2d 1341 (9th Cir. 1979) it appears that the second parcel of property was not exchanged until some five years later. In *Starker,* the Ninth Circuit Court of Appeals approved the transaction of the tax-free exchange in spite of a lack of identification of the exchange property, nonsimultaneous acts, and the fact that the seller might receive cash. This Court finds that the Plaintiff's reliance on Starker is misplaced. The pivotal point upon which this Court makes its recommendation to the District Court, with respect to the case at bar, is the escrow account. The seller, in the case at bar, had by virtue of the escrow agreement, unbridled discretion to terminate the escrow prior to the use thereof for purchasing the "contemplated" real property. In *Starker,* there was no escrow account to which the taxpayer had unrestricted access. In addition, this Court finds from the stipulated facts that the funds in the escrow were not actually used to acquire the Grand Union property. The Grand Union property was purchased from cash in the form of a purchase money mortgage. This Court is not persuaded by the Plaintiff's argument that the lawyer H. Gordon Brown "would not permit the Beneficiaries of the Trust No. 665 to obtain any of the escrowed proceeds for any reason other than obtaining exchange properties unless the tax purposes of the transaction were totally frustrated." It appears from the written document in evidence in this case that Brown could not have stopped the Beneficiaries of the Trust from demanding the funds to be paid over to them from the escrow account without having purchased like kind property. The failure to make the escrow agreement "bullet proof" is fatal to Plaintiffs' case.

Both parties, at oral argument, state that the best case in their respective favor is the case of *Earlene T. Barker, Petitioner, v. Commissioner of Internal Revenue, Respondent,* 74 T.C. 555 (June 1980). The facts of that case are very similar to the facts of the case at bar. In *Barker* the Court states that:

The exchange requirement poses an analytical problem because it runs headlong into the familiar tax law maximum that the substance of a transaction controls over form. In a sense, the substance of a transaction in which the taxpayer sells property and immediately reinvests the proceeds in a like kind property is much different from the substance of a transaction in which two parcels are exchanged without cash. *Bell Lines, Inc., v. United States,* 480 F. 2d 710, 711 (4th Cir. 1973). Yet, if the exchange requirement is to have any significance at all that perhaps formalistic difference between two types of transactions must, at least on occasions engender different results. This Court cites with approval *Starker v. United States,* 602 F.2d 1341, 1352 (9th Cir. 1979).

The Barker Court goes on to say that:

. . . at some point the confluence of some sufficient number of deviations will bring about a taxable result. Whether the cause be economic and business realities or poor tax planning, prior cases make clear that taxpayers who stray too far, run the risk of having their transactions characterized as a sale and reinvestment. At para. 74.42 P-H T.C. 74-306.

The crucial language of *Barker* is that the parties must intend that there be a like kind exchange. Barker goes on to state:

Consonant with this intent, the essence of the agreements among the parties was that petitioner would exchange the Demion property for the Casa El Camino property rather than have the petitioner sell the Demion property and reinvest the proceeds. This was accomplished through contractual arrangements which were such that petitioner did not nor could not obtain actual or constructive receipt of the cash proceeds from the sale of the Demion property to Goodyear.

The *Barker* case also requires mutually interdependent contracts which are part of an integrated plan to specifically earmark funds for particular like kind exchanges of property. This airtight escrow agreement is totally lacking in the case at bar and for that reason this Court finds that the exchange which took place was such as to render the transaction a sale of property and not a like kind exchange. Again citing *Barker:*

Under the Commissioner's administrative position, an exchange can be effected through an escrow account as long as the taxpayer cannot obtain use of the escrow monies. *Rev. Rul. 77-297.* Since the money paid into escrow here was earmarked for the Casa El Camino property and could never be made available to petitioner under the terms of the escrow agreements, this transaction meets the requirements of a like kind exchange.

Based on the foregoing finding of facts and the conclusions of law, this Court respectfully recommends to the District Court that judgment be entered for the Defendant, the United States of America, in cases 86-8446-CIV-ZLOCH and 86-8447-CIV-ZLOCH.

The parties have ten (10) days from the date of this Report and Recommendation to file their objections, if any, in writing to the Honorable William J. Zloch, United States District Court Judge.

DONE and SUBMITTED this 29th day of July, 1988, at West Palm Beach in the Northern Division of the Southern District of Florida.

FINAL ORDER OF DISMISSAL—September 16, 1988, Filed

THIS MATTER is before the Court upon the Report and Recommendation (DE 38) filed herein by the United States Magistrate, Ann E. Vitunac, dated July 29, 1988, and upon the Objections (DE 40) filed by the Plaintiffs, Mark T. Maxwell and Gertrude Maxwell, and Larry S. Bell and Nancy Bell.

Oral argument on the Report and Recommendation (DE 38) and the Objections (DE 40) thereto was held before the Court on September 9, 1988. The Court having considered argument from able counsel of record, having considered the applicable case law and having conducted an independent de novo review of the entire record herein and after due consideration, it is

ORDERED AND ADJUDGED as follows:

1. The Objections (DE 40) filed herein by the Plaintiffs, Mark T. Maxwell and Gertrude Maxwell, and Larry S. Bell and Nancy Bell, be and the same are hereby OVERRULED;

2. The Report and Recommendation (DE 38) of the United States Magistrate, Ann E. Vitunac, dated July 29, 1988, be and the same is hereby approved, ratified and adopted by the Court; and
3. The above-styled causes, 86-8446-CIV-ZLOCH and 86-8447-CIV-ZLOCH, be and the same are hereby DISMISSED, with prejudice.

DONE AND ORDERED in Chambers at Fort Lauderdale, Broward County, Florida, this 16th day of September, 1988.

nontaxable event
Transfer of property that does not result in an immediate tax consequence

capital gain or loss
Increase or decrease in value of capital asset to holder when the asset is transferred

capital asset
All property held by a taxpayer not used in the ordinary course of business

long-term capital gain or loss
Increase or decrease realized from the sale of a capital asset held for over one year

short-term capital gain or loss
Increase or decrease in the value occasioned by the sale of a capital asset held for less than one year

carried forward
Ability to continue to deduct a capital loss in tax years after the year of transfer

The determination of gain or loss is made at the time the property is sold or transferred. Certain types of transfers, however, are considered to be **nontaxable events,** meaning that no gain or loss is determined at that date. Some examples of such nontaxable trades are the like kind exchanges as discussed, transfers between spouses, and gifts. Only when the property so acquired is sold or transferred is gain or loss recognized.

To compute gain or loss, the taxpayer simply deducts the cost of the item sold or transferred from the amount or value received, including all fees, taxes, and charges. If the result is a positive number, there is a gain; if the result is a negative number, there is a loss.

The Internal Revenue Code designates two types of gains and losses: capital and ordinary. A **capital gain or loss** is a profit or loss realized from the transfer of a capital asset. A **capital asset,** as defined in section 1221 of the Internal Revenue Code, is any property a person owns and uses for personal purposes or investment. It does not include a business's inventory, either personal or real, including accounts receivable which is a noncapital asset.

Gain or loss for capital assets must be further classified by the amount of time the property was held by the taxpayer. Property held for over one year is deemed to result in a **long-term capital gain or loss** when it is sold. Property held for less than one year results in **short-term capital gain or loss** when sold. Within each category, long and short term, the taxpayer must deduct the losses from the gains to arrive at a net short- or long-term capital gain or loss. Short-term capital gains are treated as ordinary income; long-term capital gains are subject to special tax treatment. Capital losses may be **carried forward,** meaning that they may be used to offset any gains (reduce income) and, if any loss is still remaining, it may be used to offset income in future years until all of the loss is accounted for.

The following decision represents the seminal case for determining whether an asset is a capital asset or an asset used in the regular course of business.

TAX LAW & POLICY

CORN PRODUCTS REFINING CO. V. COMMISSIONER OF INTERNAL REVENUE
350 U.S. 46 (1955)

This case concerns the tax treatment to be accorded certain transactions in commodity futures. In the Tax Court, petitioner Corn Products Refining Company contended that its purchases and sales of corn futures in 1940 and 1942 were capital-asset transactions under § 117 (a) of the Internal Revenue Code of 1939. It further contended that its futures transactions came within the "wash sales" provisions of § 118. The 1940 claim was disposed of on the ground that § 118 did not apply, but for the year 1942 both the *Tax Court and the Court of Appeals for the Second Circuit, 215 F. 2d 513,* held that the futures were not capital assets under § 117. We granted certiorari, *348 U.S. 911,* because of an asserted conflict with holdings in the Courts of Appeal for the Third, Fifth, and Sixth Circuits. Since we hold that these futures do not constitute capital assets in petitioner's hands, we do not reach the issue of whether the transactions were "wash sales."

Petitioner is a nationally known manufacturer of products made from grain corn. It manufactures starch, syrup, sugar, and their by-products, feeds and oil. Its average yearly grind of raw corn during the period 1937 through 1942 varied from thirty-five to sixty million bushels. Most of its products were sold under contracts requiring shipment in thirty days at a set price or at market price on the date of delivery, whichever was lower. It permitted cancellation of such contracts, but from experience it could calculate with some accuracy future orders that would remain firm. While it also sold to a few customers on long-term contracts involving substantial orders, these had little effect on the transactions here involved.

In 1934 and again in 1936 droughts in the corn belt caused a sharp increase in the price of spot corn. With a storage capacity of only 2,300,000 bushels of corn, a bare three weeks' supply, Corn Products found itself unable to buy at a price which would permit its refined corn sugar, cerelose, to compete successfully with cane and beet sugar. To avoid a recurrence of this situation, petitioner, in 1937, began to establish a long position in corn futures "as a part of its corn buying program" and "as the most economical method of obtaining an adequate supply of raw corn" without entailing the expenditure of large sums for additional storage facilities. At harvest time each year it would buy futures when the price appeared favorable. It would take delivery on such contracts as it found necessary to its manufacturing operations and sell the remainder in early summer if no shortage was imminent. If shortages appeared, however, it sold futures only as it bought spot corn for grinding. In this manner it reached a balanced position with reference to any increase in spot corn prices. It made no effort to protect itself against a decline in prices.

In 1940 it netted a profit of $680,587.39 in corn futures, but in 1942 it suffered a loss of $109,969.38. In computing its tax liability Corn Products reported these figures as ordinary profit and loss from its manufacturing operations for the respective years. It now contends that its futures were "capital assets" under § 117 and that gains and losses therefrom should have been treated as arising from the sale of a capital asset. In support of this position it claims that its futures trading was separate and apart from its manufacturing operations and that in its futures transactions it was acting as a "legitimate capitalist." *United States v. New York Coffee & Sugar Exchange,* 263 U.S. 611, 619. It denies that its futures transactions were "hedges" or "speculative" dealings as covered by the ruling of General Counsel's Memorandum 17322, XV-2 Cum. Bull. 151, and claims that it is in truth "the forgotten man" of that administrative interpretation.

Both the Tax Court and the Court of Appeals found petitioner's futures transactions to be an integral part of its business designed to protect its manufacturing operations against a price increase in its principal raw material and to assure a ready supply for future manufacturing requirements. Corn Products does not level a direct attack on these two-court findings but insists that its futures were "property" entitled to capital-asset treatment under § 117 and as such were distinct from its manufacturing business. We cannot agree.

We find nothing in this record to support the contention that Corn Products' futures activity was separate and apart from its manufacturing operation. On the contrary, it appears that the transactions were vitally important to the company's business as a form of insurance against increases in the price of raw corn. Not only were the purchases initiated for just this reason, but the petitioner's sales policy, selling in the future at a fixed price or less, continued to leave it exceedingly vulnerable to rises in the price of corn. Further, the purchase of corn futures assured the company a source of supply which was admittedly cheaper than constructing additional storage facilities for raw corn. Under these facts it is difficult to imagine a program more closely geared to a company's manufacturing enterprise or more important to its successful operation.

Likewise the claim of Corn Products that it was dealing in the market as a "legitimate capitalist" lacks support in the record. There can be no quarrel with a manufacturer's desire to protect itself against increasing costs of raw materials. Transactions which provide such protection are considered a legitimate form of insurance. *United States v. New York Coffee & Sugar Exchange,* 263 U.S., at 619; *Browne v. Thorn,* 260 U.S. 137, 139–140. However, in labeling its activity as that of a "legitimate capitalist" exercising "good judgment" in the futures market, petitioner ignores the testimony of its own officers that in entering that market the company was "trying to protect a part of [its] manufacturing costs"; that its entry was not for the purpose of "speculating and buying and selling corn futures" but to fill an actual "need for the quantity of corn [bought] . . . in order to cover . . . what [products] we expected to market over a period of fifteen or eighteen months." It matters not whether the label be that of "legitimate capitalist" or "speculator"; this is not the talk of the capital investor but of the far-sighted manufacturer. For tax purposes petitioner's purchases have been found to "constitute an integral part of its manufacturing business" by both the Tax Court and the Court of Appeals, and on essentially factual questions the findings of two courts should not ordinarily be disturbed. *Comstock v. Group of Investors,* 335 U.S. 211, 214.

Petitioner also makes much of the conclusion by both the Tax Court and the Court of Appeals that its transactions did not constitute "true hedging." It is true that Corn Products did not secure complete protection from its market operations. Under its sales policy petitioner could not guard against a fall in prices. It is clear, however, that petitioner feared the possibility of a price rise more than that of a price decline. It therefore purchased partial insurance against its principal risk, and hoped to retain sufficient flexibility to avoid serious losses on a declining market.

Nor can we find support for petitioner's contention that hedging is not within the exclusions of § 117 (a). Admittedly, petitioner's corn futures do not come within the literal language of the exclusions set out in that section. They were not stock in trade, actual inventory, property held for sale to customers, or depreciable property used in a trade or business. But the capital-asset provision of § 117 must not be so broadly applied as to defeat rather than further the purpose of Congress. *Burnet v. Harmel,* 287 U.S. 103, 108. Congress intended that profits and losses arising from the everyday operation of a business be considered as ordinary income or loss rather than capital gain or loss. The preferential treatment provided by § 117 applies to transactions in property which are not the normal source of business income. It was intended "to relieve the taxpayer from . . . excessive tax burdens on gains resulting from a conversion of capital investments, and to remove the deterrent effect of those burdens on such conversions." *Burnet v. Harmel,* 287 U.S., at 106. Since this section is an exception from the normal tax requirements of the Internal Revenue Code, the definition of a capital asset must be narrowly applied and its exclusions interpreted broadly. This is necessary to effectuate the basic congressional purpose. This Court has always construed narrowly the term "capital assets" in § 117. See *Hort v. Commissioner,* 313 U.S. 28, 31; *Kieselbach v. Commissioner,* 317 U.S. 399, 403.

The problem of the appropriate tax treatment of hedging transactions first arose under the 1934 Tax Code revision. Thereafter the Treasury issued G.C.M. 17322, *supra,* distinguishing speculative transactions in commodity futures from hedging transactions. It held that hedging transactions were essentially to be regarded as insurance rather than a dealing in capital assets and that gains and losses therefrom were ordinary business gains and losses. The interpretation outlined in this memorandum has been consistently followed by the courts as well as by the Commissioner. While it is true that this Court has not passed on its validity, it has been well recognized for 20 years; and Congress has made no change in it though the Code has been re-enacted on three subsequent occasions. This bespeaks congressional approval. *Helvering v. Winmill,* 305 U.S. 79, 83. Furthermore, Congress has since specifically recognized the hedging exception here under consideration in the short-sale rule of § 1233 (a) of the 1954 Code.

We believe that the statute clearly refutes the contention of Corn Products. Moreover, it is significant to note that practical considerations lead to the same conclusion. To hold otherwise would permit those engaged in hedging transactions to transmute ordinary income into capital gain at will. The hedger may either sell the future and purchase in the spot market or take delivery under the future contract itself. But if a sale of the future created a capital transaction while delivery of the commodity under the same future did not, a loophole in the statute would be created and the purpose of Congress frustrated.

The judgment is *Affirmed.*

Special consideration must be given to the sale of a person's house. Under present tax law, when a person sells his or her principle residence in which he or she has resided for at least two years, $250,000 of the resulting gain from the sale is excludable from income taxes ($500,000 for a married couple). Thereafter, every two years the taxpayer may sell his or her new principle home and continue to exclude up to $250,000 in gain ($500,000 for a married couple) at each sale. Under prior law, all gain was taxable unless the proceeds of the sale were used to acquire a new home. No such "rollover" requirement now exists.

Adjustments to Income (Schedules A&B)

After the taxpayer has totaled all items of income, Form 1040 then provides for adjustments to income whereby certain deductions can be used to reduce the amount of income on which the tax will be assessed. A deduction is a subtraction, or reduction, from the amount of income on which a tax is levied. Taxable income is the difference between a person's gross income (all income from whatever source derived) less deductions and exemptions.

Taxpayers can elect to take a standard deduction or to itemize deductions. The **standard deduction** is a set amount that the IRS permits a person to subtract from his or her gross income without having to justify such amounts. The amount of the standardized deduction depends on the individual's tax status as previously discussed, except certain standard deductions apply for persons who are age 65 or older, blind, or whose spouse is either 65 years of age or older, blind, or both.

standard deduction
Deduction permitted to adjust gross income for persons who do not itemize deductions

The **itemized deductions** are computed on **Schedules A&B** (see Exhibit 2.3), which is used by taxpayers who have actual deductions in excess of the amount of the standard deduction. However, the amount of the deduction permitted by itemizing may also be beneficial for taxpayers whose adjusted gross income exceeds a specified amount. This amount changes periodically, and the tax law professional must consult the IRS tax tables in effect for the tax year in question.

For the purposes of explanation, Schedules A&B will be used.

itemized deductions
Detailing the amount of expenses incurred by a taxpayer so as to adjust the taxpayer's gross income

Schedules A&B
Attachments to Form 1040

Medical and Dental Expenses

All medical and dental bills paid by the taxpayer, either for the taxpayer's own medical or dental care or for those of the taxpayer's dependents, may be included to compute this deduction. However, only the total amount of such bills that exceed 7.5% of the taxpayer's adjusted gross income may be deducted, and the taxpayer may not include bills for which he or she was reimbursed by an employer, insurance, or otherwise.

Example

Taxpayer had medical bills of $3000. His adjusted gross income is $46,000. Thus, 7.5% of $46,000 is $3450. The taxpayer cannot use the itemized deduction because the total of his unreimbursed medical bills is less than 7.5% of his adjusted gross income.

Note also that persons who are self-employed (see Chapter 3) may deduct a percentage of the health insurance premium they pay on their own behalf. Further, any other expenses incurred in seeking and receiving medical and dental care are deductible, such as the taxpayer's meals and lodging if the taxpayer requires out-of-town medical services.

Taxes

A taxpayer is allowed a deduction for taxes he or she has already paid. The taxes that may be included in this category are:

A. State, local, and foreign income taxes
B. State, local, and foreign real estate taxes
C. State and local personal property taxes

Certain taxes imposed on a person are not deductible, such as estate taxes, federal income taxes that have been withheld during the tax year, social security taxes, and any fines levied for delinquent tax payments.

68 Chapter Two

SCHEDULES A&B (Form 1040) Department of the Treasury Internal Revenue Service (99)	Schedule A—Itemized Deductions (Schedule B is on back) ▶ Attach to Form 1040. ▶ See Instructions for Schedules A and B (Form 1040).	OMB No. 1545-0074 2003 Attachment Sequence No. 07
Name(s) shown on Form 1040		Your social security number

Medical and Dental Expenses		Caution. Do not include expenses reimbursed or paid by others.	
	1	Medical and dental expenses (see page A-2) . . .	1
	2	Enter amount from Form 1040, line 35 [2]	
	3	Multiply line 2 by 7.5% (.075)	3
	4	Subtract line 3 from line 1. If line 3 is more than line 1, enter -0-	4
Taxes You Paid (See page A-2.)	5	State and local income taxes	5
	6	Real estate taxes (see page A-2)	6
	7	Personal property taxes	7
	8	Other taxes. List type and amount ▶	8
	9	Add lines 5 through 8	9
Interest You Paid (See page A-3.) Note. Personal interest is not deductible.	10	Home mortgage interest and points reported to you on Form 1098	10
	11	Home mortgage interest not reported to you on Form 1098. If paid to the person from whom you bought the home, see page A-3 and show that person's name, identifying no., and address ▶	11
	12	Points not reported to you on Form 1098. See page A-3 for special rules	12
	13	Investment interest. Attach Form 4952 if required. (See page A-4.)	13
	14	Add lines 10 through 13	14
Gifts to Charity If you made a gift and got a benefit for it, see page A-4.	15	Gifts by cash or check. If you made any gift of $250 or more, see page A-4	15
	16	Other than by cash or check. If any gift of $250 or more, see page A-4. You **must** attach Form 8283 if over $500	16
	17	Carryover from prior year	17
	18	Add lines 15 through 17	18
Casualty and Theft Losses	19	Casualty or theft loss(es). Attach Form 4684. (See page A-5.)	19
Job Expenses and Most Other Miscellaneous Deductions (See page A-5.)	20	Unreimbursed employee expenses—job travel, union dues, job education, etc. Attach Form 2106 or 2106-EZ if required. (See page A-5.) ▶	20
	21	Tax preparation fees	21
	22	Other expenses—investment, safe deposit box, etc. List type and amount ▶	22
	23	Add lines 20 through 22	23
	24	Enter amount from Form 1040, line 35 [24]	
	25	Multiply line 24 by 2% (.02)	25
	26	Subtract line 25 from line 23. If line 25 is more than line 23, enter -0-	26
Other Miscellaneous Deductions	27	Other—from list on page A-6. List type and amount ▶	27
Total Itemized Deductions	28	Is Form 1040, line 35, over $139,500 (over $69,750 if married filing separately)? ☐ **No.** Your deduction is not limited. Add the amounts in the far right column for lines 4 through 27. Also, enter this amount on Form 1040, line 37. ▶ ☐ **Yes.** Your deduction may be limited. See page A-6 for the amount to enter.	28

For Paperwork Reduction Act Notice, see Form 1040 instructions. Cat. No. 11330X Schedule A (Form 1040) 2003

Exhibit 2.3 Schedule A&B (Form 1040)

Individual Income Taxation **69**

Schedules A&B (Form 1040) 2003 — OMB No. 1545-0074 — Page **2**

Name(s) shown on Form 1040. Do not enter name and social security number if shown on other side. | Your social security number

Schedule B—Interest and Ordinary Dividends

Attachment Sequence No. **08**

Part I
Interest

(See page B-1 and the instructions for Form 1040, line 8a.)

Note. If you received a Form 1099-INT, Form 1099-OID, or substitute statement from a brokerage firm, list the firm's name as the payer and enter the total interest shown on that form.

1. List name of payer. If any interest is from a seller-financed mortgage and the buyer used the property as a personal residence, see page B-1 and list this interest first. Also, show that buyer's social security number and address ▶

Amount
1

2. Add the amounts on line 1 . . . . | 2 |
3. Excludable interest on series EE and I U.S. savings bonds issued after 1989. Attach Form 8815 . . . . | 3 |
4. Subtract line 3 from line 2. Enter the result here and on Form 1040, line 8a ▶ | 4 |

Note. If line 4 is over $1,500, you must complete Part III.

Part II
Ordinary Dividends

(See page B-1 and the instructions for Form 1040, line 9a.)

Note. If you received a Form 1099-DIV or substitute statement from a brokerage firm, list the firm's name as the payer and enter the ordinary dividends shown on that form.

5. List name of payer ▶

Amount
5

6. Add the amounts on line 5. Enter the total here and on Form 1040, line 9a ▶ | 6 |

Note. If line 6 is over $1,500, you must complete Part III.

Part III
Foreign Accounts and Trusts

(See page B-2.)

You must complete this part if you **(a)** had over $1,500 of taxable interest or ordinary dividends; or **(b)** had a foreign account; or **(c)** received a distribution from, or were a grantor of, or a transferor to, a foreign trust. | Yes | No |

7a. At any time during 2003, did you have an interest in or a signature or other authority over a financial account in a foreign country, such as a bank account, securities account, or other financial account? See page B-2 for exceptions and filing requirements for Form TD F 90-22.1 . . . .

b. If "Yes," enter the name of the foreign country ▶ . . . .

8. During 2003, did you receive a distribution from, or were you the grantor of, or transferor to, a foreign trust? If "Yes," you may have to file Form 3520. See page B-2 . . . . . .

For Paperwork Reduction Act Notice, see Form 1040 instructions. — Schedule B (Form 1040) 2003

Exhibit 2.3 (Continued)

foreign tax
Tax paid to a country other than the United States

To determine whether a **foreign tax,** one imposed by a country other than the United States, is deductible, the tax law professional must determine the nature of the foreign tax. If the foreign tax does not fall into one of the previous categories, it may not be deducted. To determine the nature of the foreign tax, the tax law professional can contact the foreign country's embassy or consulate, or research any tax treaty that the United States may have with that foreign country. Always document the tax paid with evidence of payment and proof of the nature of the tax.

Exercise

Using the Internet or the library, determine whether the United States has a tax treaty in force with Canada, India, and the United Kingdom.

To be deductible, the tax must have been imposed on the taxpayer individually and paid during the tax year in question.

Practical tip

For foreign taxes paid, always provide evidence of the exchange rate in effect on the day of payment.

Certain items that are called real estate taxes may in fact reflect fees for services such as trash removal. These types of "taxes" are not deductible as a tax deduction; only assessments imposed on the value of the property itself may be included in this portion of the schedule.

Interest

Not all interest charges are deductible. For example, personal interest charges, such as those imposed on credit card transactions to procure personal items, are not deductible. Only the following types of interest charges are included on Schedule A.

A. Student loan interest

B. Mortgage loan interest and certain points; **points** are charges imposed when acquiring a mortgage

points
Charges imposed when acquiring a mortgage

Practical tip

The amount of the mortgage interest payments are taken from Form 1098 (see Exhibit 2.4) which is provided by the mortgagee

8181	☐ VOID ☐ CORRECTED		
RECIPIENT'S/LENDER'S name, address, and telephone number		OMB No. 1545-0901 2004 Form **1098**	**Mortgage Interest Statement**
RECIPIENT'S Federal identification no.	PAYER'S social security number	1 Mortgage interest received from payer(s)/borrower(s) $	**Copy A** **For Internal Revenue Service Center** File with Form 1096.
PAYER'S/BORROWER'S name		2 Points paid on purchase of principal residence $	For Privacy Act and Paperwork Reduction Act Notice, see the **2004 General Instructions for Forms 1099, 1098, 5498, and W-2G.**
Street address (including apt. no.)		3 Refund of overpaid interest $	
City, state, and ZIP code		4	
Account number (optional)			

Form **1098**   Cat. No. 14402K   Department of the Treasury - Internal Revenue Service

Do Not Cut or Separate Forms on This Page — Do Not Cut or Separate Forms on This Page

	☐ CORRECTED (if checked)		
RECIPIENT'S/LENDER'S name, address, and telephone number	* **Caution:** The amount shown may not be fully deductible by you. Limits based on the loan amount and the cost and value of the secured property may apply. Also, you may only deduct interest to the extent it was incurred by you, actually paid by you, and not reimbursed by another person.	OMB No. 1545-0901 2004 Form **1098**	**Mortgage Interest Statement**
RECIPIENT'S Federal identification no.	PAYER'S social security number	1 Mortgage interest received from payer(s)/borrower(s)* $	**Copy B** **For Payer**
PAYER'S/BORROWER'S name		2 Points paid on purchase of principal residence (See **Box 2** on back.) $	The information in boxes 1, 2, and 3 is important tax information and is being furnished to the Internal Revenue Service. If you are required to file a return, a negligence penalty or other sanction may be imposed on you if the IRS determines that an underpayment of tax results because you overstated a deduction for this mortgage interest or for these points or because you did not report this refund of interest on your return.
Street address (including apt. no.)		3 Refund of overpaid interest (See **Box 3** on back.) $	
City, state, and ZIP code		4	
Account number (optional)			

Form **1098**   (keep for your records)   Department of the Treasury - Internal Revenue Service

Instructions for Payer/Borrower

A person (including a financial institution, a governmental unit, and a cooperative housing corporation) who is engaged in a trade or business and, in the course of such trade or business, received from you at least $600 of mortgage interest (including certain points) on any one mortgage in the calendar year must furnish this statement to you.

If you received this statement as the payer of record on a mortgage on which there are other borrowers, furnish each of the other borrowers with information about the proper distribution of amounts reported on this form. Each borrower is entitled to deduct only the amount he or she paid and points paid by the seller that represent his or her share of the amount allowable as a deduction for mortgage interest and points. Each borrower may have to include in income a share of any amount reported in box 3.

If your mortgage payments were subsidized by a government agency, you may not be able to deduct the amount of the subsidy.

Box 1. Shows the mortgage interest received by the interest recipient during the year. This amount includes interest on any obligation secured by real property, including a home equity, line of credit, or credit card loan. This amount does not include points, government subsidy payments, or seller payments on a "buy-down" mortgage. Such amounts are deductible by you only in certain circumstances. **Caution:** If you prepaid interest in 2004 that accrued in full by January 15, 2005, this prepaid interest may be included in box 1. However, you cannot deduct the prepaid amount in 2004 even though it may be included in box 1. If you hold a mortgage credit certificate and can claim the mortgage interest credit, see **Form 8396,** Mortgage Interest Credit. If the interest was paid on a mortgage, home equity, line of credit, or credit card loan secured by your personal residence, you may be subject to a deduction limitation. For example, if a home equity loan exceeds $100,000 ($50,000 if married filing separately) or, together with other home loans, exceeds the fair market value of your home (such as in a high loan-to-value loan), your interest deduction may be limited. For more information, see **Pub. 936,** Home Mortgage Interest Deduction.

Box 2. Not all points are reportable to you. Box 2 shows points you or the seller paid this year for the purchase of your principal residence that are required to be reported to you. Generally, these points are fully deductible in the year paid, but you must subtract seller-paid points from the basis of your residence. Other points not reported in this box may also be deductible. See Pub. 936 or Schedule A (Form 1040) instructions.

Box 3. Do not deduct this amount. It is a refund (or credit) for overpayment(s) of interest you made in a prior year or years. If you itemized deductions in the year(s) you paid the interest, include the total amount shown in box 3 on the "Other income" line of your 2004 Form 1040. However, do not report the refund as income if you did not itemize deductions in the year(s) you paid the interest. No adjustment to your prior year(s) tax return(s) is necessary. For more information, see Pub. 936 and "Recoveries" in **Pub. 525,** Taxable and Nontaxable Income.

Box 4. The interest recipient may use this box to give you other information, such as the address of the property that secures the debt, real estate taxes, or insurance paid from escrow.

Exhibit 2.4 Form 1098

72 Chapter Two

☐ VOID ☐ CORRECTED			
RECIPIENT'S/LENDER'S name, address, and telephone number	OMB No. 1545-0901 2004 Form **1098**		**Mortgage Interest Statement**
RECIPIENT'S Federal identification no.	PAYER'S social security number	1 Mortgage interest received from payer(s)/borrower(s) $	**Copy C For Recipient**
PAYER'S/BORROWER'S name		2 Points paid on purchase of principal residence $	For Privacy Act and Paperwork Reduction Act Notice, see the **2004 General Instructions for Forms 1099, 1098, 5498, and W-2G.**
Street address (including apt. no.)		3 Refund of overpaid interest $	
City, state, and ZIP code		4	
Account number (optional)			

Form **1098**   Department of the Treasury - Internal Revenue Service

Instructions for Recipients/Lenders

General and specific form instructions are provided as separate products. The products you should use to complete Form 1098 are the **2004 General Instructions for Forms 1099, 1098, 5498, and W-2G** and the separate specific instructions, **2004 Instructions for Form 1098**. A chart in the general instructions gives a quick guide to which form must be filed to report a particular payment. To order these instructions and additional forms, call 1-800-TAX-FORM (1-800-829-3676).

Caution: *Because paper forms are scanned during processing, you cannot file Forms 1096, 1098, 1099, or 5498 that you download and print from the IRS website.*

Due dates. Furnish Copy B of this form to the recipient by January 31, 2005.

   File Copy A of this form with the IRS by February 28, 2005. If you file electronically, the due date is March 31, 2005.

Exhibit 2.4 (Continued)

---

investment interest
Income from a passive activity

    C. Investment interest, which represents interest the taxpayer pays on money borrowed to invest in a capital asset held as an investment
    D. Business interest, meaning any interest paid on money borrowed for the operation of a personal business; this item typically appears on a Schedule C (see Chapter 3)
    E. Interest on money borrowed to produce income

As a general rule, except for mortgage interest, deductible interest reflects the cost of borrowing money that will assist the taxpayer in producing taxable income.

Charitable Gifts

As a general definition, a **charitable gift** is a voluntary transfer of money or property to a charitable organization that is made with no expectation of producing a financial benefit. To qualify for this deduction, the recipient organization must qualify as a charitable or nonprofit organization pursuant to section 170 of the Internal Revenue Code.

charitable gift
Gift to a nonprofit organization made with no expectation of financial benefit to the donor

Practical tip

For individual gifts exceeding $500 obtain an acknowledgment from the recipient charitable organization.

Not all transfers to charitable organizations are deemed to be gifts by the IRS. For example, a transfer of money or property to a school to ensure the admission or tuition of a child will not qualify, because the gift was made with a view to seeking a financial benefit (i.e., a tuition payment couched as a "gift").

Practical tip

Gifts of property create problems with respect to valuation. To minimize such problems, present evidence of the property's fair market value along with the deduction. This is especially true of gifts whose value appreciates.

Exercise

Read *Hernandez v. Commissioner*, 490 U.S. 680 (1989) to see how the IRS views gifts to organizations that may not qualify as "charities."

Casualty and Theft Losses

To be entitled to a deduction for casualty and theft loss, the taxpayer must be able to prove that he or she actually suffered a loss. To meet this burden, the taxpayer must be able to document ownership of the property, the nature of the loss, and the value of the property lost.

To calculate the amount of the loss, the taxpayer must use the smaller of his or her adjusted basis in the property or the decrease in the fair market value occasioned by the loss. Note that any reimbursement for the loss, such as from insurance proceeds, will reduce the amount of the loss.

Each casualty or theft loss must be reduced by $100 because the first $100 of such loss is not deductible, and the amount of all such losses for the taxable year must exceed 10% of the taxpayer's adjusted gross income, known as the 10% rule.

Exercise

A man tries to take as a deduction the amount of money that he is paying his mistress to keep their affair a secret. Argue for and against the deduction.

Job and Miscellaneous Expenses

Any expense a person incurs with respect to performing his or her job that is not reimbursed by the employer may be able to be deducted from the employee-taxpayer's income. Deductible items under this category include:

- **A.** Travel expenses, those expenses incurred when the taxpayer must go on a business trip out of his or her hometown or must travel to several locations within town during the business day. Note that basic transportation to and from home to the basic worksite is not deductible. If the employee is using his or her own car, he or she may deduct gas, oil, and natural wear and tear charges that are attributable only to that job-related use; any charges associated with personal use of the vehicle are not deductible.
- **B.** Meals and lodging. If the employee-taxpayer is on a business trip, he or she may deduct the cost of lodging, airfare, and up to 50% of the meals, unless those meals are considered extravagant by the IRS. Additional expenses for such items as laundry, dry cleaning, and tips are also deductible.
- **C.** Entertainment, but only if the entertainment is job related, such as taking a customer to dinner or purchasing theatre tickets for an out-of-town client. Only 50% of this amount is deductible.
- **D.** Gifts, up to a $25 limit on each gift per donee.

Practical tip

Keep detailed records of all entertainment and gift records which are carefully scrutinized by the IRS.

- **E.** Education, if the cost is not to acquire basic skills for the job but to improve skills; the employer must require or approve of such training but not reimburse for it.

Exercise

To see how the IRS determines the deductibility of a graduate school degree, read Private Ruling 710818320D, 1971 PRL Lexis 102.

F. Union dues and license fees that must be maintained as a condition of the taxpayer's job. Note that the initial cost of becoming licensed is not deductible, such as the fees for taking a bar exam or a bar review course.

Exercise

A man pays to become a church minister so as to have tax-exempt income. May he deduct the expenses he incurred to become the minister as costs of obtaining tax advice? See *Kitcher v. Commissioner*, T.C. Memo 1986-41.

Other items that may appear in this category include fees paid for the preparation of the income tax return, and accounting and legal fees used in the production or maintaining of income. Other items that might appear in this category but which relate to the operation of a business are discussed in the following chapter.

Moving Expenses

In order to be able to deduct moving expenses, they must be incurred in moving to a new job that is at least 50 miles away from the taxpayer's current position and the job must be a full-time position that the taxpayer works at for at least 39 weeks. If the taxpayer is self-employed, he or she must work at the job for 39 of the past 12 months or 78 weeks of the past 2 years.

Credits

Once the taxpayer has adjusted his or her income by the above mentioned deductions, the tax is assessed by checking the appropriate tax tables for the taxpayer's filing status. It is important to note, however, that certain persons may be subject to an additional tax called the **alternative minimum tax.** This additional tax is imposed on persons whose taxable income exceeds a specified minimum amount, which is periodically adjusted. The tax law professional should determine this amount for the tax year in question. At this point the total amount of tax to be levied is determined.

alternative minimum tax
A tax imposed on certain high-income taxpayers

Exercise

A taxpayer claims that he should not be liable for the alternative minimum tax because although his income is above the minimum requirement, he is not wealthy and the purpose of the alternative minimum tax is to tax the rich. Argue for and against this proposition.

The following case highlights the law with respect to the alternative minimum tax.

TAX LAW & POLICY

KLAASSEN V. COMMISSIONER OF INTERNAL REVENUE
T.C. Memo 1998-241

OPINION

Our analysis necessarily begins with section 55, the section of the Internal Revenue Code that imposes the alternative minimum tax. Initially, we note that the alternative minimum tax is imposed in addition to the regular tax and that the "regular tax" is, as relevant herein, the income tax computed on taxable income by reference to the pertinent tax table. See sec. 55(a), (c)(1). In petitioners' case, the "regular tax" is $5,111; i.e., the amount reported on line 38 of petitioners' Form 1040.

Pursuant to section 55(a), the alternative minimum tax is the difference between the "tentative minimum tax" and the "regular tax." As relevant herein, the "tentative minimum tax" is 26 percent of the excess of a taxpayer's "alternative minimum taxable income" over an exemption amount of $45,000. See sec. 55(b)(1)(A)(i)(I), (b)(2), (d)(1)(A)(i).

Section 55(b)(2) defines the term "alternative minimum taxable income." As relevant herein, the term "alternative minimum taxable income" means the taxpayer's taxable income for the taxable year determined with the adjustments provided in section 56 and increased by the amount of items of tax preference described in section 57. Petitioners had no items of tax preference in 1994. Accordingly, alternative minimum taxable income means petitioners' taxable income determined with the adjustments provided in section 56.

Petitioners' taxable income for 1994 was $34,092.47, the amount reported on line 37 of Form 1040.

As relevant herein, the adjustments provided in section 56(b) are threefold. First, section 56(b)(1)(A)(ii) states that no itemized deduction for State and local taxes shall be allowed in computing alternative minimum taxable income. Second, section 56(b)(1)(B) states that in determining the amount allowable as a deduction for medical expenses, a floor of 10 percent shall be applied in lieu of the regular 7.5 percent floor. See sec. 213(a). Third, section 56(b)(1)(E) states that no personal exemptions shall be allowed in computing alternative minimum taxable income.

The effect of section 56(b)(1)(A)(ii), (b)(1)(B), and (b)(1)(E) is to increase petitioners' taxable income by: (1) $3,263.56, the amount claimed on petitioners' Schedule A for State and local taxes; (2) $2,076.41, the difference between the amount allowable as a deduction for medical expenses on Schedule A and the amount allowable as a deduction for medical expenses for purposes of the alternative minimum tax; and (3) $29,400, the amount claimed on petitioners' Form 1040 for personal exemptions.

After taking into account the foregoing three adjustments, petitioners' alternative minimum taxable income for 1994 equals $68,832.44. Alternative minimum taxable income exceeds the applicable exemption amount of $45,000 by $23,832.44. See sec. 55(d)(1)(A)(i). Petitioners' "tentative minimum tax" is therefore 26 percent of that excess, or $6,196.43. See sec. 55(b)(1)(A)(i)(I). Because petitioners' tentative minimum tax exceeds petitioners' regular tax of $5,111, petitioners are liable for the alternative minimum tax in the amount of such excess; i.e., $6,196.43 less $5,111, or $1,085.43.

Petitioners do not challenge the mechanics of the foregoing computation. Rather, petitioners contend that they are not liable for the alternative minimum tax for two independent reasons. First, petitioners contend that the elimination of personal exemptions under the alternative minimum tax adversely affects large families and results in an application of the alternative minimum tax that is contrary to congressional intent. In this regard, petitioners argue that legislative history demonstrates that the alternative minimum tax was intended to limit items of tax preference, not personal exemptions.

Second, petitioners argue that the alternative minimum tax violates various constitutional rights, particularly the right to religious freedom.

A. CONGRESSIONAL INTENT

We begin with petitioners' contention that they are not liable for the alternative minimum tax because such tax was not intended to apply to them. In this regard, petitioners emphasize that they did not have a single item of tax preference, and they argue that they are being unfairly saddled with the alternative minimum tax simply because of the size of their family.

The clearest expression of legislative intent is found in the actual language used by Congress in enacting legislation. As the Supreme Court has stated, "There is no more persuasive evidence of the purpose of a statute than the words by which the legislature undertook to give expression to its wishes." *United States v. American Trucking Associations, Inc.,* 310 U.S. 534, 543 (1940); see *Rath v. Commissioner,* 101 T.C. 196, 200 (1993) (controlling effect will generally be given to the plain language of a statute, unless to do so would produce absurd or futile results). Again as the Supreme Court has stated:

In the absence of a clearly expressed legislative intention to the contrary, the language of the statute itself must ordinarily be regarded as conclusive. Unless exceptional circumstances dictate otherwise, when we find the terms of a statute unambiguous, judicial inquiry is complete. *Burlington N. R.R. Co. v. Oklahoma*

Tax Commn., 481 U.S. 454, 461 (1987); citations and internal quotation marks omitted.

Accordingly, where, as here, a statute appears to be clear on its face, unequivocal evidence of a contrary purpose must be demonstrable if we are to construe the statute so as to override the plain meaning of the words used therein. *Estate of Owen v. Commissioner,* 104 T.C. 498, 507–508 (1995), and cases cited therein; *Huntsberry v. Commissioner,* 83 T.C. 742, 747–748 (1984).

"The statutory scheme governing the imposition and computation of the alternative minimum tax is clear and precise, and leaves, on these facts, no room for interpretation." *Okin v. Commissioner, T.C. Memo,* 1985-199, affd. per curiam 808 F.2d 1338 (9th Cir. 1987). Thus, there is no justification, in the instant case, to ignore the plain language of the statute, particularly where, as here, "we have a complex set of statutory provisions marked by a high degree of specificity." *Huntsberry v. Commissioner,* supra at 748.

The alternative minimum tax serves to impose a tax whenever the sum of specified percentages of the excess of alternative minimum taxable income over the applicable exemption amount exceeds the regular tax for the taxable year. Sec. 55(a), (b)(1)(A), (c), (d)(1); cf. *Huntsberry v. Commissioner,* supra at 744. "Alternative minimum taxable income" essentially means the taxpayer's taxable income for the taxable year determined with the adjustments provided in section 56 and increased by the amount of items of tax preference described in section 57.

In *Huntsberry v. Commissioner,* supra, we held that tax preferences are a significant, but not necessarily an indispensable component, of "alternative minimum taxable income." Accordingly, the taxpayers in that case were held liable for the alternative minimum tax computed in accordance with the specific provisions of section 55, notwithstanding the fact that the taxpayers did not have any items of tax preference for the taxable year in issue. The same result applies in the present case.

If Congress had intended to tax only tax preferences, it would have defined "alternative minimum taxable income" differently, for example, solely by reference to items of tax preference. Instead, Congress provided for a tax measured by a broader base, namely, alternative minimum taxable income, in which tax preferences are merely included as potential components.

The foregoing analysis leads to the conclusion that the alternative minimum tax is triggered by a number of factors, including the value of personal exemptions claimed on a taxpayer's return, and that respondent correctly determined such tax on the facts of this case. Accordingly, because we can understand and apply the plain meaning of unambiguous statutory text, we need not defer to legislative history. See *Calvert Anesthesia Associates v. Commissioner,* 110 T.C. 285, 289 (1998); see also *Huntsberry v. Commissioner,* supra at 745–746 ("there is no solid basis in the legislative history or otherwise for refusing to apply section 55 as written").

B. CONSTITUTIONAL CONSIDERATIONS

Having thus decided that the alternative minimum tax is otherwise applicable on the facts of this case, we turn now to petitioners' contention that such tax unconstitutionally inhibits the free exercise of religion.

Cases have held that the usual presumption of constitutionality is particularly strong in the case of a revenue measure. *Black v. Commissioner,* 69 T.C. 505 (1977). The constitutionality of the alternative minimum tax has previously been upheld by the courts. E.g., *Graff v. Commissioner,* 74 T.C. 743, 767 (1980) (and cases cited therein), affd. per curiam 673 F.2d 784 (5th Cir. 1982); see *Wallach v. United States,* 800 F.2d 1121 (Fed. Cir. 1986); *Wyly v. United States,* 662 F.2d 397, 403–406 (5th Cir. 1981); *Christine v. Commissioner,* T.C. Memo, 1993-473; *Okin v. Commissioner,* supra.

Absent clear evidence to the contrary, we are reluctant to hold that the alternative minimum tax infringes on a taxpayer's personal religious beliefs. "The fact that a law with a secular purpose may have the effect of making the observance of some religious beliefs more expensive does not render the statute unconstitutional under the First Amendment." *Black v. Commissioner,* supra at 510 (citing *Braunfeld v. Brown,* 366 U.S. 599, 605–607 (1961)). Moreover, we conclude, as in *Black,* that "religious beliefs have consistently been held not to furnish a basis for complaint about our tax system, at least where the statutory provision attacked is not specifically based, or cannot be shown to be based, upon a classification grounded on religion." *Black v. Commissioner,* supra at 510, and cases cited therein; see *Adams v. Commissioner,* 110 T.C. 137, 139 (1998) ("the Supreme Court has established that uniform, mandatory participation in the Federal income tax system, irrespective of religious belief, is a compelling governmental interest"); see also *Bob Jones Univ. v. United States,* 461 U.S. 574, 603 (1983).

In the present case, the alternative minimum tax is not based upon "a classification grounded on religion." Rather, the statute demonstrates that such tax is triggered by the value of deductions and exemptions claimed, the disallowance of which is unrelated to a taxpayer's religious beliefs. Cf. *Commissioner v. Sullivan,* 356 U.S. 27, 28 (1958); *New Colonial Ice Co. v. Helvering,* 292 U.S. 435, 440 (1934) (deductions are a matter of legislative grace; accordingly, the decision whether to permit particular deductions and under what circumstances lies within the discretion of Congress). Consequently, we do not agree that the alternative minimum tax unconstitutionally inhibits the free exercise of petitioners religion.

C. CONCLUSION

In view of the foregoing, we hold that petitioners are liable for the alternative minimum tax. Accordingly, we sustain respondent's determination of the deficiency in income tax.

Absent some constitutional defect, we are constrained to apply the law as written, see *Estate of Cowser v. Commissioner,* 736 F.2d 1168, 1171–1174 (7th Cir. 1984), affg. *80 T.C. 783, 787–788 (1983),* and we may not rewrite the law because we may deem its effects susceptible of improvement; see *Commissioner v. Lundy,* 516 U.S. 235, 252 (1996), (quoting *Badaracco v. Commissioner,* 464 U.S. 386, 398 (1984)). Accordingly, petitioners' appeal for relief must, in this instance, be addressed to their elected representatives.

To reflect our disposition of the disputed issue, as well as respondent's concession,

Decision will be entered for respondent as to the deficiency in income tax and for petitioners as to the addition to tax.

credit
Amount used to reduce amount of tax imposed

child and dependent care credit
Tax credit for expenses incurred in caring for a qualifying child or incapacitated dependent

Once the total amount of tax is calculated, the taxpayer may be entitled to certain tax credits. A tax **credit** is an amount that reduces the amount of taxes due.

The following credits are currently available to a taxpayer.

A. Child and dependent care. A taxpayer may take as a credit amounts expended to care for a child who is under 13 years of age or any disabled dependent. The credit may only be used if such care is necessary to enable the taxpayer to seek employment, and the child or dependent must reside with the taxpayer seeking the credit.

The amount of this credit is limited to a percentage of the taxpayer's expenses. To compute the credit, the taxpayer calculates all of the unreimbursed expenses incurred to provide for the care that enables the taxpayer to work. The amount of the credit cannot exceed the taxpayer's earned income for the year, nor may it exceed a specific dollar limit as established by the IRS. To deduct the amount of this care:

i. Determine the maximum dollar amount permitted for such care according to IRS guidelines.

ii. Subtract any child or dependent care benefits the taxpayer receives from his or her employer.

iii. Multiply that amount by the IRS percentage based on the taxpayer's adjusted gross income. The income percentage permitted for the lowest income levels ($0–$10,000) is 30%. These calculations are completed on Form 2441 and included as an attachment to Form 1040.

In *Poole v. Commissioner,* T.C. Summary Opinion 2001-163, petitioner taxpayer sued respondent commissioner of Internal Revenue Service after the commissioner determined deficiencies in the taxpayer's federal taxes for two years. At issue was whether the taxpayer was entitled (1) to dependency exemption deductions, (2) to file as head of household, (3) to dependent care expenses, and (4) to earned income credits.

The taxpayer did not offer any competent evidence of the total amount of support provided for each of the children for the years in question. Additionally, the children's mother had physical custody of them for the greater portion of each year. Under 26 U.S.C.S. § § 151(a) and 152(e), the taxpayer was not entitled to claim either of the children as dependents for 1997 and the taxpayer's son as a dependent for 1998. Because the court found that the children were in their mother's physical custody for the greater portion of the year, the taxpayer was not entitled to head of household filing status. Because the taxpayer was not entitled to dependency exemption deductions, he could not claim a credit for child and dependent care expenses for either of the years in question. Since the taxpayer failed to show by convincing evidence that he provided the principal place of abode for the two children for more than one-half of either of the years in issue, he did not have a qualifying child for the purposes of the earned income tax credit for either year. Because of the taxpayer's adjusted gross income, he did not qualify for the earned income tax credit for a person without a qualifying child.

The decision was entered for the commissioner of Internal Revenue.

B. Employer taxes for household help. Individuals who employ household help are required to withhold taxes from their helpers' wages and also to make certain employer contributions to IRS (see the following chapters on the federal income taxation of businesses). These employer taxes are permitted as a tax credit.

C. Credit for the elderly and disabled. This credit is available for taxpayers who are over age 65 or permanently disabled and who are either U.S. citizens or lawful permanent residents. The credit is limited by the amount of the person's adjusted gross income and of the person's nontaxable social security benefits. The credit can be determined by the taxpayer using Schedule R (see Exhibit 2.5) or having the IRS perform the calculations at the taxpayer's request.

credit for the elderly and disabled
One of the tax credits permitted to a taxpayer to reduce the amount of taxes owed

D. Child care credit. This credit, which is different from the dependant allowance, is permitted if the child is under 17 years of age, is a citizen or lawful permanent resident in the United States, and is a dependent. The maximum credit permitted is $500, and it is limited by the amount of the taxpayer's adjusted gross income. The calculations for this credit are performed on Form 8812 (see Exhibit 2.6).

child care credit
Tax credit limited to $500 to pay for the care of a child

Schedule R (Form 1040)

Credit for the Elderly or the Disabled

Department of the Treasury
Internal Revenue Service (99)

▶ Attach to Form 1040.   ▶ See Instructions for Schedule R (Form 1040).

OMB No. 1545-0074

2003

Attachment Sequence No. 16

Name(s) shown on Form 1040 | Your social security number

You may be able to take this credit and reduce your tax if by the end of 2003:

- You were age 65 or older **or**
- You were under age 65, you retired on **permanent and total** disability, and you received taxable disability income.

But you must also meet other tests. See page R-1.

TIP In most cases, the IRS can figure the credit for you. See page R-1.

Part I — Check the Box for Your Filing Status and Age

If your filing status is:	And by the end of 2003:	Check only one box:
Single, Head of household, or Qualifying widow(er)	1 You were 65 or older 1	☐
	2 You were under 65 and you retired on permanent and total disability 2	☐
Married filing jointly	3 Both spouses were 65 or older 3	☐
	4 Both spouses were under 65, but only one spouse retired on permanent and total disability 4	☐
	5 Both spouses were under 65, and both retired on permanent and total disability 5	☐
	6 One spouse was 65 or older, and the other spouse was under 65 and retired on permanent and total disability 6	☐
	7 One spouse was 65 or older, and the other spouse was under 65 and **not** retired on permanent and total disability 7	☐
Married filing separately	8 You were 65 or older and you lived apart from your spouse for all of 2003 8	☐
	9 You were under 65, you retired on permanent and total disability, and you lived apart from your spouse for all of 2003 9	☐

Did you check box 1, 3, 7, or 8?
— Yes ▶ Skip Part II and complete Part III on back.
— No ▶ Complete Parts II and III.

Part II — Statement of Permanent and Total Disability (Complete **only** if you checked box 2, 4, 5, 6, or 9 above.)

If: 1 You filed a physician's statement for this disability for 1983 or an earlier year, or you filed or got a statement for tax years after 1983 and your physician signed line B on the statement, **and**

2 Due to your continued disabled condition, you were unable to engage in any substantial gainful activity in 2003, check this box . . . . ▶ ☐

- If you checked this box, you do not have to get another statement for 2003.
- If you **did not** check this box, have your physician complete the statement on page R-4. You **must** keep the statement for your records.

For Paperwork Reduction Act Notice, see Form 1040 instructions.   Cat. No. 11359K   Schedule R (Form 1040) 2003

Exhibit 2.5 Schedule R (Form 1040)

Schedule R (Form 1040) 2003 — Page 2

Part III Figure Your Credit

10 If you checked (in Part I):   Enter:
    Box 1, 2, 4, or 7 . . . . $5,000
    Box 3, 5, or 6 . . . . $7,500   **10**
    Box 8 or 9 . . . . $3,750

Did you check box 2, 4, 5, 6, or 9 in Part I?	Yes → You **must** complete line 11.
	No → Enter the amount from line 10 on line 12 and go to line 13.

11 If you checked (in Part I):
- Box 6, add $5,000 to the taxable disability income of the spouse who was under age 65. Enter the total.
- Box 2, 4, or 9, enter your taxable disability income.
- Box 5, add your taxable disability income to your spouse's taxable disability income. Enter the total.

    11

TIP For more details on what to include on line 11, see page R-3.

12 If you completed line 11, enter the **smaller** of line 10 or line 11; **all others,** enter the amount from line 10 . . . . **12**

13 Enter the following pensions, annuities, or disability income that you (and your spouse if filing a joint return) received in 2003.
   a Nontaxable part of social security benefits and
      Nontaxable part of railroad retirement benefits treated as social security (see page R-3).   **13a**

   b Nontaxable veterans' pensions and
      Any other pension, annuity, or disability benefit that is excluded from income under any other provision of law (see page R-3).   **13b**

   c Add lines 13a and 13b. (Even though these income items are not taxable, they **must** be included here to figure your credit.) If you did not receive any of the types of nontaxable income listed on line 13a or 13b, enter -0- on line 13c **13c**

14 Enter the amount from Form 1040, line 35 . . . . **14**

15 If you checked (in Part I):   Enter:
    Box 1 or 2 . . . . $7,500
    Box 3, 4, 5, 6, or 7 . . . $10,000   **15**
    Box 8 or 9 . . . . $5,000

16 Subtract line 15 from line 14. If zero or less, enter -0- **16**

17 Enter one-half of line 16 . . . . **17**

18 Add lines 13c and 17 . . . . **18**

19 Subtract line 18 from line 12. If zero or less, **stop;** you **cannot** take the credit. Otherwise, go to line 20 . . . . **19**

20 Multiply line 19 by 15% (.15) **20**

21 Enter the amount from Form 1040, line 43 . . . . **21**

22 Add the amounts from Form 1040, lines 44 and 45, and enter the total **22**

23 Subtract line 22 from line 21 . . . . **23**

24 Credit for the elderly or the disabled. Enter the **smaller** of line 20 or line 23 here and on Form 1040, line 46 . . . . **24**

Schedule R (Form 1040) 2003

Exhibit 2.5 (Continued)

84 Chapter Two

Form **8812**	**Additional Child Tax Credit**	1040 1040A	OMB No. 1545-1620 **2003**
Department of the Treasury Internal Revenue Service	Complete and attach to Form 1040 or Form 1040A.	8812	Attachment Sequence No. **47**

Name(s) shown on return | Your social security number

Part I — All Filers

1. Enter the amount from line 3 of your Child Tax Credit Worksheet on page 41 of the Form 1040 instructions or page 38 of the Form 1040A instructions. If you used Pub. 972, enter the amount from line 10 of the worksheet on page 4 of the publication **1**

2. Enter the amount from Form 1040, line 49, or Form 1040A, line 33 . . . . **2**

3. Subtract line 2 from line 1. If zero, **stop**; you cannot take this credit **3**

4. Enter your total taxable earned income. See the instructions on back . . **4**

5. Is the amount on line 4 more than $10,500?
   ☐ **No.** Leave line 5 blank and enter -0- on line 6.
   ☐ **Yes.** Subtract $10,500 from the amount on line 4. Enter the result . **5**

6. Multiply the amount on line 5 by 10% (.10) and enter the result **6**
   Next. Do you have three or more qualifying children?
   ☐ **No.** If line 6 is zero, **stop**; you cannot take this credit. Otherwise, skip Part II and enter the **smaller** of line 3 or line 6 on line 13.
   ☐ **Yes.** If line 6 is equal to or more than line 3, skip Part II and enter the amount from line 3 on line 13. Otherwise, go to line 7.

Part II — Certain Filers Who Have Three or More Qualifying Children

7. Enter the total of the withheld social security and Medicare taxes from Form(s) W-2, boxes 4 and 6. If married filing jointly, include your spouse's amounts with yours. If you worked for a railroad, see the instructions on back . . **7**

8. **1040 filers:** Enter the total of the amounts from Form 1040, lines 28 and 56, plus any uncollected social security and Medicare or tier 1 RRTA taxes included on line 60.
   1040A filers: Enter -0-. **8**

9. Add lines 7 and 8 . . . . **9**

10. **1040 filers:** Enter the total of the amounts from Form 1040, lines 63 and 64.
    1040A filers: Enter the total of the amount from Form 1040A, line 41, plus any excess social security and tier 1 RRTA taxes withheld that you entered to the left of line 43 (see the instructions on back). **10**

11. Subtract line 10 from line 9. If zero or less, enter -0- **11**

12. Enter the **larger** of line 6 or line 11 here **12**
    Next, enter the **smaller** of line 3 or line 12 on line 13.

Part III — Your Additional Child Tax Credit

13. This is your additional child tax credit **13**

Enter this amount on Form 1040, line 65, or Form 1040A, line 42.

For Paperwork Reduction Act Notice, see back of form. | Cat. No. 10644E | Form **8812** (2003)

Exhibit 2.6 Form 8812

Form 8812 (2003) Page **2**

Instructions

Purpose of Form
Use Form 8812 to figure your additional child tax credit.

TIP: The additional child tax credit may give you a refund even if you do not owe any tax.

Who Should Use Form 8812
First, complete the Child Tax Credit Worksheet that applies to you. See the instructions for Form 1040, line 49, or Form 1040A, line 33. If you meet the condition given in the **TIP** at the end of your Child Tax Credit Worksheet, use Form 8812 to see if you can take the additional child tax credit.

Effect of Credit on Welfare Benefits
Any refund you receive as a result of taking the additional child tax credit will not be used to determine if you are eligible for the following programs, or how much you can receive from them.

- Temporary Assistance for Needy Families (TANF).
- Medicaid and supplemental security income (SSI).
- Food stamps and low-income housing.

Taxable Earned Income

1. Did you, or your spouse if filing a joint return, have net earnings from self-employment and use either optional method to figure those net earnings?

☐ **No.** Go to question 2.

☐ **Yes.** Use Pub. 972 to figure the amount to enter on Form 8812, line 4.

2. Are you claiming the earned income credit (EIC) on Form 1040, line 63, or Form 1040A, line 41?

☐ **Yes.** Use the following chart to find the amount to enter on Form 8812, line 4.

IF you are filing Form . . .	AND you completed . . .	THEN enter on Form 8812, line 4, the amount from . . .
1040	Worksheet B on page 49 of your 1040 instructions	Worksheet B, line 4b.*
1040	Step 5 on page 46 of your 1040 instructions (but not Worksheet B)	Step 5, Earned Income
1040A	Step 5 on page 42 of your 1040A instructions	Step 5, Earned Income

*If you were a member of the clergy, subtract the following from the amount on line 4b: **(a)** the rental value of a home or the nontaxable portion of an allowance for a home furnished to you (including payments for utilities) and **(b)** the value of meals and lodging provided to you, your spouse, and your dependents for your employer's convenience.

☐ **No.** 1040 filers: Go to question 3.
1040A filers: Skip question 3 and go to question 4.

3. Were you, or your spouse if filing a joint return, self-employed, or are you filing Schedule SE because you were a member of the clergy or you had church employee income, or are you filing Schedule C or C-EZ as a statutory employee?

☐ **No.** Go to question 4.

☐ **Yes.** Use Pub. 972 to figure the amount to enter on Form 8812, line 4.

4. Does the amount on line 7 of Form 1040 or Form 1040A include any of the following amounts?

- Taxable scholarship or fellowship grants not reported on a Form W-2.
- Amounts paid to an inmate in a penal institution for work (put "PRI" and the amount paid in the space next to line 7 of Form 1040 or 1040A).
- Amounts received as a pension or annuity from a nonqualified deferred compensation plan or a nongovernmental section 457 plan (put "DFC" and the amount received in the space next to line 7 of Form 1040 or 1040A). This amount may be reported in box 11 of your Form W-2. If you received such an amount but box 11 is blank, contact your employer for the amount received as a pension or annuity.
- Amounts from Form 2555, line 41, or Form 2555-EZ, line 18.

☐ **No.** Enter the amount from line 7 of Form 1040 or Form 1040A on Form 8812, line 4.

☐ **Yes.** Subtract the total of those amounts from the amount on line 7 of Form 1040 or Form 1040A. (If an amount is included in more than one of the above categories, include it only once in figuring the total amount to subtract.) Enter the result on Form 8812, line 4.

Railroad Employees
If you worked for a railroad, include the following taxes in the total on Form 8812, line 7.

- Tier 1 tax withheld from your pay. This tax should be shown in box 14 of your Form(s) W-2 and identified as "Tier 1 tax."
- If you were an employee representative, 50% of the total tier 1 tax and tier 1 Medicare tax you paid for 2003.

1040A Filers
If you, or your spouse if filing a joint return, had more than one employer for 2003 and total wages of over $87,000, figure any excess social security and tier 1 railroad retirement (RRTA) taxes withheld. See the instructions for Form 1040A, line 43. Include any excess on Form 8812, line 10.

Paperwork Reduction Act Notice. We ask for the information on this form to carry out the Internal Revenue laws of the United States. You are required to give us the information. We need it to ensure that you are complying with these laws and to allow us to figure and collect the right amount of tax.

You are not required to provide the information requested on a form that is subject to the Paperwork Reduction Act unless the form displays a valid OMB control number. Books or records relating to a form or its instructions must be retained as long as their contents may become material in the administration of any Internal Revenue law. Generally, tax returns and return information are confidential, as required by Internal Revenue Code section 6103.

The time needed to complete and file this form will vary depending on individual circumstances. The estimated average time is: **Recordkeeping,** 6 min.; **Learning about the law or the form,** 5 min.; **Preparing the form,** 28 min.; **Copying, assembling, and sending the form to the IRS,** 20 min.

If you have comments concerning the accuracy of these time estimates or suggestions for making this form simpler, we would be happy to hear from you. See the Instructions for Form 1040 or Form 1040A.

Exhibit 2.6 (Continued)

86 Chapter Two

education credit
One of two types of tax credits permitted for educational expenses paid

hope credit
Education credit permitted for students during their first two years of college

lifetime learning credit
Education credit not limited to the first two years of college

E. **Education credit.** The two types of education credits are as follows:

i. The **hope credit** permits a credit of up to $1500 for tuition and related expenses for each eligible student. An **eligible student** is one who has not completed the first two years of college and who is taking at least half of the normal full-time credit load. Further, the student cannot be a convicted felon. This credit may only be taken for a total of two years.

ii. The **lifetime learning credit** may be taken for any tuition and related expenses for any educational period and is not as restrictive as the hope credit. Computations for this credit are performed on Form 8863 (see Exhibit 2.7).

The following memorandum decision pertains to the hope scholarship credit and the lifetime learning credit.

TAX LAW & POLICY

2001 IRS CCA LEXIS 278

The taxpayer is a college student who filed as a single taxpayer in [TEXT REDACTED]. His parents, who are married and filed a joint federal income tax return for [TEXT REDACTED], were entitled to claim the taxpayer as a dependent on that return. However, the parents reported adjusted gross income (AGI) sufficiently large that they could derive no tax benefit either from claiming the taxpayer as a dependent or from claiming an education tax credit with regard to any education-related expenditures they might have made on his behalf.

On his return, the taxpayer reported an AGI of $[TEXT REDACTED], a personal exemption amount of zero, and a Hope Scholarship Credit of $[TEXT REDACTED]. The Service Center denied the education tax credit, but sent the taxpayer a letter stating that the taxpayer could claim the credit if he filed an amended return claiming himself as a dependent. The taxpayer responded that he could not claim himself as a dependent because his parents could have claimed him as a dependent on their return. However, the taxpayer continued to maintain that he is entitled to an education tax credit for the year and requested assistance from the Taxpayer Advocate in obtaining it.

Your initial understanding of the facts, when this matter was first referred to you, was that the taxpayer's parents had claimed him as a dependent on their [TEXT REDACTED] federal income tax return. Based on that understanding, your office recommended, and this office informally concurred in, denying an education tax credit to the taxpayer. However, further investigation has revealed that the taxpayer's parents did not in fact claim the taxpayer as a dependent in [TEXT REDACTED] (although they did claim a dependency exemption with respect to another of their children). Your office then requested our office's written views on whether the taxpayer was correct in claiming the education tax credit on his [TEXT REDACTED] return.

LAW AND ANALYSIS:

This case involves the relationship between the personal and dependency exemption rules (found in § § 151 and 152) and the education tax credit rules (found in § 25A). The rules operate in tandem, but a seemingly slight difference in the relevant statutory language—§ 151(d)(2) uses the word "allowable," whereas § 25A(f)(1)(A)(iii) uses the word "allowed"—is crucial to our determination that the taxpayer was correct both in treating his personal exemption amount as zero and in claiming the education tax credit.

1. Personal and dependency exemptions (§ § 151 and 152) ("allowable" as a deduction)

Sections 151 and 152 pertain to personal and dependency exemptions. Section 151(a) provides that in the case of an individual, the exemptions provided by § 151 "shall be allowed as deductions in computing taxable income." An individual and his or her spouse may each claim a personal exemption under § 151(b) for the "exemption amount." Under § 151(c)(1), an individual may also deduct the exemption amount for each of that individual's dependents if the dependent either has gross income for the relevant year of less than the exemption amount, or is a child of the taxpayer and is either under the age of 19 or, if a student, under the age of 24.

Section 152(a) generally defines a dependent as being an individual who receives (or is treated as receiving) more than half of his or her support for the calendar year from another taxpayer with whom the individual stands in a specified relationship. The first such specified relationship is between a parent and his or her son or daughter. See § 152(a)(1).

The general "exemption amount" for 1999 was $2,750. See § 151(d)(1) and (d)(4) and § 3.08 of Rev. Proc. 98-61, 1998-2 C.B. 811. However, under a special rule found in § 152(d)(2), the exemption amount applicable to an individual is zero if that individual is one "with respect to whom a deduction is **allowable** to another taxpayer" during the taxable year at issue. (Emphasis added.) In general, a deduction is allowable if it is permissible, regardless of whether the deduction is actually used or confers a tax benefit. See *Sharp v. U.S.*, 14 F.3d 583, 588–589 (Fed. Cir. 1993).

A dependency exemption was allowable to the taxpayer's parents for 1999 under § 151(c)(1) because all three conditions of § 152(a) were satisfied: (i) a specified relationship existed; (ii) the parents supplied more than half their son's support; and (iii) the son was both a student and under the age of 24. As a direct consequence of allowability under § 151(c)(1), however, the taxpayer's personal exemption amount for 1999 was pegged by § 151(d)(2) at zero: he was not entitled to the tax benefit of a personal exemption for himself because other taxpayers—his parents—were permitted to claim him on their return. The effect of § 151(c)(1) and (d)(2), when read together, is both to ensure that only one exemption can properly be claimed per individual and to mandate on which of two possible returns the claim is proper. Once the conditions of 152(a) are met, an individual will have the status of a dependent—and the concomitant personal exemption amount of zero—even if the taxpayer on whose return the dependent can be claimed chooses to forego actually claiming the dependency exemption.

Moreover, § 151(d)(2) and (d)(3)(D) will operate to mandate a personal exemption amount of zero for a dependent even if the phase out rule of § 151(d)(3) results in a zero exemption amount being available with respect to that dependent on another taxpayer's return. Section 151(d)(3) requires a phase out (or reduction) of the exemption amount for those "high income" taxpayers whose AGI exceeds a specified "threshold amount." In [TEXT REDACTED] the threshold amount for married taxpayers filing jointly began at an AGI of $189,950 of AGI, with the phaseout being complete once AGI reached $312,450. See § 3.08 of Rev. Proc. 98-21. Because the taxpayer's parents reported an AGI for [TEXT REDACTED] that was substantially in excess of $312,450, the parents' exemption amount for both personal and dependency exemptions for that year was reduced to zero. Although a zero exemption amount meant that the parents would have derived no tax benefit from claiming their son as a dependent, that lack of tax benefit was statutorily irrelevant under § 151(d)(3)(D).

In sum, because a dependency exemption with respect to their son was allowable to the parents, the taxpayer/son's personal exemption amount under § 151(d)(2) was zero. Thus, the taxpayer correctly declined to amend his 1999 return.

2. The § 25A education tax credit ("allowed" as a deduction)

Section 25A provides two credits—the Hope Scholarship Credit and the Lifetime Learning Credit—that may be claimed with respect to an individual's qualified tuition and related expenses for postsecondary education. Although the credits differ in some important respects, the statutory rule relevant here—§ 25A(f)(1)(A)—applies equally to both credits. Accordingly, the Hope Scholarship Credit and the Lifetime Learning Credit are referred to collectively in this memorandum as the education tax credit.

During 1999, the education tax credit began being phased out when a taxpayer's modified AGI reached $40,000, and was completely phased out at a modified AGI of $50,000. Section 25A(d).

Section 25A(f)(1)(A) defines qualified tuition and related expenses, in general, as tuition and fees required for the attendance or enrollment of (i) the taxpayer; (ii) the taxpayer's spouse; or (iii) any dependent of the taxpayer with respect to whom the taxpayer is allowed a deduction under section 151. In general, a deduction is "allowed" if it has been claimed on the return, regardless of whether the deduction produced a tax benefit. See *Virginian Hotel v. Helvering,* 319 U.S. 523 (1943).

As noted earlier, although the taxpayer's parents were entitled to claim the taxpayer as a dependent on their [TEXT REDACTED] tax return, they elected to forego that deduction. The consequences of the parents' forbearance were twofold: (1) a § 151 deduction was not allowed on their return; and (2) the parents were ineligible, under § 25A(f)(1)(A)(iii), to claim an education tax credit with respect to the taxpayer. By not claiming the taxpayer as a dependent, however, the parents ensured that he—who was the "taxpayer" referred to in § 25A(f)(1)(A)(i)—became the (only) person eligible to claim an education tax credit with respect to his qualified tuition and related expenses in [TEXT REDACTED]. See Notice 97-60, 1997-2 C.B. 310, 312 (Q & A 10). Moreover, the taxpayer became entitled to the credit not only for any qualified tuition and related expenses he may have paid, but also for any such amounts his parents may have paid on his behalf. See Prop. Reg. § 1.25A-(1)(f)(2), Ex. 2.

Congress deliberately chose the "allowed" standard for the education tax credit because that standard permits more flexibility to a family than does the "allowable" standard found in § 151. See H. Rep. 105-148, 105 Cong., 1st Sess., 1997-4 C.B. (Vol. 1) 319, 639–640. That flexibility is illustrated by the facts of this case. Although neither the taxpayer nor his parents could derive any tax benefit from the operation of the § 151 rules, his modified AGI was low enough that he—although not his parents—could derive some tax benefit from the education tax credit. The intrafamily allocation of the credit to the taxpayer—which the parents achieved by not claiming him as a dependent—conferred a tax advantage upon the family as a whole, in a manner consistent with congressional intent.

Accordingly, we conclude that the Service Center erred in disallowing the taxpayer's claim for the education tax credit. If we can be of further assistance, please telephone (202) 622-4920.

F. Earned income credit. This credit is available for persons whose earned income falls below a specified amount (always check the current limit in effect for the year in question). To qualify, the taxpayer must meet the following criteria:

  i. Have a valid social security card
  ii. Cannot have a filing status of "married filing separately"
  iii. Must be a U.S. citizen or lawful permanent resident
  iv. Cannot file for a foreign earned income credit for income earned outside of the United States
  v. Investment income must be below a specified amount (check current tables)

earned income credit
Tax credit for low-income taxpayers on income derived from wages, salaries, tips, and self-employment

Form **8863**	**Education Credits**	OMB No. 1545-1618
Department of the Treasury Internal Revenue Service	**(Hope and Lifetime Learning Credits)** ▶ See instructions. ▶ Attach to Form 1040 or Form 1040A.	**2003** Attachment Sequence No. **50**

Name(s) shown on return | Your social security number

Caution: *You **cannot** take both an education credit and the tuition and fees deduction (Form 1040, line 26, or Form 1040A, line 19) for the **same student** in the same year.*

Part I — Hope Credit. **Caution:** *You **cannot** take the Hope credit for more than **2** tax years for the **same student**.*

1.

(a) Student's name (as shown on page 1 of your tax return) First name Last name	(b) Student's social security number (as shown on page 1 of your tax return)	(c) Qualified expenses (see instructions). **Do not** enter more than $2,000 for each student.	(d) Enter the **smaller** of the amount in column (c) or $1,000	(e) Subtract column (d) from column (c)	(f) Enter one-half of the amount in column (e)

2. Add the amounts in columns (d) and (f) . . . . . . | **2** |
3. Tentative Hope credit. Add the amounts on line 2, columns (d) and (f). If you are taking the lifetime learning credit for another student, go to Part II; otherwise, go to Part III ▶ | **3** |

Part II — Lifetime Learning Credit

4.

Caution: *You **cannot** take the Hope credit and the lifetime learning credit for the **same student** in the same year.*

(a) Student's name (as shown on page 1 of your tax return) First name Last name	(b) Student's social security number (as shown on page 1 of your tax return)	(c) Qualified expenses (see instructions)

5. Add the amounts on line 4, column (c), and enter the total . . . . | **5** |
6. Enter the **smaller** of line 5 or $10,000 . . . . | **6** |
7. Tentative lifetime learning credit. Multiply line 6 by 20% (.20) and go to Part III ▶ | **7** |

Part III — Allowable Education Credits

8. Tentative education credits. Add lines 3 and 7 . . . . | **8** |
9. Enter: $103,000 if married filing jointly; $51,000 if single, head of household, or qualifying widow(er) . . . . | **9** |
10. Enter the amount from Form 1040, line 35*, or Form 1040A, line 22 . . . | **10** |
11. Subtract line 10 from line 9. If zero or less, **stop;** you cannot take any education credits . . . . | **11** |
12. Enter: $20,000 if married filing jointly; $10,000 if single, head of household, or qualifying widow(er) . . . . | **12** |
13. If line 11 is equal to or more than line 12, enter the amount from line 8 on line 14 and go to line 15. If line 11 is less than line 12, divide line 11 by line 12. Enter the result as a decimal (rounded to at least three places) . . . . ▶ | **13** | × . |
14. Multiply line 8 by line 13 . . . . ▶ | **14** |
15. Enter the amount from Form 1040, line 43, or Form 1040A, line 28 . . . . . . | **15** |
16. Enter the total, if any, of your credits from Form 1040, lines 44 through 46, or Form 1040A, lines 29 and 30 . . . . | **16** |
17. Subtract line 16 from line 15. If zero or less, **stop;** you cannot take any education credits . . . . ▶ | **17** |
18. **Education credits.** Enter the **smaller** of line 14 or line 17 here and on Form 1040, line 47, or Form 1040A, line 31 . . . . | **18** |

*See Pub. 970 for the amount to enter if you are filing Form 2555, 2555-EZ, or 4563 or you are excluding income from Puerto Rico.

For Paperwork Reduction Act Notice, see page 3.   Cat. No. 25379M   Form **8863** (2003)

Exhibit 2.7 Form 8863

Form 8863 (2003) Page **2**

General Instructions

A Change To Note
The maximum lifetime learning credit has increased to $2,000.

Purpose of Form
Use Form 8863 to figure and claim your education credits. The education credits are:
- The Hope credit and
- The lifetime learning credit.

Who Can Take the Credits
You may be able to take the credits if you, your spouse, or a dependent you claim on your tax return was a student enrolled at or attending an eligible educational institution. The credits are based on the amount of **qualified expenses** paid for the student in 2003 for academic periods beginning in 2003 and the first 3 months of 2004.

⚠️ **CAUTION** Qualified expenses must be reduced by any expenses paid directly or indirectly using tax-free educational assistance. See **Tax-Free Educational Assistance and Refunds of Qualified Expenses** on this page.

Note: *If a student is claimed as a dependent on another person's tax return, only the person who claims the student as a dependent may claim the credits for the student's qualified expenses. If a student is not claimed as a dependent on another person's tax return, only the student may claim the credits.*

Generally, qualified expenses paid on behalf of the student by someone other than the student (such as a relative) are treated as paid by the student. Also, qualified expenses paid (or treated as paid) by a student who is claimed as a dependent on your tax return are treated as paid by you. Therefore, you are treated as having paid expenses that were paid from your dependent student's earnings, gifts, inheritances, savings, etc.

You **cannot** take the education credits if **any** of the following apply.
- You are claimed as a dependent on another person's tax return, such as your parent's return (but see the **Note** above).
- Your filing status is married filing separately.
- Your adjusted gross income on Form 1040, line 35, or Form 1040A, line 22, is **(a)** $103,000 or more if married filing jointly or **(b)** $51,000 or more if single, head of household, or qualifying widow(er).
- You are taking a deduction for tuition and fees on Form 1040, line 26, or Form 1040A, line 19, for the same student.
- You (or your spouse) were a nonresident alien for any part of 2003 and the nonresident alien did not elect to be treated as a resident alien.

Additional Information
See **Pub. 970**, Tax Benefits for Education, for more information about these credits.

Rules That Apply to Both Credits

What Expenses Qualify?
Generally, **qualified expenses** are amounts paid in 2003 for tuition and fees **required** for the student's enrollment or attendance at an eligible educational institution. It does not matter whether the expenses were paid in cash, by check, by credit card, or with borrowed funds.

Qualified expenses **do not** include amounts paid for:
- Room and board, insurance, medical expenses (including student health fees), transportation, or other similar personal, living, or family expenses.
- Course-related books, supplies, equipment, and nonacademic activities, except for fees **required** to be paid to the institution as a condition of enrollment or attendance.
- Any course or other education involving sports, games, or hobbies, unless such course or other education is part of the student's degree program or (for the lifetime learning credit only) helps the student to acquire or improve job skills.

If you or the student take a deduction for higher education expenses, such as on Schedule A or Schedule C (Form 1040), you **cannot** use those expenses when figuring your education credits.

⚠️ **CAUTION** Any qualified expenses used to figure the education credits may not be taken into account in determining the amount of a distribution from a Coverdell ESA or a qualified state tuition program that is excluded from gross income.

Tax-Free Educational Assistance and Refunds of Qualified Expenses
Tax-free educational assistance includes a tax-free scholarship or Pell grant or tax-free employer-provided educational assistance.

You must reduce the total of your qualified expenses by any tax-free educational assistance and by any refunds of qualified expenses. If the refund or tax-free assistance is received in the same year in which the expenses were paid or in the following year before you file your tax return, reduce your qualified expenses by the amount received and figure your education credits using the reduced amount of qualified expenses. If the refund or tax-free assistance is received after you file your return for the year in which the expenses were paid, you must figure the amount by which your education credits would have been reduced if the refund or tax-free assistance had been received in the year for which you claimed the education credits. Include that amount as an additional tax for the year the refund or tax-free assistance was received on the tax line of your tax return (line 41 of the 2003 Form 1040 or line 28 of the 2003 Form 1040A). Enter the amount and "ECR" next to that line.

Example. You paid $2,250 tuition on December 26, 2002, and your child began college on January 29, 2003. You filed your 2002 tax return on February 1, 2003, and claimed a Hope credit of $1,500. After you filed your return, your child dropped two courses (but maintained one-half of a full-time workload), and you received a refund of $750. You must refigure your 2002 Hope credit using $1,500 of qualified expenses instead of $2,250. The refigured credit is $1,250. You must include the difference of $250 on line 41 of your 2003 Form 1040 or line 28 of your 2003 Form 1040A.

Exhibit 2.7 (Continued)

Form 8863 (2003)

Prepaid Expenses

Qualified expenses paid in 2003 for an academic period that **begins** in the first 3 months of 2004 can be used in figuring your 2003 education credits. For example, if you pay $2,000 in December 2003 for qualified tuition for the 2004 winter quarter that begins in January 2004, you can use that $2,000 in figuring your 2003 education credits (if you meet all the other requirements).

⚠ CAUTION You **cannot** use any amount paid in 2002 or 2004 to figure your 2003 education credits.

What Is an Eligible Educational Institution?

An **eligible educational institution** is generally any accredited public, nonprofit, or proprietary (private) college, university, vocational school, or other postsecondary institution. Also, the institution must be eligible to participate in a student aid program administered by the Department of Education. Virtually all accredited postsecondary institutions meet this definition.

Specific Instructions

Part I
Hope Credit

You may be able to take a credit of up to $1,500 for qualified expenses (defined earlier) paid for **each** student who qualifies for the Hope credit. You can take the Hope credit for a student if **all** of the following apply.

- As of the beginning of 2003, the student had not completed the first 2 years of postsecondary education (generally, the freshman and sophomore years of college), as determined by the eligible educational institution. For this purpose, **do not** include academic credit awarded solely because of the student's performance on proficiency examinations.
- The student was enrolled in 2003 in a program that leads to a degree, certificate, or other recognized educational credential.
- The student was taking at least one-half the normal full-time workload for his or her course of study for at least one academic period beginning in 2003.
- The Hope credit was **not** claimed for that student's expenses in more than one prior tax year.
- The student has not been convicted of a felony for possessing or distributing a controlled substance.

TIP If a student does not meet **all** of the above conditions, you may be able to take the lifetime learning credit for part or all of that student's qualified expenses instead.

Line 1

Complete columns (a) through (f) on line 1 for each student who qualifies for and for whom you elect to take the Hope credit.

Column (c)

Enter **only** qualified expenses paid for the student in 2003 for academic periods beginning after 2002 but before April 1, 2004, as explained earlier. If the student's expenses are more than $2,000, enter $2,000.

Note: *If you have more than three students who qualify for the Hope credit, write "See attached" next to line 1 and attach a statement with the required information for each additional student. Include the totals from line 1, columns (d) and (f), for all students in the amount you enter in columns (d) and (f) on line 2.*

Part II
Lifetime Learning Credit

The maximum lifetime learning credit for 2003 is $2,000, regardless of the number of students.

⚠ CAUTION You **cannot** take the lifetime learning credit for any student for whom you are taking the Hope credit.

Line 4

Complete columns (a) through (c) for each student for whom you are taking the lifetime learning credit.

Column (c)

Enter **only** qualified expenses paid for the student in 2003 for academic periods beginning after 2002 but before April 1, 2004, as explained earlier.

Note: *If you are taking the lifetime learning credit for more than five students, write "See attached" next to line 4 and attach a statement with the required information for each additional student. Include the totals from line 4, column (c), in the amount you enter on line 5.*

Paperwork Reduction Act Notice. We ask for the information on this form to carry out the Internal Revenue laws of the United States. You are required to give us the information. We need it to ensure that you are complying with these laws and to allow us to figure and collect the right amount of tax.

You are not required to provide the information requested on a form that is subject to the Paperwork Reduction Act unless the form displays a valid OMB control number. Books or records relating to a form or its instructions must be retained as long as their contents may become material in the administration of any Internal Revenue law. Generally, tax returns and return information are confidential, as required by Internal Revenue Code section 6103.

The time needed to complete and file this form will vary depending on individual circumstances. The estimated average time is: **Recordkeeping,** 12 min.; **Learning about the law or the form,** 8 min.; **Preparing the form,** 32 min.; **Copying, assembling, and sending the form to the IRS,** 33 min.

If you have comments concerning the accuracy of these time estimates or suggestions for making this form simpler, we would be happy to hear from you. See the Instructions for Form 1040 or Form 1040A.

Exhibit 2.7 (Continued)

vi. Must have earned income from salaries, wages, tips, or be self-employed

Once these requirements have been met, the credit amount depends on whether the taxpayer has a **qualifying child,** one who is under the age of 19 or under the age of 24 if a full-time student, or is permanently disabled, and who has lived with the taxpayer for at least one-half of the tax year and who does not qualify as a qualifying child for someone else who has a higher adjusted gross income. A taxpayer who does not have a qualifying child may still qualify for the credit if he or she is between the ages of 24 and 65, is not a dependent, and has lived in the United States for at least half of the tax year.

The earned income credit is calculated on the taxpayer's filing status and income, and may be computed either by the taxpayer using Schedule EIC or by the IRS if so requested by the taxpayer.

G. **Foreign tax credit.** An individual taxpayer may claim a credit for foreign income taxes paid instead of taking the deduction for such taxes as discussed earlier in the chapter. The decision is a financial one based on which selection provides a smaller tax liability for the taxpayer.

H. **Adoption credit.** A credit of up to $5000 may be available for expenses incurred in legally adopting someone who is under the age of 18 or who is incapable of self-care.

qualifying child
Requirement for taking the child and dependent care tax credit

Ethical Concerns

As discussed in Chapter 1, there are many potential ethical problems associated with assisting a taxpayer in the preparation of a federal income tax return. For the legal professional, possibly the most often occurring concern involves dealing with a client who the legal professional has reason to believe is underreporting or not reporting income, or who is indicating amounts for deductions that seem unrealistic. The tax law professional can never advise a taxpayer to hide income or exaggerate expenses; however, if he or she reasonably believes that a valid legal argument can be made with respect to reporting an item in a manner that favors the taxpayer, this, or course, should be done. The difference lies between reasonable argument and outright fabrication.

Chapter Review

To put matters in their most simplistic terms, individual federal income taxation law can be viewed as determining gross income, adjusting that figure to reflect valid deductions, determining the taxes due based on current Internal Revenue Service tables, and then calculating whether any credits are available to reduce that tax dollar burden. Unfortunately, putting this into practice is slightly more complicated.

The United States taxes an individual on all of his or her income from whatever source that income may be generated: from actual work through wages and salaries, to investments and appreciation in capital assets. Further, the IRS does not limit the amount of income deemed to be taxable by the geographic source of that income (although a credit for foreign income taxes paid on foreign source income is permitted). The total of all these resources is the taxpayer's gross taxable income.

For most taxpayers, this gross taxable income is reduced by their personal exemptions and the standard deduction. Because the federal government imposes certain restrictions on itemized deductions, such itemization may only become beneficial if the extent of the taxpayer's expenses exceed a given percentage of the taxpayer's income. For most individuals, these expenses rarely exceed this minimum.

The amount of tax levied on an individual is based on his or her adjusted gross income, the result of subtracting the deductions and exemptions from the gross income. Because the United States has a progressive income tax rate, the percentage of the adjusted gross income that is taken as tax is determined by the amount of that income and the filing status of the taxpayer.

Tax credits may afford some relief for qualifying taxpayers by allowing a dollar-for-dollar reduction in the amount of taxes owed for each permissible credit. However, these credits also have limited application, and few taxpayers can take advantage of their benefits.

Possibly the most important thing to remember about individual income taxation is that IRS imposes greater penalties for not filing a return than for filing a return without paying the tax due.

Key Terms

advance rent
alimony or maintenance payments
alternative minimum tax
annuity
athletic facility
barter
base amount

Individual Income Taxation

basis
cancelled debt
capital asset
capital gain or loss
carried forward
charitable gift
child and dependent care credit
child care credit
credit
credit for the elderly and disabled
de minimus rule
deduction
dependent
dividend
earned income credit
education credit
exemption
exemption for dependents
foreign tax
Form 1040
Form 1040EZ
fringe benefits
general rule
gross income
head of household
hope credit
income shift
interest
investment
investment interest
item
itemized deductions
Keogh plan
lifetime learning credit
like kind exchange
long-term capital gain or loss
married filing jointly
married filing separately
nontaxable event
passive investment
personal exemption
points
progressive income tax rate
qualified employee discount
qualified widow(er) with dependent child
qualifying child
quantify
rental income
royalty
Schedules A&B
security deposit
short-term capital gain or loss
simplified rule
single
standard deduction
taxable income
working condition fringe benefit

CHAPTER 3

Income Taxation of the Sole Proprietorship

Introduction

There is no separate income tax form used to report the income and expenses of a sole proprietorship. All such items are reported on a **Schedule C** (Exhibit 3.1) as an addendum to the Form 1040 for individual taxpayers. However, because the Schedule C concerns income derived from the operation of a business, and not all individual taxpayers own their own business enterprises, it is more appropriate that this form of income taxation be placed in its own category along with federal income taxation of other business entities.

A **sole proprietorship** involves a situation in which one person owns and operates a business for oneself. The sole proprietorship is a common form of business operating in the United States today because of its ease of formation. No jurisdiction mandates specific filings to create a sole proprietorship. Once a person declares that he or she is in business, the sole proprietorship is established. However, be aware that for operational purposes, such as using an assumed name or obtaining a tax resale number if the business merchandizes goods to the general public, certain filings may be required before operations may legally commence. Further, if the proprietorship employs workers, the **sole proprietor,** the owner of the business, must acquire a **taxpayer identification number,** a number similar to a person's social security number, which is issued by the IRS to identify a business employer and taxpayer.

Schedule C
Attachment to Form 1040 for sole proprietorships

sole proprietorship
Business owned and managed by just one person

sole proprietor
Owner of a sole proprietorship

taxpayer identification number
Number issued by IRS to identify a taxpayer, similar to a social security number

Income Taxation of the Sole Proprietorship 97

SCHEDULE C
(Form 1040)
Department of the Treasury
Internal Revenue Service (99)

Profit or Loss From Business
(Sole Proprietorship)
▶ Partnerships, joint ventures, etc., must file Form 1065 or 1065-B.
▶ Attach to Form 1040 or 1041. ▶ See Instructions for Schedule C (Form 1040).

OMB No. 1545-0074
2003
Attachment
Sequence No. **09**

Name of proprietor | Social security number (SSN)

A Principal business or profession, including product or service (see page C-2 of the instructions) | **B** Enter code from pages C-7, 8, & 9 ▶

C Business name. If no separate business name, leave blank. | **D** Employer ID number (EIN), if any

E Business address (including suite or room no.) ▶
City, town or post office, state, and ZIP code

F Accounting method: (1) ☐ Cash (2) ☐ Accrual (3) ☐ Other (specify) ▶
G Did you "materially participate" in the operation of this business during 2003? If "No," see page C-3 for limit on losses ☐ Yes ☐ No
H If you started or acquired this business during 2003, check here ▶ ☐

Part I Income

1	Gross receipts or sales. **Caution.** If this income was reported to you on Form W-2 and the "Statutory employee" box on that form was checked, see page C-3 and check here ▶ ☐	1
2	Returns and allowances	2
3	Subtract line 2 from line 1	3
4	Cost of goods sold (from line 42 on page 2)	4
5	**Gross profit.** Subtract line 4 from line 3	5
6	Other income, including Federal and state gasoline or fuel tax credit or refund (see page C-3)	6
7	**Gross income.** Add lines 5 and 6 ▶	7

Part II Expenses. Enter expenses for business use of your home **only** on line 30.

8	Advertising	8	19	Pension and profit-sharing plans	19
9	Car and truck expenses (see page C-3)	9	20	Rent or lease (see page C-5):	
			a	Vehicles, machinery, and equipment	20a
10	Commissions and fees	10	**b**	Other business property	20b
11	Contract labor (see page C-4)	11	21	Repairs and maintenance	21
			22	Supplies (not included in Part III)	22
12	Depletion	12	23	Taxes and licenses	23
13	Depreciation and section 179 expense deduction (not included in Part III) (see page C-4)	13	24	Travel, meals, and entertainment:	
			a	Travel	24a
14	Employee benefit programs (other than on line 19)	14	**b**	Meals and entertainment	
15	Insurance (other than health)	15	**c**	Enter nondeductible amount included on line 24b (see page C-5)	
16	Interest:				
a	Mortgage (paid to banks, etc.)	16a	**d**	Subtract line 24c from line 24b	24d
b	Other	16b	25	Utilities	25
17	Legal and professional services	17	26	Wages (less employment credits)	26
			27	Other expenses (from line 48 on page 2)	27
18	Office expense	18			
28	**Total expenses** before expenses for business use of home. Add lines 8 through 27 in columns ▶				28

29	Tentative profit (loss). Subtract line 28 from line 7	29
30	Expenses for business use of your home. Attach **Form 8829**	30
31	**Net profit or (loss).** Subtract line 30 from line 29.	
	• If a profit, enter on **Form 1040, line 12,** and **also** on **Schedule SE, line 2** (statutory employees, see page C-6). Estates and trusts, enter on Form 1041, line 3.	31
	• If a loss, you **must** go to line 32.	
32	If you have a loss, check the box that describes your investment in this activity (see page C-6).	
	• If you checked 32a, enter the loss on **Form 1040, line 12,** and **also** on **Schedule SE, line 2** (statutory employees, see page C-6). Estates and trusts, enter on Form 1041, line 3.	32a ☐ All investment is at risk.
	• If you checked 32b, you **must** attach **Form 6198.**	32b ☐ Some investment is not at risk.

For Paperwork Reduction Act Notice, see Form 1040 instructions.   Cat. No. 11334P   Schedule C (Form 1040) 2003

Exhibit 3.1 Schedule C (Form 1040)

98 Chapter Three

Schedule C (Form 1040) 2003 — Page **2**

Part III Cost of Goods Sold (see page C-6)

33 Method(s) used to value closing inventory: **a** ☐ Cost   **b** ☐ Lower of cost or market   **c** ☐ Other (attach explanation)

34 Was there any change in determining quantities, costs, or valuations between opening and closing inventory? If "Yes," attach explanation . . . . ☐ Yes   ☐ No

35 Inventory at beginning of year. If different from last year's closing inventory, attach explanation . . | 35 |

36 Purchases less cost of items withdrawn for personal use . . . . | 36 |

37 Cost of labor. Do not include any amounts paid to yourself . . . . | 37 |

38 Materials and supplies . . . . | 38 |

39 Other costs . . . . | 39 |

40 Add lines 35 through 39 . . . . | 40 |

41 Inventory at end of year . . . . | 41 |

42 **Cost of goods sold.** Subtract line 41 from line 40. Enter the result here and on page 1, line 4 . . | 42 |

Part IV Information on Your Vehicle. Complete this part **only** if you are claiming car or truck expenses on line 9 and are not required to file Form 4562 for this business. See the instructions for line 13 on page C-4 to find out if you must file Form 4562.

43 When did you place your vehicle in service for business purposes? (month, day, year) ▶ ....../....../......

44 Of the total number of miles you drove your vehicle during 2003, enter the number of miles you used your vehicle for:

   a Business .... **b** Commuting .... **c** Other ....

45 Do you (or your spouse) have another vehicle available for personal use? . . . . ☐ Yes   ☐ No

46 Was your vehicle available for personal use during off-duty hours? . . . . ☐ Yes   ☐ No

47a Do you have evidence to support your deduction? . . . . ☐ Yes   ☐ No

   b If "Yes," is the evidence written? . . . . ☐ Yes   ☐ No

Part V Other Expenses. List below business expenses not included on lines 8–26 or line 30.

48 Total other expenses. Enter here and on page 1, line 27 . . . . | 48 |

Schedule C (Form 1040) 2003

Exhibit 3.1 (Continued)

Exercise

Using the IRS Web site, download a copy of Form SS-4, the form used to obtain a taxpayer identification number.

For an individual who wishes to operate a business, selecting to operate that business as a sole proprietorship may provide certain federal tax advantages. This may occur because, legally, there is no distinction between the sole proprietor and the sole proprietorship. In other words, all income derived from the operation of the sole proprietorship is deemed to be direct income to the owner; but, as a potential advantage, the owner may be able to deduct as a business expense certain items which he or she as an individual taxpayer may not claim as deductions. Such items may include a portion of the taxpayer's rent, utilities, insurance, and so forth, that are directly attributable to the operation of the business.

This chapter will examine the specific items appearing on the Schedule C and relate them back to similar items appearing on the body of the Form 1040 discussed in Chapter 2.

Income

Part I of the Schedule C calls for the sole proprietor to report all income derived from the operation of the business. On line 1 the sole proprietor indicates the total of gross receipts and sales generated by the business. **Gross receipts** represents the **revenue,** or income, billed for the sale of a business's goods or services. At this stage, no provision is made to account for the cost of manufacturing those goods or providing those services. It is the total billing that the business has for the tax period that is being reported. The items of income that must appear in this section include:

gross receipts
All revenue generated from the sale of goods and services

revenue
Sales

A. *Sale of the business's product.* If the sale is made for cash, that dollar amount must be included. As discussed in Chapter 2, the fair market value of any barter transaction must also be totaled and included here.
B. *Rents.* This applies if such rental income is derived as part of the business of the sole proprietorship.

Example

As a business, a man has purchased several apartment buildings. The rent he receives from his tenants is included on Schedule C as rental income derived from the operation of a business.

Example

An advertising executive owns a country house that she only uses three weeks each year. During the part of the year when she is not residing in the country house she rents it out. This rental income is reported on her Form 1040, not a Schedule C, because she does not rent the house in the ordinary course of her business.

The following decision illustrates the court grappling with the distinction between income from a sole proprietorship versus income from a closely held corporation.

TAX LAW & POLICY

LEBOUEF v. COMMISSIONER OF INTERNAL REVENUE
T.C. Memo 2001-261

The taxpayers claimed that the gross receipts listed on their Schedule C were income of a corporate entity owned by one of the taxpayers, not income from their sole-proprietorship.

Respondent determined a Federal income tax deficiency for petitioners' 1993 taxable year in the amount of $93,957. Respondent also determined an addition to tax of $23,161 pursuant to section 6651(a)(1) and an accuracy-related penalty of $18,791 under section 6662(a).

The issues for decision are:

(1) Whether petitioners, having reported gross receipts of $244,270 on their 1993 Schedule C, Profit or Loss From Business, are entitled to offset such receipts by an identical amount as cost of goods sold;

(2) whether petitioners are entitled to deduct a claimed loss of $19,791;

(3) whether petitioners are liable for the section 6651(a)(1) addition to tax for failure timely to file their 1993 income tax return; and

(4) whether petitioners are liable for the section 6662(a) accuracy-related penalty.

Additional adjustments to petitioners' exemptions, itemized deductions, self-employment tax, and deduction for self-employment tax are computational in nature and will be resolved by our holdings on the foregoing issues.

Unless otherwise indicated, all section references are to sections of the Internal Revenue Code in effect for the year at issue, and all Rule references are to the Tax Court Rules of Practice and Procedure.

I. GENERAL FINDINGS OF FACT

On the Schedule C, petitioner Jerry LeBouef is listed as the sole proprietor of LeBouef Company, and the principal business of the entity is stated to be "CONSTRUCTION." Additionally, the question "Did you 'materially participate' in the operation of this business during 1993?" is responded to with a check in the box marked "Yes." On the Schedule C, petitioners reported gross receipts of $244,270 and cost of goods sold of $244,270. The explanation given for the cost of goods sold figure is "PROJECT COSTS." After deduction of $600 in business expenses, LeBouef Company is shown as having incurred a net loss of $600.

The record also contains petitioners' returns for the years immediately preceding and following the period at issue. The Schedule C for LeBouef Company attached to petitioners' 1992 Form 1040 shows gross receipts of $60,000, cost of goods sold "PROJECT COSTS" of $55,000, and business expenses of $1,763, for a net profit of $3,237. In 1994, petitioners reported gross receipts for LeBouef Company of $24,500, cost of goods sold "PROJECT COSTS" of $24,500, business expenses of $14,500, and a net loss of $14,500.

On their Form 4797 for 1993, petitioners claimed a loss of $19,791 with respect to business property of Toro Leasing Company. During 1993, Toro Leasing was a partnership in which Mr. LeBouef and Edward Silveri were each 50 percent general partners who shared equally in profits and losses. Toro Leasing filed a Form 1065, U.S. Partnership Return of Income, reflecting a Form 4797 loss of $39,582 on sales or exchanges of business property.

At some time prior to or during April of 1998, respondent commenced an examination of petitioners' 1993 return. Revenue Agent Ellen Nierich conducted this examination, which culminated in the issuance of a notice of deficiency to petitioners on July 6, 1999. The adjustments made in this notice are the subject of the present litigation.

II. BURDEN OF PROOF

We begin with a threshold observation regarding burden of proof. As a general rule, the Commissioner's determinations are presumed correct, and the taxpayer bears the burden of proving otherwise. Rule 142(a). Recently enacted section 7491, however, may operate in specified circumstances to place the burden on the Commissioner. Because petitioners make certain statements on brief that can be interpreted as an appeal to the benefits of section 7491, we emphasize that the statute is applicable only to court proceedings that arise in connection with examinations commencing after July 22, 1998. Internal Revenue Service Restructuring & Reform Act of 1998, Pub. L. 105-206, sec. 3001(c), 112 Stat. 685, 727. Since the record here indicates that the examination in this case was ongoing by at least April of 1998, the burden remains on petitioners to establish that respondent's determinations are erroneous.

III. SCHEDULE C REPORTING

A. General Rules

As a basic premise, the income of a sole proprietorship must be included in calculating the income and tax liabilities of the individual owning the business. Sec. 61(a)(2). The net profit or loss of such an enterprise is generally computed on Schedule C by subtracting cost of goods sold and ordinary and necessary business expenses from the gross receipts of the venture.

In this connection, taxpayers are required to maintain records sufficient to establish the existence and amount of all items reported on the tax return, including both income and offsets or deductions therefrom. Sec. 6001; *Hradesky v. Commissioner,* 65 T.C. 87, 89-90 (1975), affd. *540 F.2d 821 (5th Cir. 1976); sec. 1.6001-1(a), Income Tax Regs.* Additionally, statements made on a tax return signed by the taxpayer have long been considered admissions, and such admissions are binding on the taxpayer absent cogent evidence indicating they are wrong. *Waring v. Commissioner,* 412 F.2d 800, 801 (3d Cir. 1969), affg. T.C. Memo 1968-126; *Lare v. Commissioner,* 62 T.C. 739, 750 (1974), affd. without published opinion *521 F.2d 1399 (3d Cir. 1975); Kaltreider v. Commissioner,* 28 T.C. 121, 125-126 (1957), affd. *255 F.2d 833 (3d Cir. 1958); Smith v. Commissioner, T.C. Memo 1997-109,* affd. without published opinion *129 F.3d 1260 (4th Cir. 1997); Rankin v. Commissioner, T.C. Memo 1996-350,* affd. *138 F.3d 1286 (9th Cir. 1998); Sirrine Bldg. No. 1 v. Commissioner, T.C. Memo 1995-185,* affd. without published opinion *117 F.3d 1417 (5th Cir. 1997).*

B. Contentions of the Parties

Throughout this litigation and the earlier examination of their return, petitioners have maintained that the sole proprietorship, LeBouef Company, was inactive during the taxable year 1993 and neither earned any income nor incurred any costs of goods sold. Rather, petitioners contend that the gross receipts reflected on their Schedule C were in fact income of LeBouef Company, Inc., a corporate entity owned by Mr. LeBouef. Petitioners explain that prior to 1987 Mr. LeBouef operated his construction enterprise as a sole proprietorship and thereafter incorporated the business as LeBouef Company, Inc. They allege, however, that certain customers mistakenly continued to use the sole proprietorship's employer identification number when reporting payments for work performed to the Internal Revenue Service (IRS) on Forms 1099. Petitioners further assert that they believed such occurred in 1993 to the extent of $244,270, and they label their Schedule C reporting of this amount as gross receipts and then zeroing out that figure by an identical cost of goods sold as "disclosure" and as "a practical solution" for dealing with their situation.

Respondent, in contrast, characterizes this case as involving an unrebutted admission of income coupled with a failure to substantiate expenditures subtracted therefrom.

C. Discussion

On the record before us, we conclude that petitioners have failed to meet their burden of establishing that LeBouef Company was inactive and did not receive the reported amounts in 1993. As we explain below, our conclusion rests on two primary bases: (1) The absence of corroborating evidence beyond the testimony of Mr. LeBouef and Mr. Aulisio that the sole proprietorship did not operate in 1993, and (2) the presence of a bank deposits analysis by respondent indicating income significantly greater than petitioners' reported income would be if the $244,270 were eliminated.

First, Mr. LeBouef and Mr. Aulisio testified that LeBouef Company was not active in 1993. Neither, however, proved convincing. Mr. LeBouef was generally vague and could not specifically identify the genesis of either the $244,270 gross receipts or the $600 business deduction recorded on his Schedule C. Mr. Aulisio testified that it was common practice in the accounting industry, in order to deal with Form 1099 amounts misreported to the IRS by third parties, to "make full disclosure by putting the exact same number in and out." Aside from the questionable validity of this statement, we find it noteworthy that Mr. Aulisio did more than just report and subtract the same numerical figure. He affirmatively labeled the cost of goods sold "PROJECT COSTS," a term which connotes active operations to a far greater extent than it discloses the alleged situation of inactivity.

Webster's defines "disclose" as "to expose to view" and "to make known: open up to general knowledge * * *; esp: to reveal in words (something that is secret or not generally known): DIVULGE." *Webster's Third New International Dictionary* 645 (1976). Accordingly, we take issue with petitioners' and Mr. Aulisio's characterization of the Schedule C reporting as a form of disclosure to the IRS. To report that a particular entity earned gross receipts, incurred project costs and business expenses, and operated at a loss, all with the material participation of its proprietor, hardly exposes, makes known, reveals, or divulges that the entity was inactive, that payments were misreported by third parties, and that the income shown on the Schedule C was actually that of a corporation. If the true intent of petitioners and Mr. Aulisio had been to disclose the facts now postulated, it seems unlikely that the presentation of information in petitioners' Schedule C is the vehicle they would have selected.

Furthermore, the record is devoid of evidence which would lend credence to petitioners' purported reason for showing $244,270 of gross receipts in the first instance. None of the supposedly erroneous Forms 1099 have been produced. Mr. Aulisio even testified that he simply relied on the word of petitioners' bookkeeper in determining the total amount, and he claimed to have seen only one Form 1099 representing a small percentage of the sum in question. Significantly, the bookkeeper was not called as a witness, and we cannot assume that his or her testimony would have been favorable to petitioners. In addition, during examination of petitioners' 1993 return and upon hearing Mr. Aulisio's explanation at that time, Ms. Nierich checked the IRS records but could find no Forms 1099 issued to the sole proprietorship.

In fact, the only documents in the record which petitioners claim support their position are the combined annual reports of LeBouef Company and LeBouef Company, Inc., for 1992 and 1993. These items, however, are of little use to the Court since the balance sheets, income statements, and cashflow statements included therein do not differentiate between the entities in their presentation of financial data. Also, we note that to the extent the financials indicate that one or both of the entities operated at a loss, a loss is not necessarily equivalent to the absence of taxable activities. Moreover, although the 1992 report contains a note stating that the sole proprietorship was inactive in 1992, no similar statement was included in the 1993 report and even the 1992 remark is entitled to little weight here because of the difficulty in reconciling that assertion with other evidence in the record and because of the inherent nature of annual reports.

With regard to evidentiary discrepancies, petitioners' own return for 1992 reflects a net profit for the proprietorship of $3,237 in that year, thus obfuscating any potential correlation between claimed inactivity for financial business purposes and the receipt of taxable income. Additionally, and further calling into question claims that any inactivity which might have existed in 1992 continued throughout 1993, the record contains a copy of a check for $160,000 dated April 21, 1993, and issued to "LE BOUEF COMPANY" by "The CIT Group/Equipment Financing, Inc." The parties stipulated that this check represented "a loan made to LeBouef Company sole proprietorship for the purpose of purchasing construction equipment." Again, equipment purchases seem difficult to square with claims of inactivity.

As concerns the nature of annual reports in general, such reports are derived from the representations of management. And, while financial statements are often verified through audit, to a lesser or greater extent, we have no information as to what, if any, steps were taken to check the proprietorship's claimed inactivity in 1992 or even as to what exactly was meant by use of the term "inactive" within the context of the annual report.

We next turn to the implications of respondent's bank deposits analysis. In the course of her examination of petitioners' 1993 return, Ms. Nierich performed a bank deposits analysis in an attempt to verify petitioners' gross receipts and income. Bank deposits are considered prima facie evidence of income, and a bank deposits analysis typically encompasses the following: (1) A totaling of bank deposits; (2) the elimination from such total of any amounts derived from duplicative transfers or nontaxable sources of which the Commissioner has knowledge; and (3) the further reduction of the adjusted total by any deductible or offsetting expenditures of which the *Commissioner is aware. Clayton v. Commissioner, 102 T.C. 632, 645-646 (1994); DiLeo v. Commissioner, 96 T.C. 858, 868 (1991),* affd. *959 F.2d 16 (2d Cir. 1992).* The burden rests on the taxpayer to prove additional nontaxable sources for deposits and to substantiate greater allowable expenditures. Rule 142(a); *Clayton v. Commissioner, supra at 645.*

During 1993, four bank accounts were maintained as personal accounts of petitioners, and three were maintained in the name of the sole proprietorship. Total deposits of $943,147 were made into these accounts in 1993. After subtracting $281,708 for interaccount transfers, $269,551 for loans, $30 for overdrafts, and $7,023 for other nontaxable items, Ms. Nierich calculated net taxable deposits of $384,835. Excluding the $244,270 of gross receipts listed on the LeBouef Company Schedule C, petitioners reported total gross income on their 1993 return of less than $60,000, a difference of more than $300,000 when compared to the bank deposits analysis.

While respondent does not treat this as an unreported income case and is not attempting to tax petitioners on receipts not shown in their own return, the

> analysis performed does buttress the conclusion that petitioners and/or their sole proprietorship received substantial moneys which would escape taxation if we were to accede to their version of the facts before us. Furthermore, we note that although petitioners dispute several aspects of the bank deposits analysis, they have offered no documentary evidence tracing any particular deposits to nontaxable sources and, thus, have not substantiated their allegations that certain additional amounts should be treated as nontaxable.
>
> To summarize, petitioners have failed to overcome their initial reporting of $244,270 as gross receipts of their sole proprietorship. Moreover, because petitioners also readily concede that they have no substantiation for the identical amount claimed as cost of goods sold, we sustain respondent's determination with respect to the adjustment to petitioners' Schedule C income.
>
> IV. PARTNERSHIP LOSS [Omitted]
>
> Decision will be entered for respondent.

This rental income also includes rents derived from leasing personal property, such as a car rental agency or a hardware store that rents steam cleaners to the public. Revenue for the sole proprietorship also includes all

A. Interest and dividends for accounts that are maintained as part of the sole proprietorship. Note that if the stock or account is held for the private benefit of the sole proprietor and not as a part of the business property, the income derived therefrom must be reflected on the Form 1040, not the Schedule C.

B. Canceled debts. If the business is a debtor and that debt is forgiven, the value of that debt is deemed income to the sole proprietorship.

Example

A sole proprietorship purchases stationery on credit but cannot pay its bill. After several months, the stationery supplier tells the sole proprietor that he is forgiving one-half of the debt so that he can get paid. The amount that is forgiven by the supplier is now included as income to the sole proprietorship.

Take careful note to differentiate income to the sole proprietor from income to the sole proprietorship. Many sole proprietors are employed individuals who operate a sole proprietorship as a sideline to bring in extra income. Any wages or benefits the person receives as an employee are reported directly on the Form 1040 and are not income to the sole proprietorship.

106 Chapter Three

Similarly, not all increases in assets are income. For example, if the sole proprietor acquires a loan or mortgage to provide the enterprise with **working capital,** cash on hand used to operate the business, that money is not income because it has to be repaid.

working capital
Cash on hand used to operate a business

Exercise

A sole proprietor borrows $50,000 from a bank for his business. From that amount he pays himself a salary of $20,000, uses $10,000 to purchase raw materials to manufacture his goods, and places the remainder of the loan in a certificate of deposit. Indicate which, if any, of these uses qualifies as working capital. Explain.

From the total amount of income, the sole proprietor deducts two items in this section of the Schedule C to determine his or her gross profit. **Gross profit,** as used in this part of the Schedule C, represents all revenues less returns and allowances and the cost of the goods sold. The use of this term in its general meaning would include a subtraction of all operating expenses as well.

returns and allowances
Reduction in gross sales due to goods being returned and/or discounts given

Returns and allowances refer to the value of items that a purchaser returns to the seller after having made the initial purchase, as when a customer buys a coat in a department store and then changes his or her mind and brings it back to the store. Allowances are reductions in a sales price the seller may grant to a buyer because of the size of the order (known as a **quantity discount**) or because the buyer agrees to pay for the goods within a short time after the sale. The amount of returns and allowances reduces a business's gross sales. When returns and allowances are subtracted from the gross revenue, the result is the business's **net sales.**

quantity discount
Price reduction permitted because of the amount of goods purchased

net sales
Gross receipts less returns and allowances

Example

A law office bills a client $5000 for the preparation of a contract. The bill states that if the client pays within five days of receipt she may take a 10% discount. If the client avails herself of this allowance, her cost will be $4500 and the law firm's net sale for this item will be $4500 (5000–500).

TAX LAW & POLICY

MONTANO v. COMMISSIONER OF INTERNAL REVENUE
T.C. Memo 1997-335

There are two issues for decision. The first is whether petitioner is entitled to reduce Schedule C gross receipts or sales by claimed returns and allowances in the amount of $45,243. (Respondent's disallowance of this amount resulted in a self-employment tax liability and a corresponding deduction of one-half the amount thereof, both of which are reflected in the $11,129 income tax deficiency determined by respondent, but which must be recomputed in accordance with discussion infra.) The second issue for decision is whether petitioner is liable for the accuracy-related penalty under section 6662(a).

Some of the facts were stipulated and are so found. Petitioner resided in Corona Del Mar, California, at the time he filed his petition.

In the early 1970s petitioner was engaged in manufacturing and selling filament tape and pressure-sensitive labels. In the late 1970s, petitioner obtained a contract with the General Services Administration (GSA) under which he sold approximately $600,000 worth of filament tape to the Federal Government. The contract was canceled by GSA because the tape failed to meet contract specifications, and the defective tape was returned to petitioner. Thereafter, petitioner no longer manufactured filament tape and did not purchase any additional products for resale.

Petitioner stored the defective tape in a shed in his wife's backyard. Petitioner was married in 1949, but he and his wife have lived apart for at least 20 years. Since 1979, petitioner has attempted to sell the tape, which petitioner describes as "about $500,000 worth of material," but without success. Petitioner owed the Small Business Administration (SBA) $500,000 on a loan made in connection with his efforts in the filament tape business, and the SBA confiscated petitioner's equipment and other business assets in the early 1980s to cover some of the loans it had made to petitioner.

In 1992, petitioner placed 115,375 rolls of filament tape on consignment with Advanced Coating. In this connection, on August 26, 1992, petitioner issued an invoice to Advanced Coating showing the sale price of the tape as $80,762.50 for 115,375 rolls of filament tape, at 70 cents per roll. On his 1992 return, petitioner reported no income from the consignment to Advanced Coating.

In 1993, Advanced Coating returned all of this tape as defective. On May 12, 1993, petitioner gave Advanced Coating a credit memo for $45,243 indicating that approximately 64,633 rolls had been returned. On his 1993 return petitioner claimed $45,243 in returns and allowances in connection with the returned tape previously consigned to Advanced Coatings. Since Advanced Coating could use none of the tape, the invoice and credit memo, taken together, reflect a substantial discrepancy in the amount of tape consigned and the amount returned. Petitioner explained this discrepancy as "Well, only because it was just a book entry. It didn't really make any difference."

Petitioner paid no Federal income tax for the years 1991 through 1994.

Petitioner testified that from time to time over a number of years he attempted to dispose of his defective tape inventory. He testified that "so what I went through this whole period of time was trying to get somebody who would take some of it, any of it or all of it." But since the record is rather muddied, it is not clear that petitioner actually ever sold any of the tape.

Petitioner does not attempt to explain how Schedule C returns and allowances could exceed Schedule C gross receipts, particularly in each year over a 4-year period as reflected on the above table. Throughout 1993 and for 5 years before that, petitioner was employed by the State of California as a payroll tax auditor. We are convinced that in order to offset his State of California wage income, petitioner merely manipulated fictitious figures on his Federal income tax returns, including 1993, to make it appear that he was operating a Schedule C business that generated losses year after year. Petitioner admitted as much at trial. Accordingly, we sustain respondent's disallowance of petitioner's claimed returns and allowances on Schedule C of his 1993 return in the amount of $45,243.

Petitioner's 1993 Schedule C reflects that petitioner operated a business of filament tape manufacturer and converter as a proprietor. The Schedule C shows gross receipts of $6,417, returns and allowances of $45,243, and cost of goods sold of $6,031. Respondent disallowed the returns and allowances, but made no adjustment to cost of goods sold.

In computing petitioner's total earnings from self-employment, respondent erroneously added the $6,031 cost of goods sold to the gross receipts of $6,417, rather than reducing the latter by the former, thus erroneously arriving at total earnings from self-employment in the amount of $12,448. Based on this figure, respondent incorrectly computed petitioner's self-employment tax liability and the related self-employment tax deduction. The correct amounts will be recomputed under Rule 155.

As noted, respondent determined an accuracy-related penalty under section 6662(a) in the amount of $2,226. Section 6662(a) imposes an accuracy-related penalty of 20 percent on any portion of an underpayment of tax that is attributable to items set forth in section 6662(b). Section 6662(b) (1) provides that section 6662(a) is to apply to any portion of an underpayment attributable to negligence or disregard of rules or regulations. Section 6662(b) (2) applies section 6662(a) to any substantial understatement of income tax.

Section 6662(c) defines negligence to include any failure to make a reasonable attempt to comply with the provisions of the Internal Revenue Code, and defines "disregard" to include any careless, reckless, or intentional disregard of rules or regulations. Petitioner was an accountant who knew that he was not entitled to reduce his gross receipts by returns and allowances when he had not taken the sales price of the returned items into his income. Thus, we find and hold that petitioner demonstrated negligence or disregard of rules or regulations.

There is a substantial understatement of income tax if the amount of the understatement exceeds the greater of 10 percent of the tax required to be shown on the return for the taxable year, or $5,000. Sec. 6662(d) (1)(A).

Under section 6662(d)(2), the term "understatement" means the excess of the amount of tax required to be shown on the return over the amount of tax shown on the return, reduced by any rebate (within the meaning of section 6211(b)(2)). The computation of the correct amount of the section 6662(a) penalty will be made under Rule 155.

The **cost of goods sold (COGS)** represents all items directly associated with manufacturing a product or providing a good, such as the cost of the product's raw materials, labor, packaging, and so forth. Other expenses associated with operating the business not directly associated with creating the good or acquiring the product are considered **fixed expenses** (overhead obligations such as rent, electricity, and telephone) and are not accounted for in the net sales of the business, because they would have to be paid just to keep the business operational. These overhead expenses appear in the next section of the Schedule C.

cost of goods sold (COGS)
Cost of a business's inventory used to determine the profit realized from the sale of the product

fixed expenses
Overhead

Exercise

To understand how these items appear on the accounting books of a company, obtain the financial records of a publicly traded corporation and indicate how its items would appear on a sole proprietor's Schedule C.

To calculate the cost of goods sold, the business must start with the value of the inventory at the start of the tax period, to which is added all increases to inventory during the period in question. From this total, the business subtracts the inventory remaining at the end of the period. The difference is the cost of the goods sold.

Example

Starting inventory:	300,000
New inventory	80,000
	380,000
Less closing inventory	90,000
COGS	290,000

Note that if the business does not manufacture a product, it has no COGS item.

Expenses

Once the sole proprietor has calculated the gross income for the period in question, he or she then continues to Part II to determine the total amount of all operating expenses incurred to maintain the business entity. Many of these items are similar to those appearing in the body of the Form 1040, but here these items must be directly attributable to ordinary and necessary expenses of operating the sole proprietorship.

The following case concerns a paralegal providing her services as a sole proprietorship.

TAX LAW & POLICY

PUSATERI v. COMMISSIONER OF INTERNAL REVENUE
T.C. Memo 1997-7

Respondent determined a deficiency in petitioner's 1991 Federal income tax in the amount of $7,795, together with an accuracy-related penalty under section 6662(a) of $1,356.

We must decide: (1) Whether petitioner improperly reported income and deductions on two Schedules C and on a Schedule E attached to her 1991 Federal income tax return; (2) whether petitioner is subject to additional self-employment tax; (3) [other issues omitted].

Some of the facts have been stipulated and they are so found. Petitioner resided in Solana Beach, California, when her petition was filed. For clarity and convenience, our findings of fact and opinion have been combined.

During 1991, petitioner was married but separated from her husband. During that year, petitioner was a paralegal licensed to practice in California. She operated two paralegal businesses. On her 1991 Federal income tax return, petitioner reported income and expenses of her two paralegal businesses on two Schedules C, "Julie Pusateri-Paralegal" (Schedule C-1), and "Legal Assistance Center" (Schedule C2). The parties have used the Schedule C-1 and Schedule C-2 terminology and so shall we.

The paralegal business for Schedule C-1 was operated out of an office owned by petitioner's husband. The office was located in her husband's house. Petitioner did not pay rent to her husband or to a landlord for the use of the office. The office had a fax machine, a computer, shelves for supplies, a telephone, a printer, and similar items. Petitioner paid for her own supplies. The paralegal business for Schedule C-2 was operated out of the Legal Assistance Center.

In 1991, petitioner maintained a checking account with Union Bank. She also maintained an account with Wells Fargo Bank under the name "Legal Assistance Center." Petitioner testified that all earnings from her Schedule C-1 paralegal business were deposited into the Union Bank account, and that all earnings from her Schedule C-2 paralegal business were deposited into the Wells Fargo bank account. The parties stipulated that the total gross receipts from petitioner's Schedule C-1 paralegal business in the Union Bank checking account were $29,056 in 1991. (The $258 difference between this amount and the $29,314 reported on the Schedule C-1 was due to a mistake.)

On her Schedule E, Supplemental Income and Loss, petitioner reported "rent income" of $6,720 from "residential" property in San Diego, and "rent income" of $1,600 from "equipment and furniture," for a total of $8,320. On the Schedule E, petitioner also deducted expenses of $200 for cleaning, $100 for insurance,

$100 for utilities on the residential property in San Diego, and depreciation of $1,280 on equipment and furniture, for a total deduction of $1,680.

Respondent disallowed, for lack of substantiation, all of petitioner's expenses claimed on the Schedule C-1 and some of the expenses claimed on the Schedule C-2. Respondent disallowed all expenses claimed on the Schedule E and allocated the $8,320 of Schedule E income to petitioner's Schedule C-1.

Deductions are a matter of legislative grace. A taxpayer who seeks a deduction must be able to show that the taxpayer comes within the express provisions of the statute. *New Colonial Ice Co. v. Helvering, 292 U.S. 435, 440 (1934)*. Petitioner has the burden of proving that respondent's determinations are incorrect in all respects. Rule 142(a); *Welch v. Helvering, 290 U.S. 111, 115 (1933)*.

We first turn to the expenses deducted on the Schedule C-1 and the Schedule C-2. The parties agreed, by written and oral stipulation, that petitioner substantiated the amounts set forth below: [Omitted]

On her Schedule C-1, petitioner claimed rental expenses of $1,600 and $6,720 for a total of $8,320. Petitioner admitted that she did not pay the $1,600 rental expense on machinery. Petitioner also admitted that she did not pay $6,720 for rent for the use of her husband's office. In short, petitioner did not pay the $8,320 deducted by her on the Schedule C-1. Except to the extent the parties stipulated that the expenses were substantiated, respondent's disallowances of the Schedule C-1 and Schedule C-2 deductions are sustained.

We hold that the $8,320 reported by petitioner on the Schedule E was not rental income. Petitioner admitted that this amount was paid to her by an attorney. Petitioner claimed this was to help make up for the fact that she supplied her own facilities.

Petitioner conceded that she did not incur any of the $1,680 of expenses claimed as deductions on her Schedule E. Respondent's disallowance of that amount is sustained.

The next issue is respondent's allocation of the $8,320 of Schedule E income to petitioner's Schedule C-1. Petitioner argued that by claiming the $8,320 on her Schedule C-1 and reporting the $8,320 on her Schedule E, she merely made a "paper transfer" of the $8,320 from her Schedule C-1 to her Schedule E. It was not merely a paper transfer. We agree with respondent that this was done to avoid the payment of self-employment tax. However, petitioner further argues that by disallowing the $8,320 rent deduction on her Schedule C-1, and then attributing $8,320 from Schedule E to Schedule C-1 income, respondent has double-counted the $8,320. We find it significant that the amounts of $6,720 and $1,600 included in income on petitioner's Schedule E correspond to the amounts of $6,720 and $1,600 petitioner deducted on her Schedule C-1. We do not believe that petitioner failed to report $8,320 of income. Rather, we believe that petitioner tried to "transfer" $8,320 to her false Schedule E and to hide this by specious deductions on her Schedule C-1. On this record, we are satisfied that petitioner reported all of her income, subject to correction for the $258 mistake in her favor. Accordingly, we sustain petitioner on this issue.

Petitioner's self-employment tax was increased by respondent. A taxpayer is liable for self-employment tax on net earnings pursuant to section 1401. Net earnings are defined as "the gross income derived by an individual from any trade or business carried on by such individual," less the allowable deductions pertaining to such trade or business. Sec. 1402(a). It is not disputed that petitioner is self-employed in both her businesses. Accordingly, petitioner is liable for self-employment taxes to the extent that petitioner has net earnings under our findings. The deduction of one-half of the self-employment tax will be a computational adjustment. Sec. 164(f).

The parties stipulated that the gross receipts in the Union Bank account were $29,056, which was $258 less than the gross receipts of $29,314 reported on the Schedule C-1. We conclude that the gross receipts for the Schedule C-1 business were $29,056. When we deduct the expenses stipulated as substantiated by petitioner of $6,274, petitioner had net profit of $22,782 for her Schedule C-1 paralegal business. This is in sharp contrast to the net profit of $12,201 petitioner reported on the original Schedule C-1.

The gross receipts for the Schedule C-2 business were $3,692. When we deduct the expenses stipulated as substantiated by petitioner of $7,859, petitioner had a net loss of $4,167 for her Schedule C-2 paralegal business. This again is in sharp contrast to the $11,572 loss petitioner reported on the original Schedule C-2.

Advertising

Any amounts paid to advertise the business are deductible as a business expense. This item includes newspaper advertisements, commercials, and notices in trade and commercial journals. Each such item of expense must be evidenced by a paid receipt.

Bad Debts

bad debt
Expense permitted for business debts that cannot be collected

uncollectibles
Billings that will never be received

receivables
Amounts due from billing for sales

A **bad debt** or **uncollectible** represents the portion of the business's total **receivables** (billings) that it knows it will never in fact receive. There are several reasons why such an item may exist.

- The good was sold on credit and the credit failed.
- The debtor went bankrupt or simply refuses to pay.
- The debtor complained about the quality of the goods so that the creditor voluntarily forgave the amount owing to preserve goodwill.

The sole proprietor must be able to evidence to IRS that the debt is truly uncollectible and, to take advantage of this deduction, the item must at some time have appeared as income to the business.

Practical tip

To document to IRS that the debt is in fact uncollectible, the sole proprietor must endeavor to use all legal means to collect on the obligation, including filing appropriate lawsuits.

Example

A sole proprietorship sold a computer to a customer in exchange for a check for payment. The check was dishonored and the customer disappeared. If the business included the sale as a part of its gross receipts it may now deduct the amount as a bad debt.

The following case illustrates problems associated with the bad debt deduction.

TAX LAW & POLICY

MAYHEW v. COMMISSIONER OF INTERNAL REVENUE
T.C. Memo 1994-310

Respondent, the Commissioner of Internal Revenue, determined that petitioner taxpayers were not entitled to a bad debt deduction, certain expenses claimed on their Schedule C, and that they were liable for the additions to the tax under *I.R.C. § § 6651(a),* 6653(a), and 6661. The Commissioner issued a notice of deficiency in income tax to the taxpayers. The taxpayers filed a petition with the court. The court conducted a trial.

The taxpayer, a certified public accountant, made advances to an individual for rent on the individual's home, personal loan payments, and expenses associated with a restaurant. On Schedule C of the return, the taxpayer claimed that he was in a "financing" business, and he deducted the advances that he made to the individual as a bad debt. The Commissioner gave the taxpayers an extension to file their return. When they requested the extension, the taxpayers estimated their tax liability at $24,000. When they filed the return, they reported a tax liability of $32,760. In the notice of deficiency, the Commissioner determined that the tax liability was $45,479. The court held for the Commissioner. The court held that the advances that the taxpayer made were not loans because he did not expect to receive repayment. The court held that the taxpayers were liable for the late filing addition. The Commissioner had the authority to invalidate the extension because the liability reflected on the return was almost 35 percent higher than the estimate. The court held that the taxpayers were liable for negligence, in part, because they deducted business expenses for storing Persian rugs. The court entered the decision for the Commissioner.

Car Expenses

All transportation expenses involved in operating the business, except for travel to and from the business office, may be deducted. Make sure that the taxpayer retains all receipts for such expenses to document the total to IRS.

Exercise

How would a sole proprietor prove the expenses associated with the wear and tear on the car she used for both business and personal use? How would she evidence the allocation of these expenses? Explain.

Commissions and Fees

Commissions paid to sales personnel and/or brokers to procure income, as well as all licenses that the business must maintain in order to operate, are considered ordinary and necessary expenses of operating the sole proprietorship.

Example

An attorney works as a sole practitioner. The attorney may deduct his or her bar dues and other license fees as a cost of doing business.

Depletion

depletion
Form of depreciation for natural resources

life expectancies
Maximum amount of time an item will be of use

Depletion is a term used to account for the reduction in value of a natural resource due to use. An example is a business that operates a diamond mine. There are only a finite number of diamonds that can be extracted, and so every time a rough stone is taken out of the ground the value of the mine is decreased, or depleted, by such exploitation. All natural resources have **life expectancies**—the maximum amount of time it will have resources—and so each year the business may take a percentage of that use as a business expense. The IRS provides tables for determining the amount of such depletion.

Exercise

Locate the IRS tables for depletion and depreciation.

Depreciation

Depreciation is the method of realizing the loss in value of an item due to use or passage of time, similar to depletion. Depreciation is used to calculate such loss for personal property and buildings. Once again, the IRS provides a depreciation table. For each year of use, the sole proprietor may deduct a percentage of the item's total cost until its **useful life** is exhausted. The useful life is the period of time during which the item may be used before it becomes outdated, obsolete, or worn out. At the end of such useful life any remaining value the item may possess is referred to as its **scrap value**.

depreciation
Paper expense for the loss in value of a good due to the passage of time and wear and tear

useful life
Period of time for which an item has a perceived value

scrap value
Any remaining value on item may have at the end of its useful life

Example

A sole proprietor purchased a computer for his business. The cost of the computer was $3000. In five years the technology will be outdated and the computer will have to be replaced. At that time it will have a value of $200. Therefore, over five years the sole proprietor can depreciate the computer by $2800.

Depending on the nature of the property, the IRS permits the sole proprietor to use either the straight line method of depreciation or an accelerated depreciation method. Under the **straight line depreciation** method, a specific number of years of useful life is determined as well as the item's scrap value. The number of years of useful life is divided into the difference between the cost and the scrap value.

straight line depreciation
Depreciation allocated evenly over the entire useful life of the good

Example

Using the numbers from the previous example, straight line depreciation would produce the following result:

Cost	$3000
Scrap value	−200
	$2800/5 = $360 of depreciation for each of 5 years

accelerated depreciation
Method of depreciating an item whereby most of the depreciation is taken during the first few years of the item's useful life rather than over the entire useful life period

Using **accelerated depreciation**, the sole proprietor depreciates the item during the first few years of its useful life and then takes no further depreciation during the remainder of the item's useful life. Under this method, the business is able to take advantage of a larger depreciation expense at the beginning of an item's useful life and thereby reduce the business's taxable income.

Economic Recovery Tax Act of 1981 (ERTA)
Federal statute that, among other things, created ACRS

allocation cost recovery system (ACRS)
Statutorily determined period of useful life pursuant to the Economic Recovery Tax Act of 1981

Pursuant to the **Economic Recovery Tax Act of 1981 (ERTA),** a specified method of depreciation for tax purposes, known as the **acceleration cost recovery system (ACRS),** must be used. This system divides all depreciable property into several categories:

3 years: Automobiles and personal property used in research and development
5 years: Most other personal property
10 years: Limited real estate
20 years: Most other realty

In *Simon v. Commissioner,* 103 T.C. 247 (1994), the petitioner taxpayers claimed depreciation on two nineteenth-century violin bows under 26 U.S.C.S. § 168(b)(1). Respondent IRS disallowed the deduction and assessed a tax deficiency against the taxpayers. The taxpayers petitioned the court for a redetermination of IRS's determination that they were not entitled to deduct depreciation claimed under the ACRS.

Both of the taxpayers were orchestra performers and purchased the violin bows for their tonal quality, not their monetary value, for regular use in their professional employment as violinists. The taxpayers claimed a depreciation deduction on their income tax return under ACRS that applied to five-year property. The IRS argued that the useful lives of the bows were indeterminable because they were treasured works of art and that they were depreciable only if the taxpayers first proved that each bow had a determinable useful life within the meaning of § 167. The taxpayers countered that the bows were necessary to their profession and suffered wear and tear attributable to use in their profession. The court agreed with the taxpayers. The court held that the taxpayers could deduct depreciation on the bows because they fell within the meaning of the term *recovery property* when they were tangible property, placed in service after 1980, regularly used in the taxpayers' business as professional violinists, and the bows were subject to exhaustion, wear and tear, or obsolescence and thus, were of a character subject to the allowance for depreciation.

The court reversed the IRS's tax deficiency assessment against the taxpayers.

Employee Benefit Programs

Many services the sole proprietor provides for employees may be deducted as an ordinary and necessary business expense.

Exercise

Prepare a list of employee benefits that a sole proprietor might offer to employees. Under what circumstances would such benefits be feasible? Under what circumstances do you think IRS would disallow deductions for those benefits? Explain.

Insurance

The cost of almost all insurance except for health insurance may be deducted. Such insurance would include fire, theft, casualty, liability, malpractice, and life insurance for employees.

Interest

Any interest payments the business pays on business loans is deductible, including mortgage interest if the business has purchased the property where it operates or acquires property as part of its ordinary business, such as a real estate development company.

Legal and Professional Services

All professional fees paid in conjunction with operating the business may be deductible. All such expenses must be documented.

Office Expenses

Office expenses include those incurred in operating a business, such as furniture, computers, telephones, utilities, and so forth. Other items may also be "expensed out," which refers to the situation in which equipment with a short useful life may be deducted as an expense in total in the year of acquisition rather than being taken as a depreciation expense.

Pension and Profit Sharing Plans

Any business contribution to pension funds and profit sharing plans on behalf of the business's employees is includable as a deductible expense.

Rent

Any facility leased for the purpose of operating the business is deductible as an ordinary and necessary business expense. For the sole proprietor who operates the business from his or her own home, that portion of the residence that is used exclusively for operating the sole proprietorship may be deducted, up to a limit of 30% of the total rent. The calculations for determining the amount of the deductible rent for combined residential and business uses are performed on Form 8829 (Exhibit 3.2).

Exercise

What would be the advantages for a sole proprietor in renting separate business space? When would such a decision be detrimental? Explain.

118 Chapter Three

Form 8829
Department of the Treasury
Internal Revenue Service (99)

Expenses for Business Use of Your Home
▶ File only with Schedule C (Form 1040). Use a separate Form 8829 for each home you used for business during the year.
▶ See separate instructions.

OMB No. 1545-1266
2003
Attachment Sequence No. **66**

Name(s) of proprietor(s) — Your social security number

Part I — Part of Your Home Used for Business

1. Area used regularly and exclusively for business, regularly for day care, or for storage of inventory or product samples (see instructions) **1**
2. Total area of home **2**
3. Divide line 1 by line 2. Enter the result as a percentage . . . . **3** %
   - For day-care facilities not used exclusively for business, also complete lines 4–6.
   - All others, skip lines 4–6 and enter the amount from line 3 on line 7.
4. Multiply days used for day care during year by hours used per day . **4**   hr.
5. Total hours available for use during the year (365 days × 24 hours) (see instructions) **5** 8,760 hr.
6. Divide line 4 by line 5. Enter the result as a decimal amount . . . **6** .
7. Business percentage. For day-care facilities not used exclusively for business, multiply line 6 by line 3 (enter the result as a percentage). All others, enter the amount from line 3 . . . . ▶ **7** %

Part II — Figure Your Allowable Deduction

8. Enter the amount from Schedule C, line 29, **plus** any net gain or (loss) derived from the business use of your home and shown on Schedule D or Form 4797. If more than one place of business, see instructions **8**

See instructions for columns (a) and (b) before completing lines 9–20.
(a) Direct expenses | (b) Indirect expenses

9. Casualty losses (see instructions) **9**
10. Deductible mortgage interest (see instructions) . **10**
11. Real estate taxes (see instructions) **11**
12. Add lines 9, 10, and 11 . . . . **12**
13. Multiply line 12, column (b) by line 7 . . . . **13**
14. Add line 12, column (a) and line 13 . . . . . **14**
15. Subtract line 14 from line 8. If zero or less, enter -0- . **15**
16. Excess mortgage interest (see instructions) . . **16**
17. Insurance **17**
18. Repairs and maintenance **18**
19. Utilities **19**
20. Other expenses (see instructions) **20**
21. Add lines 16 through 20 . . . . **21**
22. Multiply line 21, column (b) by line 7 . . . . **22**
23. Carryover of operating expenses from 2002 Form 8829, line 41 . . **23**
24. Add line 21 in column (a), line 22, and line 23 . . . . **24**
25. Allowable operating expenses. Enter the **smaller** of line 15 or line 24 . . . . **25**
26. Limit on excess casualty losses and depreciation. Subtract line 25 from line 15 . . . . . **26**
27. Excess casualty losses (see instructions) **27**
28. Depreciation of your home from Part III below **28**
29. Carryover of excess casualty losses and depreciation from 2002 Form 8829, line 42 **29**
30. Add lines 27 through 29 . . . . **30**
31. Allowable excess casualty losses and depreciation. Enter the **smaller** of line 26 or line 30 . . **31**
32. Add lines 14, 25, and 31 . . . . **32**
33. Casualty loss portion, if any, from lines 14 and 31. Carry amount to **Form 4684**, Section B . . **33**
34. Allowable expenses for business use of your home. Subtract line 33 from line 32. Enter here and on Schedule C, line 30. If your home was used for more than one business, see instructions ▶ **34**

Part III — Depreciation of Your Home

35. Enter the **smaller** of your home's adjusted basis or its fair market value (see instructions) . . **35**
36. Value of land included on line 35 . . . . **36**
37. Basis of building. Subtract line 36 from line 35 . . . . **37**
38. Business basis of building. Multiply line 37 by line 7 . . . . **38**
39. Depreciation percentage (see instructions) . . . . **39** %
40. Depreciation allowable (see instructions). Multiply line 38 by line 39. Enter here and on line 28 above **40**

Part IV — Carryover of Unallowed Expenses to 2004

41. Operating expenses. Subtract line 25 from line 24. If less than zero, enter -0- **41**
42. Excess casualty losses and depreciation. Subtract line 31 from line 30. If less than zero, enter -0- . **42**

For Paperwork Reduction Act Notice, see page 4 of separate instructions.   Cat. No. 13232M   Form **8829** (2003)

Exhibit 3.2 Form 8829

Practical tip

IRS carefully scrutinizes expenses for home offices. Be sure that the client documents all expenses and that the portion of the residence that is claimed for a business use is used exclusively for such purposes.

Example

An attorney rents an apartment that has five rooms. She uses one of the rooms exclusively as her office. She may deduct one-fifth of her rent as a business expense on her Schedule C.

The full rental cost of any property leased for use by the business is also deductible on this line, such as renting a truck for deliveries.

TAX LAW & POLICY

WILLIAMS v. COMMISSIONER OF INTERNAL REVENUE
T.C. Memo 1994-63

The issues for decision for each of the taxable years are:
(1) Whether petitioner is entitled to Schedule C returns and allowances, cost of goods sold, and deductions in excess of the amounts allowed by respondent; (2) whether petitioner is entitled to deductions for a home office; (3) [other issues].

Petitioner received a B.A. degree from the University of Illinois at Urbana and an M.A. degree from Chicago State University. During the taxable years at issue, petitioner was employed by the Chicago Board of Education as an elementary school teacher. In addition to his full-time employment as a teacher, petitioner was engaged in the business of buying and selling new and used books.

RETURNS AND ALLOWANCES, COST OF GOODS SOLD, AND DEDUCTIONS

On Schedule C attached to his Federal income tax return for each taxable year, petitioner reported gross income from his business activity and reduced this amount by returns and allowances, cost of goods sold, and business deductions. Respondent determined that petitioner had not substantiated, in full, the amounts claimed on his Schedules C. In the notice of deficiency, respondent disallowed all of the claimed returns and allowances, and a portion of the cost of goods sold and deductions. For each taxable year, the respective amounts claimed by petitioner in each category and disallowed by respondent in the notice of deficiency are as follows: [Omitted]

We begin by noting that deductions are strictly a matter of legislative grace, and a taxpayer has the burden of establishing that he or she is entitled to any deduction claimed on the return. Rule 142(a); *Deputy v. du Pont,* 308 U.S. 488, 493 (1940); *New Colonial Ice Co. v. Helvering,* 292 U.S. 435, 440 (1934); *Welch v. Helvering,* 290 U.S. 111, 115 (1933).

Generally, taxpayers are required to substantiate claimed deductions and credits by maintaining some type of records. See sec. 1.6001-1(c), Income Tax Regs. Under certain circumstances, where a taxpayer has no records to substantiate claimed deductions, we are permitted to estimate expenses when we are convinced from the record that the taxpayer has incurred such expenses. *Cohan v. Commissioner,* 39 F.2d 540 (2d Cir. 1930). However, in order to make an estimation, "there [must] be sufficient evidence to satisfy the trier that at least the amount allowed in the estimate was in fact spent or incurred for the stated purpose." *Williams v. United States,* 245 F.2d 559, 560 (5th Cir. 1957). Until the trier has that assurance from the record, relief to the taxpayer would be "unguided largesse." Id.; *Cohan v. Commissioner,* supra at 544; accord *Vanicek v. Commissioner,* 85 T.C. 731, 742-743 (1985).

Petitioner argues that although he cannot substantiate all of the items claimed on his Schedules C, the lack of documentation should not be "fatal." As a consequence, based on his testimony, petitioner contends that he should be allowed all the returns and allowances, cost of goods sold, and deductions that respondent disallowed. This Court is not bound to accept the unverified, undocumented testimony of petitioner. See *Hradesky v. Commissioner,* 65 T.C. 87, 90 (1975), affd. per curiam 540 F.2d 821 (5th Cir. 1976). We stress that in order for this Court to apply the rationale of *Cohan v. Commissioner,* supra, to any particular disallowed expenditure, there must be sufficient evidence to permit us to make an estimation. *Williams v. United States,* supra. Self-serving, vague, and undocumented testimony is insufficient.

Other than his own testimony, petitioner presented no evidence to support his contention that he is entitled to amounts in excess of the amounts allowed by respondent for returns and allowances, cost of goods sold, and deductions. Petitioner explained that some of his business records had been lost when he was evicted from his rented bookstore location, but he also testified that "a receipt is something I never thought I would actually need. So when I put gas in the car, I paid for the gas, but I didn't get receipts because I really didn't anticipate that this day would come." The amounts claimed by petitioner on his Schedules C appear in most instances to be estimates. For example, on the 1986 Schedule C, petitioner claimed deductions of $800 for advertising, $800 for car and truck expenses, $200 for dues and publications, $200 for laundry and dry cleaning, $280 for legal and professional services, $4,000 for rent on business property, $1,000 for repairs, $1,200 for supplies, $800 for travel and entertainment, and $2,500 for utilities and telephone. The deductions claimed for the other taxable years are similarly set forth in round numbers. Further, some of the items deducted by petitioner, such as laundry and dry cleaning expenses for maintaining clothing suitable for everyday street wear and depletion for books in inventory that were out of date, would not be deductible as claimed, even if properly substantiated as to amount. Sec. 262; (sec. 611 allowance for depletion applies to mines, oil and gas wells, other natural deposits, and timber); *Dawkins v. Commissioner,* T.C. Memo. 1991-225 (laundry expense for clothing suitable for everyday street wear not allowable).

In sum, petitioner's testimony at trial consisted primarily of a restatement of the estimates shown on the returns. As such, it was general, vague, and lacking in specificity. Respondent allowed reasonable amounts for deductible expenses and cost of goods sold considering petitioner's lack of documentation. On this record, respondent's determinations with respect to the Schedule C returns and allowances, cost of goods sold, and deductions are sustained for each year.

DEDUCTION FOR HOME OFFICE

At trial, petitioner argued that a portion of the amounts he deducted on Schedules C as "rent on business property" should be allowed as deductions for a home office. Petitioner deducted expenses for rent for 1986, 1987, 1988, and 1989 in the amounts of $4,000, $3,600, $3,600, and $4,500, respectively. Of these amounts, respondent allowed $2,100 for 1986, and $3,600 for each of the years 1987, 1988, and 1989, the amounts substantiated by petitioner for rental of the bookstore premises. On the 1986 and 1987 Schedules C attached to his returns, petitioner indicated that he deducted no expenses for an office in his home. Petitioner failed to answer the question concerning whether he had claimed a deduction for a home office on the 1988 and 1989 Schedules C.

Section 280A, in general, denies deductions with respect to the use of a dwelling unit which is used by the taxpayer during the taxable year as a residence. Section 280A(c) permits the deduction of expenses allocable to a portion of the dwelling unit which is exclusively used on a regular basis as "the principal place of business" for any trade or business of the taxpayer. Sec. 280A(c)(1)(A).

In deciding this case, we must employ the definition of "principal place of business" put forth in *Commissioner v. Soliman,* 506 U.S., 113 S. Ct. 701, 703 (1993). [HN7] The term "principal place of business" means not merely an important or necessary place of business, but the "most important, consequential, or influential" one. Petitioner stored some books at home, but did not sell books from his home. Petitioner rented separate commercial space for his bookstore beginning in July of 1986, and continuing until he was evicted sometime in 1989. During the time that petitioner did not have rented store space, he sold books on Saturdays from a table set up at Operation PUSH meetings. On this record, we find that petitioner's home office was not his principal place of business. Accordingly, we hold that petitioner is not entitled to claim deductions for a home office for any of the taxable years at issue.

Exemption for Son [Omitted]

Decision will be entered for respondent.

Repairs and Maintenance

The cost of repairing and maintaining equipment used for the business is deductible. The taxpayer must retain all paid receipts to evidence this expense.

Example

A sole proprietor uses his computer for both business and personal use. He needs to upgrade the computer, and so spends $1000 on software and hiring a technician to install the programs. Can he deduct this amount on his Schedule C? Explain.

The following case discusses the method IRS uses to determine whether a taxpayer truly is engaged in a self-employed business and is thereby entitled to certain business deductions.

TAX LAW & POLICY

PETTY v. COMMISSIONER OF INTERNAL REVENUE
T.C. Memo 2001-59

On April 5, 1997, petitioners signed Form 1040, U.S. Individual Income Tax Return, for 1993 (petitioners' joint return), which respondent received on April 9, 1997. Attached to petitioners' joint return was Schedule C, Profit or Loss From Business (Schedule C), in which petitioner Larry Petty (Mr. Petty) reported his principal business or profession as "Truck Service." In Schedule C, petitioners reported gross income of $5,820 and claimed expenses of $30,268 and a net loss of $24,448. Included in the expenses claimed in Schedule C were $7,902 for "Repair parts," $3,748 for "Repairs and maintenance," $6,205 for "Depreciation," and $3,208 for "Fuel."

During 1993, petitioners paid the amounts indicated with respect to the following expenses that they claim are part of the total expenses that they deducted for 1993 in Schedule C for "Repair parts":[Omitted]

During 1993, petitioners paid the amounts indicated with respect to the following expenses that they claim are deductible for 1993 as Schedule C expenses for "Repairs and maintenance":[Omitted]

At some time around December 1993 or January 1994, petitioners traveled from Alaska to Texas to purchase certain farm equipment. After purchasing such equipment, petitioners discovered that the truck and the trailer that they had driven to Texas were not large enough to transport all of that equipment back to Alaska. Consequently, at a time not established by the record, petitioners purchased another truck and another trailer to use in transporting to Alaska the farm equipment that they had purchased in Texas.

In the notice of deficiency issued to petitioners for 1992 and 1993 (notice), respondent determined, inter alia, to disallow deductions for 1993 for certain of the total expenses claimed in Schedule C because petitioners did not establish that Mr. Petty was engaged in a trade or business during 1993, that such expenses were paid or incurred during 1993, and that such expenses were ordinary and necessary expenses within the meaning of section 162(a). Respondent further determined, inter alia, that petitioners are liable for 1993 for the addition to tax under section 6651(a)(1) for their failure to file timely petitioners' joint return. . . .

SCHEDULE C DEDUCTIONS

Deductions are strictly a matter of legislative grace, and petitioners bear the burden of proving that they are entitled to any deductions claimed. See *INDOPCO, Inc. v. Commissioner,* 503 U.S. 79, 84, 117 L. Ed. 2d 226, 112 S. Ct. 1039 (1992). At trial, petitioners attempted to satisfy that burden through Mr. Petty's testimony and certain documentary evidence. We found Mr. Petty's testimony to be general, vague, conclusory, and/or questionable in certain material respects. Under these circumstances, we are not required to, and we shall not, rely on Mr. Petty's testimony to sustain petitioners' burden of proving that they are entitled to any Schedule C deductions in excess of those conceded by respondent. See *Lerch v. Commissioner,* 877 F.2d 624, 631-632 (7th Cir. 1989), affg. T.C. Memo 1987-295; *Geiger v. Commissioner,* 440 F.2d 688, 689-690 (9th Cir. 1971), affg. per curiam T.C. Memo 1969-159; *Tokarski v. Commissioner,* 87 T.C. 74, 77 (1986).

As for the documentary evidence on which petitioners rely, some of that evidence establishes that petitioners paid certain amounts for various expenditures. However, we find that that documentary evidence does not show that any of those paid amounts is deductible for 1993.

On brief, respondent concedes that during 1993 Mr. Petty operated a truck service Schedule C business. However, respondent contends on brief that petitioners have failed to establish their entitlement for 1993 to the claimed Schedule C deductions at issue.

Section 162(a) generally allows a deduction for ordinary and necessary expenses paid during the taxable year in carrying on a trade or business. The determination of whether an expenditure satisfies the requirements for deductibility under section 162 is a question of fact. See *Commissioner v. Heininger,* 320 U.S. 467, 475, 88 L. Ed. 171, 64 S. Ct. 249 (1943). In general, an expense is ordinary if it is considered normal, usual, or customary in the context of the particular business out of which it arose. See *Deputy v. du Pont,* 308 U.S. 488, 495, 84 L. Ed. 416, 60 S. Ct. 363 (1940). Ordinarily, an expense is necessary if it is appropriate and helpful to the operation of the taxpayer's trade or business. See *Commissioner v. Tellier,* 383 U.S. 687, 689, 16 L. Ed. 2d 185, 86 S. Ct. 1118 (1966); *Carbine v. Commissioner,* 83 T.C. 356, 363 (1984), affd. 777 F.2d 662 (11th Cir. 1985).

With respect to the deductions for 1993 totaling $7,902 claimed in Schedule C for "Repair parts," respondent concedes that petitioners are entitled to deduct $5,214 of those claimed expenses. However, respondent contends that petitioners are not entitled to deduct the balance (i.e., $2,688) of those claimed Schedule C expenses because they have not shown that such expenses are ordinary and necessary expenses paid during 1993 in carrying on Mr. Petty's truck service business. Of the $2,688 of claimed Schedule C expenses for "Repair parts" that are at issue, petitioners have shown that during 1993 they paid only $183.59 of such claimed expenses. We find on the instant record that petitioners have failed to establish that during 1993 they paid more than $183.59 of the claimed Schedule C expenses for "Repair parts" that are at issue. We further find on the record before us that petitioners have failed to establish that the $2,688 of Schedule C expenses at issue claimed as deductions for 1993 for "Repair parts" are ordinary and necessary expenses paid during that year in carrying on Mr. Petty's truck service business.

Based on our examination of the entire record before us, we find that petitioners have failed to prove that they are entitled for 1993 to deduct under section 162(a) $2,688 of their claimed Schedule C expenses for "Repair parts" that remain at issue or any other amount in excess of that conceded by respondent.

With respect to the deductions for 1993 totaling $3,748 claimed in Schedule C for "Repairs and maintenance," respondent concedes that petitioners are entitled to deduct $865 of those claimed expenses. However, respondent contends that petitioners are not entitled to deduct the balance (i.e., $2,883) of those claimed Schedule C expenses because they have not shown that such expenses are ordinary and necessary expenses paid during 1993 in carrying on Mr. Petty's truck service business. On the record before us, we agree with respondent.

We note initially that the documentary evidence on which petitioners rely to establish their entitlement to deduct for 1993 the expenses remaining at issue that they claimed in Schedule C for "Repairs and maintenance" shows that they paid amounts during 1993 totaling $5,020.68. However, petitioners claimed a deduction in Schedule C for "Repairs and maintenance" of only $3,748, of which, as noted above, respondent conceded $865 at trial, leaving only $2,883 which remains at issue. Furthermore, the documentary evidence on which petitioners rely to support their entitlement to deduct for 1993 the $2,883 of claimed Schedule C expenses for "Repairs and maintenance" that remain at issue included a number of checks which do not even involve or relate to repair and/or maintenance expenses. On the instant record, we find that petitioners have failed to establish that the entire amount of $5,020.68 that the record establishes they paid during 1993 relates to "Repairs and maintenance." We further find on the record before us that petitioners have failed to prove that such paid amounts are ordinary and necessary expenses paid during 1993 in carrying on Mr. Petty's truck service business.

Based on our examination of the entire record before us, we find that petitioners have failed to prove that they are entitled for 1993 to deduct under section 162(a) $2,883 of their claimed Schedule C expenses for "Repairs and maintenance" that remain at issue or any other amount in excess of that conceded by respondent.

With respect to the deductions for 1993 totaling $6,205 claimed in Schedule C for depreciation, respondent concedes that petitioners are entitled under section 167(a) to deduct $2,055. However, respondent contends that petitioners are not entitled to deduct the remaining amount (i.e., $4,150) of claimed Schedule C depreciation. Section 167(a) allows a deduction for a reasonable allowance for the exhaustion, wear and tear, and obsolescence of property used in a trade or business or held for the production of income. The basis on which a depreciation deduction is allowable with respect to any property under section 167(a) is the adjusted basis of the property, determined under section 1011 for the purpose of determining gain on the sale or other disposition of such property. See sec. 167(c). Petitioners introduced no evidence to support the $4,150 of claimed Schedule C depreciation deductions at issue for 1993 other than Mr. Petty's testimony that "my Schedule C was filled out by my accountant, and I stand by [that] as correct."

Based on our examination of the entire record before us, we find that petitioners have failed to prove that they are entitled for 1993 to deductions under section 167(a) for $4,150 of their claimed Schedule C depreciation deductions that remain at issue or any other amount in excess of that conceded by respondent.

At trial, petitioners raised a new issue with respect to the purchase of a truck and a trailer, which they contend they purchased in 1993. Although petitioners do not claim a specific total dollar amount for any deductions with respect to that purchase, it is our understanding that petitioners are claiming depreciation on the truck and the trailer and all of the expenses that they paid during their round trip from Alaska to Texas. Mr. Petty initially testified that the purchase price of the truck and the trailer was approximately $40,000. He thereafter testified that he did not remember the purchase price of the truck and the trailer. The only documentary evidence petitioners submitted with respect to the purchase in question was a check dated January 7, 1994 (check), in the amount of $500 that was payable to Bledsoe Ford. The signature line on that check bore the name "Larry Petty," and a notation on the check stated: "down on 93 F350." Petitioners contend that the check was for the purchase of the extended warranty on the truck and not for the purchase of the truck itself. On the record before us, we find that petitioners have failed to establish that they paid specified amounts of expenses during their round trip from Alaska to Texas, that any such amounts were paid in 1993, that any such amounts were for ordinary and necessary expenses paid in 1993 in carrying on any trade or business of Mr. Petty or petitioners, and that any such amounts were not already included as part of the expenses conceded by respondent. We further find on the instant record that petitioners have failed to establish their entitlement for 1993 to any deduction for depreciation under section 167(a) with respect to their purchase in Texas of a truck and a trailer.

Based on our examination of the entire record before us, we find that petitioners have failed to prove that they are entitled for 1993 to deductions under sections 162(a) and 167(a) in excess of any such deductions conceded by respondent with respect to amounts that they claim they paid during their round trip from Alaska to Texas and for the purchase of a truck and a trailer in Texas.

To reflect the foregoing and the concessions of the parties, Decision will be entered under Rule 155.

Supplies

All office and business supplies not otherwise accounted for on the Schedule C may be deducted on this line.

Taxes and Licenses

Many localities impose business taxes on enterprises, and such taxes or license fees paid by the sole proprietor to operate the business are deductible expenses.

Exercise

Determine whether your locality imposes a business tax on sole proprietors. If so, obtain the appropriate filing forms.

Travel, Meals, and Entertainment

As discussed in Chapter 2, such expense items as travel, meals, and entertainment are deductible only if they are necessary to maintain and expand the business and are not reimbursed. Certain limitations apply with respect to meals as discussed therein.

In *King v. Commissioner,* T.C. Memo 1980-373, the petitioner taxpayer sought review of a decision of respondent commissioner of Internal Revenue (commissioner), who determined deficiencies in his income tax.

The taxpayer's wife had started a wholesale costume jewelry business as a sole proprietorship which was later incorporated. The taxpayer and his wife did not draw salaries for several years from the company but each eventually drew a salary. The wife handled day-to-day administration and traveled to purchase goods and resolve personnel problems. The husband was based out of town for his primary job and flew home frequently. They claimed business expense deductions on their income tax return and the commissioner disallowed the expenses on the ground that they were not shown to be ordinary and necessary business expenses. He determined a deficiency. On the taxpayer's appeal, the court held that the home office expenses incurred while the business was a sole proprietorship were deductible as long as they were substantiated. The court held that travel expenses for the taxpayer to return home during that time were not deductible because they were for the purpose of visiting home rather than business. The court held that the expenses incurred after the business was incorporated were the corporation's expenses and not expenses the taxpayer and his wife incurred in a trade or business.

The court held that expenses incurred by the taxpayer and his wife after their business was incorporated and certain travel expenses the taxpayer incurred while the business was a sole proprietorship were not deductible. All other expenses incurred while the business was a sole proprietorship were deductible.

Utilities

Utilities are deductible in the same manner as rent discussed previously.

Wages

All wages and salaries paid to persons employed by the sole proprietor are deductible.

Exercise

A sole proprietor, like any other business, is responsible for withholding taxes on wages paid. Obtain a copy of a withholding tax schedule to see how much of an employee's wages must be withheld.

TAX LAW & POLICY

DIETRICK v. COMMISSIONER OF INTERNAL REVENUE
T.C. Memo 1988-180 (1988)

In these consolidated cases, respondent determined deficiencies in petitioners' Federal income tax for the calendar years 1980 and 1982 as follows:

Docket No.	Year	Deficiency
13616-84	1980	$70,864.55
42129-84	1982	38,490.19

After a concession by petitioners, the issues for decision are:

(1) Whether the taxpayer, who incurs and pays expenses for his closely held corporation from which his sole proprietorship possibly may later derive income, is protecting or promoting his sole proprietorship and so may deduct the corporation's expenses on his Schedule C.

(2) If the taxpayer is found to be protecting or promoting his sole proprietorship, whether he may deduct the corporation's expenses when the corporation has transferred funds to him. This depends upon whether the corporation's transfers of funds to him are loans or reimbursements for the corporate expenses he has paid.

(3) Whether the taxpayer may deduct under section 162 a certain percentage of the wages paid to an employee of a corporation if the employee did work for the taxpayer's sole proprietorship as an agent of the corporation.

FINDINGS OF FACT

Some of the facts have been stipulated and are so found. The stipulation of facts, supplemental stipulation of facts, and the exhibits attached thereto are incorporated herein by this reference.

Petitioners Gerald Patrick Dietrick and Anita Lea Dietrick resided in Florence, Kentucky, at the time of the filing of their petitions. Petitioners filed their joint Federal income tax returns (Forms 1040) for the taxable years 1980, 1981, and 1982, and an amended individual income tax return (Form 1040X) for the taxable year 1982 with the Internal Revenue Service Center in Memphis, Tennessee. Petitioner Anita Lea Dietrick is a party in this case solely because she filed joint income tax returns with her husband for each of the years in issue. All further references to "petitioner" are to Gerald Patrick Dietrick.

In approximately 1959 petitioner began operating a sole proprietorship known as Dietrick Sales and Service. This business provided a wide variety of engineering services, which primarily included the sales and service of filtration equipment, water waste treatment, tramp oil systems and oil water separators, generally referred to as the filtration operation.

Petitioner became interested in the Windecker Eagle airplane (hereinafter referred to as the Eagle) in 1973 when he bought an Eagle from Windecker Industries, Inc. The Eagle is a single engine, high performance aircraft constructed of a composite material known as NUF, or nonwoven, unidirectional fiberglass material. The Eagle was first conceived by Dr. Leo J. Windecker, a dentist who devoted substantial time to aircraft research and development. Dr. Windecker incorporated Windecker Industries, Inc. in 1967 primarily for the purpose of developing, manufacturing, and marketing the Eagle.

Petitioner had no experience in the aircraft industry other than as a private pilot. Petitioner became convinced that the Eagle could be commercially successful and proceeded to acquire certain indebtedness of the financially troubled Windecker Industries, Inc. The indebtedness petitioner acquired was secured by various assets of Windecker Industries, Inc. that were required to manufacture the Eagle. Windecker Industries, Inc. had obtained a Federal Aviation Administration (FAA) Type Certificate on the Eagle and had manufactured seven of the aircraft before it defaulted on its indebtedness. Petitioner then foreclosed on his security interests and obtained machine tools, production molds, the FAA Type Certificate on the Eagle, aircraft tooling, the machine that manufactured NUF, trademarks and registered trade names, and engineering specifications. Petitioner then purchased substantial aircraft inventory that Windecker Industries, Inc. had on hand. Petitioner sold most of the machine tools, but retained the FAA Type Certificate and aircraft tooling, unique machine tools and production molds, as well as the machine that manufactured NUF.

Petitioner initially attempted to market the Eagle on his own through his sole proprietorship, Dietrick Sales and Service. Petitioner later decided to set up a corporation for the manufacture and sale of the Eagle. Petitioner decided to incorporate for several reasons, including his belief that his Schedule C operation had become too complex and his desire to separate his various enterprises. Other reasons were his belief that the best way to finance the production of the Eagle was through contributing shareholders and his desire for an entity that would continue even if something were to happen to him. Thus, petitioner hired an engineer to take over the Dietrick Sales and Service filtration operation so petitioner could incorporate a company, Composite Aircraft Corporation, to produce the Eagle aircraft and devote his full time to the aircraft business.

On April 1, 1979, Composite Aircraft Corporation (hereinafter referred to as Composite) was organized under the laws of the State of Delaware. Composite filed a corporation income tax return (Form 1120) for the taxable years 1980, 1981, and 1982, with the Memphis Service Center. In addition, Composite filed Employer's Quarterly Federal Tax Returns (Forms 941) for the four quarters of the calendar year 1980 with the Memphis Service Center.

At the time Composite was organized petitioner transferred to Composite all of the assets required for the production of the Eagle, except the NUF machine, that he had acquired from Windecker Industries, Inc., as well as know-how and engineering data in exchange for 310 shares of common stock in Composite. Under the FAA Type Certificate, Composite had the right to use the name "Windecker" in connection with the Eagle. Petitioner retained ownership of the NUF machine. The NUF machine was kept at the Dietrick Sales and Service plant in Midland, Texas. However, petitioner entered into a contract with Composite to supply Composite with its requirements of NUF "at his cost."

In addition to the assets transferred to Composite by petitioner, Composite sold a few shares of stock through three private offerings on April 1, 1979, March 1, 1980, and January 20, 1981, to obtain financing for the Eagle project. Each of the three offering circulars warned potential investors that "If Windecker Industries, which was larger and better capitalized than [Composite], was unable to manufacture and market the Eagle on a commercially successful basis, there can be no assurance that [Composite] will be able to manufacture and market the

Eagle successfully." Petitioner was the controlling shareholder of Composite, owning over 90 percent of the issued and outstanding stock at all times. Moreover, the purchasers of the stock were required to execute a Voting Trust Agreement authorizing petitioner to act as voting trustee and to vote all of their shares subject to the voting trust. These three offerings resulted in capital contributions to Composite from shareholders of $75,000 (12 shares × $6,250 per share) as of September of 1979, $85,800 (11 shares × $7,800 per share) as of June of 1980, and $9,750 (one share × $9,750 per share) as of February of 1981, for a total capital contribution of $170,550. These contributions fell far short of the $1.25 million that Composite had set as its original goal. Composite placed these funds in interest-bearing accounts and Treasury bills so the funds could earn interest. Petitioner used his own funds to pay the corporation's expenses, using Account 22 of Dietrick Sales and Service for that purpose.

Petitioner believed that the only way the Eagle could become commercially feasible was if the wing of the Eagle that Windecker Industries, Inc., had originally manufactured was redesigned. In September of 1979, Composite hired a full-time aeronautical engineer and hired the original designer, Dr. Leo J. Windecker, as a consultant. Composite hired George Alther (hereinafter referred to as Alther) as its aeronautical engineer. Alther had once been the chief engineer on the Eagle's original design team at Windecker Industries, Inc. Due to the risky nature of the new enterprise, petitioner and Alther orally agreed to a contingency plan under which Alther could switch to the filtration operation at the Dietrick Sales and Service plant in Midland, Texas, if Composite could not attract sufficient financing for the Eagle project.

Since petitioner and Alther wanted to promote the Composite name, in early 1980 they decided to operate only under the Composite name in Midland, Texas, and to close out any reference to Dietrick Sales and Service in Midland. By 1981 all references made to the Midland, Texas, plant referred to Composite only.

In 1980, petitioner paid Alther to perform services for Dietrick Sales and Service. Petitioner drew twelve checks on his Dietrick Sales and Service account to Alther, each of which was for $2,864.35 with the notation "payroll," for a total of $34,372.20. Petitioner deducted these payments on his Schedule C as part of his cost of goods sold. In addition, petitioner drew a check on the Dietrick Sales and Service account in the amount of $1,650 with the notation "Fed. Tax Deposit for Composite Aircraft" for withholding taxes relative to Alther's salary. See supra. Petitioner also deducted this expenditure on his Schedule C as part of his cost of goods sold. Petitioner also recorded Alther's salary payments in Account 22, which was the account petitioner used to record the amounts he spent to pay Composite's expenses. The total amount of expenditures that petitioner included in Account 22 for 1980 was $137,638.31.

Since Composite was still unable to begin production of the Windecker Eagle due to the lack of financial capital, in 1981 Alther was assigned to do consulting work in the oil industry in which he had had experience before he became an employee of Composite. Although Alther was an employee of Composite, he did consulting work using the name "Alther Engineering" because his name was well known in the oil industry while Composite's name was not. During the years in issue here, all of Alther's W-2 forms were issued by Composite. The record does not disclose whether Composite had a separate bank account in 1980, but by 1981 it apparently did have one. Some of the consulting fees that Alther generated as Alther Engineering were deposited in the Composite corporate bank account and used to help pay Alther's salary and expenses for the year. During 1981, petitioner also wrote eight checks on the Dietrick Sales and Service account payable to George Alther totaling $20,050.45, which he classified as "wages," included in Account 22, and deducted on his Schedule C as cost of goods sold.

In early 1982, petitioner incorporated the filtration operations of Dietrick Sales and Service, and also incorporated Tailwinds Aviation, Inc., an aircraft service organization. The record does not disclose which of petitioner's various assets were transferred to each of these corporations. In particular, the record does not establish whether the NUF machine was transferred to the new Dietrick Sales and Service Corporation or Tailwinds Aviation or was retained by petitioner individually. There had been some sales of NUF in 1979, but there were no sales of such material during any of the years before the Court. The NUF machine had never been used to produce any NUF material for Composite up to the time of the trial. Neither petitioner nor Composite had ever produced an Eagle plane up to the time of the trial.

As president, director, and principal shareholder of Composite, petitioner spent a great deal of the time attempting to obtain financing for the airplane project through publicity for the plane. In this effort petitioner agreed to let Composite use his Eagle for demonstration and promotional purposes. Publicity for Composite included exhibiting the Eagle at air shows, taking part in races, and publishing the "Tail Feather," a newsletter about the Eagle. Each of Composite's Confidential Offering Circulars specified that since Composite did not have a full-time sales force, it would rely on petitioner's efforts to obtain orders for the Eagle at air shows and through personal contact with prospective customers. In 1982 petitioner negotiated a lease with the United States Army in which the Army would pay Composite $15,000 per month to lease petitioner's Eagle and Composite would then pay petitioner for the use of the airplane. Petitioner agreed to devote substantially all of his time to Composite's affairs and work initially without compensation.

In its Confidential Offering Circulars, Composite included expenditures for air show travel expenses when specifying how the proceeds would be disbursed. The Circulars specifically stated that petitioner would make his Eagle available to Composite for demonstration and promotional purposes and would be reimbursed for his expenses in connection therewith. The Confidential Offering Circulars also specified that petitioner had previously advanced funds to cover

Composite's expenses and that petitioner would be reimbursed from the proceeds of the offering. The initial circular expressly stated that petitioner could also elect in the future to advance funds on behalf of Composite to cover expenses, and Composite would reimburse petitioner for such advances from the proceeds of the offering available at that time.

In 1980 Composite transferred a total of $91,000 to petitioner. Petitioner executed no notes in favor of the corporation, no interest was specified, and no unconditional promise to repay existed. In addition, in late December of 1980 Composite obtained a loan from a financial institution in the amount of $65,000 that was secured by Treasury bills Composite owned, which were not due until March and June of 1982. Composite then transferred the $65,000 to petitioner. In the 1981 Offering Circular, the above transfers, plus another bringing the total to $160,800, were characterized as loans from Composite to petitioner. Petitioner was not sure how he would ultimately treat the $65,000 transfer from Composite to himself. If Composite were to be liquidated or sold, petitioner wanted the loan amount taken out of the proceeds and petitioner would then report the loan as income to himself. If Composite proved successful, petitioner wanted to repay the loan to Composite or use it as the basis for the cost of additional shares in Composite.

As with the previous transfer of $91,000 from Composite to petitioner, no note existed between Composite and petitioner as to the $65,000, no interest was charged, and no unconditional promise to repay existed. That was the situation as to the entire $160,800 "loan" referred to in the 1981 circular.

On his 1980 Schedule C, petitioner deducted as part of his cost of goods sold or as expense the $137,638.31 he recorded in Account 22 as expenses he paid for Composite. On March 15, 1984, respondent issued a statutory notice of deficiency to petitioner for the 1980 tax year. Respondent disallowed most of the Account 22 expenditures that petitioner had claimed as deductions on his Schedule C as cost of goods sold and as expenses. Except possibly the wages paid to Alther, discussed above, the disallowed Account 22 expenditures represented corporate expenses of Composite Aircraft Corporation that petitioner had paid. In addition, respondent disallowed a medical deduction of $2,018.77 due to the increase in the amount of petitioner's adjusted gross income because of the disallowed deductions.

On October 31, 1984, respondent issued a statutory notice of deficiency to petitioner for the 1982 tax year. In this notice of deficiency respondent disallowed a net operating loss carryover of $84,392.97 from petitioner's 1981 tax year that petitioner had used on his 1982 individual income tax return. This net operating loss carryover was the result of petitioner's claiming deductions in 1981 on his Schedule C as cost of goods sold and as expenses of amounts recorded on Account 22. Except possibly the wages paid to Alther, discussed above, these Account 22 expenditures represented corporate expenses of Composite Aircraft Corporation that petitioner had paid. Respondent also disallowed expenditures totaling $4,082.37 for the 1982 year, which were recorded on Account 22 for Composite's expenses for that year, that petitioner claimed as deductions on his Schedule C as part of his cost of goods sold.

OPINION § 162(a) allows a taxpayer to deduct all "ordinary and necessary expenses paid or incurred during the taxable year in carrying on any trade or business." Under section 162 the payment by one taxpayer of an expense of another taxpayer's trade or business is not deductible. *Deputy v. du Pont*, 308 U.S. 488, 494 (1940); *Welch v. Helvering*, 290 U.S. 111, 115 (1933). As a general rule, the trade or business of a corporation is not also a trade or business of its shareholders. *Whipple v. Commissioner*, 373 U.S. 193, 202 (1963). Shareholders do not engage in a trade or business when they invest in the stock of a corporation. 373 U.S. at 202. Thus, a shareholder is generally not permitted to deduct from his personal income his payment of the corporation's expenses. *Deputy v. du Pont*, supra; *Betson v. Commissioner*, 802 F.2d 365, 368 (9th Cir. 1986), affg. on this issue a Memorandum Opinion of this Court; *Rink v. Commissioner*, 51 T.C. 746, 751 (1969). The expenditures, if not loans, are considered capital contributions under 263. *Betson v. Commissioner*, supra, 802 F.2d at 368. Sums advanced with the intent of yielding income from business operations in future years are generally considered capital contributions. *Betson v. Commissioner*, supra, 802 F.2d at 371.

An exception to this general rule exists if the taxpayer pays the expenses of another to protect or promote his own trade or business. *Gould v. Commissioner*, 64 T.C. 132, 134-135 (1975); *Lohrke v. Commissioner*, 48 T.C. 679, 684-685 (1967); *Pepper v. Commissioner*, 36 T.C. 886, 895 (1961). In that instance the taxpayer may take the deduction, even though the transaction that gives rise to the payments originated with another person and would have been deductible by that other person if that other person had made the payment. *Gould v. Commissioner*, supra, 64 T.C. at 134-135; *Lohrke v. Commissioner*, supra, 48 T.C. at 684-685; *Pepper v. Commissioner*, supra, 36 T.C. at 895; *Dinardo v. Commissioner*, 22 T.C. 430, 436 (1954); *L. Heller & Son, Inc. v. Commissioner*, 12 T.C. 1109, 1112 (1949).

The first issue for decision is whether petitioner paid his corporation's expenses in order to protect or promote his sole proprietorship and so may deduct his payments of the expenses of another taxpayer, Composite. Respondent argues that petitioner is not entitled to deduct Composite's expenses because petitioner may not deduct the expenses of another taxpayer and does not come within any exception to that general rule. On the other hand, petitioner contends that his payment of Composite's expenses is fully deductible since petitioner paid these expenses to protect or promote his sole proprietorship.

Under the exception the taxpayer must make the payments to retain or protect the taxpayer's existing, ongoing business rather than to acquire, invest in, or establish a new business. *Pepper v. Commissioner*, supra, 36 T.C. at 895; *Snow v. Commissioner*, 31 T.C. 585, 591 (1958). In *Dodd v. Commissioner*, 298 F.2d 570 (4th Cir. 1962), affg. a Memorandum Opinion of this Court, the taxpayer operated his sole proprietorship and a corporation from the same address with the same employees and many of the same customers. Due to the fact that the corporation was undercapitalized, the taxpayer advanced funds to the corporation to meet current operating expenses. The corporation reimbursed the taxpayer for some of the funds the taxpayer advanced for the corporation's benefit. The taxpayer, however, deducted the unreimbursed amounts and stated that the payments were made to protect and preserve the credit and goodwill of his sole proprietorship. The Fourth Circuit stated that the taxpayer's position reduced itself "to the contention that his own individual business and that of the corporation were so intertwined as to be virtually one, and the expenses of the corporation (to the extent of the advances not repaid) presumably deductible by the corporation itself, were also deductible expenses of the taxpayer's separate business." 298 F.2d at 573. The Fourth Circuit disagreed. The Fourth Circuit disallowed the deductions, finding that the taxpayer's purpose in making the advances was to establish a new business and pay the current expenses of the corporation in order to keep it in existence. 298 F.2d at 578. The court found that any benefits to the credit rating or goodwill of the taxpayer's sole proprietorship were incidental, and that the taxpayer's payments of the corporate expenses were just contributions to capital. 298 F.2d at 578.

In addition to the fact that the payment must be made to retain or protect the taxpayer's existing business, the other entity that incurred the expense must previously have provided the taxpayer's trade or business with income or other benefits. In *Dinardo v. Commissioner,* 22 T.C. 430 (1954), we held that the taxpayer's medical partnership could deduct payments it made to cover the operating deficits of a nonprofit corporation that the taxpayer had previously organized to operate a private hospital. The taxpayer had initially organized the hospital to protect and augment the taxpayer's medical practice. The Court found that the taxpayer made the payments in question to keep the hospital in operation so that the taxpayer could continue to earn medical fees from patients who would come or be sent to the taxpayer because of the taxpayer's access to the hospital. 22 T.C. at 435-436. The Court reasoned that the payments were not capital advances made to finance a new enterprise but payments so the taxpayer could continue to receive the additional medical fees from his medical practice. 22 T.C. at 438.

In *Lohrke v. Commissioner,* supra, 48 T.C. at 688, the above standards were refined and restated by this Court. The Court specified that two elements must be met before a taxpayer can deduct the ordinary and necessary business expenses of another taxpayer under the protect-or-promote exception. In that case the taxpayer received a substantial amount of royalty income from the licensing of a patent on a process used in the synthetic fiber industry. The taxpayer also had a substantial interest in a corporation that used the patented process in the conversion of synthetic fibers into fabrics. When the corporation made a shipment of defective fiber to a customer, the taxpayer agreed to be held personally liable. The taxpayer agreed to this because the corporation could not afford to lose the sale of the fiber and the taxpayer did not want to lose the benefits that he, as a licensor and inventor of the patented process, derived from having access to the manufacturing facilities of the corporation. The taxpayer tried to deduct the payments he made for the resulting losses.

This Court in *Lohrke v. Commissioner,* supra, 48 T.C. at 688, established two elements or a two-prong test to determine whether a taxpayer could deduct the expenses of another person. The first element is whether the taxpayer's purpose or motive for paying the obligation of the other entity is to protect or promote the taxpayer's own trade or business. 48 T.C. at 688. The second element is whether the expenditure is an ordinary and necessary expense of the taxpayer's own trade or business. 48 T.C. at 688.

In *Lohrke v. Commissioner* we found that the taxpayer's primary motive for paying the obligation of the corporation was to protect his individual licensing business, which was receiving several benefits from the continued existence of the corporation. 48 T.C. at 689. These benefits included using the corporation as a pilot plant so prospective licensees could sample the fiber processed by the patented process and using the corporation to gain a sufficiently intimate knowledge of trade activities so the taxpayer would know whether companies were using the patented process without a license or paying inadequate royalties.

As to the second element or prong of the test, in determining what is an ordinary and necessary business expense, necessary means appropriate and helpful. *Welch v. Helvering,* 290 U.S. 111, 113 (1933). Ordinary does not mean that the payments must be habitual or normal to the taxpayer but, instead, denotes payments that are a common and accepted means of protecting or promoting the taxpayer's own trade or business. *Welch v. Helvering,* supra, 290 U.S. at 114. In *Lohrke v. Commissioner,* supra, 48 T.C. at 689, we found that the taxpayer's payment was proximately related to his individual licensing business and so was ordinary and necessary. 48 T.C. at 689. Thus, the taxpayer was entitled to deduct the payment as an ordinary and necessary business expense of carrying on his licensing business.

In this case petitioner attempts to defend his deductions for payments he made for Composite by claiming that he comes within the protect-or-promote exception to section 162. Petitioner claims that he was trying to protect or promote his sole proprietorship, Dietrick Sales and Service, when he paid the expenses of Composite. Under the general rule of Section 162, once petitioner incorporated Composite he was no longer entitled to deduct the payment of Composite's expenses on his individual income tax return. To determine whether the exception applies we will apply the two-prong test of *Lohrke v. Commissioner,* supra. Petitioner bears the burden of demonstrating that he satisfies each prong of the test. Rule 142(a).

Under the first element of the two-prong test in *Lohrke v. Commissioner,* supra, 48 T.C. at 688, petitioner must demonstrate that his purpose or motive for making the payment was to protect or promote petitioner's sole proprietorship. Petitioner argues that he paid Composite's expenses to both financially benefit his sole proprietorship and protect the goodwill or reputation of his own business. Petitioner first argues that the expenses he paid were incurred to organize and obtain financing for Composite so that his sole proprietorship could later derive income by selling NUF to Composite to make the Eagle airplanes. Since petitioner owned the machine that produced the NUF material, petitioner contends that it was critical for him to insure Composite's success so he could earn money on his investment in the machine.

We find that petitioner's primary motive for paying Composite's expenses was to establish a new business rather than protect or promote his sole proprietorship. Petitioner wants the best of both worlds in which he can take advantage of the benefits of incorporation while personally deducting the expenses of the corporation. Under the protect-or-promote exception to section 162, petitioner's payments are not deductible since the payments were made so petitioner could establish a new business rather than protect or promote his sole proprietorship. The protect-or-promote exception only applies if the payments are made to retain or protect an existing business rather than establish a new business. *Dodd v. Commissioner,* supra, 298 F.2d at 573.

Petitioner initially attempted to market the Eagle on his own through his sole proprietorship. However, petitioner decided to set up a corporation for production of the Eagle for a number of good business reasons: his belief that the best way to finance production of the Eagle was through contributing shareholders; his wish to separate the Eagle aircraft project from his sole proprietorship, which dealt primarily with oil filtration; and his desire for continuity of the Eagle aircraft business in case anything happened to him. The expenses of Composite that petitioner paid included expenses incurred in organizing the new corporation and trying to obtain adequate financing so Composite could commence production of the Eagle. In addition, petitioner, as the president, director, and principal shareholder, agreed to advance funds to Composite until such time as Composite could reimburse him from the proceeds of the private offerings or otherwise. The fact that petitioner (either through his sole proprietorship or perhaps through his other corporations—Dietrick Sales and Service or Tailwinds Aviation) might benefit from Composite's possible future success is not sufficient to bring this case within the protect-or-promote exception.

In addition, in *Lohrke v. Commissioner,* supra, and *Dinardo v. Commissioner,* supra, we held that the taxpayers could deduct the expenses of another legal entity because the taxpayer's own trade or business had previously received benefits from the corporations whose expenses they paid. The taxpayers in those cases paid the corporations' expenses only when the taxpayers thought that their own trade or businesses might lose those benefits. In this case neither petitioner's sole proprietorship nor his other two corporations had ever received any benefits from Composite. Petitioner never furnished any NUF material to Composite and had he done so, it would have been furnished "at his cost" (see n.3, supra); petitioner never received any compensation for consulting services rendered to Composite. Hence, petitioner's argument that payment of Composite's expenses was to protect or promote "his business of supplying N.U.F. and consulting services to Composite" is merely theory without a factual basis.

Petitioner also speculates that Dietrick Sales and Service (sole proprietorship or closely held corporation) runs the risk of being placed in "severe financial straits" unless Composite proves successful. Petitioner has offered no proof that Dietrick Sales and Service would be placed in any financial danger if petitioner had not paid Composite's expenses. In fact, Dietrick Sales and Service has been in business since 1959 and its principal business was the filtration operations, not the fledgling aircraft business Mr. Dietrick was trying to launch. Without any sale of NUF to Composite, Dietrick Sales and Service continued its profitable filtration business and was incorporated in 1982. In fact the record does not establish whether the NUF machine was transferred to the new Dietrick Sales and Service Corporation in 1982, was transferred to Tailwinds Aviation, or remained as one of Mr. Dietrick's personal assets.

Petitioner contends that by specifying both "protect" and "promote" in the exception to section 162 in *Lohrke v. Commissioner,* supra, this Court intended to include both the protection of prior benefits or income and the promotion of possible future income or benefits. Petitioner argues that his payment of composite's expenses falls within the exception since he intended to promote his sole proprietorship through Composite's use of NUF material in the future. We disagree with this analysis factually for the reasons stated above and also legally. This Court did not intend to include benefits that had never materialized prior to the taxpayer's payment of expenses under the protect-or-promote exception. It is too speculative to guess whether benefits that have not materialized by the time the taxpayer pays his corporation's expenses might have benefited the taxpayer's own separate trade or business. Thus, we find that petitioner's primary motive for paying Composite's expenses was not to financially benefit his sole proprietorship or his other corporations since they had never received any financial benefits from Composite, either prior to the payment of these expenses or up to the time of trial.

Petitioner also argues that his motive for paying Composite's expenses was to protect or promote his trade or business through the protection of his own business' goodwill or reputation, relying on *Jenkins v. Commissioner,* T.C. Memo. 1983-667. In that case this Court held that one means of protecting a taxpayer's trade or business was to protect that trade or business' reputation. In *Jenkins v. Commissioner* the taxpayer, country music entertainer Conway Twitty, repaid the investors, who included the taxpayer's friends and business associates, the amounts they invested in Twitty Burger after he decided to shut down the financially troubled Twitty Burger corporation. We found that the taxpayer made those payments with the primary motive of protecting his personal business reputation in his ongoing business of being a country music entertainer. The Court found that the possibility of extensive adverse publicity concerning the taxpayer's involvement in the defunct corporation, which would reflect on the taxpayer's reputation for integrity, was a very likely possibility. The Court based this determination on both the taxpayer's testimony that allegations of fraud against him, with several investors threatening to sue him, could ruin the positive image that he had carefully built over the years, and the expert testimony of the Director of Country Music Foundation who testified that a country music entertainer's character, personality, and credit reputation are part of his role as a country singer and have an effect on the popularity of that singer.

Petitioner bears the burden of proving that the nonpayment of Composite's expenses would have adversely affected petitioner's business reputation. Rule 142(a). Petitioner has not established that he paid Composite's expenses to maintain his own or his other corporations' reputation or goodwill. Petitioner claims that he was an entrepreneur who relied on his reputation for good business acumen to attract investors to his business enterprises. Unlike the taxpayer in *Jenkins v. Commissioner,* supra, petitioner offered no evidence to demonstrate that the failure of Composite to pay its expenses would reflect unfavorably on either the reputation of Dietrick Sales and Service or the reputation of petitioner himself as a businessman. Without such evidence petitioner has failed to meet his burden of proof.

Moreover, we note that each of the private Offering Circulars expressly warned potential investors that Mr. Dietrick had no experience in the aircraft industry other than as a private pilot. Those circulars also warned potential investors that if Windecker Industries which was larger and better capitalized than [Composite] was unable to manufacture and market the Eagle on a commercially successful basis, there can be no assurance that [Composite] will be able to manufacture and market the Eagle successfully.

In other words, there is no evidence that anyone was relying upon the business reputation of Mr. Dietrick or of his sole proprietorship/corporation, Dietrick Sales and Service. Likewise, there is no evidence that the success or failure of Composite's Eagle aircraft business would have any impact on petitioner or his other business activities. Thus, petitioner has failed to prove that his primary motive for paying Composite's expenses was to protect or promote petitioner, his sole proprietorship, or his other corporations, either financially or through their reputation.

The second element of the two-prong test in *Lohrke v. Commissioner,* supra, 48 T.C. at 688, is whether the payment was an ordinary and necessary expense of the taxpayer's own trade or business. Since both prongs of the test must be met and we have determined that petitioner has not met the first prong, we need not determine whether this second element has been met. However, the same facts discussed at length above establish that petitioner also could not meet this test.

Petitioner's payment of Composite's expenses was not proximately related to his own separate trade or business.

Even if the protect-or-promote exception were applicable to petitioner, and we have concluded it was not, petitioner still could not deduct the payment of expenses for which he was reimbursed by Composite. A taxpayer cannot deduct payments for expenses for which he has been reimbursed by the corporation. In Composite's Confidential Offering Circulars, Composite included air show travel expenses as one of the purposes for which the proceeds would be disbursed. The circulars specifically stated that Mr. Dietrick would use his own Eagle airplane "for demonstration and promotional purposes and will be reimbursed for his expenses in connection therewith." In addition, Composite specified in its Confidential Offering Circulars that petitioner would be reimbursed for payments he made on behalf of Composite. Petitioner attempted to deduct on his own Schedule C payments of $137,638.31 for 1980, $87,959.27 for 1981, and $4,082.37 for 1982. However, Composite transferred a total of $156,000 to petitioner in 1980, and an additional amount in 1981 to bring the total up to $160,800, the total capital contributions received in the first two stock offerings. The parties in this case disagree as to the proper characterization of these transfers of funds. Petitioner says these transfers of funds were loans to him from Composite. Respondent says these transfers of funds were reimbursements to petitioner for the corporate expenses he had paid.

The third Offering Circular in early 1981 characterized the $160,800 transfers as "loans" from Composite to petitioner. Thus, petitioner argues the funds were not reimbursements of expenses he had paid. The primary test used to determine whether a distribution from a corporation is a dividend or a loan is the intent to repay or retain the amounts. Estate of *Chism v. Commissioner,* 322 F.2d 946, 960 (9th Cir. 1963), affg. a Memorandum Opinion of this Court; *Pierce v. Commissioner,* 61 T.C. 424, 430 (1974); *Nasser v. United States,* 257 F. Supp. 443, 447 (N.D. Cal. 1966). This determination is a question of fact to be determined from all of the circumstances. *Estate of Chism v. Commissioner,* supra, 322 F.2d at 960. The taxpayer bears the burden of proof. *Welch v. Helvering,* 290 U.S. 111, 115 (1933). Although this case does not deal with the dividend versus loan issue, the same intent test applies to determine whether a transfer is a loan or a reimbursement for the shareholder's payment of the corporation's expenses. Frequently, the inquiry is whether an amount paid to a corporation by a shareholder is a loan or a contribution to capital. Here, with a corporation that is vastly undercapitalized for its business of developing, manufacturing, and selling a new type of airplane, we have the anomalous situation of the corporation making a distribution of its limited funds to the principal shareholder, purportedly as "loans."

An inquiry into the subjective intent of petitioner requires an examination of both his testimony and the objective evidence of intent. This objective evidence includes: (1) whether the transferor corporation was closely held, (2) whether notes were executed, (3) whether the purported obligation was secured by collateral, (4) whether there were fixed dates or a schedule for payment, (5) whether interest was paid or accrued, (6) whether there was a limit to the amount that could be advanced to a shareholder, (7) whether the corporation took steps to collect on overdue "loan," (8) whether any part of the advances were repaid, (9) how the transfers were treated on the books and records, the tax returns and financial statements of the corporation and shareholder, and (10) whether there was a specific business purpose for making the advances. *Alterman Foods, Inc. v. United States,* 505 F.2d 873, 878-879 (5th Cir. 1974); *Berthold v. Commissioner,* 404 F.2d 119, 121-122 (6th Cir. 1968), affg. a Memorandum Opinion of this Court; *Pierce v. Commissioner,* 61 T.C. 424, 430-431 (1974).

In this case, although the transfers were labeled as "loans" in the third Offering Circular and although petitioner testified to that effect, we conclude on the basis of the record as a whole that petitioner has failed to establish that he had any obligation to repay, or intent to repay, these funds to Composite. Petitioner claims that the transfers were loans, pointing out that he repaid $25,000 of the $65,000 loan Composite had borrowed from a bank when Composite's note to the bank came due. Petitioner offered no objective evidence to prove that the transfers to him were loans. No note was ever executed by petitioner, no agreement existed between Composite and petitioner stating that the transfers were loans, no mention of collateral was made, no schedule existed for repayment, no interest was specified, and the loan transaction was not recorded as such on the corporate books or records. In fact, petitioner testified that he was uncertain as to how he would ultimately characterize the $65,000 transfer. In light of this, petitioner's testimony that the transfers were loans and the characterization of the transfers as a loan in Composite's third Offering Circular do not satisfy petitioner's burden of proof. Thus, we conclude that the transfers were reimbursements to petitioner. We hold that even if the protect-or-promote exception applied to petitioner, he still could not deduct those expenses for which he received reimbursement from Composite.

Lastly, petitioner claims that even if he cannot deduct the payments under the protect-or-promote exception, he properly deducted Alther's salary on Schedule C of his individual income tax return. Petitioner contends that he should be allowed to deduct 90 percent of Alther's salary since Alther spent at least 90 percent of his time working for the sole proprietorship, the filtration operations, in 1980 and 1981. Respondent argues that salaries of employees who are in the employ of a separate and distinct corporate entity are only deductible by that entity, citing *Columbia Rope Co. v. Commissioner,* 42 T.C. 800, 815 (1964); and *Young & Rubicam, Inc. v. United States,* 410 F.2d 1233, 1237 (Cl. Ct. 1969). Respondent says taxpayer has the burden of proving that a particular individual was involved in a specific activity clearly for the proximate and direct benefit of the taxpayer rather than of that other entity. *Young & Rubicam, Inc. v. United States,* supra, 410 F.2d at 1239.

In this case, at the time Composite hired Alther as an aeronautical engineer, petitioner and Alther agreed to a contingency plan under which Alther would work for the filtration operation if Composite could not attract sufficient financing to commence production of the Eagle. Composite never received the amount of capital contributions that were necessary to begin production of the Eagle. Although Alther remained an employee of Composite throughout the years in issue and received his W-2's from that corporation, he spent most of his time working for the filtration business and his wages were actually paid by Mr. Dietrick in 1980 and 1981.

To a minor extent in 1981 and in 1982 and subsequent years, Alther's engineering services rendered under the name of "Alther Engineering" apparently produced income that was deposited into Composite's corporate account, and used to pay at least part of Alther's salary and expenses. However, the only Alther wages in dispute in this case are those amounts paid by Mr. Dietrick in 1980 and 1981. See nn. 4,5,8,9,10, supra.

Petitioner argues that when Composite could not obtain adequate financing to begin production of the Eagle, Alther was reassigned, according to his agreement with petitioner, to do consulting work for Dietrick Sales and Service. Although Alther used the name "Alther Engineering," we find that he only did so because his name was better known than Composite's and not because he was no longer working for Composite.

However, assuming Alther was Composite's employee and worked in the filtration business as an agent of Composite, that does not mean petitioner would not be entitled to deduct any amounts he actually paid for services actually rendered to his sole proprietorship. The parties seemed to argue this issue as if only Composite or only petitioner could deduct Alther's wage expense. This case is factually distinguishable from *Columbia Rope Co. v. Commissioner,* supra. This case does not involve a section 482 reallocation of expenses as in *Young & Rubicam, Inc. v. United States,* supra. However, even under that case, a taxpayer who can show that the employee worked part of the time for the proximate and direct benefit of the taxpayer may deduct a percentage of the earnings for the time the employee devoted solely to the taxpayer. *Young & Rubicam, Inc. v. United States,* supra, 410 F.2d at 1240-1241. The fact situation in the instant case is more like the "Kelly Girl" or leased employee case. Petitioner can deduct on his Schedule C any reasonable amounts he paid Composite for services actually rendered by Alther to the filtration operation; Composite should then report that income on its tax return and in turn deduct the amount it actually paid Alther as its corporate employee. That is not exactly what happened, but in essence that is the substance of the transaction.

Accordingly, we hold that petitioner is entitled to deduct on his Schedule C 90 percent of the $36,022.20 he paid for Alther's wages and withholding tax in

1980, and 90 percent of the $20,050.45 that he paid for Alther's wages in 1981. However, those amounts must be reduced to the extent that petitioner was reimbursed for such expenditures by Composite.

Except for some portion of Alther's wages, petitioner cannot deduct any payments he made on behalf of Composite on his Schedule C since those expenses were those of another taxable entity and petitioner was not protecting or promoting his own trade or business in making the payments.

To reflect the concession and the foregoing holdings,

Decisions will be entered under Rule 155.

Other Expenses

Any other items of expense incurred in operating the business not appearing on another line may be included here, such as subscriptions to trade journals and business gifts.

The following case discusses a taxpayer's ability to deduct certain expenses on a Schedule C for costs involved in operating a presumptive consulting business.

TAX LAW & POLICY

MAERKI v. COMMISSIONER OF INTERNAL REVENUE
T.C. Memo 1995-460

Respondent determined a deficiency in petitioners' 1990 Federal income tax in the amount of $11,280 and an addition to tax in the amount of $564, pursuant to section 6651(a)(1).

The issues for decision are: (1) Whether petitioners underreported gross income in the amount of $4,398; (2) whether petitioners are entitled to deduct $38,271 for expenses, which they claimed on Schedule C, for a business known as the Registry; (3) whether petitioners are entitled to deduct $8,951 for expenses, which they claimed on Schedule C, for a business known as Express Network Technologies (ENT); and (4) whether petitioners are liable for the addition to tax pursuant to section 6651(a)(1).

Some of the facts have been stipulated and are so found. The stipulation of facts and attached exhibits are incorporated herein by this reference. At the time the petition was filed, petitioners resided in Scottsdale, Arizona. During the year in issue, petitioners were married, and they filed a joint return for that year.

For convenience, we will combine our findings of fact and opinion with respect to each of the issues presented. Respondent's determination is presumed correct, and petitioners bear the burden of proving otherwise. Rule 142(a); *Welch v. Helvering,* 29 U.S. 111 (1933).

ISSUE 1. UNDERREPORTED GROSS INCOME

Respondent determined that petitioners failed to report income from the following sources:

Arizona State lottery winnings	$1,409
Interest from Valley Bank of Nevada	1,119
Dividend from the Franklin Fund	1,651
Dividend from Dreyfus Worldwide MM Fund	190
Dividend from American Capital Growth	19
Dividend from Value Line Fund	10
Increase to income	4,398

Petitioners do not seriously dispute the fact that they received and failed to report these amounts. However, in an attempt to offset this unreported income, petitioners contend that they erroneously reported a $5,200 loan as income on their Schedule C for the Registry. The Registry was a business operated by Mr. Maerki (hereinafter referred to as petitioner) whose purpose was to raise capital and do consulting work for other businesses.

Petitioner was the only witness who testified at trial. He testified that $5,200 had been borrowed and produced a printout of his computerized records showing a $5,200 deposit to the Registry account with the description "Equipment Loan Other Income." Petitioners produced no other corroborating evidence of the transaction such as loan documents. In answer to his attorney's questions concerning whether he overreported income by this amount, petitioner stated: "If this was put on the tax return, which I understand it was, we overstated it, yes." Based on the record before us, petitioners have not met their burden of proof to show that they erroneously reported $5,200 in loan proceeds as gross receipts.

ISSUE 2. SCHEDULE C EXPENSES FOR THE REGISTRY

On the Schedule C for the Registry, petitioners deducted expenses of over $126,000. Respondent has disallowed $38,271 of those Schedule C deductions.

Respondent disallowed $8,521, which was deducted as employee benefits on petitioners' Schedule C for the Registry. Petitioner agreed at trial that he had no substantiation for $2,168 of this amount. Of the remaining amount, petitioners claim they are entitled to deduct $4,256 for medical expenses, $1,497 for child care, and $600 for travel reimbursement.

Medical expenses paid as part of an employee benefit plan can be deducted as a business expense. Sec. 1.162-10(a), Income Tax Regs. Of the medical expenses claimed as a business deduction by petitioners, all but $22 was spent for medical services for petitioners. Petitioners have not proven that an employee plan existed for the Registry. Except for petitioner's conclusory testimony that a plan existed, there is no evidence of such a plan or its terms of coverage. Medical expenses are normally considered to be personal, and an employer's payment of medical expenses for employees would normally constitute taxable income. Section 105 provides for the exclusion of employer-paid medical expenses if certain conditions are met. However, even if some type of plan did exist, petitioners have not established (or even argued) that it would meet the conditions of section 105. We sustain respondent's disallowance of the claimed medical expenses.

Petitioner testified that the $1,497 of child care expenses deducted as employee benefits was paid for the care of petitioners' child. Petitioners provided checks for child care totaling only $818. Such expenses would normally be considered personal, and an employer's payment of its employees' child care expenses would normally be includable in the employees' taxable income. Section 129 provides an exception for qualified dependent care programs. Petitioners have neither proven nor argued that their situation meets the requirements of section 129. We sustain respondent's disallowance of the deduction for child care expenses.

Petitioner testified that $600 of the amount claimed as employee benefits was a reimbursement to petitioner Kathleen Turner for travel expenses she incurred as a member of the board of directors for Crystal Communications, a client of the Registry. Petitioners produced a $600 check payable to Ms. Turner. There was no explanation on the check, and petitioners produced no other documentation showing the nature of the alleged travel. Petitioners did not explain why this was classified as an employee benefit rather than a travel expense, nor have they shown that the $600 expense was not included in the $1,558 of travel expenses allowed as a deduction on the Schedule C for the Registry. Petitioners have failed to prove entitlement to the $600 deduction.

On Schedule C for the Registry, petitioners claimed a deduction for "other expenses" in the amount of $29,750, which respondent also disallowed. These "other expenses" included expenses for bank charges of $1,881, seminars/education of $5,549, dues of $1,187, business gifts of $53, casual labor of $350, and "other" in the amount of $20,730.

With respect to the portion of bank charges related to credit cards, petitioner testified that he used credit cards in his name for both business and personal affairs. With respect to bank charges related to an escrow account, petitioner testified that they related to an escrow account that was opened for a client. Petitioners produced no records showing which portion of the bank charges for credit cards related to business or personal matters, nor did they produce any records to show the nature of the escrow account and related charges. Petitioners have not shown that they are entitled to a business deduction for these bank charges.

The education expenses deducted were paid to Lamson College, apparently for petitioner Kathleen Turner. Petitioner testified that he required his wife to take courses that would help her perform services for the business. Except for petitioner's testimony at trial, no evidence was produced to show that the expenditures incurred for education were ordinary and necessary business expenses of the Registry. Petitioners failed to produce any documents to show which specific courses were taken or the nature of the courses, and petitioner Kathleen Turner did not testify. Petitioners have failed to carry their burden of showing that respondent's determination is incorrect.

With respect to the disallowance of the deduction for "dues," petitioners provided copies of checks that appear to be for various magazines, periodicals, and other publications. Petitioner testified that some of these checks were for magazines needed for business purposes. Petitioner testified that a portion of the amount deducted for "dues" also included advertisements in at least four magazines and/or periodicals. Petitioners have not shown that these alleged advertising expenses were not included in amounts already allowed for advertising. The Schedule C for the Registry shows a separate deduction for advertising in the amount of $617. Petitioner also testified that a portion of the expenses for "dues" consisted of payments to United Cable for cable television. Petitioner testified that approximately one-third of petitioners' house was used for business and that the cable television service was provided for the whole house. Based on this, we are unable to determine what portion, if any, of the cable television costs might be applicable to the business of the Registry. Petitioner also testified that a portion of the expenses for "dues" consisted of payments for supplies, even though on the Schedule C for the Registry, petitioners deducted $2,063 for supplies. Again, petitioners have not shown that these amounts were not included in the deduction allowed for supplies on Schedule C. Petitioners have failed to establish their entitlement to the claimed "dues" deduction.

With respect to the deductions for gifts, petitioners produced a check for $53, which indicates on its face that it was for Godiva chocolates. This was recorded on the business records as a gift, and petitioner testified that it was for a gift to one of the Registry's customers. We hold that petitioners have established that the $53 was a deductible business expense.

With respect to $350 claimed as a labor expense, petitioners produced seven canceled checks to Lorraine S. Whipps, each in the amount of $50. The dates of these checks indicated that they were issued approximately every 2 weeks from September 14 to December 14, 1990. The records of the Registry record these checks as "Contract Wages," and petitioner testified that they were paid for miscellaneous labor for the business. We hold that petitioners have established that these items were deductible expenses.

With respect to the "other" expenses claimed in the amount of $20,730, petitioners now apparently claim that $16,755 of this amount actually represents trust preparation fees, which should have been claimed on the Schedule C for ENT rather than the Schedule C for the Registry. Petitioner testified that he operated ENT and that ENT did "business consulting, living trust, and also was involved in starting a couple of other businesses; a legal preparation services business and some others." The checks making up the $16,755 were all drawn on ENT's account. Petitioner gave no explanation of how checks drawn on ENT's account were deducted as expenses of the Registry, nor is it clear whether or not these amounts were already deducted on ENT's Schedule C. There was no other documentation (such as invoices or contracts) presented showing the nature and purpose of these payments. Petitioners again simply failed to prove entitlement to the deductions claimed.

Petitioners appear to argue that the remainder of the "other" expenses was interest of $3,255.29 paid on a home equity loan. Petitioner testified that the loan proceeds from this loan were used in his business, but he provided no supporting documents to establish this. We also find it curious that a deduction for $3,255.29 of alleged business interest would be buried in a $20,110.29 business deduction classified as "other" when the Schedule C provides a specific line for interest deductions. In any event, based on the record before us, petitioners have failed to prove entitlement to a business deduction for interest.

ISSUE 3. EDUCATION EXPENSES ON SCHEDULE C FOR ENT

On the Schedule C for ENT, petitioners deducted expenses of over $135,000. Respondent has disallowed $8,951 of those Schedule C deductions.

Petitioners claimed a deduction for education expenses on the Schedule C for ENT in the amount of $8,951. Petitioner testified that $5,000 of this amount was attributable to the cost of a training seminar for Jon Palmieri, an ENT employee. Petitioners produced a canceled check to "The Estate Plan" that indicates it was for training for Mr. Palmieri. The "Profit and Loss" statement for ENT for the year ended December 31, 1990, shows total expenses for education in the amount of $5,000. In her brief, respondent notes the fact that this statement shows only $5,000—rather than the $8,951—that petitioners claimed on the Schedule C for ENT. Respondent argues that this shows that the other items of education expenses should be disallowed, but respondent makes no argument on brief that specifically addresses the $5,000 amount. Based on the record before us, we hold that petitioners are entitled to a $5,000 education expense deduction with respect to ENT.

Petitioner testified that the claimed education expenses also include expenses for other items, such as the rental of rooms from the Arizona Club and the rental of booths for home shows. Petitioner admitted that he had a personal account with the Arizona Club and that he visited that establishment for non-business purposes. In addition, the Schedule C for ENT already claimed a deduction for the rental of other business property in the amount of $3,569.63. Petitioners have not shown that the amount of rental expenses claimed as education expenses is not included in the deduction allowed for rents on the Schedule C. As previously noted, petitioners' own disbursement journal shows that only $5,000 was spent for education. Except for the $5,000, petitioners have failed to overcome the presumption that respondent's determination is correct.

Other cases have dealt with the issues of deductible expenses on a Schedule C. In *Hood v. Commissioner,* 115 T.C. 172 (2000), the petitioners challenged notices of deficiency issued by respondent that determined that (1) petitioner sole proprietorship was not entitled to deduct legal fees incurred during its 1991 taxable year to defend petitioner husband (its sole shareholder), and (2) petitioner couple received a constructive dividend equal to the legal fees paid by petitioner sole proprietorship during calendar year 1991.

The central issue in these consolidated cases was whether petitioner sole proprietorship could deduct the legal fees it paid for petitioner husband's defense against criminal tax evasion and false declaration charges arising from his reporting of the Schedule C, Profit or Loss from Business, income of a predecessor sole proprietorship. Respondent contended that petitioner sole proprietorship could not deduct the legal fees because their payment constituted a constructive dividend to petitioner husband. The court concluded that payment of the legal fees was a constructive dividend, not deductible to petitioner sole proprietorship during its 1991 taxable year, and taxable to petitioner husband as a dividend to the extent paid during calendar year 1991. The court further held that petitioner sole proprietorship was not entitled to a deduction for the legal fees it paid because they were the expenses of another, and petitioner sole proprietorship did not show that the payment was made to protect or promote its own trade or business.

The court held that (1) petitioner sole proprietorship could not deduct legal fees it paid to defend petitioner husband (its sole shareholder) against criminal tax charges, (2) petitioner husband was required to report the legal fees, which constituted a constructive dividend, and (3) petitioner sole proprietorship was not liable for the accuracy-related penalty related to the deduction of the legal fees.

Once all of the expenses are determined, they are totaled as the sole proprietor's operating expenses. When this figure is subtracted from the gross income, a net profit or loss is the result. If the sole proprietor operates several sole proprietorships, these calculations must be completed for each such business.

If the business generates a net profit, the amount of the profit appears as part of the sole proprietor's income on page 1 of Form 1040. If the business generates a loss, that loss may be used to offset the sole proprietor's regular income, and may be carried forward as a loss for future years.

Ethical Concerns

The most common ethical problem associated with the taxation of a sole proprietorship occurs when the sole proprietor attempts to include as business expenses what are in fact personal expenses. This is especially prevalent when the business is operated from the owner's home. IRS carefully scrutinizes all expenses for home-operated sole proprietorships, and so the tax law professional must be sure to document all items of business expense claimed by the taxpayer client.

Practical tip

If a sole proprietor has a regular source of income and continually operates the sole proprietorship at a loss to offset such income, IRS is likely to treat the "business" as a hobby and disallow all losses.

CHAPTER REVIEW

A sole proprietorship is a business that is owned and operated by just one person. Legally there is no differentiation between the owner and the business and therefore, for federal income tax purposes, all income of the business is deemed to be income to the owner.

No separate federal income tax return is required for a sole proprietorship. Rather, the sole proprietor reports his or her income and expenses associated with operating the business on a Schedule C as an attachment to his or her individual income tax return, the Form 1040.

Because there is no legal distinction between the business and the business owner, all profits derived from the operation of the business are considered ordinary income to the sole proprietor. Conversely, if the business suffers a loss, the sole proprietor may use such loss to reduce his or her taxable income.

Profit or loss derived from operating the sole proprietorship is calculated by determining the business's gross sales less returns and allowances to arrive at its net income. From this figure all expenses associated with maintaining and operating the enterprise are deducted to arrive at the business's gain or loss for the period in question.

If a taxpayer operates several businesses as sole proprietorships, a separate Schedule C must be prepared for each such business.

Key Terms

accelerated depreciation

allocation cost recovery system (ACRS)

bad debt

cost of goods sold (COGS)

depletion

depreciation

Economic Recovery Tax Act of 1981 (ERTA)

fixed expenses

gross receipts

life expectancies

net sales

quantity discount

receivables

returns and allowances

revenue

Schedule C

scrap value

sole proprietor

sole proprietorship

straight line depreciation

taxpayer identification number

uncollectibles

useful life

working capital

CHAPTER 4

Income Taxation of Partnerships

Introduction

Most partnerships fall into one of two broad classifications: general or limited. A **general partnership** is an association of two or more persons engaged in business for profit as co-owners. A **limited partnership** is an association of two or more persons engaged in business for profit as co-owners, with one or more general partners and one or more limited partners. The distinguishing characteristic of a partnership, either general or limited, is that the general partner retains unlimited personal liability for the obligations of the partnership business. The limited partner in a limited partnership is only responsible for the business's debts to the extent of his or her contribution to the business. In other words, limited partners are considered investors whose liability is limited by the extent of their investment, whereas general partners are owners in the same fashion as a sole proprietor (Chapter 3).

general partnership
An association of two or more persons engaged in business as co-owners for profit

limited partnership
An association of two or more persons as co-owners in a business for profit with one or more general partners and one or more limited partners

Example

Two sisters decide to open a small restaurant which they operate as a general partnership. Each sister will retain unlimited personal liability for any obligations of the business. If a customer slips on some spilt food, breaks his leg, and sues the restaurant, if successful in court the customer can attach the personal assets of each sister to satisfy his claim if the business's assets are themselves insufficient.

Income Taxation of Partnerships   **151**

Example

The two sisters from the previous example need to finance the restaurant and their mother agrees to contribute $20,000. To protect their mother, the sisters form a limited partnership and the mother becomes the limited partner. Now if a customer injures himself and sues the restaurant, the mother could only lose her $20,000 investment; all of her other personal assets are secure from attachment.

Each state has established requirements for creating both general and limited partnerships, and therefore each state's statutes must be individually analyzed to determine whether a business qualifies as a general or limited partnership. However, for federal income tax purposes, the Internal Revenue Code (IRC), pursuant to sections 761(a) and 7701(a)(2), define *partnership* to include not only lawfully formed general and limited partnerships, but also syndicates, joint ventures, and unincorporated associations. Under this definition, **limited liability companies (LLCs)** may also be treated as a partnership for federal income tax purposes.

Exercise

Determine the requirements for creating a general and limited partnership in your jurisdiction.

Practical tip

When deciding whether an entity is a lawfully formed partnership, be aware that many jurisdictions do not require any formalized writing to create a general partnership. However, the legal professional should determine whether such loosely formed entities are legally enforceable or a violation of the statute of frauds.

> **limited liability company (LLC)**
> An unincorporated association whose owners have limited personal liability and which may be taxed either as a partnership or a corporation

---

TAX LAW & POLICY

REV RUL 88-76
1988-2 C.B. 360; 1988 IRB LEXIS 3773; 1988-38 I.R.B. 14

Partnership classification. An unincorporated organization operating under the Wyoming Limited Liability Company Act is classified as a partnership for federal tax purposes under section 301.7701-2 of the regulation
   ISSUE

Whether a Wyoming limited liability company, none of whose members or designated managers are personally liable for any debts of the company, is classified for federal tax purposes as an association or as a partnership.

LAW AND ANALYSIS

Section 7701(a)(2) of the Internal Revenue Code provides that the term "partnership" includes a syndicate, group, pool, venture, or other unincorporated organization, through or by means of which any business, financial operation, or venture is carried on, and which is not a trust or estate or a corporation.

Section 7701(a)(3) of the Code provides that the term "corporation" includes associations, joint-stock companies, and insurance companies.

Section 301.7701-1(b) of the Procedure and Administration Regulations states that the Code prescribes certain categories, or classes, into which various organizations fall for purposes of taxation. These categories, or classes, include associations (which are taxable as corporations), partnerships, and trusts. The tests, or standards, that are to be applied in determining the classification of an organization are set forth in sections 301.7701-2 through 301.7701-4.

Section 301.7701-2(a)(1) of the regulations sets forth the following basic characteristics of a corporation: (1) associates, (2) an objective to carry on business and divide the gains therefrom, (3) continuity of life, (4) centralization of management, (5) liability for corporate debts limited to corporate property, and (6) free transferability of interests. Whether a particular organization is to be classified as an association must be determined by taking into account the presence or absence of each of these corporate characteristics. In addition to the six major characteristics, other factors may be found in some cases which may be significant in classifying an organization as an association, a partnership, or a trust.

Section 301.7701-2(a)(2) of the regulations further provides that characteristics common to partnerships and corporations are not material in attempting to distinguish between an association and a partnership. Since associates and an objective to carry on business and divide the gains therefrom are generally common to corporations and partnerships, the determination of whether an organization which has such characteristics is to be treated for tax purposes as a partnership or as an association depends on whether there exists centralization of management, continuity of life, free transferability of interests, and limited liability.

Section 301.7701-2(a)(3) of the regulations provides that if an unincorporated organization possesses more corporate characteristics than noncorporate characteristics, it constitutes an association taxable as a corporation.

In interpreting section 301.7701-2 of the regulations, the Tax Court, in *Larson v. Commissioner,* 66 T.C. 159 (1976), acq., 1979-1 C.B. 1, concluded that equal weight must be given to each of the four corporate characteristics of continuity of life, centralization of management, limited liability, and free transferability of interests.

In the present situation, M has associates and an objective to carry on business and divide the gains therefrom. Therefore, M must be classified as either an association or a partnership. M is classified as a partnership for federal tax purposes unless the organization has a preponderance of the remaining corporate characteristics of continuity of life, centralization of management, limited liability, and free transferability of interests.

Section 301.7701-2(b)(1) of the regulations provides that if the death, insanity, bankruptcy, retirement, resignation, or expulsion of any member will cause a dissolution of the organization, continuity of life does not exist. Section 301.7701-2(b)(2) provides that an agreement by which an organization is established may provide that the business will be continued by the remaining members in the event of the death or withdrawal of any member, but such agreement does not establish continuity of life if under local law the death or withdrawal of any member causes a dissolution of the organization.

Under the Act, unless the business of M is continued by the consent of all the remaining members, M is dissolved upon the death, retirement, resignation, expulsion, bankruptcy, dissolution of a member or occurrence of any other event that terminates the continued membership of a member in the company. If a member of M ceases to be a member of M for any reason, the continuity of M's not assured, because all remaining members must agree to continue the business. Consequently, M lacks the corporate characteristic of continuity of life.

Under section 301.7701-2(c)(1) of the regulations an organization has the corporate characteristic of centralized management if any person (or group of persons that does not include all the members) has continuing exclusive authority to make management decisions necessary to the conduct of the business for which the organization was formed.

Under the Act, a limited liability company has the discretion to be managed either by a designated manager or managers, or to be managed by its members. Because M is managed by its designated managers, A, B, and C, M possesses the corporate characteristic of centralized management.

Section 301.7701-2(d)(1) of the regulations provides that an organization has the corporate characteristic of limited liability if under local law there is no member who is personally liable for the debts of, or claims against, the organization. Personal liability means that a creditor of an organization may seek personal satisfaction from a member of the organization to the extent that the assets of such organization are insufficient to satisfy the creditor's claim.

Under the Act, neither the managers nor the members of M are personally liable for its debts and obligations. Consequently, M possesses the corporate characteristic of limited liability.

Under section 301.7701-2(e)(1) of the regulations, an organization has the corporate characteristic of free transferability of interests if each of the members or those members owning substantially all of the interests in the organization have the power, without the consent of other members, to substitute for themselves in the same organization a person who is not a member of the organization. In order for this power of substitution to exist in the corporate sense, the member must be able, without the consent of other members, to confer upon the member's substitute all the attributes of the member's interest in the organization. The characteristic of free transferability does not exist if each member can, without the consent of the other members, assign only the right to share in the profits but cannot assign the right to participate in the management of the organization.

Under the terms of the Act, a member of M can assign or transfer that member's interest to another who is not a member of the organization. However, the assignee or transferee does not become a substitute member and does not acquire all the attributes of the member's interest in M unless all the remaining members approve the assignment or transfer. Therefore, M lacks the corporate characteristic of free transferability of interests.

M has associates and an objective to carry on business and divide the gains therefrom. In addition, M possesses the corporate characteristic of centralized management and limited liability. M does not, however, possess the corporate characteristics of continuity of life and free transferability of interests.

HOLDING

M has associates and an objective to carry on business and divide the gains therefrom, but lacks a preponderance of the four remaining corporate characteristics. Accordingly, M is classified as a partnership for federal tax purposes.

subchapter K
Section of the Internal Revenue Code regulating the taxation of partnerships

aggregate approach
Treating a partnership as a conglomeration of the individual partners

The legal practitioner should be aware that, pursuant to current federal tax law, an LLC may elect to be treated either as a partnership or as a corporation for income tax purposes. For the purposes of this textbook, however, taxation of LLCs will be discussed in Chapter 5.

The federal tax rules with respect to partnerships appear in **Subchapter K** of the Internal Revenue Code, which consists of sections 701 through 777 inclusive. Subchapter K provides for an **aggregate approach** to the taxation of partnership income and expenses. This approach treats the partnership as an amalgam of the individual partners, meaning that the partnership itself is not liable for income taxes. Rather, all profits and losses are passed through to the partners themselves who are personally responsible for reporting their shares of the partnership income and paying any taxes due thereon. To determine the business's profits and losses, however, IRS mandates that, for accounting purposes only, the partnership maintain records as a separate entity (IRC secs. 701–705).

Example

To determine whether the business has operated with a profit or a loss, all business income and expenses are calculated, thereby treating the partnership as a separate entity. The partnership may not take as a deductible expense deductions that are permitted an individual partner on his or her personal income tax return. Once the business's profit or loss is determined, however, the partner may take those personal deductions when reporting income on his or her personal income tax return to reduce the portion of the profits he or she receives from the partnership's operation.

Partnership income, gains, and losses are reported on **Form 1065-B, Schedule K-1** (see Exhibit 4.2), which acts as an informational return. A copy of this form is given to each partner who attaches it to his or her own individual income tax return to report any profit or loss from the operation of the business. In this fashion the partnership acts merely as a conduit to pass through income to the individual partners [IRC sec. 772(a)]. The portion of the profit or loss that attaches to each partner is referred to as the partner's **distributive share**.

For federal tax purposes, partners have two types of profit and loss. The first represents income from the operation of the partnership business and is treated as ordinary income or loss for federal income tax purposes. The second represents a return of capital on the partner's investment in the partnership, and is treated as a capital gain or loss. Form 1065 (Exhibit 4.1) specifies the nature of the gain or loss for reporting purposes, and such determinations are made at the partnership level; the individual partners may not decide how to classify a given item.

To determine gains or losses, two distinct interests in the partnership property are deemed to exist: an outside basis and an inside basis. The **outside basis** (IRC sec. 722) reflects the contribution to the business the partner made in order to become a partner. This figure is used, as will be discussed later in the chapter, to determine the extent, if any, of the partner's profit or loss from the operation of the business. The **inside basis** (IRC sec. 723) represents the value of the assets of the business as it operated over time and is used to determine gain or loss for the partnership (IRC sec. 741). In other words, the outside basis reflects the partner's interest and the inside basis reflects the partnership's overall value.

Form 1065-B, Schedule K-1
Federal tax form for partnerships

distributive share
Portion of a distribution allocated to each partner

outside basis
Value of partner's interest in the partnership

inside basis
Value of the partnership

Practical tip

When a partner transfers assets to the partnership, it is important to determine and document whether that transfer represents a capital contribution or a loan to the business. A capital contribution increases the partner's basis and the partnership's assets, whereas a loan does not affect the basis and represents a liability of the business.

156 Chapter Four

Form **1065**	U.S. Return of Partnership Income	OMB No. 1545-0099
Department of the Treasury Internal Revenue Service	For calendar year 2002, or tax year beginning ...., 2002, and ending ...., 20..... ▶ See separate instructions.	**2002**

A Principal business activity	Use the IRS label. Otherwise, print or type.	Name of partnership	**D** Employer identification number
B Principal product or service		Number, street, and room or suite no. If a P.O. box, see page 14 of the instructions.	**E** Date business started
C Business code number		City or town, state, and ZIP code	**F** Total assets (see page 14 of the instructions) $

G Check applicable boxes: (1) ☐ Initial return (2) ☐ Final return (3) ☐ Name change (4) ☐ Address change (5) ☐ Amended return
H Check accounting method: (1) ☐ Cash (2) ☐ Accrual (3) ☐ Other (specify) ▶ ....
I Number of Schedules K-1. Attach one for each person who was a partner at any time during the tax year ▶ ....

Caution: *Include only trade or business income and expenses on lines 1a through 22 below. See the instructions for more information.*

Income

1a	Gross receipts or sales	1a	
b	Less returns and allowances	1b	1c
2	Cost of goods sold (Schedule A, line 8)		2
3	Gross profit. Subtract line 2 from line 1c		3
4	Ordinary income (loss) from other partnerships, estates, and trusts *(attach schedule)*		4
5	Net farm profit (loss) *(attach Schedule F (Form 1040))*		5
6	Net gain (loss) from Form 4797, Part II, line 18		6
7	Other income (loss) *(attach schedule)*		7
8	**Total income (loss).** Combine lines 3 through 7		8

Deductions (see page 15 of the instructions for limitations)

9	Salaries and wages (other than to partners) (less employment credits)		9
10	Guaranteed payments to partners		10
11	Repairs and maintenance		11
12	Bad debts		12
13	Rent		13
14	Taxes and licenses		14
15	Interest		15
16a	Depreciation (if required, attach Form 4562)	16a	
b	Less depreciation reported on Schedule A and elsewhere on return	16b	16c
17	Depletion **(Do not deduct oil and gas depletion.)**		17
18	Retirement plans, etc.		18
19	Employee benefit programs		19
20	Other deductions *(attach schedule)*		20
21	**Total deductions.** Add the amounts shown in the far right column for lines 9 through 20		21
22	**Ordinary income (loss)** from trade or business activities. Subtract line 21 from line 8		22

Sign Here
Under penalties of perjury, I declare that I have examined this return, including accompanying schedules and statements, and to the best of my knowledge and belief, it is true, correct, and complete. Declaration of preparer (other than general partner or limited liability company member) is based on all information of which preparer has any knowledge.

▶ Signature of general partner or limited liability company member   Date

May the IRS discuss this return with the preparer shown below (see instructions)? ☐ Yes ☐ No

Paid Preparer's Use Only

Preparer's signature		Date	Check if self-employed ▶ ☐	Preparer's SSN or PTIN
Firm's name (or yours if self-employed), address, and ZIP code	▶		EIN ▶ Phone no. ( )	

For Paperwork Reduction Act Notice, see separate instructions.   Cat. No. 11390Z   Form **1065** (2002)

Exhibit 4.1 Form 1065

Form 1065 (2002) Page **2**

Schedule A — Cost of Goods Sold (see page 19 of the instructions)

1	Inventory at beginning of year	1
2	Purchases less cost of items withdrawn for personal use	2
3	Cost of labor	3
4	Additional section 263A costs *(attach schedule)*	4
5	Other costs *(attach schedule)*	5
6	**Total.** Add lines 1 through 5	6
7	Inventory at end of year	7
8	**Cost of goods sold.** Subtract line 7 from line 6. Enter here and on page 1, line 2	8

9a Check all methods used for valuing closing inventory:
  (i) ☐ Cost as described in Regulations section 1.471-3
  (ii) ☐ Lower of cost or market as described in Regulations section 1.471-4
  (iii) ☐ Other (specify method used and attach explanation) ▶ ....
b Check this box if there was a writedown of "subnormal" goods as described in Regulations section 1.471-2(c). ▶ ☐
c Check this box if the LIFO inventory method was adopted this tax year for any goods *(if checked, attach Form 970)* ▶ ☐
d Do the rules of section 263A (for property produced or acquired for resale) apply to the partnership? ☐ Yes ☐ No
e Was there any change in determining quantities, cost, or valuations between opening and closing inventory? ☐ Yes ☐ No
  If "Yes," attach explanation.

Schedule B — Other Information

		Yes	No
1	What type of entity is filing this return? Check the applicable box:		

  a ☐ Domestic general partnership   **b** ☐ Domestic limited partnership
  c ☐ Domestic limited liability company   **d** ☐ Domestic limited liability partnership
  e ☐ Foreign partnership   **f** ☐ Other ▶ ....

2 Are any partners in this partnership also partnerships?
3 During the partnership's tax year, did the partnership own any interest in another partnership or in any foreign entity that was disregarded as an entity separate from its owner under Regulations sections 301.7701-2 and 301.7701-3? If yes, see instructions for required attachment
4 Is this partnership subject to the consolidated audit procedures of sections 6221 through 6233? If "Yes," see **Designation of Tax Matters Partner** below
5 Does this partnership meet **all three** of the following requirements?
  a The partnership's total receipts for the tax year were less than $250,000;
  b The partnership's total assets at the end of the tax year were less than $600,000; **and**
  c Schedules K-1 are filed with the return and furnished to the partners on or before the due date (including extensions) for the partnership return.
  If "Yes," the partnership is not required to complete Schedules L, M-1, and M-2; Item F on page 1 of Form 1065; or Item J on Schedule K-1
6 Does this partnership have any foreign partners? If "Yes," the partnership may have to file Forms 8804, 8805 and 8813. See page 20 of the instructions
7 Is this partnership a publicly traded partnership as defined in section 469(k)(2)?
8 Has this partnership filed, or is it required to file, **Form 8264**, Application for Registration of a Tax Shelter?
9 At any time during calendar year 2002, did the partnership have an interest in or a signature or other authority over a financial account in a foreign country (such as a bank account, securities account, or other financial account)? See page 20 of the instructions for exceptions and filing requirements for Form TD F 90-22.1. If "Yes," enter the name of the foreign country. ▶ ....
10 During the tax year, did the partnership receive a distribution from, or was it the grantor of, or transferor to, a foreign trust? If "Yes," the partnership may have to file Form 3520. See page 20 of the instructions
11 Was there a distribution of property or a transfer (e.g., by sale or death) of a partnership interest during the tax year? If "Yes," you may elect to adjust the basis of the partnership's assets under section 754 by attaching the statement described under **Elections Made By the Partnership** on page 8 of the instructions
12 Enter the number of **Forms 8865**, Return of U.S. Persons With Respect to Certain Foreign Partnerships, attached to this return ▶ ....

Designation of Tax Matters Partner (see page 21 of the instructions)
Enter below the general partner designated as the tax matters partner (TMP) for the tax year of this return:

Name of designated TMP ▶		Identifying number of TMP ▶	
Address of designated TMP ▶			

Form **1065** (2002)

Exhibit 4.1 (Continued)

158 Chapter Four

Form 1065 (2002)   Page **3**

Schedule K	Partners' Shares of Income, Credits, Deductions, etc.		
	(a) Distributive share items		**(b) Total amount**

Income (Loss)
1. Ordinary income (loss) from trade or business activities (page 1, line 22) . . . . | 1 |
2. Net income (loss) from rental real estate activities (attach Form 8825) . . . . . . | 2 |
3a. Gross income from other rental activities . . . . | 3a |
  b. Expenses from other rental activities (attach schedule) . . . . | 3b |
  c. Net income (loss) from other rental activities. Subtract line 3b from line 3a . . . . . | 3c |
4. Portfolio income (loss):   **a** Interest income . . . . | 4a |
  b. Ordinary dividends . . . . | 4b |
  c. Royalty income . . . . | 4c |
  d. Net short-term capital gain (loss) (attach Schedule D (Form 1065)) . . . . . | 4d |
  e. (1) Net long-term capital gain (loss) (attach Schedule D (Form 1065)) . . . . | 4e(1) |
    (2) 28% rate gain (loss) ▶ .... (3) Qualified 5-year gain ▶ .... | |
  f. Other portfolio income (loss) (attach schedule) . . . . | 4f |
5. Guaranteed payments to partners . . . . | 5 |
6. Net section 1231 gain (loss) (other than due to casualty or theft) (attach Form 4797) . . | 6 |
7. Other income (loss) (attach schedule) . . . . | 7 |

Deductions
8. Charitable contributions (attach schedule) . . . . | 8 |
9. Section 179 expense deduction (attach Form 4562) . . . . . . | 9 |
10. Deductions related to portfolio income (itemize) . . . . | 10 |
11. Other deductions (attach schedule) . . . . | 11 |

Credits
12a. Low-income housing credit:
    (1) From partnerships to which section 42(j)(5) applies . . . . . . | 12a(1) |
    (2) Other than on line 12a(1) . . . . | 12a(2) |
  b. Qualified rehabilitation expenditures related to rental real estate activities (attach Form 3468) | 12b |
  c. Credits (other than credits shown on lines 12a and 12b) related to rental real estate activities | 12c |
  d. Credits related to other rental activities . . . . | 12d |
13. Other credits . . . . | 13 |

Investment Interest
14a. Interest expense on investment debts . . . . | 14a |
  b. (1) Investment income included on lines 4a, 4b, 4c, and 4f above . . . . | 14b(1) |
    (2) Investment expenses included on line 10 above . . . . . . | 14b(2) |

Self-Employment
15a. Net earnings (loss) from self-employment . . . . | 15a |
  b. Gross farming or fishing income . . . . | 15b |
  c. Gross nonfarm income . . . . | 15c |

Adjustments and Tax Preference Items
16a. Depreciation adjustment on property placed in service after 1986 . . . . | 16a |
  b. Adjusted gain or loss . . . . | 16b |
  c. Depletion (other than oil and gas) . . . . | 16c |
  d. (1) Gross income from oil, gas, and geothermal properties . . . . | 16d(1) |
    (2) Deductions allocable to oil, gas, and geothermal properties . . . . | 16d(2) |
  e. Other adjustments and tax preference items (attach schedule) . . . . | 16e |

Foreign Taxes
17a. Name of foreign country or U.S. possession ▶ ....
  b. Gross income from all sources . . . . | 17b |
  c. Gross income sourced at partner level . . . . | 17c |
  d. Foreign gross income sourced at partnership level:
    (1) Passive ▶ .... (2) Listed categories (attach schedule) ▶ ....(3) General limitation ▶ | 17d(3) |
  e. Deductions allocated and apportioned at partner level:
    (1) Interest expense ▶ .... (2) Other . . . . ▶ | 17e(2) |
  f. Deductions allocated and apportioned at partnership level to foreign source income:
    (1) Passive ▶ .... (2) Listed categories (attach schedule) ▶ ....(3) General limitation ▶ | 17f(3) |
  g. Total foreign taxes (check one): ▶ Paid ☐ Accrued ☐ . . . . . . | 17g |
  h. Reduction in taxes available for credit (attach schedule) . . . . . | 17h |

Other
18. Section 59(e)(2) expenditures: **a** Type ▶ .... **b** Amount ▶ | 18b |
19. Tax-exempt interest income . . . . | 19 |
20. Other tax-exempt income . . . . | 20 |
21. Nondeductible expenses . . . . | 21 |
22. Distributions of money (cash and marketable securities) . . . . . | 22 |
23. Distributions of property other than money . . . . . . | 23 |
24. Other items and amounts required to be reported separately to partners (attach schedule) . . | |

Form **1065** (2002)

Exhibit 4.1 (Continued)

Income Taxation of Partnerships

Form 1065 (2002) — Page 4

Analysis of Net Income (Loss)

1. Net income (loss). Combine Schedule K, lines 1 through 7 in column (b). From the result, subtract the sum of Schedule K, lines 8 through 11, 14a, 17g, and 18b . . . . 1 _____

2. Analysis by partner type:

	(i) Corporate	(ii) Individual (active)	(iii) Individual (passive)	(iv) Partnership	(v) Exempt organization	(vi) Nominee/Other
a General partners						
b Limited partners						

Note: Schedules L, M-1 and M-2 are not required if Question 5 of Schedule B is answered "Yes."

Schedule L — Balance Sheets per Books

Assets	Beginning of tax year (a)	(b)	End of tax year (c)	(d)
1 Cash				
2a Trade notes and accounts receivable				
b Less allowance for bad debts				
3 Inventories				
4 U.S. government obligations				
5 Tax-exempt securities				
6 Other current assets *(attach schedule)*				
7 Mortgage and real estate loans				
8 Other investments *(attach schedule)*				
9a Buildings and other depreciable assets				
b Less accumulated depreciation				
10a Depletable assets				
b Less accumulated depletion				
11 Land (net of any amortization)				
12a Intangible assets (amortizable only)				
b Less accumulated amortization				
13 Other assets *(attach schedule)*				
14 **Total** assets				

Liabilities and Capital

15 Accounts payable				
16 Mortgages, notes, bonds payable in less than 1 year				
17 Other current liabilities *(attach schedule)*				
18 All nonrecourse loans				
19 Mortgages, notes, bonds payable in 1 year or more				
20 Other liabilities *(attach schedule)*				
21 Partners' capital accounts				
22 **Total** liabilities and capital				

Schedule M-1 — Reconciliation of Income (Loss) per Books With Income (Loss) per Return

1. Net income (loss) per books _____
2. Income included on Schedule K, lines 1 through 4, 6, and 7, not recorded on books this year (itemize): _____
3. Guaranteed payments (other than health insurance) _____
4. Expenses recorded on books this year not included on Schedule K, lines 1 through 11, 14a, 17g, and 18b (itemize):
   a Depreciation $ _____
   b Travel and entertainment $ _____
5. Add lines 1 through 4 _____
6. Income recorded on books this year not included on Schedule K, lines 1 through 7 (itemize):
   a Tax-exempt interest $ _____
7. Deductions included on Schedule K, lines 1 through 11, 14a, 17g, and 18b, not charged against book income this year (itemize):
   a Depreciation $ _____
8. Add lines 6 and 7 _____
9. Income (loss) (Analysis of Net Income (Loss), line 1). Subtract line 8 from line 5 _____

Schedule M-2 — Analysis of Partners' Capital Accounts

1. Balance at beginning of year _____
2. Capital contributed: a Cash _____
   b Property _____
3. Net income (loss) per books _____
4. Other increases (itemize): _____
5. Add lines 1 through 4 _____
6. Distributions: a Cash _____
   b Property _____
7. Other decreases (itemize): _____
8. Add lines 6 and 7 _____
9. Balance at end of year. Subtract line 8 from line 5 _____

Form **1065** (2002)

Exhibit 4.1 (Continued)

160 Chapter Four

Exhibit 4.2 Schedule K-1 (Form 1065-B)

Exhibit 4.2 (Continued)

Exercise

A partner contributes $10,000 to join a partnership. The partnership still needs additional capital, and the partner agrees to loan the partnership another $10,000. Prepare documents evidencing this loan to the enterprise. Indicate what provisions would be needed to protect the partner and the partnership.

When an individual contributes cash or property to become a partner, the amount or value of that contribution is "tax free" to the partnership (IRC sec. 721), meaning that it is not considered income to the business for determining profit or loss. If a partner contributes services or expertise, however, the value of that service or expertise may be taxable according to **Rev. Proc. 93-27.**

TAX LAW & POLICY

REV PROC 93-27

SECTION 1. PURPOSE

This revenue procedure provides guidance on the treatment of the receipt of a partnership profits interest for services provided to or for the benefit of the partnership.

SEC. 2. DEFINITIONS

The following definitions apply for purposes of this revenue procedure.

.01 A capital interest is an interest that would give the holder a share of the proceeds if the partnership's assets were sold at fair market value and then the proceeds were distributed in a complete liquidation of the partnership. This determination generally is made at the time of receipt of the partnership interest.

.02 A profits interest is a partnership interest other than a capital interest.

SEC. 3. BACKGROUND

Under section 1.721-1(b)(1) of the Income Tax Regulations, the receipt of a partnership capital interest for services provided to or for the benefit of the partnership is taxable as compensation. On the other hand, the issue of whether the receipt of a partnership profits interest for services is taxable has been the subject of litigation. Most recently, in *Campbell v. Commissioner,* 943 F.2d 815 (8th Cir. 1991), the Eighth Circuit in dictum suggested that the taxpayer's receipt of a partnership profits interest received for services was not taxable, but decided the case on valuation. Other courts have determined that in certain circumstances the receipt of a partnership profits interest for services is a taxable event under section 83 of the Internal Revenue Code. See, e.g., *Campbell v. Commissioner,* T.C.M. 1990-236, rev'd, 943 F.2d 815 (8th Cir. 1991); *St. John v. United States,* No. 82-1134 (C.D. Ill. Nov. 16, 1983). The courts have also found that typically the profits interest received has speculative or no determinable value at the time of receipt. See *Campbell,* 943 F.2d at 823; *St. John.* In *Diamond v. Commissioner,* 56 T.C. 530 (1971), aff'd, 492 F.2d 286 (7th Cir. 1974), however, the court assumed that the interest received by the taxpayer was a partnership profits interest and found the value of the interest was readily determinable. In that case, the interest was sold soon after receipt.

SEC. 4. APPLICATION

.01 Other than as provided below, if a person receives a profits interest for the provision of services to or for the benefit of a partnership in a partner capacity or in anticipation of being a partner, the Internal Revenue Service will not treat the receipt of such an interest as a taxable event for the partner or the partnership.

.02 This revenue procedure does not apply:

(1) If the profits interest relates to a substantially certain and predictable stream of income from partnership assets, such as income from high-quality debt securities or a high-quality net lease;

(2) If within two years of receipt, the partner disposes of the profits interest; or

(3) If the profits interest is a limited partnership interest in a "publicly traded partnership" within the meaning of section 7704(b) of the Internal Revenue Code.

Exercise

A lawyer contributes his expertise in forming the partnership and drafting form contracts for the business. How would such "expertise" be valued?

When the partnership makes a distribution to each partner, the distribution must be allocated according to that partner's contribution to the business. As a general rule, many partnerships are formed by a written agreement in which each partner's allocated interest is specified. However, for IRS purposes, if challenged, the partnership must substantiate that the allocation of such interests is made according to the "substantial economic effect" generated by each partner's contribution [IRC sec. 704(b)]. If IRS determines that the allocation of interests is not reflective of a partner's economic effect on the business, it may reallocate the distribution for income tax purposes.

Example

Three people decide to form a partnership to operate a clothing manufacturing business. Two of the people have substantial assets but no experience in the industry, whereas the third is a well-known designer who has worked in the field for 10 years. When they form the partnership, they allocate one-third of the business to each partner, even though only two have contributed cash. In this instance, because of the economic effect of the designer's expertise on the business's success, such allocation would probably be deemed consistent with IRC sec. 704.

Exercise

Obtain a copy of a partnership agreement and analyze its allocation provisions.

publically traded partnership
Partnership whose shares may be acquired by anyone

One final introductory note: Pursuant to section 7704(a) of the IRC, a **publically traded partnership,** one whose partnership interests may be purchased by anyone, is treated as a corporation for tax purposes (Chapter 5), unless substantially all of its income is derived from passive sources (i.e., investments in other enterprises with no actual operational activities).

Example

To produce a Broadway show, three producers form a limited partnership to sell limited partnership shares to anyone interested in investing in the show. This partnership would be considered a publically traded partnership and thus be taxed as a corporation.

This chapter examines the provisions of Form 1065 and the special accounting rules that IRS mandates partnerships to follow, the determination of partnership income and losses, the taxation of distributions made to individual partners, and the tax effect of the termination of the partnership.

Form 1065

All domestic partnerships, including LLCs that are classified as partnerships for federal income tax purposes, are required to file Form 1065. The entities that must meet this filing requirement include foreign partnerships that have gross income connected with the carrying on of a trade or business in the United States as well as religious organizations that are otherwise tax exempt under section 501(d) of the Internal Revenue Code which have taxable income allocated to its members as dividends. Partnerships with more than 100 partners are required to file Form 1065 electronically. This electronic filing requirement may be waived if the partnership can demonstrate that such e-filing would cause it an undue hardship. Form 1065 must be signed either by a general partner or a member of the LLC.

Practical tip

Form 1524 has the necessary information connected with electronic filing.

Practical tip

In addition to Form 1065, the partnership may be required to file a host of other forms incident to the operation of its trade or business, such as those for excise taxes and employees. A detailed list of these additional forms can be found in the instructions to Form 1065.

In addition to the partnership determining the accounting and depreciation methods it will use (see later in the chapter), the partnership must also make the following elections.

A. Selection to expense certain tangible property (IRC sec. 179)
B. Definition of mines, wells, and other natural deposits for depletion allowances (IRC sec. 614)
C. Involuntary conversions (loss of property without the will or consent of the partnership) (IRC sec. 1032)
D. Optional adjustment to basis (IRC sec. 754)

When preparing the tax form, the partnership may group one or more trades or activities to reflect a reasonable financial method of operation. Otherwise, each such activity must be listed individually. IRS retains the right to disallow the grouping or to regroup if it does not believe such grouping accurately reflects one type of endeavor.

Example

A partnership operates movie theatres and restaurants in New York, Los Angeles, and Miami. The partnership may elect to group these activities in two groups of theatres and restaurants, three groups of activities in New York, Los Angeles, and Miami, or treat the activities as totally separate. However, once the election is made, the partnership must continue to use that grouping on all subsequent returns.

Exercise

A partnership is engaged in the lease of apartments and commercial space as well as renting trucks and heavy equipment. How may these activities be grouped? Substantiate your answer by reference to the appropriate code and regulation sections.

For federal income tax purposes, pursuant to Temporary Regulations 1.469-T2(f) and Regulations sec. 1.469-2(f), the net passive income must be treated as nonpassive, or ordinary, income. **Net passive income** is the gross income derived from passive activities, less expenses incurred in connection with those activities, such as the following:

1. **Significant participation passive activities,** those in which the partner participates more than 100 hours per year
2. Nondepreciable rental property activity, if less than 30% of the property is used for such activity is subject to the depreciation rules under IRC sec. 167
3. Passive equity-financed lending

net passive income
Gross income from passive activities less incident expenses

significant participation passive activity
Activity in which a partner is engaged more than 100 days per year

4. Rental property incidental to a development activity
5. Rental of property to a nonpassive activity
6. Acquisition of an interest in a pass-through entity that licenses intangible property, which generally refers to receiving royalties from an entity whose major activity is to license intellectual property

For all passive income activity, the partnership is required to provide an attachment for each such activity.

For the most part, Form 1065 follows a similar format as the individual income tax return, Form 1040, along with Schedule C.

Line 1(a) requires reporting all gross income, except for passive activity income, derived from the operation of the partnership's business. Passive income, rental income, and tax exempt income are reported on Schedules K and K-1.

From line 1(a) all returns and allowances, previously discussed in Chapter 3, are deducted as are the costs of the goods sold. To determine the amount of COGS, the tax professional must complete Schedule A which appears as an attachment to Form 1965. The result, appearing on line 3, represents the partnership's gross profit or loss. To determine the partnership's total income or loss, the partnership then includes any gain or loss resulting from farm operations, other sources of income, and gains or losses resulting from involuntary conversions (Form 4797).

The second section of Form 1065 provides for deductions the partnership may take to adjust its total income or loss. The permissible items of deductions are:

- Salaries and wages paid to persons other than partners (line 9)
- Guaranteed payments to partners (line 10) which are distributions the partnership is required to make to each partner pursuant to the partnership agreement
- Repairs and maintenance (line 11)
- Bad debts (line 12)
- Rent (line 13)
- Taxes and licenses (line 14)
- Interest (line 15)
- Depreciation (line 16)
- Depletion, except for oil and gas depletion (line 17)
- Contributions to retirement plans (line 18)

- Contributions to employee benefit plans (line 19)

- Other deductions, such as legal fees, supplies, insurance premiums, and so forth, provided that such items do not appear elsewhere on the return (line 20). The partnership must attach a schedule listing each such deduction by type.

The definitions and calculations for these items have been previously discussed in Chapter 3.

The total amount of the deductions is then subtracted from the total income or loss to arrive at the partnership's ordinary income or loss from operating its trade or business (line 22).

The distribution of the partners' shares of this income or loss is calculated on Schedule K. Schedule K is divided into eight sections:

Income (loss). This section of Schedule K not only indicates the total amount of income or loss attributable to the partners, but also establishes the character of such income or loss as ordinary, passive, or capital. As stated, these characterizations are made at the partnership level and are not subject to recharacterization by the individual partners.

Deductions. These deductions include those for charitable contributions and other expenses. These deductions are permitted for the individual partners but not the partnership, which is why they appear on the Schedule K.

Credits. For partners, credits are allowed for businesses that engage in low-income housing, rehabilitation of real estate, and other real estate and rental activities. These credits are similar to those permitted a sole proprietor engaged in similar activities.

Investment interest. IRS permits a credit for interest expenses on investment loans.

Self-employment. The partner must report income or loss derived from self-employed activities.

Adjustment and tax preference items. These include depreciation and depletion allowances

Foreign taxes. To take this credit, Schedule K requires the name of each country for which the credit is claimed, the source of the partnership income, and all deductions permitted from such income at the partnership level by the foreign country.

Other. This section includes lines for tax exempt income, nondeductible expenses, and distributions. Partnership distributions are discussed in detail later in the chapter.

The major difference between Form 1065 and Form 1040 with a Schedule C attachment is that Form 1065 requires the preparation of a balance sheet to substantiate all of the foregoing operations of the partnership. The format for this balance sheet, Schedules L, M-1, and M-2, do not have to be completed if the following requirements are met.

1. The partnership's total receipts for the tax year are less than $250,000.
2. The partnership's total assets at the end of the tax year are less than $600,000.
3. Schedule Ks are filed with the return and forwarded to the partners on or before the due date of the partnership return.

A **balance sheet** primarily reflects the basic accounting equation: Assets = Liabilities + Equity. **Assets** represent all items of value that are owned by the partnership or over which it has control and the right of assignment. **Liabilities** reflect all debts of the partnership, and **equity** represents the partners' contributions to the partnership as well as all net gains or losses resulting from the operation of the business.

balance sheet
Financial document reflecting the basic accounting equation: Assets = Liabilities + Equity

assets
Items of value owned or over which an entity has control and the right of assignment

liabilities
Debt portion of a balance sheet

equity
Portion of balance sheet reflecting owners' contributions and income or loss from business operations

Exercise

Classify the following items as an asset, liability, or equity.

A. Utility bill
B. Legal fee
C. Proceeds from the sale of a partnership share
D. Inventory
E. Royalty income

It is beyond the scope of this textbook to provide a detailed analysis of balance sheets; however, the following chapter on corporate income taxation does include a fuller discussion of the subject.

Practical tip

For a complete discussion of financial documents incident to operating a business, refer to *Financial Documents and Accounting for Legal Professionals* by Helewitz, published by West Legal Studies, an imprint of Thomson Delmar Learning.

Exercise

Obtain a copy of the balance sheet for a publically traded partnership and compare it to the items appearing on Schedule L. Which items appear on both, and which appear on only one or the other?

Tax Accounting for Partnerships

Because of the pass-through nature of the taxation of partnerships, certain special accounting rules have been created for partnerships to ensure that the business as well as the individual partners maintain accurate financial records indicating the income and expenses for the business and the business owners. However, before these accounting rules are discussed, it is important to note that certain types of partnerships are excluded from fulfilling these partnership rules.

Exclusion from Partnership Accounting Rules

If the partnership in question is not actually engaged in operating an ongoing business, it may be able to be totally or partially excluded from being treated as a partnership. To do so, all of the partners must agree, and each must be able to calculate his, her, or its own income without reference to the partnership's taxable income. However, even if the partnership elects to be excluded, it still must demonstrate a valid business purpose if it wishes to report its taxes on a fiscal rather than a calendar year basis. To avail itself of this exclusion, the partnership must make the election within the mandated time for filing the partnership return [Regs. Sec. 1.761-2(b)].

Basically, two types of partnerships would qualify for this exclusion:

1. **Operating agreement partnership** [IRC sec. 761(a)(2)], which is a partnership formed for the production, extraction, or use of property but not for the selling of the services or property so produced or extracted. This type of partnership may elect to be excluded from Subchapter K if all of the following requirements are met.
   A. The partners own the property as co-owners.
   B. Each partner retains the right to dispose of his or her share of any property produced or extracted.
   C. The partners do not jointly sell the property produced or extracted.
2. **Investing partnerships** [IRC sec. 761(a)(1)], which are partnerships that do not actually operate a business but

operating agreement partnership Partnership formed with a formal partnership agreement

investing partnership Partnership doesn't operate a business, only invests in other enterprises.

merely invest in other enterprises. This type of partnership may only elect to be excluded if all of the following requirements are met.

A. The partners own the property as co-owners.
B. Each partner retains the right to dispose of the share of any property acquired or retained.
C. The partnership does not engage in conducting a business, either directly or indirectly.

Example

A group of suburban couples form an investment club as a partnership, each couple contributing $10,000. The purpose of the partnership is to invest in the stock and futures markets. When investments are bought, they are purchased in the name of the partnership so that each partner is a co-owner, and their agreement permits each partner to dispose of his or her share of the property. In this instance, this partnership may elect to be excluded from the partnership tax rules.

Accounting Principles

For all partnerships which either must follow Subchapter K or elect not to be excluded, the following accounting and tax principles apply.

Pursuant to section 446 of the Internal Revenue Code, a partnership may elect either a cash or accrual method of accounting *unless* one of the partners is a C corporation (Chapter 5), in which instance only a cash method is permitted.

Each partner is taxed according to his or her distributive share as determined at the partnership level [IRC sec. 702(b)]. This means that the collective partnership determines the amount of the partnership property that is to be distributed to each partner; the individual partner alone does not control such determination. Further, all tax elections that affects the computation of partnership income must be made by the partnership [IRC sec. 703(a)].

All partners must report on their own individual income tax return the amount of profit or loss from the partnership that is deemed to be their own distributive share. However, individuals may not take a loss for their partnership interest that causes their own outside basis to fall below zero. What that means is that the extent of the loss that partners may take on their individual income tax return is limited to the amount of their own outside basis.

Example

A partner contributed $1000 to become a partner, which represents his outside basis. At the start of its business the partnership operates at a loss. If the partner's distributive share of the loss is $800, he may take that entire loss in that tax year. If the amount of his distributive loss is $1200, he may only take a loss of $1000 in that tax year, the extent of his outside basis.

Practical tip

The outside basis is subject to adjustment as the business develops. Always determine the amount of a partner's outside basis for the tax year in question.

In computing its profit or loss, a partnership is not entitled to take the following deductions.

A. Personal exemption
B. Foreign taxes paid
C. Charitable contributions
D. Net operating loss
E. Other itemized deductions [IRC sec. 703(a)]

This is true even though the individual partners may take such deductions on their own income tax returns. The character of these items are determined at the partnership level [IRC sec. 702(b); Regs. Sec. 1.702-1(b)]. The reason why such deductions are not allowed is, because the individual partner may take such deductions as well as the partnership, it would create a "double" deduction—one for the partnership and one for the partner.

Example

A partnership sells property that is considered to be a noncapital asset (Chapter 2) in its hands so that any resulting profit from the sale would be ordinary income. If that same property were held by the individual partners it would be considered a capital asset and the resulting profit would be a capital gain. Because the determination of such items is made at the partnership level, the profit is considered ordinary income to both the partnership and the partner.

A partnership may not take as a deduction any of the expenses associated with the creation of the partnership or the selling of its shares [IRC sec. 709(a)]. However, the partnership may elect to amortize these expenses over a 60-month period. What this means, in practical terms, is that such expenses may not be used to reduce the partnership gains in the year they are expended, but one-sixtieth of such expenses may be used to reduce partnership income each month for a total of 60 months.

To determine the extent of any profit or loss for the individual partner, certain rules have been established.

ordering rules
Method of determining distributions

1. **Ordering rules.** These rules are used to adjust a partner's outside basis (IRC sec. 731). Any upward adjustment caused by an increase in partnership assets is decided on the last day of the partnership's taxable year. Any downward movement is determined when the actual distribution is made.

   Any actual increase in excess of a partner's outside basis is treated as an ordinary gain [IRC sec. 731(a)(1)].

Practical tip

Calculate any increases first to adjust the basis before determining losses so that the losses do not cause the outside basis to fall below zero.

TAX LAW & POLICY

REV RUL 94-4
1994-1 C.B. 196; 1994 IRB LEXIS 2; 1994-2 I.R.B. 21;

Recognition of gain on deemed distribution of money. A deemed distribution of money under section 752(b) of the Code resulting from a decrease in a partner's share of liabilities is treated as an advance or drawing of money under section 1.731-1(a)(1)(ii) of the regulations to the extent of the partner's distributive share of income for the partnership taxable year.

ISSUE

If a deemed distribution of money under § 752(b) of the Internal Revenue Code occurs as a result of a decrease in a partner's share of the liabilities of a partnership, is the deemed distribution taken into account at the time of the distribution or at the end of the partnership taxable year?

LAW

Under § 752(b), a decrease in a partner's share of partnership liabilities is considered a distribution of money to the partner by the partnership. The partner will recognize gain under § 731(a)(1) if the distribution of money exceeds the adjusted basis of the partner's interest immediately before the distribution.

Section 1.731-1(a)(1)(ii) of the Income Tax Regulations provides that for purposes of §§ 731 and 705, advances or drawings of money or property against a partner's distributive share of income are treated as current distributions made on the last day of the partnership taxable year with respect to that partner.

Rev. Rul. 92-97, 1992-2 C.B. 124, treats a deemed distribution of money to a partner resulting from a cancellation of debt as an advance or drawing under § 1.731-1(a)(1)(ii) against that partner's distributive share of cancellation of indebtedness income.

HOLDING

A deemed distribution of money under § 752(b) resulting from a decrease in a partner's share of the liabilities of a partnership is treated as an advance or drawing of money under § 1.731-1(a)(1)(ii) to the extent of the partner's distributive share of income for the partnership taxable year. An amount treated as an advance or drawing of money is taken into account at the end of the partnership taxable year. A deemed distribution of money resulting from a cancellation of debt may qualify for advance or drawing treatment under this revenue ruling and under Rev. Rul. 92-97.

2. **At risk rule** (IRC sec. 465). A partner may only deduct losses to the extent that he or she is "at risk" (i.e., has personal financial liability for the partnership's loss). This means that the partner's percentage of loss distributable to him or her cannot exceed his or her personal liability for the partnership.

at risk rule
Method of determining the allocation of distributions based on the distributee partner's degree of financial risk for the partnership obligations

Exercise

Read the regulations associated with IRC sec. 465 to determine what factors constitute a partner being "at risk."

3. **Passive loss limitation** [IRC sec. 469(a)]. Pursuant to this rule, losses from passive activities may not be used to offset increases derived from other, nonpassive, activities. However, losses that exceed the amount that may be taken in a given tax year may be carried over indefinitely [IRC sec. 469(b)].

passive loss limitation
Losses from passive activities cannot offset increases from non-passive activities

Example

In a given tax year a partnership has passive activity losses of $8500 and passive activity gains of $5000. In that tax year the partnership may use $5000 of its passive activity loss to offset its passive activity gain, and carry forward $3500 as passive losses to future tax years to offset passive activity gains in those future years.

Bearing these rules in mind, the partnership computes its profits and/or losses for each tax year.

Practical tip

Publication 538 details the various accounting rules for partnerships.

Partnership Income or Loss

To calculate the extent of a partnership's income or loss for a given tax year, the partnership is required to report on Form 1065 (Schedule K) certain items which must be separately stated. These items include:

A. Ordinary profit or loss from the partnership's activities

Example

A partnership operates a linen manufacturing company. For each year the partnership must total all of its income from sales, based on the cash or accrual method elected by the partnership, and then deduct all items of expense to determine profit or loss. Recall that not all deductions are permitted to a partnership, primarily those that may be taken by the individual partners on their own individual tax returns.

B. Net profit or loss from real estate activities. If the partnership's business is exclusively involved in renting real estate, this item would be its only source of profit or loss. If the partnership is engaged in various commercial endeavors, however, income from this activity would be indicated separately.

C. Net profit or loss from rental activities not involving real estate. This activity could include the renting of equipment such as cars, tractors, or heavy machinery.

D. Gains or losses from the sale or exchange of a capital asset. Remember, not all items maintained by a business are capital assets. Review Chapter 2 for a discussion of the difference between a capital and a noncapital asset.

E. Gain or loss from the sale or exchange of IRC sec. 1231 property.

TAX LAW & POLICY

IRC SEC. 1231
§ 1231. PROPERTY USED IN THE TRADE OR BUSINESS AND INVOLUNTARY CONVERSIONS.

(a) General rule.
  (1) Gains exceed losses. If—
  (A) the section 1231 gains for any taxable year, exceed
  (B) the section 1231 losses for such taxable year,

such gains and losses shall be treated as long-term capital gains or long-term capital losses, as the case may be.

(2) Gains do not exceed losses. If—

(A) the section 1231 gains for any taxable year, do not exceed

(B) the section 1231 losses for such taxable year,

such gains and losses shall not be treated as gains and losses from sales or exchanges of capital assets.

(3) Section 1231 gains and losses. For purposes of this subsection—

(A) Section 1231 gain. The term "section 1231 gain" means—

(i) any recognized gain on the sale or exchange of property used in the trade or business, and

(ii) any recognized gain from the compulsory or involuntary conversion (as a result of destruction in whole or in part, theft or seizure, or an exercise of the power of requisition or condemnation or the threat or imminence thereof) into other property or money of—

(I) property used in the trade or business, or

(II) any capital asset which is held for more than 1 year and is held in connection with a trade or business or a transaction entered into for profit.

(B) Section 1231 loss. The term "section 1231 loss" means any recognized loss from a sale or exchange or conversion described in subparagraph (A).

(4) Special rules. For purposes of this subsection—

(A) In determining under this subsection whether gains exceed losses—

(i) the section 1231 gains shall be included only if and to the extent taken into account in computing gross income, and

(ii) the section 1231 losses shall be included only if and to the extent taken into account in computing taxable income, except that section 1211 shall not apply.

(B) Losses (including losses not compensated for by insurance or otherwise) on the destruction, in whole or in part, theft or seizure, or requisition or condemnation of—

(i) property used in the trade or business, or

(ii) capital assets which are held for more than 1 year and are held in connection with a trade or business or a transaction entered into for profit,

shall be treated as losses from a compulsory or involuntary conversion.

(C) In the case of any involuntary conversion (subject to the provisions of this subsection but for this sentence) arising from fire, storm, shipwreck, or other casualty, or from theft, of any—

(i) property used in the trade or business, or

(ii) any capital asset which is held for more than 1 year and is held in connection with a trade or business or a transaction entered into for profit,

this subsection shall not apply to such conversion (whether resulting in gain or loss) if during the taxable year the recognized losses from such conversions exceed the recognized gains from such conversions.

(b) Definition of property used in the trade or business. For purposes of this section—

(1) General rule. The term "property used in the trade or business" means property used in the trade or business, of a character which is subject to the allowance for depreciation provided in section 167, held for more than 1 year, and real property used in the trade or business, held for more than 1 year, which is not—

(A) property of a kind which would properly be includible in the inventory of the taxpayer if on hand at the close of the taxable year,

(B) property held by the taxpayer primarily for sale to customers in the ordinary course of his trade or business,

(C) a copyright, a literary, musical, or artistic composition, a letter or memorandum, or similar property, held by a taxpayer described in paragraph (3) of section 1221(a), or

(D) a publication of the United States Government (including the Congressional Record) which is received from the United States Government, or any agency thereof, other than by purchase at the price at which it is offered for sale to the public, and which is held by a taxpayer described in paragraph (5) of section 1221(a).

(2) Timber, coal, or domestic iron ore. Such term includes timber, coal, and iron ore with respect to which section 631 applies.

(3) Livestock. Such term includes—

(A) cattle and horses, regardless of age, held by the taxpayer for draft, breeding, dairy, or sporting purposes, and held by him for 24 months or more from the date of acquisition, and

(B) other livestock, regardless of age, held by the taxpayer for draft, breeding, dairy, or sporting purposes, and held by him for 12 months or more from the date of acquisition.

Such term does not include poultry.

(4) Unharvested crop. In the case of an unharvested crop on land used in the trade or business and held for more than 1 year, if the crop and the land are sold or exchanged (or compulsorily or involuntarily converted) at the same time and to the same person, the crop shall be considered as "property used in the trade or business."

(c) Recapture of net ordinary losses.

(1) In general. The net section 1231 gain for any taxable year shall be treated as ordinary income to the extent such gain does not exceed the non-recaptured net section 1231 losses.

(2) Non-recaptured net section 1231 losses. For purposes of this subsection, the term "non-recaptured net section 1231 losses" means the excess of—

(A) the aggregate amount of the net section 1231 losses for the 5 most recent preceding taxable years beginning after December 31, 1981, over

(B) the portion of such losses taken into account under paragraph (1) for such preceding taxable years.

(3) Net section 1231 gain. For purposes of this subsection, the term "net section 1231 gain" means the excess of—

(A) the section 1231 gains, over
(B) the section 1231 losses.

(4) Net section 1231 loss. For purposes of this subsection, the term "net section 1231 loss" means the excess of—

(A) the section 1231 losses, over
(B) the section 1231 gains.

(5) Special rules. For purposes of determining the amount of the net section 1231 gain or loss for any taxable year, the rules of paragraph (4) of subsection (a) shall apply.

F. Charitable contributions. Recall that the partnership may not deduct the value of these contributions because the partners may do so. The partners are allocated a proportion of the partnership's charitable contributions that appear on this form [IRC sec. 703(a)].

G. Deductions that pass through to corporate partners

H. Foreign taxes paid [IRC sec. 703(a)]

I. Other items of income, loss, and deduction such as nonbusiness expenses and soil and conservation expenses.

To calculate and report the partnership's profit or loss, the partnership is required to make certain tax elections designed to reflect the financial operations of the business in the most appropriate manner. Certain of these elections have been discussed previously, such as the election of accounting methods—cash or accrual—and the amortization of organizational fees and start-up costs. In addition to those elections, however, the partnership must determine the following:

A. Depreciation method

B. Nonrecognition of gain or loss from involuntary conversion

C. Depletion method

Example

A partnership, under state law, must file a business certificate in order to operate. Because the cost of preparing and filing this form is an item of expense associated with the formation of the business, it is not a deductible expense for federal income tax purposes.

> *Practical tip*
> IRS publishes Publication 946 which details the various depreciation methods available for partnerships.

Each of these items appears on the Schedule K, copies of which are maintained by the partnership, distributed to each partner, and reported to the Internal Revenue Service.

Partnership Distributions

Generally, partnership distributions take one of two forms: Either they represent a distribution of annual profits and losses from earnings or a distribution of partnership assets upon the dissolution of the business or termination of a partner's interest. Partnership distributions are deemed to be a sale or exchange of the partner's interest in the partnership, provided that they do not represent a current distribution.

A **current distribution** is any distribution which is not in liquidation of a partner's entire interest in the enterprise [Regs. Sec. 1.761-1(d)]. Current distributions include proceeds from:

current distribution
Distribution of current income, profit, and losses

1. Current earnings (or earnings from prior years) not needed for working capital (Working capital represents cash on hand that a business needs in order to meet expenses.)
2. Return of capital
3. Distribution of the partner's contribution to the business resulting in a decrease in his or her percentage share of the partnership (IRC sec. 752)

When a current distribution is made to a partner, the partnership itself recognizes no gain or loss [IRC sec. 731(b)]. For the partner, however, the distribution reduces his or her adjusted basis in the partnership by the money and property so distributed, but in no event may that basis fall below a zero value.

The partner will generally only recognize a gain to the extent that any money so distributed to him or her exceeds that adjusted basis, which is generally treated as a capital gain for the sale of that partnership interest on the date of distribution [IRC sec. 731(a)]. Note, however, that such recognition of gain only applies to distributions of cash and marketable securities. If a distribution to a partner consists of property, no gain is recognized until the partner disposes of that property (IRC sec. 732).

Example

A partner's outside basis in the partnership equals $15,000. The partner receives a current distribution of $8000 in cash and $2000 in marketable securities. The partner does not have to report any gain, but his outside basis is reduced to $5000 ($15,000 − 8000 − 2000).

Exercise

A partnership distributes to its partner's inventory that it could not sell in the preceding year. Determine how a partner could calculate a basis in this property so as to determine gain or loss at its eventual sale.

A partner must also recognize any gain on the distribution of property that was contributed by that partner to the partnership within seven years prior to the distribution.

Practical tip

A five-year, rather than a seven-year, period applies to property contributed prior to June 9, 1997, or pursuant to a binding contract that was in effect on June 8, 1997, and specifies the contribution of a fixed amount of property.

The gain that the partner must recognize is the lesser of either:

A. The difference between the fair market value of the property and the partner's adjusted basis in the partnership, or

B. The **net precontribution gain** of the partner, which is the gain the partner would recognize if all of the property he or she contributed within seven years (five years if prior to June 9, 1997) prior to the distribution were distributed to another partner.

The result of the recognition of this gain is an upward adjustment in the partner's basis of his or her interest in the partnership.

A partner will not be able to recognize a loss resulting from a partnership distribution unless the following requirements are met.

1. The partner's outside basis exceeds the distribution.
2. The partner's entire interest in the partnership is extinguished.
3. The distribution takes the form of cash, unrealized receivables, or inventory. **Unrealized receivables** are amounts owing to the partnership from customers.

net precontribution gain
Gain a partner would recognize if all of his or her contributions made within seven years of the distribution in question were distributed to another partner

unrealized receivables
Amounts owing to partnership from customers

Example

A partner has an outside basis in the partnership of $10,000. The loss occasioned by the distribution equals $8000. Because the outside basis exceeds the loss, the partner can recognize a complete loss of $8000.

To determine a partner's basis in the partnership, that basis is only adjusted to reflect the cash and marketable securities he or she has received.

Example

A partner has a basis in the partnership valued at $20,000. She receives a distribution of $4000 in cash and marketable securities and property with $8000. Her adjusted basis in the partnership is now $16,000 ($20,000 − 4,000).

Generally, a partner's basis is adjusted for property distributions only when there is a complete liquidation of the partnership interest (see later in the chapter).

Note that if a partner acquires interest in the partnership by inheritance or by sale or exchange with a former partner, he or she may select a special basis adjusted for property formerly distributed by the partnership. To avail oneself of the special basis, the interest must have been acquired within two years of the distribution in question [IRC sec. 732(d)]. Further, if the following conditions exist, the special adjusted basis is mandatory.

A. The fair market value of all of the partnership property, other than cash, exceeds 110% of its adjusted basis.
B. If the partner's interest had been liquidated immediately after its acquisition, under the general rules for determining bases, the basis would have been decreased by the value of property that could not be depreciated, depleted, or amortized and increased by the value of the property that could be depreciated, depleted, or amortized.
C. The optional basis adjustment would have changed the partner's basis for the property that was actually distributed.

If the special basis adjustment applies, either by choice or requirement, the partnership must supply the partner with a statement containing information necessary for the partner to complete the special basis adjustment forms.

A **liquidating distribution** occurs when the partner or the partnership terminates the partner's interest in the enterprise [Regs. Sec.

liquidating distribution
Distribution made at the termination of a partner's interest in the partnership

1.761-(1)(d)]. In a liquidating distribution, the liquidating partner recognizes any gain for cash so distributed that exceeds his or her adjusted basis in the partnership [IRC sec. 731(a)(1)]. Loss is only recognized if the partner receives *only* cash, unrealized receivables, or inventory, referred to as **hot assets** because they are immediately reducible to cash. The loss that is recognized equals the excess of the partner's outside basis over the sum of any cash and hot assets distributed.

hot assets
Assets that are immediately convertible to cash

Exercise

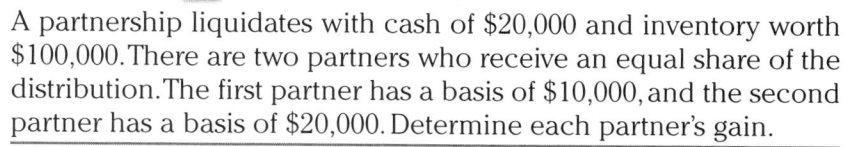

A partnership liquidates with cash of $20,000 and inventory worth $100,000. There are two partners who receive an equal share of the distribution. The first partner has a basis of $10,000, and the second partner has a basis of $20,000. Determine each partner's gain.

Allocation of Distributions

In making distributions to the partners, the partnership must see that each partner receives a percentage share of the total distribution. These allocations of distributions are governed by section 704(a) of the Internal Revenue Code, which states that the allocation is determined by the provisions of the partnership agreement, or, if no such agreement exists, pursuant to the provisions of section 704(b) of the code. Under section 704(b), IRS requires the partner's allocation to be consistent with his or her proportionate "substantial economic effect" on the partnership. Basically, this means that a partnership may not distribute all losses to one partner and all income to another, resulting in a tax loss to one and a gain to the other, unless there is a logical financial reason for such allocation that has some relationship to the partner's interest and financial liability in the partnership.

TAX LAW & POLICY

ORRISCH V. COMMISSIONER OF INTERNAL REVENUE
55 T.C. 395 (1970)

The only issue presented for decision is whether tax effect can be given the agreement between petitioners and the Crisafis that, beginning with 1966, all the partnership's depreciation deductions were to be allocated to petitioners for their use in computing their individual income tax liabilities. In our view, the answer must be in the negative, and the amounts of each of the partners' deductions for the depreciation of partnership property must be determined in accordance with the ratio used generally in computing their distributive shares of the partnership's profits and losses.

Among the important innovations of the 1954 Code are limited provisions for flexibility in arrangements for the sharing of income, losses, and deductions arising from business activities conducted through partnerships. The authority for special allocations of such items appears in section 704(a), which provides that a partner's share of any item of income, gain, loss, deduction, or credit shall be determined by the partnership agreement. That rule is coupled with a limitation in section 704(b), however, which states that a special allocation of an item will be disregarded if its "principal purpose" is the avoidance or evasion of Federal income tax. See *Smith v. Commissioner,* 331 F. 2d 298 (C.A. 7, 1964), affirming a Memorandum Opinion of this Court; *Jean V. Kresser,* 54 T.C. 1621 (1970). In case a special allocation is disregarded, the partner's share of the item is to be determined in accordance with the ratio by which the partners divide the general profits or losses of the partnership. Sec. 1.704-1(b)(2), Income Tax Regs.

The report of the Senate Committee on Finance accompanying the bill finally enacted as the 1954 Code (S. Rept. No. 1622, to accompany H.R. 8300 (Pub.L. No. 591), 83d Cong., 2d Sess., p. 379 (1954)) explained the tax-avoidance restriction prescribed by section 704(b) as follows:

Subsection (b) * * * provides that if the principal purpose of any provision in the partnership agreement dealing with a partner's distributive share of a particular item is to avoid or evade the Federal income tax, the partner's distributive share of that item shall be redetermined in accordance with his distributive share of partnership income or loss described in section 702(a)(9) [i.e., the ratio used by the partners for dividing general profits or losses]. * * *

Where, however, a provision in a partnership agreement for a special allocation of certain items has substantial economic effect and is not merely a device for reducing the taxes of certain partners without actually affecting their shares of partnership income, then such a provision will be recognized for tax purposes. * * *

This reference to "substantial economic effect" did not appear in the House Ways and Means Committee report (H. Rept. No. 1337, to accompany H.R. 8300 (Pub.L. No. 591), 83d Cong., 2d Sess., p. A223 (1954)) discussing section 704(b), and was apparently added in the Senate Finance Committee to allay fears that special allocations of income or deductions would be denied effect in every case where the allocation resulted in a reduction in the income tax liabilities of one or more of the partners. The statement is an affirmation that special allocations are ordinarily to be recognized if they have business validity apart from their tax consequences. Driscoll, "Tax Problems of Partnerships—Special Allocation of Specific Items," 1958 So. Cal. Tax Inst. 421, 426.

In resolving the question whether the principal purpose of a provision in a partnership agreement is the avoidance or evasion of Federal income tax, all the facts and circumstances in relation to the provision must be taken into account. Section 1.704-1(b)(2), Income Tax Regs., lists the following as relevant circumstances to be considered:

Whether the partnership or a partner individually has a business purpose for the allocation; whether the allocation has "substantial economic effect," that is, whether the allocation may actually affect the dollar amount of the partners' shares of the total partnership income or loss independently of tax consequences; whether related items of income, gain, loss, deduction, or credit from the same source are subject to the same allocation; whether the allocation was made without recognition of normal business factors and only after the amount of the specially allocated item could reasonably be estimated; the duration of the allocation; and the overall tax consequences of the allocation. * * *

Applying these standards, we do not think the special allocation of depreciation in the present case can be given effect.

The evidence is persuasive that the special allocation of depreciation was adopted for a tax-avoidance rather than a business purpose. Depreciation was the only item which was adjusted by the parties; both the income from the buildings and the expenses incurred in their operation, maintenance, and repair were allocated to the partners equally. Since the deduction for depreciation does not vary from year to year with the fortunes of the business, the parties obviously knew what the tax effect of the special allocation would be at the time they adopted it. Furthermore, as shown by our findings, petitioners had large amounts of income which would be offset by the additional deduction for depreciation; the Crisafis, in contrast, had no taxable income from which to subtract the partnership depreciation deductions, and, due to depreciation deductions which they were obtaining with respect to other housing projects, could expect to have no taxable income in the near future. On the other hand, the insulation of the Crisafis from at least part of a potential capital gains tax was an obvious tax advantage. The inference is unmistakably clear that the agreement did not reflect normal business considerations but was designed primarily to minimize the overall tax liabilities of the partners.

Petitioners urge that the special allocation of the depreciation deduction was adopted in order to equalize the capital accounts of the partners, correcting a disparity ($14,000) in the amounts initially contributed to the partnership by them ($26,500) and the Crisafis ($12,500). But the evidence does not support this contention. Under the special allocation agreement, petitioners were to be entitled, in computing their individual income tax liabilities, to deduct the full amount of the depreciation realized on the partnership property. For 1966, as an example, petitioners were allocated a sum ($18,904) equal to the depreciation on the partnership property ($18,412) plus one-half of the net loss computed without regard to depreciation ($492). The other one-half of the net loss was, of course, allocated to the Crisafis. Petitioners' allocation ($18,904) was then applied to reduce their capital account. The depreciation specially allocated to petitioners ($18,412) in 1966 alone exceeded the amount of the disparity in the contributions. Indeed, at the end of 1967, petitioners' capital account showed a deficit of $25,187.11 compared with a positive balance of $405.65 in the Crisafis' account. By the time the partnership's properties are fully depreciated, the amount of the reduction in petitioners' capital account will approximate the remaining basis for the buildings as of the end of 1967. The Crisafis' capital account will be adjusted only for contributions, withdrawals, gain or loss, without regard to depreciation, and similar adjustments for these factors will also be made in petitioners' capital account. Thus, rather than correcting an imbalance in the capital accounts of the partners, the special allocation of depreciation will create a vastly greater imbalance than existed at the end of 1966. In the light of these facts, we find it incredible that equalization of the capital accounts was the objective of the special allocation.

Petitioners rely primarily on the argument that the allocation has "substantial economic effect" in that it is reflected in the capital accounts of the partners. Referring to the material quoted above from the report of the Senate Committee on Finance, they contend that this alone is sufficient to show that the special allocation served a business rather than a tax-avoidance purpose.

According to the regulations, an allocation has economic effect if it "may actually affect the dollar amount of the partners' shares of the total partnership income or loss independently of tax consequences." The agreement in this case provided not only for the allocation of depreciation to petitioners but also for gain on the sale of the partnership property to be "charged back" to them. The charge back would cause the gain, for tax purposes, to be allocated on the books entirely to petitioners to the extent of the special allocation of depreciation, and their capital account would be correspondingly increased. The remainder of the gain, if any, would be shared equally by the partners. If the gain on the sale were to equal or exceed the depreciation specially allocated to petitioners, the increase in their capital account caused by the charge back would exactly equal the depreciation deductions previously allowed to them and the proceeds of the sale of the property would be divided equally. In such circumstances, the only effect of the allocation would be a trade of tax consequences, i.e., the Crisafis would relinquish a current depreciation deduction in exchange for exoneration from all or part of the capital gains tax when the property is sold, and petitioners would enjoy a larger current depreciation deduction but would assume a larger ultimate capital gains tax liability. Quite clearly, if the property is sold at a gain, the special allocation will affect only the tax liabilities of the partners and will have no other economic effect.

To find any economic effect of the special allocation agreement aside from its tax consequences, we must, therefore, look to see who is to bear the economic burden of the depreciation if the buildings should be sold for a sum less than their original cost. There is not one syllable of evidence bearing directly on this crucial point. We have noted, however, that when the buildings are fully depreciated, petitioners' capital account will have a deficit, or there will be a disparity in the capital accounts, approximately equal to the undepreciated basis of the buildings as of the beginning of 1966. Under normal accounting procedures, if the buildings were sold at a gain less than the amount of such disparity petitioners would either be required to contribute to the partnership a sum equal to the remaining deficit in their capital account after the gain on the sale had been added back or would be entitled to receive a proportionately smaller share of the partnership assets on liquidation. Based on the record as a whole, we do not think the partners ever agreed to such an arrangement. On dissolution, we think the partners contemplated an equal division of the partnership assets which would be adjusted only for disparities in cash contributions or withdrawals. Certainly there is no evidence to show otherwise. That being true, the special allocation does not "actually affect the dollar amount of the partners' share of the total partnership income or loss independently of tax consequences" within the meaning of the regulation referred to above.

Our interpretation of the partnership agreement is supported by an analysis of a somewhat similar agreement, quoted in material part in our findings, which petitioners made as part of a marital property settlement agreement in 1968. Under this agreement, Orrisch was entitled to deduct all the depreciation for 1968 in computing his income tax liability, and his wife was to deduct none; but on the sale of the property they were to first reimburse Orrisch for "such moneys as he may have advanced," and then divide the balance of the "profits or proceeds" of the sale equally, each party to report one-half of the capital gain or loss on his income tax return. In the 1969 amendment to this agreement the unequal allocation of the depreciation deduction was discontinued, and a provision similar to the partnership "charge back" was added, i.e., while the proceeds of the sale were to be divided equally, only Orrisch's basis was to be reduced by the depreciation allowed for 1968 so that he would pay taxes on a larger portion of the gain realized on the sale. Significantly, in both this agreement and the partnership agreement, as we interpret it, each party's share of the sales proceeds was determined independently from his share of the depreciation deduction.

In the light of all the evidence we have found as an ultimate fact that the "principal purpose" of the special allocation agreement was tax avoidance within the meaning of section 704(b). Accordingly, the deduction for depreciation for 1966 and 1967 must be allocated between the parties in the same manner as other deductions.

Generally, such an uneven distribution would only be viewed as appropriate if the partner receiving the "losses" has personal liability to restore any deficit to the partnership [IRC sec. 704(b)]. However, special rules are permitted for limited partnerships and LLCs because, by definition, their partners and members have limited

alternative economic effect test
Requires that the allocation does not cause or create a deficit in the partner's capital assets and the partnership agreement provides for a qualified income offset

liability. Pursuant to section 704(b), such operations may make differing distributions if they meet the **alternative economic effect test,** which requires that the allocation does not cause or create a deficit in the partner's capital assets and the partnership agreement provides for a qualified income offset [Regs. Sec. 1.704-1(b)(2)(ii)(d)], which is interpreted as a limited deficit obligation to the extent of the limited partner's or member's contribution.

Termination of a Partnership

Section 1.708-1(b) of the Regs. explains the termination of a partnership. Generally, a partnership is considered terminated if all of its operations are suspended or at least 50% of its total interest in the partnership capital and profits are sold or exchanged within a 12-month period.

For reporting requirements, the partnership's tax year ends on the date of its termination. If the partnership ceases its operations, that date is considered to be the date on which all of its affairs are wound up. If the partnership terminates by the sale or exchange of 50% of its capital and profit, the tax year ends on the date at which at least 50% of such interest has been exchanged.

Practical tip

Form 1065 must be filed if the partnership terminates prior to the end of its regular tax year.

Note that if the partnership converts to an LLC that is classified as a partnership for federal tax purposes, no termination is deemed to have occurred, although there may be an adjustment to the partners' bases. The same termination rules apply if an LLC, taxed as a partnership, converts to a formal partnership.

Ethical Concerns

Two of the ethical concerns that apply particularly to partnerships involves the use of the partnership format to attempt to income shift and to create inappropriate tax shelters. Simply by indicating that a person holds a partnership interest may not be sufficient to allocate income to him or her, especially if he or she has contributed nothing to become a partner and is not actively engaged in operating the business. Further, as a titular partner, that individual may wind up liable for the partnership liabilities.

Until stringent controls were placed on tax shelters, one of the most prevalent forms such shelters took was that of a partnership. A tax shelter, in theory, provides a paper loss to the partners which they can use to offset other income. Because of the change in the tax law, tax practitioners should be wary of creating a partnership in the hopes that it will permit the partners such paper deductions from income.

CHAPTER REVIEW

The most important fact to remember about the federal taxation of a partnership is that the IRS treats the partnership as an aggregate, meaning that the partnership itself is a nontaxable entity but each partner is individually liable for reporting income and paying any taxes due thereon.

The partnership tax return, Form 1065, primarily acts as an informational return, specifying income and losses for the business and indicating how such items are identified and distributed to each partner. IRS carefully scrutinizes the allocation method employed by the partnership to ensure that the distribution reflects each partner's share of financial risk associated with the enterprise. Further, the nature of the distribution, representing either ordinary or capital gain or loss, is determined at the partnership level, not by the individual partners.

When distributions are made to each partner, that distribution has the effect of adjusting the partner's outside basis in the partnership. Gains above that outside basis are treated as ordinary income. Losses may only be recognized by the partner to the extent of his or her outside basis, that is, the outside basis cannot fall below zero. However, any excess losses may be carried over to future years to offset gains that would adjust the basis upwards.

A partnership terminates if all of its operations are suspended or if it sells off at least 50% of its interest within a 12-month period.

KEY TERMS

aggregate approach	distributive share
alternative economic effect test	equity
assets	Form 1065
at risk rule	Form 1065-B, Schedule K-1
balance sheet	general partnership
current distribution	hot assets

inside basis
investing partnership
investment
liabilities
limited liability company (LLC)
limited partnership
liquidating distribution
net passive income
net precontribution gain
operating agreement
partnership

ordering rules
outside basis
passive loss limitation
publically traded partnership
significant participation passive activity
subchapter K
termination
unrealized receivables

CHAPTER 5

Income Taxation of Corporations

Introduction

A **corporation** is a legal entity separate and distinct from its shareholder-owners. Because the corporation is a separate entity, it is responsible for all of its own obligations, including taxes, and its shareholders are immune from personal financial liability for corporate indebtedness above the extent of their purchase price for their shares. It is this aspect of limited liability that has made the corporate format one of the most favored for investors.

Pursuant to federal tax law, a corporation is responsible for reporting and paying any taxes due on its taxable income. Once these corporate income taxes have been paid, any resulting net profit may be distributed to the shareholders who are in turn subject to individual income taxation on these distributed dividends (see Chapter 2). These two tiers of taxation have often been referred to as an example of **double taxation,** because the same income is taxed twice: once at the corporate level and then again at the individual level. Such a view is, in fact, specious, because the corporation is a separate entity. For tax and all other legal purposes, it is a distinct individual from its shareholders. Therefore, two persons are being taxed, not one person being taxed twice.

corporation
A legal entity separate and distinct from its shareholder owners

double taxation
Theory that corporate income is taxed twice—once at the corporate level and again at the individual shareholder level

Example

A tenant pays rent to his landlord who must report such rental income and pay any taxes due thereon. From his after-tax dollars the landlord buys groceries, and the grocer must report such income and pay his own taxes on any profit. Because the landlord and the grocer are two separate people, their tax situation is not considered double taxation. Legally, the corporation and the shareholder are also two separate individuals, the corporation paying taxes on its income and the shareholder paying taxes on her income.

Just because the corporation is owned by the shareholders does not negate its legal status as a separate entity, which in turn enables it to offer its owners limited personal liability.

Most business corporations fall under **Subchapter C** of the Internal Revenue Code, which provides the statutory rules for the taxation of business transactions. It is important to note that under current tax law not all business transactions subject the corporation to immediate income taxation. If the transaction under scrutiny is one in which assets and investments of the corporation are merely being changed, such change may be treated as being nonrecognized. For federal tax purposes, **nonrecognition** refers to financial changes that do not give rise to immediate taxation. This is to be contrasted with **nonrealization**, which refers to situations in which the taxable entity must report the transaction but does not receive any cash or item of value for income tax purposes [IRC sec. 7701(a)(42)–(44)].

To determine whether a given transaction is covered under the nonrecognition provisions, certain tests have been established by the IRS:

- **Business purpose test.** If the transaction does not further a legitimate business purpose of the corporation, it will be subject to immediate taxation since it would appear to be a scheme designed only to avoid taxation.
- **Substance test.** IRS will scrutinize the substance of the transaction, not its purported form, to determine whether it is a legitimate reorganization of corporate assets or a tax avoidance scheme.
- **Step transaction doctrine.** Under this doctrine a series of transactions will be viewed as a single transaction to determine the actual intent and purpose of the exchange. The courts have used three tests to determine this doctrine:

Subchapter C
Section of IRC concerning corporations

nonrecognition
Gain or loss not accounted for tax purposes

nonrealization
Gain recognized but no funds produced thereby

business purpose test
IRS will not recognize gain if the restructuring furthers a legitimate business purpose

substance test
IRS will not recognize gain if the substance of the transaction, rather than its form, does not warrant recognition

step transaction doctrine
IRS will not recognize gain if multiple transactions can be viewed as a whole

i. **Binding commitment test.** At the first step the court looks to see whether the parties entered into a binding commitment to perform the subsequent steps.

ii. **Mutual interdependence test.** The court determines whether the initial step would be meaningless without the subsequent steps.

iii. **End result test.** The court looks at the initial intent of the parties to see whether they themselves viewed all of the steps as a single integrated transaction.

The courts apply these tests and doctrines to determine whether the corporation can avail itself of the nonrecognition provisions of the IRC, which could in turn provide favorable tax treatment for the investors by deferring any gain on the transaction.

These nonrecognition provisions relating to corporate reorganizations (see later in the chapter) have made the corporate format one of the most desirable for creating tax shelters. Generally, a **tax shelter** can be viewed as a method of avoiding or minimizing federal income taxation either for the corporation, its shareholders, or both. It is beyond the scope of this textbook to detail and examine tax shelters and all of their ramifications; however, certain characteristics have been observed incident to most tax shelters of which the tax law professional should be aware:

1. Pretax profits that are insignificant in respect to the tax advantage of the scheme
2. Parties who can absorb any gains without a negative tax consequence, such as a tax exempt entity
3. Minimum economic risk
4. Transactions that bear little relationship to the taxpayer's normal business and endeavors
5. High promoter fees
6. Usually requiring the parties to the deal to maintain strict confidentiality

binding commitment test
IRS will not recognize a gain if the restructuring can be shown to bind the parties

mutual interdependence test
IRS will not recognize a gain in a restructuring if the entities are mutually dependent

end result test
IRS will not recognize gains of a restructure if the end result of the process furthers the corporate purpose

tax shelter
Business formed primarily to provide tax benefits to its owners

Practical tip

IRS requires the registration of listed tax shelters and has established reporting requirements for them pursuant to Temp. Regs. Secs. 1.6011-4T and 301.6111-2T.

192 Chapter Five

small corporation
Corporation that meets the definition of IRC sec. 55

Subchapter S corporation
Domestic corporation that has only one class of stock, no more than 75 shareholders, and no shareholder is a nonresident alien

Form 1120
Income tax return filed by C corporations

Form 1120S
Income tax return for Subchapter S corporations

accumulated earnings tax
Tax imposed on undistributed operational profits

The entities that qualify as a "corporation" for federal tax purposes are defined in section 7701(a)(3) of the IRC. Under this provision, any business entity that is recognized as a separate entity for federal tax purposes, except for trusts (see Chapter 7), may qualify to be taxed as a corporation. This classification includes limited liability companies (LLCs) and certain publicly traded partnerships [IRC sec. 7704(a)]. At the top of the tax return, the entity simply has to check a box to indicate its tax status. For the purposes of this chapter, the term *corporation* will be used to denote all entities that qualify for corporate tax treatment under section 7701(a) of the IRC.

In addition to regular taxation, a corporation, like an individual, may be subject to an alternative minimum tax to ensure that the entity does not reduce its taxable income to a minimal level by using certain permitted exclusions (IRC sec. 55). Even so, there is an exemption for **small corporations,** those corporations with average gross receipts of less than $7.5 million for the preceding three years [IRC sec. 55(e)(1)(B)]. If a corporation qualifies as a small corporation for an initial three-year period, it may continue to so qualify as long as its average gross receipts do not exceed $7.5 million for subsequent years [IRC sec. 55(e)(1)(A)].

This chapter will examine the federal income taxation of corporations, not only those subject to the provisions of Subchapter C but also ones classified as **Subchapter S corporations,** those with few shareholders which are treated as partnerships for federal income tax purposes. The chapter will discuss the mechanics of the basic financial documents that the corporation must produce to determine its tax liabilities, the tax implications of dividends and distributions to shareholders, corporate reorganizations, and the tax forms these entities must complete, **Form 1120** (Exhibit 5.1) and **Form 1120S** (Exhibit 5.2).

It should be noted at the outset that, in addition to regular income taxation, corporations are subject to certain special corporate taxes. Although they will not be discussed in this textbook, the tax professional should be aware of the two most commonly encountered ones.

1. **Accumulated earnings tax.** A corporation is only permitted to accumulate approximately $250,000 of earnings without distributing them to its shareholders. Any excess above this amount subjects the corporation to an additional tax. The purpose of this tax is to force corporations to distribute earnings to the shareholders who can then be taxed on these dividends (IRC secs. 531-535).

Income Taxation of Corporations 193

Form 1120 — U.S. Corporation Income Tax Return
Department of the Treasury
Internal Revenue Service

For calendar year 2002 or tax year beginning ...., 2002, ending ...., 20....
▶ Instructions are separate. See page 20 for Paperwork Reduction Act Notice.

OMB No. 1545-0123

2002

A Check if a:
1 Consolidated return (attach Form 851) ☐
2 Personal holding co. (attach Sch. PH) ☐
3 Personal service corp. (as defined in Regulations sec. 1.441-3(c)—see instructions) ☐

Use IRS label. Otherwise, print or type.

Name
Number, street, and room or suite no. (If a P.O. box, see page 7 of instructions.)
City or town, state, and ZIP code

B Employer identification number
C Date incorporated
D Total assets (see page 8 of instructions)

E Check applicable boxes: (1) ☐ Initial return (2) ☐ Final return (3) ☐ Name change (4) ☐ Address change $

Income

1a	Gross receipts or sales _____ **b** Less returns and allowances _____ **c** Bal ▶	1c
2	Cost of goods sold (Schedule A, line 8)	2
3	Gross profit. Subtract line 2 from line 1c	3
4	Dividends (Schedule C, line 19)	4
5	Interest	5
6	Gross rents	6
7	Gross royalties	7
8	Capital gain net income (attach Schedule D (Form 1120))	8
9	Net gain or (loss) from Form 4797, Part II, line 18 (attach Form 4797)	9
10	Other income (see page 9 of instructions—attach schedule)	10
11	**Total income.** Add lines 3 through 10 ▶	11

Deductions (See instructions for limitations on deductions.)

12	Compensation of officers (Schedule E, line 4)	12
13	Salaries and wages (less employment credits)	13
14	Repairs and maintenance	14
15	Bad debts	15
16	Rents	16
17	Taxes and licenses	17
18	Interest	18
19	Charitable contributions (see page 11 of instructions for 10% limitation)	19
20	Depreciation (attach Form 4562) ... 20	
21	Less depreciation claimed on Schedule A and elsewhere on return ... 21a	21b
22	Depletion	22
23	Advertising	23
24	Pension, profit-sharing, etc., plans	24
25	Employee benefit programs	25
26	Other deductions (attach schedule)	26
27	**Total deductions.** Add lines 12 through 26 ▶	27
28	Taxable income before net operating loss deduction and special deductions. Subtract line 27 from line 11	28
29	Less: **a** Net operating loss (NOL) deduction (see page 13 of instructions) 29a	
	b Special deductions (Schedule C, line 20) 29b	29c

Tax and Payments

30	**Taxable income.** Subtract line 29c from line 28	30
31	**Total tax** (Schedule J, line 11)	31
32	Payments: **a** 2001 overpayment credited to 2002 32a	
	b 2002 estimated tax payments 32b	
	c Less 2002 refund applied for on Form 4466 32c ( ) **d** Bal ▶ 32d	
	e Tax deposited with Form 7004 32e	
	f Credit for tax paid on undistributed capital gains (attach Form 2439) 32f	
	g Credit for Federal tax on fuels (attach Form 4136). See instructions 32g	32h
33	Estimated tax penalty (see page 14 of instructions). Check if Form 2220 is attached ▶ ☐	33
34	**Tax due.** If line 32h is smaller than the total of lines 31 and 33, enter amount owed	34
35	**Overpayment.** If line 32h is larger than the total of lines 31 and 33, enter amount overpaid	35
36	Enter amount of line 35 you want: **Credited to 2003 estimated tax** ▶ **Refunded** ▶	36

Sign Here
Under penalties of perjury, I declare that I have examined this return, including accompanying schedules and statements, and to the best of my knowledge and belief, it is true, correct, and complete. Declaration of preparer (other than taxpayer) is based on all information of which preparer has any knowledge.

Signature of officer   Date   Title

May the IRS discuss this return with the preparer shown below (see instructions)? ☐ Yes ☐ No

Paid Preparer's Use Only
Preparer's signature ▶
Firm's name (or yours if self-employed), address, and ZIP code ▶
Date
Check if self-employed ☐
Preparer's SSN or PTIN
EIN
Phone no. ( )

Cat. No. 11450Q   Form **1120** (2002)

Exhibit 5.1 Form 1120

Form 1120 (2002)   Page **2**

Schedule A — Cost of Goods Sold (see page 14 of instructions)

1	Inventory at beginning of year	1
2	Purchases	2
3	Cost of labor	3
4	Additional section 263A costs (attach schedule)	4
5	Other costs (attach schedule)	5
6	**Total.** Add lines 1 through 5	6
7	Inventory at end of year	7
8	**Cost of goods sold.** Subtract line 7 from line 6. Enter here and on line 2, page 1	8

9a Check all methods used for valuing closing inventory:
    (i) ☐ Cost as described in Regulations section 1.471-3
    (ii) ☐ Lower of cost or market as described in Regulations section 1.471-4
    (iii) ☐ Other (Specify method used and attach explanation.) ▶ ....
  b Check if there was a writedown of subnormal goods as described in Regulations section 1.471-2(c) ▶ ☐
  c Check if the LIFO inventory method was adopted this tax year for any goods (if checked, attach Form 970) ▶ ☐
  d If the LIFO inventory method was used for this tax year, enter percentage (or amounts) of closing inventory computed under LIFO   9d
  e If property is produced or acquired for resale, do the rules of section 263A apply to the corporation?   ☐ Yes   ☐ No
  f Was there any change in determining quantities, cost, or valuations between opening and closing inventory? If "Yes," attach explanation   ☐ Yes   ☐ No

Schedule C — Dividends and Special Deductions (see instructions beginning on page 15)

		(a) Dividends received	(b) %	(c) Special deductions (a) × (b)
1	Dividends from less-than-20%-owned domestic corporations that are subject to the 70% deduction (other than debt-financed stock)		70	
2	Dividends from 20%-or-more-owned domestic corporations that are subject to the 80% deduction (other than debt-financed stock)		80	
3	Dividends on debt-financed stock of domestic and foreign corporations (section 246A)		see instructions	
4	Dividends on certain preferred stock of less-than-20%-owned public utilities		42	
5	Dividends on certain preferred stock of 20%-or-more-owned public utilities		48	
6	Dividends from less-than-20%-owned foreign corporations and certain FSCs that are subject to the 70% deduction		70	
7	Dividends from 20%-or-more-owned foreign corporations and certain FSCs that are subject to the 80% deduction		80	
8	Dividends from wholly owned foreign subsidiaries subject to the 100% deduction (section 245(b))		100	
9	**Total.** Add lines 1 through 8. See page 16 of instructions for limitation			
10	Dividends from domestic corporations received by a small business investment company operating under the Small Business Investment Act of 1958		100	
11	Dividends from certain FSCs that are subject to the 100% deduction (section 245(c)(1))		100	
12	Dividends from affiliated group members subject to the 100% deduction (section 243(a)(3))		100	
13	Other dividends from foreign corporations not included on lines 3, 6, 7, 8, or 11			
14	Income from controlled foreign corporations under subpart F (attach Form(s) 5471)			
15	Foreign dividend gross-up (section 78)			
16	IC-DISC and former DISC dividends not included on lines 1, 2, or 3 (section 246(d))			
17	Other dividends			
18	Deduction for dividends paid on certain preferred stock of public utilities			
19	**Total dividends.** Add lines 1 through 17. Enter here and on line 4, page 1 ▶			
20	**Total special deductions.** Add lines 9, 10, 11, 12, and 18. Enter here and on line 29b, page 1 ▶			

Schedule E — Compensation of Officers (see instructions for line 12, page 1, on page 10 of instructions)

Note: *Complete Schedule E only if total receipts (line 1a plus lines 4 through 10 on page 1) are $500,000 or more.*

(a) Name of officer	(b) Social security number	(c) Percent of time devoted to business	Percent of corporation stock owned		(f) Amount of compensation
			(d) Common	(e) Preferred	
1		%	%	%	
		%	%	%	
		%	%	%	
		%	%	%	
		%	%	%	

2   Total compensation of officers
3   Compensation of officers claimed on Schedule A and elsewhere on return
4   Subtract line 3 from line 2. Enter the result here and on line 12, page 1

Form **1120** (2002)

Exhibit 5.1 (Continued)

Form 1120 (2002)   Page **3**

Schedule J   Tax Computation (see page 17 of instructions)

1. Check if the corporation is a member of a controlled group (see sections 1561 and 1563) . . . . ▶ ☐
   Important: Members of a controlled group, see instructions on page 17.
2a. If the box on line 1 is checked, enter the corporation's share of the $50,000, $25,000, and $9,925,000 taxable income brackets (in that order):
   (1) $ _____ (2) $ _____ (3) $ _____
 b. Enter the corporation's share of: **(1)** Additional 5% tax (not more than $11,750) $ _____
                                  (2) Additional 3% tax (not more than $100,000) $ _____
3. Income tax. Check if a qualified personal service corporation under section 448(d)(2) (see page 17) . ▶ ☐   **3**
4. Alternative minimum tax (attach Form 4626) **4**
5. Add lines 3 and 4 . . . . **5**
6a. Foreign tax credit (attach Form 1118) **6a**
 b. Possessions tax credit (attach Form 5735) **6b**
 c. Check: ☐ Nonconventional source fuel credit   ☐ QEV credit (attach Form 8834)   **6c**
 d. General business credit. Check box(es) and indicate which forms are attached.
      ☐ Form 3800   ☐ Form(s) (specify) ▶ **6d**
 e. Credit for prior year minimum tax (attach Form 8827) **6e**
 f. Qualified zone academy bond credit (attach Form 8860) **6f**
7. **Total credits.** Add lines 6a through 6f **7**
8. Subtract line 7 from line 5 . . . . **8**
9. Personal holding company tax (attach Schedule PH (Form 1120)) **9**
10. Other taxes. Check if from: ☐ Form 4255   ☐ Form 8611   ☐ Form 8697
                                      ☐ Form 8866   ☐ Other (attach schedule) **10**
11. **Total tax.** Add lines 8 through 10. Enter here and on line 31, page 1 . . . . **11**

Schedule K   Other Information (see page 19 of instructions)

		Yes	No
1	Check method of accounting: **a** ☐ Cash **b** ☐ Accrual **c** ☐ Other (specify) ▶		
2	See page 21 of the instructions and enter the:		
a	Business activity code no. ▶		
b	Business activity ▶		
c	Product or service ▶		
3	At the end of the tax year, did the corporation own, directly or indirectly, 50% or more of the voting stock of a domestic corporation? (For rules of attribution, see section 267(c).)		
	If "Yes," attach a schedule showing: **(a)** name and employer identification number (EIN), **(b)** percentage owned, and **(c)** taxable income or (loss) before NOL and special deductions of such corporation for the tax year ending with or within your tax year.		
4	Is the corporation a subsidiary in an affiliated group or a parent-subsidiary controlled group?		
	If "Yes," enter name and EIN of the parent corporation ▶		
5	At the end of the tax year, did any individual, partnership, corporation, estate, or trust own, directly or indirectly, 50% or more of the corporation's voting stock? (For rules of attribution, see section 267(c).)		
	If "Yes," attach a schedule showing name and identifying number. (Do not include any information already entered in **4** above.) Enter percentage owned ▶		
6	During this tax year, did the corporation pay dividends (other than stock dividends and distributions in exchange for stock) in excess of the corporation's current and accumulated earnings and profits? (See sections 301 and 316.) . . .		
	If "Yes," file **Form 5452,** Corporate Report of Nondividend Distributions.		
	If this is a consolidated return, answer here for the parent corporation and on **Form 851,** Affiliations Schedule, for each subsidiary.		

		Yes	No
7	At any time during the tax year, did one foreign person own, directly or indirectly, at least 25% of **(a)** the total voting power of all classes of stock of the corporation entitled to vote or **(b)** the total value of all classes of stock of the corporation?		
	If "Yes," enter: **(a)** Percentage owned ▶ .... and **(b)** Owner's country ▶		
c	The corporation may have to file **Form 5472,** Information Return of a 25% Foreign-Owned U.S. Corporation or a Foreign Corporation Engaged in a U.S. Trade or Business. Enter number of Forms 5472 attached ▶		
8	Check this box if the corporation issued publicly offered debt instruments with original issue discount . ▶ ☐		
	If checked, the corporation may have to file **Form 8281,** Information Return for Publicly Offered Original Issue Discount Instruments.		
9	Enter the amount of tax-exempt interest received or accrued during the tax year ▶ $		
10	Enter the number of shareholders at the end of the tax year (if 75 or fewer) ▶		
11	If the corporation has an NOL for the tax year and is electing to forego the carryback period, check here ▶ ☐		
	If the corporation is filing a consolidated return, the statement required by Regulations section 1.1502-21(b)(3)(i) or (ii) must be attached or the election will not be valid.		
12	Enter the available NOL carryover from prior tax years (Do not reduce it by any deduction on line 29a.) ▶ $		
13	Are the corporation's total receipts (line 1a plus lines 4 through 10 on page 1) for the tax year **and** its total assets at the end of the tax year less than $250,000? . . .		
	If "Yes," the corporation is not required to complete Schedules L, M-1, and M-2 on page 4. Instead, enter the total amount of cash distributions and the book value of property distributions (other than cash) made during the tax year. ▶ $		

Note: *If the corporation, at any time during the tax year, had assets or operated a business in a foreign country or U.S. possession, it may be required to attach* **Schedule N (Form 1120),** *Foreign Operations of U.S. Corporations, to this return. See Schedule N for details.*

Form **1120** (2002)

Exhibit 5.1 (Continued)

Form 1120 (2002) Page **4**

Note: *The corporation is not required to complete Schedules L, M-1, and M-2 if Question 13 on Schedule K is answered "Yes."*

Schedule L — Balance Sheets per Books

		Beginning of tax year		End of tax year	
		(a)	(b)	(c)	(d)
	Assets				
1	Cash				
2a	Trade notes and accounts receivable				
b	Less allowance for bad debts	( )		( )	
3	Inventories				
4	U.S. government obligations				
5	Tax-exempt securities (see instructions)				
6	Other current assets (attach schedule)				
7	Loans to shareholders				
8	Mortgage and real estate loans				
9	Other investments (attach schedule)				
10a	Buildings and other depreciable assets				
b	Less accumulated depreciation	( )		( )	
11a	Depletable assets				
b	Less accumulated depletion	( )		( )	
12	Land (net of any amortization)				
13a	Intangible assets (amortizable only)				
b	Less accumulated amortization	( )		( )	
14	Other assets (attach schedule)				
15	Total assets				
	Liabilities and Shareholders' Equity				
16	Accounts payable				
17	Mortgages, notes, bonds payable in less than 1 year				
18	Other current liabilities (attach schedule)				
19	Loans from shareholders				
20	Mortgages, notes, bonds payable in 1 year or more				
21	Other liabilities (attach schedule)				
22	Capital stock: a Preferred stock				
	b Common stock				
23	Additional paid-in capital				
24	Retained earnings—Appropriated (attach schedule)				
25	Retained earnings—Unappropriated				
26	Adjustments to shareholders' equity (attach schedule)				
27	Less cost of treasury stock		( )		( )
28	Total liabilities and shareholders' equity				

Schedule M-1 — Reconciliation of Income (Loss) per Books With Income per Return (see page 20 of instructions)

1	Net income (loss) per books		7	Income recorded on books this year not included on this return (itemize):
2	Federal income tax per books			Tax-exempt interest $ ....
3	Excess of capital losses over capital gains			....
4	Income subject to tax not recorded on books this year (itemize):		8	Deductions on this return not charged against book income this year (itemize):
	....		a	Depreciation . . . . $...........
5	Expenses recorded on books this year not deducted on this return (itemize):		b	Charitable contributions $.........
a	Depreciation . . . $			....
b	Charitable contributions $		9	Add lines 7 and 8
c	Travel and entertainment $		10	Income (line 28, page 1)—line 6 less line 9
6	Add lines 1 through 5			

Schedule M-2 — Analysis of Unappropriated Retained Earnings per Books (Line 25, Schedule L)

1	Balance at beginning of year		5	Distributions: a Cash
2	Net income (loss) per books			b Stock
3	Other increases (itemize):			c Property
	....		6	Other decreases (itemize): ....
			7	Add lines 5 and 6
4	Add lines 1, 2, and 3		8	Balance at end of year (line 4 less line 7)

Form **1120** (2002)

Exhibit 5.1 (Continued)

Income Taxation of Corporations   197

Form 1120S

U.S. Income Tax Return for an S Corporation

Department of the Treasury
Internal Revenue Service

▶ Do not file this form unless the corporation has timely filed Form 2553 to elect to be an S corporation.
▶ See separate instructions.

OMB No. 1545-0130

2002

For calendar year 2002, or tax year beginning _____ , 2002, and ending _____ , 20 ___

A Effective date of election as an S corporation

B Business code no. (see pages 29-31)

Use IRS label. Otherwise, print or type.

Name

Number, street, and room or suite no. (If a P.O. box, see page 11 of the instructions.)

City or town, state, and ZIP code

C Employer identification number

D Date incorporated

E Total assets (see page 11)
$

F Check applicable boxes: (1) ☐ Initial return (2) ☐ Final return (3) ☐ Name change (4) ☐ Address change (5) ☐ Amended return
G Enter number of shareholders in the corporation at end of the tax year . . . . ▶

Caution: Include **only** trade or business income and expenses on lines 1a through 21. See page 11 of the instructions for more information.

Income

1a	Gross receipts or sales _____	**b** Less returns and allowances _____	**c** Bal ▶	1c
2	Cost of goods sold (Schedule A, line 8)		2
3	Gross profit. Subtract line 2 from line 1c		3
4	Net gain (loss) from Form 4797, Part II, line 18 (attach Form 4797)		4
5	Other income (loss) (attach schedule)		5
6	**Total income (loss).** Combine lines 3 through 5 . . . . ▶		6

Deductions (see page 12 of the instructions for limitations)

7	Compensation of officers	7
8	Salaries and wages (less employment credits)	8
9	Repairs and maintenance	9
10	Bad debts	10
11	Rents	11
12	Taxes and licenses	12
13	Interest	13
14a	Depreciation (if required, attach Form 4562) 14a	
b	Depreciation claimed on Schedule A and elsewhere on return . . 14b	
c	Subtract line 14b from line 14a	14c
15	Depletion **(Do not deduct oil and gas depletion.)**	15
16	Advertising	16
17	Pension, profit-sharing, etc., plans	17
18	Employee benefit programs	18
19	Other deductions (attach schedule)	19
20	**Total deductions.** Add the amounts shown in the far right column for lines 7 through 19 . ▶	20
21	Ordinary income (loss) from trade or business activities. Subtract line 20 from line 6 . .	21

Tax and Payments

22	**Tax: a** Excess net passive income tax (attach schedule) . . .	22a	
	b Tax from Schedule D (Form 1120S)	22b	
	c Add lines 22a and 22b (see page 16 of the instructions for additional taxes)		22c
23	**Payments: a** 2002 estimated tax payments and amount applied from 2001 return	23a	
	b Tax deposited with Form 7004	23b	
	c Credit for Federal tax paid on fuels (attach Form 4136) . . .	23c	
	d Add lines 23a through 23c		23d
24	Estimated tax penalty. Check if Form 2220 is attached . . . . ▶ ☐		24
25	**Tax due.** If the total of lines 22c and 24 is larger than line 23d, enter amount owed. See page 4 of the instructions for depository method of payment . . . . ▶		25
26	**Overpayment.** If line 23d is larger than the total of lines 22c and 24, enter amount overpaid ▶		26
27	Enter amount of line 26 you want: **Credited to 2003 estimated tax** ▶ _____ **Refunded** ▶		27

Sign Here

Under penalties of perjury, I declare that I have examined this return, including accompanying schedules and statements, and to the best of my knowledge and belief, it is true, correct, and complete. Declaration of preparer (other than taxpayer) is based on all information of which preparer has any knowledge.

▶ _____ _____ ▶ _____
Signature of officer   Date   Title

May the IRS discuss this return with the preparer shown below (see instructions)? ☐ Yes ☐ No

Paid Preparer's Use Only

Preparer's signature	▶	Date		Check if self-employed ☐	Preparer's SSN or PTIN
Firm's name (or yours if self-employed), address, and ZIP code	▶			EIN	
				Phone no. ( )	

For Paperwork Reduction Act Notice, see the separate instructions.   Cat. No. 11510H   Form **1120S** (2002)

Exhibit 5.2 Form 1120S

Form 1120S (2002) Page **2**

Schedule A — Cost of Goods Sold (see page 17 of the instructions)

1	Inventory at beginning of year	1
2	Purchases	2
3	Cost of labor	3
4	Additional section 263A costs *(attach schedule)*	4
5	Other costs *(attach schedule)*	5
6	**Total.** Add lines 1 through 5	6
7	Inventory at end of year	7
8	**Cost of goods sold.** Subtract line 7 from line 6. Enter here and on page 1, line 2	8

9a Check all methods used for valuing closing inventory: (i) ☐ Cost as described in Regulations section 1.471-3
   (ii) ☐ Lower of cost or market as described in Regulations section 1.471-4
   (iii) ☐ Other (specify method used and attach explanation) ▶ ....
 b Check if there was a writedown of "subnormal" goods as described in Regulations section 1.471-2(c) . . . . ▶ ☐
 c Check if the LIFO inventory method was adopted this tax year for any goods *(if checked, attach Form 970)* . . . ▶ ☐
 d If the LIFO inventory method was used for this tax year, enter percentage (or amounts) of closing inventory computed under LIFO . . . . | 9d |
 e Do the rules of section 263A (for property produced or acquired for resale) apply to the corporation? . . . . ☐ Yes ☐ No
 f Was there any change in determining quantities, cost, or valuations between opening and closing inventory? . . ☐ Yes ☐ No
   If "Yes," attach explanation.

Schedule B — Other Information

		Yes	No
1	Check method of accounting: **(a)** ☐ Cash **(b)** ☐ Accrual **(c)** ☐ Other (specify) ▶		
2	Refer to the list on pages 29 through 31 of the instructions and state the corporation's principal: **(a)** Business activity ▶ .... **(b)** Product or service ▶		
3	Did the corporation at the end of the tax year own, directly or indirectly, 50% or more of the voting stock of a domestic corporation? (For rules of attribution, see section 267(c).) If "Yes," attach a schedule showing: **(a)** name, address, and employer identification number and **(b)** percentage owned		
4	Was the corporation a member of a controlled group subject to the provisions of section 1561?		
5	Check this box if the corporation has filed or is required to file **Form 8264,** Application for Registration of a Tax Shelter ▶ ☐		
6	Check this box if the corporation issued publicly offered debt instruments with original issue discount . . ▶ ☐ If so, the corporation may have to file **Form 8281,** Information Return for Publicly Offered Original Issue Discount Instruments.		
7	If the corporation: **(a)** was a C corporation before it elected to be an S corporation **or** the corporation acquired an asset with a basis determined by reference to its basis (or the basis of any other property) in the hands of a C corporation **and (b)** has net unrealized built-in gain (defined in section 1374(d)(1)) in excess of the net recognized built-in gain from prior years, enter the net unrealized built-in gain reduced by net recognized built-in gain from prior years (see page 17 of the instructions) . . . . ▶ $		
8	Check this box if the corporation had accumulated earnings and profits at the close of the tax year (see page 18 of the instructions) . . . . ▶ ☐		
9	Are the corporation's total receipts (see page 29 of the instructions) for the tax year **and** total assets at the end of the tax year less than $250,000? If "Yes," the corporation is not required to complete Schedules L and M-1.		

Note: *If the corporation had assets or operated a business in a foreign country or U.S. possession, it may be required to attach Schedule N (Form 1120), Foreign Operations of U.S. Corporations, to this return. See Schedule N for details.*

Schedule K — Shareholders' Shares of Income, Credits, Deductions, etc.

	(a) Pro rata share items		(b) Total amount
	1 Ordinary income (loss) from trade or business activities (page 1, line 21)		1
	2 Net income (loss) from rental real estate activities *(attach Form 8825)*		2
	3a Gross income from other rental activities	3a	
	b Expenses from other rental activities *(attach schedule)*	3b	
Income (Loss)	c Net income (loss) from other rental activities. Subtract line 3b from line 3a		3c
	4 Portfolio income (loss):		
	a Interest income		4a
	b Ordinary dividends		4b
	c Royalty income		4c
	d Net short-term capital gain (loss) *(attach Schedule D (Form 1120S))*		4d
	e (1) Net long-term capital gain (loss) *(attach Schedule D (Form 1120S))*		4e(1)
	(2) 28% rate gain (loss) ▶ .... (3) Qualified 5-year gain ▶		
	f Other portfolio income (loss) *(attach schedule)*		4f
	5 Net section 1231 gain (loss) (other than due to casualty or theft) *(attach Form 4797)*		5
	6 Other income (loss) *(attach schedule)*		6

Form **1120S** (2002)

Figure 5.2 (Continued)

Form 1120S (2002) Page **3**

Schedule K Shareholders' Shares of Income, Credits, Deductions, etc. *(continued)*

	(a) Pro rata share items		(b) Total amount
Deductions	7 Charitable contributions *(attach schedule)*	7	
	8 Section 179 expense deduction *(attach Form 4562)*	8	
	9 Deductions related to portfolio income (loss) (itemize)	9	
	10 Other deductions *(attach schedule)*	10	
Investment Interest	11a Interest expense on investment debts	11a	
	b (1) Investment income included on lines 4a, 4b, 4c, and 4f above	11b(1)	
	(2) Investment expenses included on line 9 above	11b(2)	
Credits	12a Credit for alcohol used as a fuel *(attach Form 6478)*	12a	
	b Low-income housing credit:		
	(1) From partnerships to which section 42(j)(5) applies	12b(1)	
	(2) Other than on line 12b(1)	12b(2)	
	c Qualified rehabilitation expenditures related to rental real estate activities *(attach Form 3468)*	12c	
	d Credits (other than credits shown on lines 12b and 12c) related to rental real estate activities	12d	
	e Credits related to other rental activities	12e	
	13 Other credits	13	
Adjustments and Tax Preference Items	14a Depreciation adjustment on property placed in service after 1986	14a	
	b Adjusted gain or loss	14b	
	c Depletion (other than oil and gas)	14c	
	d (1) Gross income from oil, gas, or geothermal properties	14d(1)	
	(2) Deductions allocable to oil, gas, or geothermal properties	14d(2)	
	e Other adjustments and tax preference items *(attach schedule)*	14e	
Foreign Taxes	15a Name of foreign country or U.S. possession ▶		
	b Gross income from all sources	15b	
	c Gross income sourced at shareholder level	15c	
	d Foreign gross income sourced at corporate level:		
	(1) Passive	15d(1)	
	(2) Listed categories *(attach schedule)*	15d(2)	
	(3) General limitation	15d(3)	
	e Deductions allocated and apportioned at shareholder level:		
	(1) Interest expense	15e(1)	
	(2) Other	15e(2)	
	f Deductions allocated and apportioned at corporate level to foreign source income:		
	(1) Passive	15f(1)	
	(2) Listed categories *(attach schedule)*	15f(2)	
	(3) General limitation	15f(3)	
	g Total foreign taxes (check one): ▶ ☐ Paid ☐ Accrued	15g	
	h Reduction in taxes available for credit *(attach schedule)*	15h	
Other	16 Section 59(e)(2) expenditures: a Type ▶ .... b Amount ▶	16b	
	17 Tax-exempt interest income	17	
	18 Other tax-exempt income	18	
	19 Nondeductible expenses	19	
	20 Total property distributions (including cash) other than dividends reported on line 22 below	20	
	21 Other items and amounts required to be reported separately to shareholders *(attach schedule)*		
	22 Total dividend distributions paid from accumulated earnings and profits	22	
	23 **Income (loss).** (Required only if Schedule M-1 must be completed.) Combine lines 1 through 6 in column (b). From the result, subtract the sum of lines 7 through 11a, 15g, and 16b	23	

Form **1120S** (2002)

Exhibit 5.2 (Continued)

Form 1120S (2002) Page **4**

Note: The corporation is not required to complete Schedules L and M-1 if question 9 of Schedule B is answered "Yes."

Schedule L — Balance Sheets per Books

	Assets	Beginning of tax year (a)	(b)	End of tax year (c)	(d)
1	Cash				
2a	Trade notes and accounts receivable				
b	Less allowance for bad debts				
3	Inventories				
4	U.S. Government obligations				
5	Tax-exempt securities				
6	Other current assets (attach schedule)				
7	Loans to shareholders				
8	Mortgage and real estate loans				
9	Other investments (attach schedule)				
10a	Buildings and other depreciable assets				
b	Less accumulated depreciation				
11a	Depletable assets				
b	Less accumulated depletion				
12	Land (net of any amortization)				
13a	Intangible assets (amortizable only)				
b	Less accumulated amortization				
14	Other assets (attach schedule)				
15	Total assets				
	Liabilities and Shareholders' Equity				
16	Accounts payable				
17	Mortgages, notes, bonds payable in less than 1 year				
18	Other current liabilities (attach schedule)				
19	Loans from shareholders				
20	Mortgages, notes, bonds payable in 1 year or more				
21	Other liabilities (attach schedule)				
22	Capital stock				
23	Additional paid-in capital				
24	Retained earnings				
25	Adjustments to shareholders' equity (attach schedule)				
26	Less cost of treasury stock		( )		( )
27	Total liabilities and shareholders' equity				

Schedule M-1 — Reconciliation of Income (Loss) per Books With Income (Loss) per Return

1	Net income (loss) per books		5	Income recorded on books this year not included on Schedule K, lines 1 through 6 (itemize):	
2	Income included on Schedule K, lines 1 through 6, not recorded on books this year (itemize):		a	Tax-exempt interest $	
3	Expenses recorded on books this year not included on Schedule K, lines 1 through 11a, 15g, and 16b (itemize):		6	Deductions included on Schedule K, lines 1 through 11a, 15g, and 16b, not charged against book income this year (itemize):	
a	Depreciation $		a	Depreciation $	
b	Travel and entertainment $				
			7	Add lines 5 and 6	
4	Add lines 1 through 3		8	Income (loss) (Schedule K, line 23). Line 4 less line 7	

Schedule M-2 — Analysis of Accumulated Adjustments Account, Other Adjustments Account, and Shareholders' Undistributed Taxable Income Previously Taxed (see page 26 of the instructions)

		(a) Accumulated adjustments account	(b) Other adjustments account	(c) Shareholders' undistributed taxable income previously taxed
1	Balance at beginning of tax year			
2	Ordinary income from page 1, line 21			
3	Other additions			
4	Loss from page 1, line 21	( )		
5	Other reductions	( )	( )	
6	Combine lines 1 through 5			
7	Distributions other than dividend distributions			
8	Balance at end of tax year. Subtract line 7 from line 6			

Form **1120S** (2002)

Exhibit 5.2 (Continued)

2. **Personal holding company tax.** This tax is imposed on **personal holding companies,** corporations of which more than half of its stock is owned by not more than five individuals if at least 60% of the corporation's gross income is derived from passive income sources. If the corporation meets this definition, an additional tax equal to the highest individual income tax rate is imposed above the corporate taxes due (IRC sec. 541-545). Note that this definition is deemed to apply to certain corporations that market the personal services of professional athletes and actors.

personal holding company
Corporation that has no more than five shareholders and at least 60% of its income is derived from passive sources

Example
A well-known hip-hop performer decides to incorporate to take advantage of limiting her personal liability. She is the sole shareholder of the corporation. All of her professional income is paid through the corporation. Even though the corporation's income is derived from personal services, it still qualifies as a personal holding company.

The Balance Sheet and Income Statement

To substantiate the items that appear on the corporation's tax return, IRS requires that a simplified balance sheet be included as part of the Form 1120, similar to the one required for partnership returns discussed in Chapter 4. A balance sheet is a written summary of what is referred to as the **basic accounting equation:** Assets = Liabilities + Equity. The balance sheet is created by taking all of the financial data that the business has maintained and placing them into categories that correspond to the accounting equation. This is a much more formalized approach to record keeping than is required for an individual income tax return, the preparation of a Schedule C for sole proprietorships, or tax returns mandated for estates and trusts (Chapters 6 and 7). Those returns may be prepared by reference to simply journal entries, notes, and check stubs.

basic accounting equation
Assets = Liabilities + Equity

Exercise
Obtain the balance sheet of a publicly traded corporation and compare it with the balance sheet required to be attached to Form 1120 (Schedule L). What, if any, differences exist?

The categories that appear as part of the basic accounting equation can be defined as follows:

Asset: all property that can be converted to cash to which the entity has a transferable title. Accounts that appear under this category may include cash, bank accounts, real property, securities (stocks and bonds issued by other entities held by the corporation), inventory and equipment, receivables (work that has been performed by the corporation and billed for but not yet paid), and prepaid expenses (services that the corporation has been paid for but not used).

Liabilities: all expenses of the business, such as rent, utilities, wages and salaries, supplies, and taxes and fees. All accounts that fall into this category usually include the word *payable* to indicate that it is an item of expense for which the corporation is financially liable, such as "rent payable."

Equity: all funds that the owners have contributed to the corporation to acquire their ownership interests, evidenced by shares of stock, as well as any profit or loss the corporation shows from the operation of its business. Generally, equity is divided into two subaccounts: capital and retained earnings. **Capital** reflects the starting funds of the corporation, those amounts initially paid by investors to acquire shares in the company as well as cash and property paid by investors to acquire shares after the corporation is operational. Acquisition of these funds is not considered income to the corporation because they are used to create the enterprise [IRC sec. 351, and IRC sec. 118(a)]. If an investor receives cash or other property as well as stock when he or she contributes capital to the corporation, this property is called **boot** and is also subject to the nonrecognition rules, meaning that the value of this boot is added to the person's basis in the stock received, and is only subject to taxation when the shareholder eventually sells or transfers the shares [IRC sec. 351(b)]. Retained earnings represents profit for the operation of the business.

capital
Account representing the investors' contribution to the corporation

boot
Cash and other property given along with stock when a person invests in a corporation

The basic premise behind a balance sheet is that it must balance. Unlike a checkbook, in which deposits and withdrawals are noted and at the end of a given period a single total remains, with a balance sheet, at the end of the period in question, the equation must balance, that is, the total value of all of the corporation's assets *must* equal the total of all of its liabilities combined with the value of all of its equity. To maintain this balance, a second document must be prepared, known as the income statement. The **income statement** is a financial document on which the corporation posts all of its items of income and from which it deducts all of its items of expense, including taxes, to determine whether the business is operating at a profit or a loss. This final number from the income statement is then placed

income statement
Document prepared along with the balance sheet to indicate sales and expenses incurred in operating the business

on the balance sheet as "retained earnings" under the equity account. In a manner of speaking, the income statement may be viewed in a manner similar to the Schedule C discussed previously with respect to sole proprietors (Chapter 3).

It is well beyond the scope of this textbook to examine accounting systems and documents in detail, but all tax law professionals should have a basic understanding of the accounts created as the basis for reporting income, profits, and losses to the IRS. It is also important to note that the IRS uses these documents to uncover unlawful activities such as tax fraud, as evidenced in the following judicial decision.

In *Pittman v. Commissioner of Internal Revenue* the court highlighted the tax problems that may ensue from a failure to maintain appropriate records and accounts.

TAX LAW & POLICY

PITTMAN v. COMMISSIONER OF INTERNAL REVENUE
100 F.3d 1308 (7th CIR. 1996)

Pittman was president and 50 percent shareholder of BBL during 1986 and 1987, the tax years in issue. Judith A. Boyd held the balance of the stock in BBL and served as its secretary-treasurer. Pittman incorporated BBL in 1979. From its inception in 1979 through 1987, BBL operated a school bus service serving the Milwaukee metropolitan area. During 1986 and 1987, BBL provided busing services to the Milwaukee Public Schools ("MPS") and Heritage Christian Schools ("Heritage"), among others. Both school systems paid for BBL's busing services by checks. The checks from MPS, BBL's principal source of income, totaled $667,015 in 1986 and $429,967 in 1987. The checks from Heritage totaled $67,241 in 1986 and $79,036 in 1987. As explained below, the checks from these two sources were handled quite differently.

BBL maintained two checking accounts at Bank One (formerly Marine Bank) and a third checking account at Park State Bank. Pittman maintained two personal savings accounts at Columbia Savings and Loan Association. BBL did not maintain any accounts at Columbia. During 1986 and 1987, BBL recorded the checks from MPS on ledger sheets labeled "Accounts Receivable" and deposited them into its checking account at Bank One. BBL treated the checks it received from MPS in 1984 and 1985 in the same manner. Consistent with its treatment of the MPS checks, BBL included the MPS checks as gross receipts on its corporate income tax returns for 1984 and 1985, and BBL included the checks as gross receipts on its prepared, but unfiled, corporate income tax returns for 1986 and 1987. Indeed, the gross receipts reported on BBL's corporate tax returns for 1984 and 1985 matched within a few hundred dollars the receipts listed on BBL's accounts receivable ledgers. The gross receipts entry on BBL's 1987 prepared but unfiled tax return matches identically its accounts receivable ledger reflecting 1987 payments from MPS. The gross receipts entry on BBL's 1986 prepared but unfiled tax return differs from its 1986 accounts receivable ledger by $228.

The checks from Heritage were handled in a much different fashion. BBL did not deposit the Heritage checks into BBL's Bank One checking account and did not record them in its ledger along with the MPS entries. Instead, Pittman endorsed all the checks from Heritage as "Bee Bus Line/James A. Pittman" (or a variation thereof) and then either cashed or deposited the checks at Columbia, where he maintained personal bank accounts.

During the relevant years, BBL received checks totaling thousands of dollars for busing services provided to a number of other schools and deposited these checks into its Park State Bank account. Like the Heritage checks, these checks were not reflected on BBL's books and records, and they were not reported as gross receipts on BBL's prepared but unfiled tax returns for 1986 and 1987. Also, checks drawn on BBL's Park State Bank account were not reflected in BBL's records nor on its prepared but unfiled returns for 1986 and 1987. In June 1987, BBL issued a check payable to Pittman in the amount of $7,000. The check was drawn by Pittman on behalf of BBL on its Park State Bank account. In November 1987, BBL issued a check payable to cash in the amount of $1,000. The check was drawn by Pittman on BBL's Park State Bank account. Pittman later endorsed the check and negotiated it at Columbia. In March 1987, Pittman drew a check on BBL's Park State Bank account in the amount of $500 payable to his personal Visa charge account with Bank Card Associates.

During 1986 and 1987, BBL made 20 separate mortgage payments of $269.37 on Pittman's personal residence. Also during 1986 and 1987, BBL paid actual dividends to Pittman in the amount of $13,928 and $10,000, respectively. The dividends were paid by check from BBL's Bank One account. Boyd received like distributions on the same dates.

Pittman did not report any of the foregoing distributions (i.e., the Heritage checks, Park State Bank checks totaling $8,000, actual dividends, personal expenses paid by BBL) as income on his individual tax returns for 1986 and 1987. On June 26, 1992, the Commissioner issued a notice of deficiency to Pittman determining income tax deficiencies in the amounts of $35,488 and $32,818 for 1986 and 1987, respectively. Among other things not relevant here, the Commissioner determined that Pittman received but failed to report constructive dividends from BBL based upon: (1) his diversion of corporate receipts from Heritage in the amounts of $67,241 and $79,036 during 1986 and 1987, respectively; (2) his receipt of checks totaling $8,000 from BBL's Park State Bank account during 1987; and (3) BBL's payment of Pittman's personal expenses including mortgage payments in the amount of $2,963 in 1986 and $2,424 in 1987, as well as $933 in 1986 real estate taxes and a $500 Visa charge card payment in 1987. The

Commissioner also determined that Pittman received but failed to report actual dividends from BBL in the amounts of $13,928 and $5,000 in 1986 and 1987, respectively. Last, the Commissioner determined that Pittman was liable for additions to tax for fraud and substantial understatement of income tax liability for these years. The Tax Court sustained the Commissioner's determinations in all material respects.

The core of Pittman's appeal consists of three separate but related arguments all to the effect that the Tax Court erred in according the customary presumption of correctness to the Commissioner's determination that he received unreported income in the form of constructive dividends—principally from the Heritage receipts. Pittman first argues that the Commissioner failed generally to establish that he diverted the proceeds from the Heritage checks to personal use. His second contention is merely a more refined version of the first, namely, that the Commissioner failed to establish that he personally benefitted from the Heritage receipts that he allegedly diverted from BBL. Finally, Pittman faults the Tax Court for according the presumption of correctness to the Commissioner's determination of BBL's earnings and profits. [Argument omitted]

Pittman's first contention on appeal is that the Tax Court erred in determining that the payments received by BBL from Heritage in 1986 and 1987 were diverted by him to his personal use. This factual determination by the Tax Court is far from clearly erroneous. To the contrary, the finding is amply supported by the record. The uncontroverted evidence established that Pittman took the Heritage checks to Columbia Savings and Loan—where he, and not BBL, maintained accounts—and either cashed or deposited them. The evidence also revealed that the Heritage payments were not recorded or otherwise reflected on any of BBL's accounts receivable ledger sheets or other balance sheets. In short, there is not a shred of evidence that BBL ever received any of the value of the Heritage payments. In light of this substantive evidence linking Pittman to the Heritage payments and revealing that BBL received none of the value of those payments, the Commissioner clearly had a rational foundation for her determination that Pittman diverted the funds to personal use. Accordingly, the presumption of correctness properly attached to the Commissioner's determination and it was Pittman's burden to prove by a preponderance of the evidence that her determination was erroneous. See *Zuhone,* 883 F.2d at 1327; *Ruth v. United States,* 823 F.2d at 1093-1094 (7th Cir. 1987).

Here Pittman relied solely on his cross-examination of the government's expert to sustain his burden, and that examination completely failed to undermine the Commissioner's factual foundation for her determination. Nothing in that cross-examination affirmatively demonstrated that the money from the Heritage checks remained within BBL's corporate dominion. At most, the cross-examination on this issue revealed that a book or folder (or perhaps both) labeled "Heritage" was included among the records seized from BBL by IRS criminal investigation agents and that the government's summary witness, revenue agent Benham, was not familiar with the contents of that book or folder. Pittman argues that absent a review by the Commissioner of these documents, the determination that Pittman diverted the Heritage funds was arbitrary and excessive and therefore the Commissioner bore the burden of proof on the issue. See *Zuhone,* 883 F.2d 1317, 1327. Not so. Benham testified at length as to the fact that the BBL financial records she reviewed, which included accounts receivable ledger sheets, balance sheets, and income statements, agreed (within a few hundred dollars) with BBL's corporate income tax returns for the years 1979 through 1985 as well as the prepared but unfiled returns for 1986 and 1987. She concluded quite reasonably that this agreement between the records and the returns indicated that these records were used to prepare BBL's returns. A reasonable inference from this testimony is that the financial records reviewed by Benham constituted the entirety of BBL's corporate financial records. As Benham put it, there was "no room" for any other corporate financial records given the close agreement between those records that were reviewed and the corporation's returns. When the evidence as a whole is viewed in the light most favorable to the Commissioner, the most reasonable inference from the fact that there was a separately maintained set of records for the Heritage receipts (if, in fact, that is what was contained in the book or folder—and Pittman made no affirmative showing on this point), is that Pittman was maintaining two sets of records in furtherance of his fraudulent under-reporting of income. See *Spies v. United States,* 317 U.S. 492, 499, 87 L. Ed. 418, 63 S. Ct. 364 (listing the maintenance of a double set of books as an indication of fraud). Far from suggesting that the Commissioner's determination was arbitrary and excessive, this evidence is substantial evidence of his liability. The Tax Court's finding that the diverted Heritage receipts constituted a constructive dividend is a finding of fact that will not be set aside unless clearly erroneous. *Crowley v. Commissioner,* 962 F.2d 1077, 1080 (1st Cir. 1992); *Hagaman v. Commissioner,* 958 F.2d 684, 690 (6th Cir. 1992); *Loftin & Woodard, Inc. v. United States,* 577 F.2d 1206, 1215 (5th Cir. 1978). And, again, the finding here is amply supported.

Pittman's second ground for arguing that the Tax Court erred in determining that the Heritage receipts he diverted were taxable to him as constructive dividends, is that in order to be treated as a constructive dividend, an alleged distribution must inure to the personal benefit of the taxpayer and the Commissioner failed to demonstrate that Pittman enjoyed any such personal benefit. In this regard, he asserts that there was no evidence of any unusual expenditures by him or evidence of unexplained increases in his net worth. Accordingly, Pittman concludes that the Commissioner's deficiency assessment is not entitled to the presumption of correctness. As should be evident, this argument is simply a makeover of his first, adding as a twist a requirement that the Commissioner must demonstrate the taxpayer's benefit from the diverted funds before they can be considered a constructive dividend.

Pittman misapprehends the nature of the showing required to overcome the presumption of correctness here and mistakenly places the burden of proof on the Commissioner. In large measure, the foregoing analysis rejecting Pittman's first attack on the presumption also defeats the second. The evidence in this case linking Pittman to the Heritage checks is far more than a naked assertion by the Commissioner that he diverted the receipts. The evidence establishes that Pittman took the checks to his personal bank, not that of the corporation, and either cashed or deposited them. Moreover, there is no trace of the funds in the corporation's financial records. That evidence provided a rational foundation for the Commissioner to conclude that Pittman personally benefitted from the receipts and received a constructive dividend. At that point the burden was on Pittman to disprove this determination by a preponderance of the evidence. Because Pittman made no showing whatsoever that the Heritage receipts remained in corporate possession, the Tax Court reasonably concluded from the record as a whole that Pittman personally benefitted from the Heritage receipts and that they constituted a constructive dividend to him.

Although there is language in these Tax Court decisions noting the absence of evidence of lavish expenditures or unexplained increases in net worth, the opinions do not purport to establish that such a showing is a necessary prerequisite for according the Commissioner's determination a presumption of correctness. Perhaps recognizing this shortcoming in his showing, Pittman points to several other unreported income cases in which the court refused to accord the Commissioner's determination of unreported income the usual presumption of correctness, *Jackson v. Commissioner,* 73 T.C. 394 (1979); *Portillo v. Commissioner,* 932 F.2d 1128 (5th Cir. 1991); *Weimerskirch v. Commissioner,* 596 F.2d 358 (9th Cir. 1979), and he urges us to do the same here. However, those cases also have no relevance to this case. As explained in the Jackson opinion, "on rare occasions . . . in cases involving unreported income *where the respondent introduced no substantive evidence but rested on the presumption of correctness* and the petitioner challenged the notice of deficiency on the grounds that it was arbitrary," courts have declined to follow the general rule of not looking behind the notice of deficiency to examine the evidence used in making the determination. 73 T.C. at 401 (emphasis added). Thus in *Weimerskirch,* "the Commissioner called no witnesses and introduced no evidence." 596 F.2d at 359. "In view of the total absence of any substantive evidence in the record which could support the Commissioner's deficiency determination," id. at 362, the Ninth Circuit reversed the judgment of the Tax Court, which had accorded the presumption of correctness to that determination.

The Commissioner's case against Pittman stands on a much different footing than in *Weimerskirch* and *Portillo.* As has been emphasized repeatedly above, the evidence linking Pittman to the Heritage receipts is ample. The Commissioner's undisputed evidence—in fact it was stipulated to in the Tax Court (see Stipulation of Facts PP 19, 20)—established that Pittman took the Heritage checks and either cashed or deposited them at Columbia Savings and Loan where he held personal accounts and BBL held none. Thus this is not a case like *Portillo* where there was no factual basis establishing that the taxpayer had received the subject income or like *Weimerskirch* where there was absolutely no evidence supporting the Commissioner's determination that the taxpayer had received unreported income. Rather the facts in this case clearly provide a rational foundation for the Commissioner's determination that Pittman received a constructive dividend in the form of the Heritage receipts and that determination was entitled to the presumption of correctness. Pittman bore the burden of proving by a preponderance of the evidence that he did not receive a constructive dividend. In light of his complete failure to satisfy his burden, the Tax Court correctly found that the Heritage receipts constituted a constructive dividend that was taxable to Pittman as ordinary income.

For the foregoing reasons, the judgment of the Tax Court is affirmed in all respects.

AFFIRMED.

Dividends

A dividend is a distribution made by a corporation to its shareholders representing the profits the corporation has generated from its operations. Basically, a dividend represents the yield on the shareholder's investment in the same way that interest payments represent the yield on the lender's loan. Similarly to partnership distributions as discussed in the preceding chapter, dividends fall into two distinct categories: liquidating and nonliquidating. A **liquidating** dividend occurs when the corporation is terminating its existence, either by dissolution or reorganization (discussed in the next section of this chapter) and represents a capital gain or loss to the shareholder based on his or her basis in the corporate stock. A **nonliquidating** dividend is the typical dividend as defined above, representing a distribution of ordinary income to the investor.

For federal income tax purposes, dividends are defined in section 316 of the Internal Revenue Code. Nonliquidating dividend distributions may only be made from the current or accumulated earnings and profits of the corporation. These funds appear on the corporate balance sheet as its retained earnings. This source of funds is often referred to as the enterprise's **earnings and profits (E&P)**. Dividends may take the form of either cash, property, or stock, and the nature of this distribution has distinct tax implications:

> *Cash.* If a shareholder receives a nonliquidating dividend of cash, he or she must report such dividend as ordinary income and pay any taxes due thereon, based on the

liquidating dividend
Occurs when a corporation is terminated and is a capital gain or loss to the shareholder

nonliquidating dividend
Distribution of ordinary income

earnings and profits (E&P)
Net income derived from the operations of the business

shareholder's overall tax situation. The corporation makes this distribution directly from its retained earnings account and, as a consequence, the corporation no longer has access to these funds.

Example

A corporation issues a dividend of $0.25 per share. A shareholder owns 100 shares, and so receives a cash dividend of $25. This amount must appear on the shareholder's Form 1040 as dividend income.

Property. As a generalization, a distribution of corporate property only occurs with **closely held corporations,** those with relatively few shareholders whose shares are not publicly traded. Note, not all closely held corporations qualify for tax treatment under Subchapter S of the Internal Revenue Code, as will be discussed later in this chapter. With a property distribution, the corporation distributes to its shareholders property it already owns that appears on its balance sheet as assets, such as unsold inventory or equipment. Because dividends may only be paid from current or accumulated earnings and profits, the corporation uses the funds in its retained earnings account to "purchase" from itself the assets designated for distribution to the shareholders. In this fashion the corporation is able to use its E&P as ready cash, in the same way as if it had sold this property to disinterested third parties.

closely held corporation
A corporation owned by a limited number of shareholders and whose shares are not publicly traded

However, for the shareholder, when property is distributed to him or her as a nonliquidating distribution, the shareholder is required to report the fair market value of that property as ordinary income on the individual income tax return. Note that, because of depreciation rules permitted to all business enterprises by IRS (see Chapter 3), the value of this distributed property as it appears on the company books may be less than its fair market value.

Example

A closely held corporation that manufactures ladies' dresses has been unable to sell one of its models. The cost of each of these garments to the corporation is $10. It decides to distribute these dresses to its shareholders as a dividend. Each dress has a fair market value of $20. The shareholders must report income of $20 for each dress they receive, reflecting the fair market value, not the book value, of the item.

Shares of stock. If the corporation distributes shares of stock to its shareholders as a dividend, the shareholders do not recognize any income or gain on the value of those shares until the shares are sold or exchanged [IRC sec. 305(a)]. Basically, it is a nontaxable event, because when a shareholder receives shares of stock it merely changes his or her proportionate interest in the corporation. Because all shareholders are required by law to receive a proportionate share of the stock distribution, depending upon class of stock, in reality the shareholder's interest in the company has not changed but is simply reflected by a different number of shares [IRC sec. 307(a)].

However, if the shareholders are given the option to take a dividend in the form of cash or stock, the value of the stock is treated as ordinary income to the shareholder even if the shareholder elects to take the dividend in stock, and the dividend must be reported as such on his or her individual income tax return [IRC sec. 305(b)(1)]. The same result is true if the corporation makes a disproportionate stock distribution so that the shareholder's proportionate ownership is affected [IRC sec. 305(b)(2)].

Example

A shareholder owns 100 shares of stock in a corporation that represents a 1% ownership of the corporation. As a dividend the corporation distributes 1 share of stock for every 10 shares owned by the shareholders. After distribution the shareholder now owns 110 shares in the corporation, but her percentage ownership in the company remains at 1%, because all shareholders received a dividend of one-tenth of a share of stock for each share owned.

Exercise

What is your opinion of IRS differentiating the tax consequences of a cash, property, and share dividend? How do you think each of these distributions should be treated for tax purposes? Explain.

The following judicial decision indicates how the tax court views certain distributions to its shareholders for tax purposes.

TAX LAW & POLICY

KINCH v. COMMISSIONER
1942 TAX CT. MEMO LEXIS 67 (1942)

The Commissioner determined deficiencies in 1938 income tax of $3,398.05 as to Kinch and $1,490.98 as to Dark. The petitioners owned all the preferred and common shares of a corporation, and contend that part of a distribution to them which exceeded the corporation's available earnings should be treated as a reduction of cost of the preferred shares and not as capital gain, as respondent treats it. The facts are all stipulated and are hereby found as stipulated. Both returns were filed in the 28th District of New York.

Rock Asphalt & Construction Co., Inc., had outstanding 6,000 7 per cent preferred and 3,000 common shares. Each petitioner was an officer and director and owned one-half the shares of each class. The corporation's earnings available for dividends were $173,336.14. Dividends were declared and paid of $42,000 on the preferred and $150,000 on the common of which each petitioner received half. The total of these dividends exceeded the available earnings by $18,773.86. The cost to each petitioner of his preferred shares was $300,000, and none of this had been recovered by him through capital distributions; the entire cost of the common had been recovered through earlier distributions in excess of earnings and "accumulated surplus."

The petitioners argue that, since they were the only shareholders, the amount of $18,773.86, which was distributed to them in excess of available earnings, must be regarded, not as a dividend on common, as it was declared to be (albeit excessive), but as a recovery by them of part of the cost of their preferred. This theory cannot be supported on the evidence. There is no evidence of the financial or operating condition of the corporation, no explanation for the dividends, and no explanation of the earlier recovery of the cost of the common and not of the preferred. Petitioners simply argue that because the distribution on the common was in excess of earnings, the excess should, as a matter of law, be held to be a partial capital distribution on the preferred. This would reduce the tax basis of their preferred for the determination of future gain or loss. The argument upon the rights of the preferred shares is made as if this were a lawsuit to determine whether the common shareholders or the directors should be required to account for an improper distribution in derogation of the rights of the preferred shareholders. What might be the claims or defenses in such a suit could only be the subject of speculation; but if the evidence were no more than is here stipulated, the petitioners' demands would not necessarily be sustained, or petitioners' rationale adopted.

The facts stipulated are squarely within section 115 (d), Revenue Act of 1938, upon which respondent relies. The distribution of $150,000 made by the corporation to its common shareholders was not made in partial or complete liquidation, not out of pre-1913 increase in value, not, as to $18,773.86, a dividend in the statutory sense; and since the basis is, because of prior distributions, *nil,* and the $18,773.86 is therefore in excess of the basis, each shareholder's part of "such excess shall be taxable in the same manner as a gain from the sale or exchange of property." Whether petitioners, who controlled the corporation, were free to cause the distribution of the excessive amount as a liquidation of preferred, is speculative, as we have said; for the preferred was receiving its 7 per cent dividend, and perhaps, under the circumstances, that was all it was entitled to. From the bare figures alone, one could not conclude that the corporation's capital was being impaired. The determination is sustained.

Decision will be entered for the respondent.

Each corporation is regulated by the state statute of the state in which it is incorporated. Some jurisdictions mandate that the corporation only distribute shares of the same class of stock as a dividend, while some permit distributions of different classes of stock. Regardless, the tax consequences are the same: nonrecognition until sold or exchanged. However, the value of the shareholder's basis in the stock is increased by the value of the share so distributed on the date of the distribution.

Exercise

Determine whether your state permits its corporations to make share distributions of different classes of stock. Under what authority does this occur?

Exercise

How would a shareholder determine the value of the share distributed as a dividend? Indicate the difference in valuing the shares of a publicly traded corporation from one that is closely held.

intercorporate dividend
Dividend paid by one corporation to an interconnected corporation

Special rules apply if the shareholder is itself a separate corporation. In these situations, the provisions of section 243 of the IRC apply, which provide for certain dividend deductions to avoid the effects of multiple taxation on these **intercorporate dividends.** The amount of the deduction depends on the percentage ownership of the distributing corporation by the corporate shareholder. If the corporate shareholder owns less than 20% of the distributing corporation, it may deduct 70% of the dividend from its own taxable income. If it owns at least 20% but less than 80% of the distributing corporation, it may deduct 80% of the dividend. If the corporate shareholder owns at least 80% of the distributing corporation, it may deduct 100% of the dividend distributed to it.

Example

Acme Corporation has purchased 5000 shares of Beta, Inc. These 5000 shares represent a 2% interest in Beta. When Beta pays a dividend to its shareholders, Acme may deduct 70% of the dividend it receives pursuant to section 243 of the code because it owns less than 20% of Beta.

Sometimes a corporation will reacquire its shares from its shareholders, either because of contractual obligations or as part of a financial restructuring. This process is known as **redemption** and occurs when a corporation exchanges cash or property for its own shares that are held by shareholders [IRC sec. 317(b)]. Two tax implications are possible when a redemption occurs. Either the redemption will be treated as an exchange of property for stock or it will be treated as a nonliquidating distribution. The difference depends on whether the redemption falls within the purview of section 302(b) or 302(d) (redemptions allocation as dividend and return or capital) of the IRC.

redemption
Process by which a corporation repurchases its own shares

Section 302(b) lists four tests used to determine whether the redemption falls within its subsection:

1. The redemption will be treated as an exchange if the redemption does not have essentially the same effect as a dividend [IRC sec. 302(b)(1)].

2. The redemption will be treated as an exchange if its effect will be to substantially reduce the shareholder's interest in the corporation [IRC sec. 302(b)(2)]. To fulfill this requirement, after the redemption the shareholder must own less than 50% of the voting shares of the corporation and have had his or her percentage ownership reduced by 20% of both voting stock and common stock.

3. The redemption will be treated as an exchange if it results in a complete redemption of all of the shareholder's stock in the corporation [IRC sec. 302(b)(3)].

TAX LAW & POLICY

REV. RUL. 85-14
1985-1 C.B. 93 (1985)

ISSUE

Should qualification under *section 302(b)(2) of the Internal Revenue Code* of a redemption of one shareholder be measured immediately after that redemption, or after a second redemption of another shareholder that followed soon after the first redemption, under the following acts?

FACTS

X, a corporation founded by *A*, is engaged in an ongoing business. As of January 1, 1983, *X*'s sole class of stock, voting common stock, was held by *A*, *B*, *C*, and *D*, who are unrelated to each other. *A* owned 1,466 shares, *B* owned 210 shares, *C* owned 200 shares, and *D* owned 155 shares of *X* stock. *A* was president and *B* was vice-president of *X*.

X has a repurchase agreement with all *X* shareholders, except *A*. This agreement provides that if any such shareholder ceases to be actively connected with the business operations of *X*, such shareholder must promptly tender to *X* the then-held *X* shares for an amount equal to the book value of such stock. *X* has a reciprocal obligation to purchase such shares at book value within 6 months of such shareholder's ceasing to be actively connected with *X*'s business operations.

On January 1, 1983, *B* informed *A* of *B*'s intention to resign as of March 22, 1983. Based on this information, *A* caused *X* to adopt a plan of redemption and to redeem 902 shares of *A*'s *X* stock, on March 15, 1983, for which *A* received 700x dollars. Thus, *A* then held 564 shares of the 1129 shares (49.96 percent) of the *X* stock still outstanding, temporarily yielding majority control over the affairs of *X* until *B* ceased to be a shareholder. On March 22, 1983, *B* resigned from *X* and, in accordance with the *X* stock purchase agreement, *X* redeemed for cash all of *B*'s shares within the next 6 months, thus, leaving 919 shares of *X* stock outstanding, restoring majority control to *A*.

LAW AND ANALYSIS

Section 302(a) of the Code provides that if a corporation redeems its stock and if one of the paragraphs of subsection (b) applies, then such redemption will be treated as a distribution in part or full payment in exchange for the stock.

Section 302(b)(2) of the Code provides that a redemption will be treated as an exchange pursuant to section 302(a) if the redemption is substantially disproportionate with respect to the shareholder, but that this paragraph will not apply unless immediately after the redemption the shareholder owns less than 50 percent of the total combined voting power of all classes of stock entitled to vote.

Under section 302(b)(2)(C) of the Code, one of the requirements for the distribution to be substantially disproportionate is that the ratio that the voting stock of the corporation owned by the shareholder immediately after the redemption bears to all the voting stock of the corporation at such time, is less than 80 percent of the ratio that the voting stock of the corporation owned by the shareholder immediately before the redemption bears to all the voting stock of the corporation at such time.

Section 302(b)(2)(D) of the Code, in dealing with a series of redemptions, provides that section 302(b)(2) is not applicable to any redemption made pursuant to a plan the purpose or effect of which is a series of redemptions resulting in a distribution which (in the aggregate) is not substantially disproportionate with respect to the shareholder.

The percentage provisions contained in sections 302(b)(2)(B) and 302(b)(2)(C) of the Code provide "safe harbor" exchange treatment. Examined separately, the transaction that occurred on March 15, 1983, would qualify as a substantially disproportionate redemption because (i) A's ownership of X's voting stock immediately after the redemption was less than 50 percent of the total combined voting power of all the X stock and (ii) A's ownership of X's voting stock was reduced from 72.18 percent to 49.96 percent, which meets the 80 percent requirement of section 302(b)(2)(C). However, if A's redemption is considered to be part of a section 302(b)(2)(D) series of redemptions which included X's redemption of B's shares, then A's redemption would not constitute a substantially disproportionate redemption because (i) A's ownership of X's voting stock after the redemptions exceeded 50 percent of the total combined voting power of X and (ii) A's ownership of X"s voting stock after the redemptions was reduced from 72.18 percent to 61.37 percent, which does not meet the 80 percent requirement of section 302(b)(2)(C).

Section 1.302-3(a) of the Income Tax Regulations states that whether or not a plan described in section 302(b)(2)(D) of the Code exists will be determined from all the facts and circumstances.

In the present situation, although A and B had no joint plan, arrangement, or agreement for a series of redemptions, the redemption of A's shares was causally related to the redemption of B's shares in that A was an apparent opportunity to secure exchange treatment under section 302(b)(2) of the Code by temporarily yielding majority control over the affairs of X.

Nothing in section 302(b)(2)(D) of the Code or in the legislative history of this section (S. Rep. 1622, 83d Cong., 2d Sess., 234-235 (1954)) indicates that the existence of a plan depends upon an agreement between two or more shareholders. Thus, a "plan" for purposes of section 302(b)(2)(D) need be nothing more than a design by a single redeemed shareholder to arrange a redemption as part of a sequence of events that ultimately restores to such shareholder the control that was apparently reduced in the redemption.

Under the facts and circumstances here, section 302(b)(2)(D) of the Code requires that the redemptions of A and B be considered in the aggregate.

Accordingly, *A*'s redemption meets neither the 50 percent limitation of section 302(b)(2)(B) nor the 80 percent test of section 302(b)(2)(C). Thus, the redemption of *A*'s shares was not substantially disproportionate within the meaning of section 302(b)(2).

HOLDING

Under the facts of this ruling, qualification under section 302(b)(2) of the Code of *A*'s redemption should not be measured immediately after that redemption, but, instead, should be measured after *B*'s redemption that followed soon after *A*'s redemption.

4. The redemption will be treated as an exchange if it is in partial liquidation of the corporation [IRC sec. 302(b)(4)].

When the distribution is a liquidating distribution, the value of the distribution has the effect of adjusting the shareholder's basis in the corporation [IRC sec. 1001(a) and (b)]. The shareholder will then report any gain or loss as a capital gain or loss on his or her individual income tax return.

Reorganizations

The concept of a corporate reorganization is that a business is able to transfer and exchange assets without having to recognize any gain or loss at the time of such transfer or exchange. This nonrecognition applies at both the corporate and shareholder level (IRC secs. 354 and 361). The rationale for this nonrecognition treatment is that the business is continuing to operate but with different assets (and sometimes with a different focus), and therefore the investment in the enterprise continues and remains the same. Typically, in order to avail itself of the corporate reorganization provisions of the IRC, the corporation will apply for a private ruling letter indicating the IRS's willingness to treat the transfer as a nontaxable event.

Basically, corporate reorganizations fall into six main categories, depending on the nature of the reorganization.

Exercise

Explain why a corporation would want to obtain a private ruling letter prior to effecting the reorganization.

"A" reorganization
Corporate restructuring by a merger or consolidation

"A" Reorganizations

An **"A" reorganization** is a classical merger or consolidation, as defined under the appropriate state law [IRC sec. 368(a)(1)(A)]. Gener-

Income Taxation of Corporations

ally, a **merger** is a situation in which one corporation takes over and absorbs all of the assets and liabilities of another organization (referred to as the **target corporation** or **company**). The target corporation ceases to exist as a separate entity. In a **consolidation,** two or more corporations come together to form a new, separate corporation, transferring all of their assets, liabilities, and business to the new entity. In this situation the original corporations cease to exist and become part and parcel of the newly created entity. The tests used to determine whether these transfers qualify as a type-A reorganization are as follows:

A. If there is a continuity in the shareholders' interests in the new entity, meaning that they continue to have an ownership interest in the new entity
B. If the business enterprise continues to exist as a viable business entity [Regs. Sec. 1.368-1(d)(1)]

Example

A corporate publisher decides to acquire another, smaller publishing house. The publisher purchases the shares of the smaller house, and absorbs all of that house's assets and liabilities. The two publishers have merged, with the smaller house ceasing to have a separate existence.

"B" Reorganizations

A **"B" reorganization** can best be described as a corporate exchange, in which one corporation swaps stock for a controlling interest in a second corporation, represented by a controlling block of voting stock [IRC sec. 368(a)(1)(B)]. This exchange creates a **parent-subsidiary relationship** in which the acquired corporation is controlled by the acquiring corporation. The test used by IRS to determine whether the transaction falls within this category is whether the exchange is solely used to acquire the voting stock of the acquired entity.

Example

A television network makes an offer to the shareholders of a local newspaper to acquire their shares. Once the network purchases enough shares to control election of the board of directors, it has acquired a subsidiary corporation.

"C" Reorganizations

A **"C" reorganization** is another type of exchange in which one corporation swaps "substantially all of its assets" for shares of another

---

merger
One corporation absorbs another corporation; the one absorbed ceases its individual existence

target corporation or company
Company taken over as part of a merger

consolidation
Two or more corporations pool their resources and transfer them to a new entity; the original entities cease to exist

"B" reorganization
Corporate restructuring by an exchange

parent-subsidiary relationship
One corporation owning a controlling block of stock in another corporation

"C" reorganization
Corporate restructuring by an exchange that creates a holding company

holding company
A company whose income is derived solely from investments in other entities

corporation [IRC sec. 368(a)(1)(C)]. The result of this exchange is to create a **holding company,** by which the corporation that exchanged substantially all of its assets to acquire stock now no longer operates a business but produces income by receiving dividends from the corporation that acquired its assets.

Example

Many years ago a man started a manufacturing corporation of which he is the sole shareholder. He now wishes to retire, but still wants an income. He agrees to exchange all of the corporation's assets for shares of stock in one of his former competitors. The man has created a holding company from his former manufacturing corporation. Now all of that corporation's assets consist of shares of another company, and its income is derived from dividends that company distributes.

"D" reorganization
Corporate restructuring that creates a spin-off or a split-off

divisive transaction
Reorganization that creates a spin-off or split-off

spin-off
A corporation distributes to its shareholders stock in one of its controlled companies

split-up
Shareholders of a corporation relinquish their shares to acquire shares of a newly created corporation

nondivisive transfer
Transfer of assets that is similar to a "C" reorganization

"D" Reorganizations

A **"D" reorganization** requires that one corporation transfer all or part of its assets to another, controlled, corporation and then distribute the stock so acquired for the transfer of the assets in either a divisive or nondivisive transaction [IRC sec. 368(a)(1)(D)]. A **divisive transaction** is one in which one corporation forms a spin-off or split-up corporation from one of its divisions. A **spin-off** occurs when the corporation distributes to its shareholders stock in one of its controlled subsidiaries A **split-up** is similar to a spin-off except that the shareholders relinquish some of their stock to acquire the shares of the newly created corporation (IRC sec. 355). To qualify under this section of the IRC, the following requirements must be met.

A. The corporation that makes the distribution must be in control of the subsidiary prior to the transaction (have at least 80% voting power).
B. Both corporations must be actively engaged in business.
C. The corporations must have been actively engaged in business for at least the preceding five years.
D. The corporation making the distribution must distribute all of its securities in the controlled corporation, or at least enough to relinquish its controlling interest.
E. The distribution cannot be used simply as a method of attempting to distribute earnings and profits "tax free" [IRC sec. 355(a)(1)(B)].

A **nondivisive transaction** results when the transferor corporation's assets are placed with the transferee corporation, similarly to the exchange qualifying as a "C" reorganization. With an exchange that falls within this subsection, however, the transferor corporation also distributes any assets and securities it has received from the transferee corporation pursuant to the exchange.

"E" Reorganizations

An **"E" reorganization** is simply a recapitalization of the corporation's finances, primarily within the corporation's capital account [IRC sec. 368(a)(1)(E)]. Examples would be exchanges of stock for stock as in a corporate **stock split,** in which the shareholder's percentage ownership in the corporation remains the same but is represented by a different amount of stock, or exchanging bonds for stock, thereby reducing the corporate long-term debt and replacing it with equity.

"E" reorganization Corporate restructuring that changes the capital account of the corporation

stock split Method of restructuring capital whereby the same dollar amount represents a different number of shares than it did prior to the split

Example

Widget, Inc. has 1000 shares of stock outstanding with a capital account of $10,000. Each share has a value of $10. Widget announces a 2 for 1 split, meaning that each shareholder will receive 2 shares for each 1 share of stock he or she currently holds. After the split, there are 20,000 shares outstanding, but the capital account remains the same so that each of the shares now has a value of $5.

"F" Reorganizations

An **"F" reorganization** occurs when a corporation changes its identity, form, or place of incorporation, for example, if a New York corporation decides to reincorporate in Delaware because of Delaware's favorable antitakeover statutes, or a corporation reforms itself into an LLC.

As stated at the outset of this section of the chapter, the importance of these reorganizations is that they qualify for nonrecognition treatment for both the corporation and the shareholders.

"F" reorganization Corporate restructuring resulting in a change in the format of the entity

Exercise

Discuss how the nonrecognition tests discussed at the beginning of this chapter could be used to avoid recognition of gain for the six types of reorganizations discussed in this section.

Form 1120

Unless otherwise exempt, all domestic corporations must file Form 1120 regardless of whether they have taxable income. IRS also provides **Form 1120-A** (Exhibit 5.3), a short form income tax return,

Form 1120-A Simplified income tax return for C corporations

Form 1120-A — U.S. Corporation Short-Form Income Tax Return

OMB No. 1545-0890

Department of the Treasury, Internal Revenue Service

For calendar year 2002 or tax year beginning ...., 2002, ending ...., 20......
See separate instructions to make sure the corporation qualifies to file Form 1120-A.

2002

A Check this box if the corp. is a personal service corp. (as defined in Regulations section 1.441-3(c)—see instructions) ☐

Use IRS label. Otherwise, print or type.
- Name
- Number, street, and room or suite no. (If a P.O. box, see page 7 of instructions.)
- City or town, state, and ZIP code

B Employer identification number
C Date incorporated
D Total assets (see page 8 of instructions) $

E Check applicable boxes: (1) ☐ Initial return (2) ☐ Name change (3) ☐ Address change
F Check method of accounting: (1) ☐ Cash (2) ☐ Accrual (3) ☐ Other (specify) ▶

Income

1a	Gross receipts or sales	**b** Less returns and allowances	**c** Balance ▶ 1c
2	Cost of goods sold (see page 14 of instructions)	2
3	Gross profit. Subtract line 2 from line 1c	3
4	Domestic corporation dividends subject to the 70% deduction	4
5	Interest	5
6	Gross rents	6
7	Gross royalties	7
8	Capital gain net income (attach Schedule D (Form 1120))	8
9	Net gain or (loss) from Form 4797, Part II, line 18 (attach Form 4797)	9
10	Other income (see page 9 of instructions)	10
11	**Total income.** Add lines 3 through 10 ▶	11

Deductions (See instructions for limitations on deductions.)

12	Compensation of officers (see page 10 of instructions)	12
13	Salaries and wages (less employment credits)	13
14	Repairs and maintenance	14
15	Bad debts	15
16	Rents	16
17	Taxes and licenses	17
18	Interest	18
19	Charitable contributions (see page 11 of instructions for 10% limitation)	19
20	Depreciation (attach Form 4562)	20
21	Less depreciation claimed elsewhere on return	21a	21b
22	Other deductions (attach schedule)	22
23	**Total deductions.** Add lines 12 through 22 ▶	23
24	Taxable income before net operating loss deduction and special deductions. Subtract line 23 from line 11	24
25	Less: **a** Net operating loss deduction (see page 13 of instructions)	25a	
	b Special deductions (see page 13 of instructions)	25b	25c
26	**Taxable income.** Subtract line 25c from line 24	26
27	Total tax (from page 2, Part I, line 6)	27

Tax and Payments

28 Payments:
- **a** 2001 overpayment credited to 2002 — 28a
- **b** 2002 estimated tax payments — 28b
- **c** Less 2002 refund applied for on Form 4466 — 28c ( ) Bal ▶ 28d
- **e** Tax deposited with Form 7004 — 28e
- **f** Credit for tax paid on undistributed capital gains (attach Form 2439) — 28f
- **g** Credit for Federal tax on fuels (attach Form 4136). See instructions — 28g
- **h** Total payments. Add lines 28d through 28g — 28h

29 Estimated tax penalty (see page 14 of instructions). Check if Form 2220 is attached ▶ ☐ — 29
30 **Tax due.** If line 28h is smaller than the total of lines 27 and 29, enter amount owed — 30
31 **Overpayment.** If line 28h is larger than the total of lines 27 and 29, enter amount overpaid — 31
32 Enter amount of line 31 you want: Credited to 2003 estimated tax ▶ | Refunded ▶ 32

Sign Here
Under penalties of perjury, I declare that I have examined this return, including accompanying schedules and statements, and to the best of my knowledge and belief, it is true, correct, and complete. Declaration of preparer (other than taxpayer) is based on all information of which preparer has any knowledge.

Signature of officer   Date   Title

May the IRS discuss this return with the preparer shown below (see instructions)? ☐ Yes ☐ No

Paid Preparer's Use Only
- Preparer's signature ▶
- Date
- Check if self-employed ☐
- Preparer's SSN or PTIN
- Firm's name (or yours if self-employed), address, and ZIP code ▶
- EIN
- Phone no. ( )

For Paperwork Reduction Act Notice, see page 20 of the instructions.   Cat. No. 11456E   Form **1120-A** (2002)

Exhibit 5.3 Form 1120-A

Form 1120-A (2002) Page **2**

Part I — Tax Computation (see page 17 of instructions)

1. Income tax. If the corporation is a qualified personal service corporation (see page 17), check here ▶ ☐ ... **1**
2a. General business credit. Check box(es) and indicate which forms are attached.
   ☐ Form 3800 ☐ Form(s) (specify) ▶ **2a**
 b. Credit for prior year minimum tax (attach Form 8827) ... **2b**
3. **Total credits.** Add lines 2a and 2b ... **3**
4. Subtract line 3 from line 1 ... **4**
5. Other taxes. Check if from: ☐ Form 4255 ☐ Form 8611 ☐ Form 8697 ☐ Form 8866
   ☐ Other (attach schedule) ... **5**
6. **Total tax.** Add lines 4 and 5. Enter here and on line 27, page 1 ... **6**

Part II — Other Information (see page 19 of instructions)

1. See page 21 and enter the:
   a. Business activity code no. ▶ ....
   b. Business activity ▶ ....
   c. Product or service ▶ ....

2. At the end of the tax year, did any individual, partnership, estate, or trust own, directly or indirectly, 50% or more of the corporation's voting stock? (For rules of attribution, see section 267(c).) ... ☐ Yes ☐ No
   If "Yes," attach a schedule showing name and identifying number.

3. Enter the amount of tax-exempt interest received or accrued during the tax year ... ▶ $

4. Enter total amount of cash distributions and the book value of property distributions (other than cash) made during the tax year ... ▶ $

5a. If an amount is entered on line 2, page 1, enter from worksheet on page 14 instr.:
   (1) Purchases
   (2) Additional 263A costs (attach schedule)
   (3) Other costs (attach schedule)
 b. If property is produced or acquired for resale, do the rules of section 263A apply to the corporation? ... ☐ Yes ☐ No
6. At any time during the 2002 calendar year, did the corporation have an interest in or a signature or other authority over a financial account (such as a bank account, securities account, or other financial account) in a foreign country? ... ☐ Yes ☐ No
   If "Yes," the corporation may have to file Form TD F 90-22.1.
   If "Yes," enter the name of the foreign country ▶ ....
7. Are the corporation's total receipts (line 1a plus lines 4 through 10 on page 1) for the tax year **and** its total assets at the end of the tax year less than $250,000? ... ☐ Yes ☐ No
   If "Yes," the corporation is **not** required to complete Parts III and IV below.

Part III — Balance Sheets per Books

		(a) Beginning of tax year	(b) End of tax year
Assets			
1	Cash		
2a	Trade notes and accounts receivable		
b	Less allowance for bad debts	( )	( )
3	Inventories		
4	U.S. government obligations		
5	Tax-exempt securities (see instructions)		
6	Other current assets (attach schedule)		
7	Loans to shareholders		
8	Mortgage and real estate loans		
9a	Depreciable, depletable, and intangible assets		
b	Less accumulated depreciation, depletion, and amortization	( )	( )
10	Land (net of any amortization)		
11	Other assets (attach schedule)		
12	Total assets		
Liabilities and Shareholders' Equity			
13	Accounts payable		
14	Other current liabilities (attach schedule)		
15	Loans from shareholders		
16	Mortgages, notes, bonds payable		
17	Other liabilities (attach schedule)		
18	Capital stock (preferred and common stock)		
19	Additional paid-in capital		
20	Retained earnings		
21	Adjustments to shareholders' equity (attach schedule)		
22	Less cost of treasury stock	( )	( )
23	Total liabilities and shareholders' equity		

Part IV — Reconciliation of Income (Loss) per Books With Income per Return

1. Net income (loss) per books
2. Federal income tax per books
3. Excess of capital losses over capital gains
4. Income subject to tax not recorded on books this year (itemize) ....
5. Expenses recorded on books this year not deducted on this return (itemize) ....
6. Income recorded on books this year not included on this return (itemize) ....
7. Deductions on this return not charged against book income this year (itemize) ....
8. Income (line 24, page 1). Enter the sum of lines 1 through 5 less the sum of lines 6 and 7

Form **1120-A** (2002)

Exhibit 5.3 (Continued)

which may be used by a corporation that meets all of the following requirements.

A. Gross receipts under $500,000
B. Total income under $500,000
C. Total assets under $500,000
D. Only dividend income comes from domestic corporations which qualifies for the 70% dividends received deduction and are not from debt-financed securities
E. Small corporation that is exempt from the alternative minimum tax
F. No "write in" addition to tax (see later in the chapter)
G. No refundable tax credit other than the general business credit or credit for the prior year minimum tax
H. Not a member of a controlled group or a personal holding company
I. No ownership in a foreign corporation or partnership or trust and no foreign shareholders who own 25% or more of its shares

In addition, corporations may be required to file returns other than the 1120 or 1120-A. For a complete list of such corporations and the forms they must file, see the IRS instructions to Form 1120.

As with partnerships discussed in Chapter 4, the corporation, as a business entity that employs workers, may be required to file other forms and statements, especially if the corporation is a member of an affiliated group that would require the filing and attachment of a consolidated return, or if the source of the corporation's income falls within certain enumerated categories. However, a discussion of these additional forms is beyond the scope of this textbook, which is designed to discuss basic federal income taxation.

Practical tip

For a complete list and explanation of the additional potential filing requirements for corporations, obtain a copy of the instructions for Form 1120 and 1120-A from the IRS Web site.

It is important to note that all corporations that expect to pay at least $500 in income taxes are required to file quarterly estimated income taxes to ensure that at least 90% of all taxes due are paid in to the government by the fifteenth day of the last month of the corporation's tax year. Interest and penalties may be assessed for late estimated payment or if the amount of estimated taxes paid in falls below 90% of the total taxes due.

Practical tip

Use Form 1120-W to compute the amount of estimated taxes that will be due, and Form 4466 if the corporation has overpaid its estimated taxes and is due a refund.

The top of Form 1120 asks the corporation to indicate whether it is filing a consolidated return as part of (1) a controlled group, in which case it must attach Form 851 and supporting documents, (2) a personal holding company, in which case it must attach **Schedule PH** (*holding company* is defined earlier in the chapter), or (3) a **personal services corporation,** whose principal activity is to provide personal services such as law, accounting, and medicine. Generally, any corporation that is formed as a professional corporation under its state's laws would fall into this category.

The last section on the top of the return, question D, requires the corporation to indicate its total assets, as determined by the accounting method it has previously selected.

The basic portion of Form 1120 consists of three sections to report all income, deductions, and taxes and payments. To substantiate these figures, Form 1120 provides eight attachments, each of which will be discussed in turn. The return must be signed by an officer or director of the corporation, or a member of the LLC for those that have elected to be taxed as a corporation.

Schedule PH Attachment for personal holding companies

personal services corporation Company that only provides services, such as law or accounting

Income

Line 1 is used to report all gross sales and to indicate all returns and allowances. However, this item of gross receipts is not to include income from dividends, interest, rents, or royalties, each of which must be reported on lines 4 through 7 inclusive.

Line 2 permits the corporation to deduct from its gross receipts (less returns and allowances) the costs of its goods sold. To calculate this figure, the corporation must complete and attach Schedule A (see later in the chapter). The concepts of *gross receipts, returns and allowances,* and *cost of goods sold* have been discussed in previous chapters and do not need reiteration here.

Line 3 represents the corporation's gross profit, determined by deducting line 2 from line 1.

On line 8 the corporation states all of its net capital gain income. This amount is calculated on Schedule D, which is attached as a supporting document (see later in the chapter).

Line 9 is used to report the net gain or loss from the sale of business property that does not qualify either for capital gains treatment or regular sales income.

All other income is reported on line 10. For each item of such income, the corporation must attach a schedule indicating the source of the income and any deductions that were taken to arrive at a net amount. If the corporation has only one such item, it may be described in parentheses on this line. Examples of such other income would include:

- Recovery of bad debts, deductions for which were taken in prior years
- Amount of any recovery for previous deductions

Example

A corporation took a depreciation deduction for an item of equipment. The original cost of the item was $50,000, and it had depreciated it to a value of $20,000. At this point the corporation sold the equipment for $25,000. It must now report $5000 as "other income" for a depreciation deduction that it has "recaptured" in the sale.

- Ordinary income from partnership activity in which the corporation engaged during the taxable year
- Recaptured LIFO

LIFO stands for "last in, first out," and is a method used to calculate the cost of goods sold. Because materials used to create the company's goods are purchased over time, the cost of such items will vary. When valuing inventory, one method that may be used is LIFO, in which it is assumed that the most recently produced or purchased goods are the first that were sold. This item of other income will have to be calculated if the corporation used the LIFO method in the last tax year prior to its electing to be a Subchapter S corporation. The amount of this income is computed as the amount of the corporation's inventory calculated under the FIFO method that exceeds its value under the LIFO method. **FIFO** stands for "first in, first out," the exact reverse of LIFO.

LIFO
Last in, first out; method of valuing inventory sold

FIFO
First in, first out; method of valuing inventory sold

Example

A wholesaler purchases widgets for resale to retailers. Its purchase history is as follows:

January 2004: 1000 widgets at $5 per widget

February 2004: 1000 widgets at $6 per widget

March 2004: 1000 widgets at $7 per widget

When the wholesaler sells 1500 widgets in April 2004, its COGS would be $8000 according to the FIFO (1000 at $5 per widget and 500 at $6 per widget) method, or $10,000 according to the LIFO method (1000 at $7 per widget and 500 at $6 per widget).

Line 11 indicates the corporation's total income by adding lines 3 through 10.

Deductions

There is a limitation imposed on deductions for corporations. Unlike the sole proprietor, as discussed in Chapter 3, the corporation must capitalize certain costs incurred with the production of the following: real property and tangible personal property held (a) in inventory, (b) for use in its trade or business, or (c) in an activity engaged in for profit and real or personal property held for resale. This means that these items may not be included as an expense but must be calculated as part of the enterprise's basis in the property (IRC sec. 263A). Such items could include interest charges, taxes, compensation paid to officers for services rendered, and so forth. A detailed list appears in sec. 263A of the IRC and its accompanying regulations. These rules impact this second section of Form 1120, which concerns deductions permitted the corporation to reduce its taxable income.

Line 12 requires the inclusion of compensation paid to officers of the corporation provided that such item does not appear elsewhere on the return, such as in the computation of the cost of goods sold. Further, the corporation is not entitled to take a deduction for officers' compensation which exceeds $1 million during the tax year.

Practical tip

The officers whose compensation exceeds $1 million include the chief executive officer and those whose compensation must be reported to shareholders pursuant to the Securities Exchange Act of 1934.

Note that this compensation line relates only to publicly traded corporations.

Line 14 reflects all other salaries and wages paid to employees, reduced by the following credits:

- Work opportunity credit, reported on Form 5884
- Employment zone and community renewal employment credit, reported on Form 8844
- Indian employment credit, reported on Form 8845
- Welfare-to-work credit, reported on Form 8861
- New York City Liberty Zone business employee credit, reported on Form 8884

The amounts appearing on this line would include all fringe benefits paid to employees, but would not include amounts appearing as depreciation or other expenses associated with such benefits.

Example

A corporation provides an automobile to its employee as a fringe benefit. The depreciation the company takes on the car as well as its expenses for maintaining the car, because it holds title to the car, appears on lines 20 and 26 rather than as part of its employee's salary and wages on line 12.

Line 14 is used to deduct the costs of repairs and maintenance that do not appear elsewhere on the return and that do not add to the value of the property. Any expense that adds to the property's value must be depreciated or amortized, not expensed.

Lines 15 and 16 are used to indicate bad debt and rent expenses, items that have been addressed in earlier chapters.

Line 17 indicates tax and license expenses, but these items do not include the following:

A. Federal income taxes
B. Foreign income taxes if a credit is claimed
C. Taxes paid as part of the acquisition or disposition of property (basically what are referred to as transfer taxes), which are added to the corporation's basis instead
D. Local benefit taxes
E. Taxes that are deducted elsewhere on the return, such as in the calculation of COGS

Line 18 concerns interest payments made by the corporation. Note that if the loan was used for more than one purpose, the corporation must indicate the allocation of the proceeds of the loan, such as 25% for research and development and 75% to upgrade equipment. Certain items of interest are not deductible, including:

1. Interest that is exempt from income taxes
2. Prepaid interest if the corporation is a cash basis taxpayer
3. Interest on "straddles" [IRC sec. 263(g)]
4. Interest on a loan used to produce property that is used by the corporation for its own use or sale. These charges are capitalized (Regs. sec. 1.263A-8 et seq.)
5. Interest on which no tax is imposed [IRC sec. 163(j)]

6. Foregone interest on below-market loans
7. Original issue discount on certain high yield obligations [IRC sec. 163(e)]

Charitable contributions appear on line 19. Be aware that the total amount of the contributions claimed cannot exceed 10% of the corporation's taxable income before net operating loss (NOL) calculations (see later in the chapter). The amount of any contribution over this 10% limitation may be carried over for deductions for the following five years. The corporation must obtain a written confirmation of the contribution for all contributions valued at over $250. Also, if the contribution is one of property rather than cash, and the contributed property has a value of over $500, it must attach a schedule to indicate the type of property contributed and the method used to calculate its fair market value.

Practical tip

Certain appraisers specialize in determining the value of appreciated property given as a charitable contribution. These people should be employed to provide documentation to IRS, especially if artwork is the subject of the contribution.

The value of the contribution must be reduced by the income or capital gain the corporation would have realized if the property were sold at its fair market value [IRC sec. 170(e)(5)], and an increased deduction is permitted for computer equipment donated for educational purposes. The instructions provided with Form 1120 detail the exact manner of determining these decreases and increases for these contributions.

Exercise

Discuss the effects of different tax consequences of making charitable contributions by an individual, a partnership, and a corporation.

Lines 20, 21, and 22 concern depreciation and depletion, as discussed elsewhere in this textbook. Line 23 permits the corporation to take a deduction for its advertising expenses.

Contributions made to qualified pension, profit sharing, and other funded deferred compensation plans are reported on line 24. The corporation may also be required to file Form 5500 or Form 5500-EZ, for certain plans, and such filings are mandatory even if the corporation is not claiming a deduction for such contributions. These filings generally apply to plans that cover more than one participant or those that only cover the owner, provided that he or she owns 100% of the corporation.

Contributions to employee benefit programs that are not deducted elsewhere appear on Line 25.

All other deductions are reported on Line 26. Such items include insurance premiums, legal fees, utilities, and other such items as discussed in connection with partnership returns in Chapter 4.

The total amount of these deductions is then subtracted from the corporation's total income to arrive at its taxable income.

Line 29 permits the corporation to further reduce its taxable income by deducting its net operating loss and certain special deductions. A **net operating loss (NOL)** is a loss a business sustains that exceeds its income from operations. In any given tax year the business may only take this deduction to the extent that it does not exceed its taxable income. For any excess NOL, the corporation may carry it forward to use in succeeding tax years, once again limited to the amount of taxable income for that tax year.

net operating loss (NOL)
Loss occasioned to the operation of the business

Practical tip

Certain rules apply to specific situations with respect to net operating loss deductions. For details, obtain Publication 542.

Special deductions, as the term is applied on Form 1120, refers to certain deductions permitted with respect to dividends. These deductions appear on Form 1120 Schedule C, which will be discussed in the next section dealing with corporate income tax schedules.

Taxes and Payments

The final section of the main portion of Form 1120 consists of the computation of the corporation's taxes due. Line 30 notes the corporation's total taxable income, computed by subtracting the results of line 29 from line 28. If this amount is zero or less, the corporation has a net operating loss for the tax year in question. This NOL is first carried back for two tax years, and any excess may be carried forward. Using the NOL as a carryback requires the corporation to file amended returns for the previous tax years. However, the corporation may elect not to carry back any NOL, but use the NOL for deductions in future tax years. The corporation is also permitted to take a deduction for funds it places in a capital construction fund.

Exercise

Why do you believe IRS permits businesses to take a net operating loss carryback and carryforward, but does not allow an individual whose income is insufficient to meet expenses and who must use savings to cover the difference to do the same? Discuss.

Practical tip

For details on the capital construction fund deduction, obtain Publication 595.

The amount of tax due is then indicated on line 31 which is picked up from Schedule J (see later in the chapter).

Line 32 adjusts the amount of tax due by the amount of taxes the corporation has already paid toward that liability by means of estimated payments, credits for overpayment for the preceding year, and any refund due. The tax liability also is reduced by taxes deposited and credits for taxes paid on undistributed capital gains and the federal tax on fuels. If the corporation has not made any estimated tax payments, or its estimated tax payments do not equal either its current tax liability or its tax liability for the preceding year, it is subject to an estimated tax penalty, provided its tax liability is $500 or more. To determine whether the corporation owes such a penalty and, if so, the amount of the penalty, the tax professional must complete and attach Form 2220.

Line 34 states the amount of tax that the corporation still owes. If the amounts from line 32, when subtracted from line 31, result in an overpayment, the corporation indicates such overpayment on line 35. The corporation may elect to take this overpayment as a refund or to have it credited to its estimated taxes for the following tax year by indicating its choice on line 36.

The main body of Form 1120 is now complete, except for the appropriate signatures and date.

Form 1120 Schedules

Schedule A, Cost of Goods Sold If the corporation is either a "qualifying taxpayer" or a "qualifying small business" it may change its accounting method during the tax year, which could have a direct effect on how its inventory is accounted. A **qualified taxpayer** is one whose average annual gross receipts for the three prior

qualified taxpayer
Individual who completes Schedule A

qualified small business
Business that meets the definition of IRC sec. 448

tax years is $1 million or less and whose business is not a tax shelter. A **qualified small business** is one whose average annual gross receipts for the three prior tax years are more than $3 million but less than $10 million, whose business is not a tax shelter, and whose principal activity is not "ineligible" as defined in Rev. Proc. 2002-28 [IRC sec. 448(d)(3)]. Those taxpayers who fall within these categories may deduct the cost of raw materials and goods purchased for resale in the year the goods are sold. All other corporations must determine the cost of goods sold by reference to the goods on hand at the end of the tax year compared with the goods on hand at the start of the tax year (Regs. Sec. 1.471-1). These rules apply to the first three lines of this schedule: inventory, purchases, and labor.

TAX LAW & POLICY

REGS. SEC. 448

Sec. 448. Limitation on use of cash method of accounting
    (a) General rule
Except as otherwise provided in this section, in the case of a—
    (1) C corporation,
    (2) partnership which has a C corporation as a partner, or
    (3) tax shelter,
taxable income shall not be computed under the cash receipts and disbursements method of accounting.
    (b) Exceptions
    (1) Farming business
Paragraphs (1) and (2) of subsection (a) shall not apply to any farming business.
    (2) Qualified personal service corporations
Paragraphs (1) and (2) of subsection (a) shall not apply to a qualified personal service corporation, and such a corporation shall be treated as an individual for purposes of determining whether paragraph (2) of subsection (a) applies to any partnership.
    (3) Entities with gross receipts of not more than $5,000,000
Paragraphs (1) and (2) of subsection (a) shall not apply to any corporation or partnership for any taxable year if, for all prior taxable years beginning after December 31, 1985, such entity (or any predecessor) met the $5,000,000 gross receipts test of subsection (c).
    (c) $5,000,000 gross receipts test
For purposes of this section—
    (1) In general

A corporation or partnership meets the $5,000,000 gross receipts test of this subsection for any prior taxable year if the average annual gross receipts of such entity for the 3-taxable-year period ending with such prior taxable year does not exceed $5,000,000.

(2) Aggregation rules

All persons treated as a single employer under subsection (a) or (b) of *section 52* or subsection (m) or (o) of *section 414* shall be treated as one person for purposes of paragraph (1).

(3) Special rules

For purposes of this subsection—

(A) Not in existence for entire 3-year period

If the entity was not in existence for the entire 3-year period referred to in paragraph (1), such paragraph shall be applied on the basis of the period during which such entity (or trade or business) was in existence.

(B) Short taxable years

Gross receipts for any taxable year of less than 12 months shall be annualized by multiplying the gross receipts for the short period by 12 and dividing the result by the number of months in the short period.

(C) Gross receipts

Gross receipts for any taxable year shall be reduced by returns and allowances made during such year.

(D) Treatment of predecessors

Any reference in this subsection to an entity shall include a reference to any predecessor of such entity.

(d) Definitions and special rules

For purposes of this section—

(1) Farming business

(A) In general

The term "farming business" means the trade or business of farming (within the meaning of *section 263A(e)(4)*).

(B) Timber and ornamental trees

The term "farming business" includes the raising, harvesting, or growing of trees to which *section 263A(c)(5)* applies.

(2) Qualified personal service corporation

The term "qualified personal service corporation" means any corporation—

(A) substantially all of the activities of which involve the performance of services in the fields of health, law, engineering, architecture, accounting, actuarial science, performing arts, or consulting, and

(B) substantially all of the stock of which (by value) is held directly (or indirectly through 1 or more partnerships, S corporations, or qualified personal service corporations not described in paragraph (2) or (3) of subsection (a)) by—

(i) employees performing services for such corporation in connection with the activities involving a field referred to in subparagraph (A),

(ii) retired employees who had performed such services for such corporation,

(iii) the estate of any individual described in clause (i) or (ii), or

(iv) any other person who acquired such stock by reason of the death of an individual described in clause (i) or (ii) (but only for the 2-year period beginning on the date of the death of such individual).

To the extent provided in regulations which shall be prescribed by the Secretary, indirect holdings through a trust shall be taken into account under subparagraph (B).

(3) Tax shelter defined

The term "tax shelter" has the meaning given such term by *section 461(i)(3)* (determined after application of paragraph (4) thereof). An S corporation shall not be treated as a tax shelter for purposes of this section merely by reason of being required to file a notice of exemption from registration with a State agency described in *section 461(i)(3)(A)*, but only if there is a requirement applicable to all corporations offering securities for sale in the State that to be exempt from such registration the corporation must file such a notice.

(4) Special rules for application of paragraph (2)

For purposes of paragraph (2)—

(A) community property laws shall be disregarded,

(B) stock held by a plan described in *section 401(a)* which is exempt from tax under *section 501(a)* shall be treated as held by an employee described in paragraph (2)(B)(i), and

(C) at the election of the common parent of an affiliated group (within the meaning of section 1504(a)), all members of such group may be treated as 1 taxpayer for purposes of paragraph (2)(B) if 90 percent or more of the activities of such group involve the performance of services in the same field described in paragraph (2)(A).

(5) Special rule for certain services—

(A) In general—

In the case of any person using an accrual method of accounting with respect to amounts to be received for the performance of services by such person, such person shall not be required to accrue any portion of such amounts which (on the basis of such person's experience) will not be collected if—

(i) such services are in fields referred to in paragraph (2)(A), or

(ii) such person meets the gross receipts test of subsection (c) for all prior taxable years.

(B) Exception—

This paragraph shall not apply to any amount if interest is required to be paid on such amount or there is any penalty for failure to timely pay such amount.

(C) Regulations—

The Secretary shall prescribe regulations to permit taxpayers to determine amounts referred to in subparagraph (A) using computations or formulas which, based on experience, accurately reflect the amount of income that will not be collected by such person. A taxpayer may adopt, or request consent of the Secretary to change to, a computation or formula that clearly reflects the taxpayer's experience. A request under the preceding sentence shall be approved if such computation or formula clearly reflects the taxpayer's experience.

(6) Treatment of certain trusts subject to tax on unrelated business income

For purposes of this section, a trust subject to tax under *section 511(b)* shall be treated as a C corporation with respect to its activities constituting an unrelated trade or business.

(7) Coordination with *section 481*

In the case of any taxpayer required by this section to change its method of accounting for any taxable year—

(A) such change shall be treated as initiated by the taxpayer,

(B) such change shall be treated as made with the consent of the Secretary, and

(C) the period for taking into account the adjustments under *section 481* by reason of such change—

(i) except as provided in clause (ii), shall not exceed 4 years, and

(ii) in the case of a hospital, shall be 10 years.

(8) Use of related parties, etc.

The Secretary shall prescribe such regulations as may be necessary to prevent the use of related parties, pass-thru entities, or intermediaries to avoid the application of this section.

Line 4 applies only to those corporations that have elected to use a simplified method of accounting. For one such method, the **simplified production method,** certain costs are required to be capitalized. Such costs are detailed in Regs. Sec. 1.263A-2(b). For the other simplified method, the **simplified resale method,** additional costs are permitted to be used to determine the cost of goods sold. Such costs include:

simplified production method
Certain costs are required to be capitalized rather than taken as an expense

1. Offsite storage and warehousing
2. Purchasing, handling, repackaging, processing, and transporting
3. General administrative costs [Regs. Sec. 1.638A-3(d)]

simplified resale method
Allocation of costs to determine COGS

Other costs appear on line 5, which must be substantiated by an attached schedule. Lines 1 through 5 are then totaled, from which amount the inventory remaining at the end of the year is then subtracted. The resulting figure represents the corporation's cost of goods sold.

The remainder of this schedule requires the corporation to specify its method of accounting to indicate how the numbers appearing on the schedule were determined.

The number appearing on this schedule on line 8 is placed on the main body of Form 1120 on line 2.

Schedule C, Dividends and Special Deductions This schedule is used to account for the dividends the corporation receives as a shareholder of other corporate entities. It is divided into lines to reflect the source of the dividends received by the corporate taxpayer.

Lines 1 and 2 reflect dividends received by the corporate shareholder whose interest is less than 20% ownership in the distributing domestic corporation. These dividends are subject to the percentage deductions that have been discussed earlier in this chapter.

Line 3 is used to indicate dividends received by the corporation when such shares were acquired by means of debt financing, and lines 4 and 5 report dividends from public utilities to which the taxpayer owns less than or more than 20% of the utilities preferred stock respectively.

Lines 6 and 7 indicate dividends received from foreign corporations and line 9 accounts for dividends from wholly owned foreign subsidiaries of the corporation for which the corporation is permitted to take a 100% deduction [IRC sec. 245(b)].

The next three lines are used to report dividends received for which the corporate taxpayer is permitted a 100% deduction. The first is for dividends received from a domestic corporation by a small business investment company that operates under the Small Business Investment Act of 1958; the second is for dividends from FSCs [IRC sec. 245©(1)]; and the third is for dividends from affiliated groups [IRC sec. 243(a)(3)].

Exercise

Discuss the rationale behind the special deductions permitted the corporate shareholder. Do you agree with this policy? Why or why not?

The remaining lines reflect dividend income from other sources as specified on each such line (see Exhibit). Finally, public utilities may take a 40% deduction for dividends paid for the smaller of the dividends, paid on their preferred stock of their taxable income, without regard to any net operating losses [IRC sec. 172(d)].

Schedule E, Compensation of Officers This schedule is only completed if the corporation's total receipts equal at least $500,000.

Schedule J, Tax Computation The first two lines of this schedule are used to determine the tax liability of controlled groups, corporations that are interrelated by share ownership. The instructions accompanying Form 1120 provide a worksheet for such entities to compute their taxes, as well as the current tax rate schedule.

Qualified personal service corporations are taxed at a flat rate of 35%, and this appears on line 3 of this schedule. A corporation is a qualified personal service corporation if substantially all of its activities involve providing services in health, law, engineering, architecture, accounting, actuarial science, performing arts, or consulting, and at least 95% of its stock is owned by persons performing those services, retired employees who used to perform such services, or heirs of deceased employees who performed such services (IRC sec. 448).

Line 4 is used to indicate the alternative minimum tax (AMT), which is the minimum tax that would be owed unless the corporation qualifies as a small corporation. This means that it was treated as a small corporation for all tax years beginning after 1997 and its average gross receipts for the three tax years prior to the year in question did not exceed $7.5 million ($5 million if it had only one preceding tax year).

Line 6 and its subparts provide for recognition of various tax credits to which the corporation may be entitled. The nature of these credits has been discussed in earlier chapters in this textbook.

From the total tax due, appearing on line 5, all of the credits are subtracted to arrive at the tax due. However, certain adjustments may be necessary if the corporation is a personal holding company, as defined in IRC section 542 as previously discussed. Various other taxes may be due from the corporation as well, such as:

- Recapture of investment credit if the corporation disposed of the subject property before the end of its useful life [Form 4255]

- Recapture of low-income housing credit if the corporation disposed of the subject property [Form 8611]

- Recapture of Indian employment credit if the employee was terminated before one year [Form 8845]

These additional taxes, as may be inferred, are imposed when a corporation has received a tax benefit for engaging in a particular activity and has stopped that activity before the period mandating to receive that benefit.

The total of these adjustments results in the amount of total tax owed by the corporation, which appears as line 31 on the front page of Form 1120.

Schedule K, Other Information This schedule is used to provide IRS with general information regarding the operation of the corporation, and is self-explanatory by reference to Exhibit.

Schedule L, Balance Sheet As discussed earlier in the chapter, the corporation is required to provide IRS with a balance sheet to substantiate the figures it reports. This schedule is the form attachment for the production of that balance sheet. The items appearing on the balance sheet have been previously discussed.

Schedule M-1, Reconciliation This schedule is used to reconcile the amounts appearing on the balance sheet and the amount appearing on the tax return. This reconciliation is necessary because not all items posted to the balance sheet are reported on the tax return, and this schedule explains any discrepancy.

Schedule M-2, Analysis of Unappropriated Retained Earnings This schedule is used to indicate the distribution of the corporation's retained earnings and to ascertain whether the corporation might be liable for any excess business holdings tax, as discussed.

This completes the analysis of Form 1120, which is used to report income for "C" corporations.

Subchapter S Corporations

As discussed previously in the chapter, a Subchapter OL corporation is a domestic corporation that has only one class of stock and no more than 75 shareholders [IRC sec. 1361(a)(1)]. To qualify, the shareholders of the corporation must be individuals, excluding nonresident aliens, estates, trusts, or certain tax exempt organizations. For the purposes of Subchapter S treatment, a husband and wife are treated as a single shareholder.

Sections 1361 through 1379 of the Internal Revenue Code govern the treatment of Subchapter S corporations. The purpose behind the sections is to provide these qualifying small corporations the ability to be taxed, for federal income tax purposes, as a partnership rather than as a corporation, thereby permitting pass-through tax treatment, as discussed in Chapter 4. The election to be taxed as a Subchapter S corporation may be made each year that the corporation meets the definitional requirements of section 1361 [IRC sec. 1362(b)(1)]. To be valid, on the day the election is made all shareholders must agree to the election, because that choice has a direct and immediate impact on individual tax liability [Regs. Sec. 1.1362-6(b)(3)]. However, the election may be revoked by a vote of shareholders who own more than half of the outstanding shares. Also, the Subchapter S election may be terminated involuntarily if the corporation ceases to meet the definitional requirements as stated [IRC sec. 1362(d)(2)].

As with partnerships, once the corporation has qualified and elected to be taxed as a Subchapter S corporation, it is taxed in the same manner as a partnership, with all income, profits, and losses attributed to each partner according to his or her proportionate share of ownership. However, section 1366(d)(1) of the IRC limits the amount of losses that may pass through to the shareholder to that shareholder's aggregate basis in his or her shares. Any loss or deduction that cannot be taken in the tax year it is suffered, because of the loss limitation imposed by the IRC, may be carried over indefinitely and subsequently used when the shareholder's basis in the stock increases. It should be noted that such carryovers are deemed to be personal to the shareholder and are not transferred should the shareholder sell or exchange his or her stock.

Individual shareholders of the Subchapter S corporations, as distinct from trusts, estates, and so forth, are subject to the same at-risk rules specified for partners as detailed in Chapter 4. [IRC sec. 465]. Further, individual shareholders are limited to passive activity loss limitations under section 469 of the IRC. These passive activity limitations apply to any rental or passive income activity of the corporation in which the individual shareholder does not "materially participate." What qualifies as "material participation" is specified in Temp. Regs. sec. 1.469-5T(a). Generally, these passive activity losses may only be used to offset passive activity gains, but an exception exists that permits a shareholder to offset up to $25,000 against nonpassive income for real estate rental losses in which he or she actively participated. Any passive losses not used up in the year in which they were occasioned may be carried over indefinitely.

Despite the preceding, a Subchapter S corporation may still be subject to corporate-level taxation if it has accumulated earnings and profits and its passive investment income exceeds 25% of its gross receipts [IRC sec. 1375(a)]. To determine this potential tax liability, the total amount of the passive investment income is reduced by the expenses directly attributable to it. This figure is called the corporation's net

excess net passive income
Income derived from passive activities after expenses have been deducted

passive income. This number is then multiplied by the percent of the passive investment income that exceeds 25% of the gross receipts, which is then divided by the passive investment income for the year. The result is called the **excess net passive income,** and this amount is taxed at the highest corporate tax rate in effect.

The following judicial decision is presented to underscore the problems of passive activity losses and carryforwards with respect to corporate taxation, particularly with Subchapter S corporation.

TAX LAW & POLICY

ST. CHARLES INVESTMENT CO. v. COMMISSIONER
110 T.C. 46 (1998)

This case comes before us on cross-motions for partial summary judgment by the parties under Rule 121. The issues for decision are:

(1) Whether suspended passive activity losses (PAL's) incurred by a closely held C corporation that later elects to be an S corporation may be deducted by the then S corporation in the year the corporation disposes of its entire interest in the activity generating the losses, and if not,

(2) whether the basis of the assets used in the activity may be recomputed to restore amounts for portions of the suspended PAL's attributable to depreciation (and the gain or loss from the disposition commensurately recalculated).

BACKGROUND

At the time the petition was filed, Burton C. Boothby (petitioner) resided in Denver, Colorado, and St. Charles Investment Company (St. Charles) had its principal place of business in Englewood, Colorado. St. Charles filed its 1991 U.S. Income Tax Return as an S corporation with the Internal Revenue Service at Odgen, Utah.

Prior to 1991, St. Charles was a closely held C corporation as defined under section 469(j)(1). St. Charles operated rental real estate giving rise to PAL's under section 469 in 1988, 1989, and 1990. St. Charles elected S corporation status effective January 1, 1991. Immediately prior to the effective date of the S corporation election, St. Charles had suspended PAL's from its real estate activities.

During 1991, St. Charles disposed of certain of the rental properties (the properties). St. Charles reported the sales of the properties and deducted the suspended PAL's arising from the properties on its 1991 S corporation tax return. Six of the seven properties sold produced losses of $9,237,752; the seventh produced a gain of $6,161.

A portion of the suspended PAL's was attributable to depreciation for which St. Charles had adjusted the bases of the properties. St. Charles used these adjusted bases in calculating its gain or loss from the sales of the properties.

Effective March 30, 1995, St. Charles elected to terminate its S corporation status and reverted to C corporation status.

DISCUSSION

The parties have locked horns on the impact of sections 469(b) and 1371(b)(1). St. Charles contends that section 469 governs and that section 1371(b) has no application under the circumstances herein. Respondent takes a diametrically opposed position and contends that section 1371(b) controls and that therefore section 469 is inapplicable.

Section 469(a) disallows the PAL for the taxable year to any individual, estate or trust, any closely held C corporation, and any personal service corporation. The term "passive activity loss" generally means the amount by which the aggregate losses from all passive activities for the taxable year exceed the aggregate income from all passive activities for such year. Sec. 469(d)(1). However, a closely held C corporation, unlike the other taxpayers to whom section 469 applies, also may use its PAL for a taxable year to offset net active income for such year, and the amount so used will not be disallowed under section 469(a) Sec. 469(e)(2). The term "passive activity" includes any rental activity, with exceptions not relevant herein. Sec. 469(c)(2). Although section 469(a) disallows PAL's, section 469(b) provides: "Except as otherwise provided in this section, any loss or credit from an activity which is disallowed under subsection (a) shall be treated as a deduction or credit allocable to such activity in the next taxable year."

Section 469(f)(2) provides:

(2) Change in status of closely held C corporation or personal corporation.—If a taxpayer ceases for any taxable year to be a closely held C corporation or personal service corporation, this section shall continue to apply to losses and credits to which this section applied for any preceding taxable year in the same manner as if such taxpayer continued to be a closely held C corporation or personal service corporation, whichever is applicable.

Section 469(g)(1)(A) provides that, in the taxable year in which a taxpayer disposes of his entire interest in any passive activity in a transaction where all the gain or loss realized on such disposition is recognized, then generally, the excess of—

(i) any loss from such activity for such taxable year (determined after the application of subsection (b)), over

(ii) any net income or gain for such taxable year from all other passive activities (determined after the application of subsection (b)),

shall be treated as a loss which is not from a passive activity.

Thus, the usual result upon a taxable disposition of a passive activity is that the taxpayer may use any remaining suspended PAL allocated to that activity first against passive income from the same activity, then against net passive income from other passive activities, and then as a nonpassive loss.

The effect of making an election to be an S corporation is that, generally, an S corporation is not subject to income tax; instead, the shareholders are taxed on their respective shares of the items constituting the S corporation's taxable income. Secs. 1363, 1366. Section 1371(b)(1) provides that "No carryforward, and no carryback, arising for a taxable year for which a corporation is a C corporation may be carried to a taxable year for which such corporation is an S corporation." On the basis of this provision, respondent disallowed the deduction of the suspended PAL's.

Before proceeding to discuss the specific arguments of the parties, we think it important to recognize the purposes which underlay the enactment of sections 469 and 1371 and the overall context applicable to those sections. Section 469 was enacted in 1986 by section 501(a) of the Tax Reform Act of 1986, Pub. L. 99-514, 100 Stat. 2233, in response to legislative concern that certain categories of taxpayers were engaging in activities which generated losses and using those losses to shelter income from other activities. See *Schaefer v. Commissioner,* 105 T.C. 227, 230 (1995). It is essentially a TRANSACTIONAL provision, i.e., it deals with the tax treatment of particular activities. In determining the existence of a PAL, section 469 treats each activity separately.

Section 1371 was enacted in 1982 by section 2 of the Subchapter S Revision Act of 1982, Pub. L. 97-354, 96 Stat. 1669, as part of a continuing effort by the Congress to provide a statutory framework whereby shareholders of closely held corporations could obtain substantially the same tax treatment as they would have received if they had conducted their activities as a partnership without being required to accept the personal liability attaching to a partner. Thus, subchapter S, of which section 1371 was a part, dealt with the STATUS OF A TAXPAYER by permitting a corporation to continue as the same corporate entity but treating its income and deductions as those of its shareholders and taxing them accordingly. As we observed in *Frederick v. Commissioner,* 101 T.C. 35, 43 (1993):

> conversion from a C corporation to an S corporation does not create a new taxpayer or otherwise involve a transfer of assets and liabilities from one entity to another. Following its S corporation election, Quanta is still the same taxpayer; Quanta merely has subjected its income and expenses to a new taxing regime for Federal income tax purposes. * * *

This structural difference, i.e., transactional versus taxpayer status, is a significant element in synthesizing the application of sections 469(b) and 1371(b)(1). It facilitates our ability to take into account the objectives of Congress, namely, (1) including section 469(b) to ease the restrictive thrust of section 469 generally by limiting, but not necessarily eliminating, use of PAL's, and (2) including section 1371(b)(1) to narrow the liberalizing thrust of subchapter S generally, and to prevent abuse by limiting, but not necessarily eliminating, the ability of a corporation to utilize subchapter S status to pass on its C status losses to its shareholders, see *Rosenberg v. Commissioner,* 96 T.C. 451, 455 (1991).

Respondent's position is straightforward. Respondent maintains that section 1371(b)(1) is clear on its face and that the word "carryforward" in that section is not limited and encompasses PAL's. Respondent argues that nothing in the legislative history of either section 1371(b)(1) or 469 casts doubt on respondent's position and that petitioner's attempts to accord a narrow interpretation to the word "carryforward," both directly and by interpolating section 469, are unavailing.

Petitioner's arguments fall into two categories: (1) Suspended PAL's are not "carryforwards" within the meaning of section 1371(b)(1), because the PAL rules, set forth in section 469, constitute an accounting method which St. Charles should continue to use after its conversion to an S corporation; and (2) pursuant to principles of statutory construction, the specific language of section 469, particularly subsections (f)(2) and (g)(1)(A), precludes the application of section 1371(b)(1). Petitioner asserts that, unless it is permitted to utilize the suspended PAL's in the year of disposition of the activities giving rise to them, its right to use those PAL's will be lost forever.

We deal first with petitioner's position in respect of the proper interpretation of section 1371(b)(1). Clearly, Congress could not have had PAL's specifically in mind when it enacted section 1371(b)(1) in 1982, since section 469 was not enacted until 1986. But even petitioner does not suggest that this factor, in and of itself, is determinative. Rather, petitioner goes on to argue that the word "carryforward" was intended to refer only to those items which are specifically so described in other provisions of the Code. We disagree.

In construing the meaning of a statute, we seek the plain meaning of its language, assuming that Congress uses common words in their popular meaning, and relying on the words as generally understood. *Norfolk S. Corp. v. Commissioner,* 104 T.C. 13, 36-37 (1995) and cases cited thereat, modified 104 T.C. 417 (1995). The language of section 1371(b) ("No carryforward, and no carryback") is broad, unlike that of other sections which specify certain types of carryforwards and carrybacks. See supra note 4. The legislative history of section 1371(b) supports a broad interpretation in that the prohibition reflected in this provision appears in similar terms and follows a list of specific examples of passthrough items. S. Rept. 97-640 (1982), 1982-2 C.B. 718, 725; H. Rept. 97-826 (1982), 1982-2 C.B. 730, 737. Although section 469(b) does not use the term "carryforward," we think the phrase "shall be treated as a deduction * * * allocable to such activity in the next taxable year" has the same meaning. We think this is particularly true in the case of a closely held C corporation where passive losses are available as deductions against active losses. Our view in this respect is reinforced by that fact that the Senate Finance Committee report, accompanying the enactment of section 469, states that "Suspended passive activity losses for the year are CARRIED FORWARD indefinitely, but are not carried back" (emphasis added). S. Rept. 99-313 (1986), 1986-3 C.B. (Vol. 3) 1, 722; see also H. Conf. Rept. 99-841 (Vol. II) (1986), 1986-3 C.B. (Vol. 4) 1, 137, describing the Senate version of section 469 (there was no House of Representatives version) as providing that "Disallowed losses and credits are CARRIED FORWARD" (emphasis added). Moreover, while we recognize that the use of captions is limited, see section 7806(a), we think it not amiss, in the context of this case, to note that section 469(b) is entitled "Disallowed Loss or Credit CARRIED to Next Year" (emphasis added).

Petitioner points to Congress' placement of section 469 within subchapter E, part II of the Code, entitled "Methods of Accounting." Petitioner argues that the PAL rules, like other methods of accounting, such as basis and depreciation, are to be continued after a C corporation becomes an S corporation. As the subject of an accounting method, petitioner argues, PAL's are not carryovers within the meaning of section 1371(b)(1).

"The term 'method of accounting' includes not only the overall method of accounting of the taxpayer but also the accounting treatment of any item." Sec. 1.446-1(a)(1), Income Tax Regs. A material item, for purposes of a method of accounting, is any item which involves the proper time for the inclusion of the item in income or the taking of a deduction. Sec. 1.446-1(e)(2)(ii), Income Tax Regs. The legislative history of section 469 expresses concern over the mismatching of deductions and income from passive activities which leads to the sheltering of other income. S. Rept. 99-313, supra, 1986-3 C.B. (Vol. 3) at 716-717.

An accounting method addresses the TIMING of the deduction of an item, it does not provide for any deduction per se. Sec. 1.446- 1(a)(1), Income Tax Regs., states: "These methods of accounting for special items include the accounting treatment prescribed for research and experimental expenditures, soil and water conservation expenditures, depreciation, net operating losses, etc." Section 1371(b)(1) clearly precludes the carryover of net operating losses (NOLs). *Rosenberg v. Commissioner, supra;* cf. sec. 1374(b)(2) (allowing NOL carryforward "Notwithstanding section 1371(b)(1)"). Similarly, it appears Congress intended section 1371(b)(1) to apply to carryover of research and other business credits. See sec. 1374(b)(3)(B) (allowing business credit carryforwards "Notwithstanding section 1371(b)(1)"). In short, Congress evinced an intention to recognize specific exceptions, rather than a general exception to the application of section 1371(b)(1). It does not follow, as petitioner suggests, from the fact that the statute specifies certain items to be excluded from the application of section 1371(b) for one purpose, namely built-in gains under section 1374, that other items are excluded from the application of section 1371(b) for other purposes.

Thus, even if section 469 is treated as an accounting method, we are still left with the question whether section 1371(b)(1) applies to a particular item, in this case, PAL's. Moreover, we note that, although Congress placed section 469 in a part of the Code entitled "Methods of Accounting," the legislative history indicates that such treatment is not as significant as petitioner would have us believe. The statute itself and the legislative history treat section 469 separately from the provisions dealing with accounting matters. Compare title V entitled "Tax Shelter Limitations; Interest Limitations," which includes the provisions of section 469, with title VIII "Accounting Provisions" of the Tax Reform Act of 1986, Pub. L. 99-514, 100 Stat. 2085, 2233–2249, 2345–2375; H. Conf. Rept. 99-841 (Vol. II), supra, 1986-3 C.B. (Vol. 4) at 134, 285.

We are not impressed by petitioner's attempt to reinforce the "method of accounting" argument that PAL's should not be treated in the same fashion as NOL's under section 1371(b)(1) by pointing to the fact that the regulations under section 469 disallow ratably the deductions which enter into the determination of whether the taxpayer has incurred a PAL. The regulations upon which petitioner bases this argument provide:

(ii) ALLOCATION WITHIN LOSS ACTIVITIES—(A) IN GENERAL. If all or any portion of a taxpayer's loss from an activity is disallowed under paragraph (f)(2)(i) of this section for the taxable year, A RATABLE PORTION OF EACH PASSIVE ACTIVITY DEDUCTION (OTHER THAN AN EXCLUDED DEDUCTION (within the meaning of paragraph (f)(2)(ii)(B) of this section)) of the taxpayer from such activity IS DISALLOWED. * * *

* * *

(iii) SEPARATELY IDENTIFIED DEDUCTIONS. "In identifying the deductions from an activity that are disallowed under this paragraph (f)(2), the taxpayer need not account separately for a deduction unless such deduction may, if separately taken into account, result in an income tax liability for any taxable year different from that which would result were such deduction not taken into account separately. * * * Sec. 1.469-1T(f)(2), Temporary Income Tax Regs., 53 Fed. Reg. 5706 (Feb. 25, 1988); emphasis added.

According to petitioner, these regulations make it clear that deductions do not lose their character in determining a PAL but are the items that are carried over under section 469(b) whereas such deductions lose their character in the case of an NOL. We think petitioner reads too much into the regulations and in effect ignores the word "loss" in section 469(b). In this connection, we note that, with respect to section 469, the conference report on the Tax Reform Act of 1986 speaks of "Deductions in excess of income (i.e. losses)" and states: "DISALLOWED LOSSES and credits are carried forward and treated as deductions and credits from passive activities in the next taxable year." (Emphasis added.) H. Conf. Rept. 99-841 (Vol. II), 1986-3 C.B. (Vol. 4) at 137. In sum, we view section 469 as denying the PAL deduction with the regulations merely supplying the mechanics for allocating expenses among the taxpayer's various activities in order to calculate the amount of expenses to be deducted in computing the PAL from a particular activity.

Going beyond the "method of accounting" argument, petitioner points to specific provisions of section 469 to support the position that PAL's are not carryovers for purposes of section 1371(b)(1). Petitioner argues that, since PAL's are not personal to the taxpayer but may follow the property as basis adjustments in certain types of transfers, PAL's more closely resemble basis (which does "carry over" from C corporation to S corporation) than NOL's (which do not).

In the cases of a disposition of an interest in a passive activity by gift or distribution of such an interest by an estate or trust, the basis of the interest is increased by the suspended PAL's allocated to that activity. Sec. 469(j)(6), (12).

However, while the increase in basis affords the recipient the benefit of using the equivalent of the suspended PAL's upon the recipient's disposition of the activity, the original taxpayer is denied any deduction of the suspended PAL's in any taxable year. Sec. 469(j)(6), (12). Where the taxpayer transfers the interest in the passive activity by reason of death, the suspended PAL's allocated to that activity are treated as if there were a sale, but only to the extent that the PAL's allocated to that activity exceed the step-up in basis by reason of death to the transferee. Sec. 469(g)(2). The taxpayer is denied the deduction in any taxable year of the amount of the PAL's allocated to the disposed of activity which equal the amount of the basis step-up. Id.

We are not convinced by petitioner's arguments that suspended PAL's of St. Charles should be treated as basis adjustments and therefore should not be considered carryforwards within the meaning of section 1371(b)(1).

Finally, petitioner argues that, even if PAL's are carryforwards, section 469 is a specific provision which should prevail over the general provisions reflected by section 1371(b)(1). It is a basic principle of statutory construction that a specific statute controls over a general provision. *Bulova Watch Co. v. United States,* 365 U.S. 753, 758, 6 L. Ed. 2d 72, 81 S. Ct. 864 (1961). However, when two statutes are capable of coexistence, "it is the duty of the courts, absent a clearly expressed congressional intention to the contrary, to regard each as effective." *Vimar Seguros Y. Reaseguros, S.A. v. M/V Sky Reefer,* 515 U.S. 528, 533, 132 L. Ed. 2d 462, 115 S. Ct. 2322 (1995); see *DeSalvo v. IRS,* 861 F.2d 1217, 1219 (10th Cir. 1988).

Petitioner points to section 469(b), (f)(2), and (g)(1) to sustain this position. Petitioner argues that the clause "Except as otherwise provided IN THIS SECTION" (emphasis added) in section 469(b) dictates the conclusion that section 1371(b)(1), not being in section 469, does not apply to PAL's and, therefore, St. Charles should be allowed to use the suspended PAL's.

As previously noted, see supra p. 5, section 469(b) provides: "Except as otherwise provided in this section, any loss or credit from an activity which is disallowed under subsection (a) shall be treated as a deduction or credit allocable to such activity in the next taxable year."

Section 469(b) accomplishes two things: (1) It maintains the deductibility of suspended PAL's activity by activity, important to the overall working of section 469, and (2) it allows the taxpayer further opportunity to take such a loss. Even without the interplay of section 1371(b)(1), section 469(b) does not mean the taxpayer must recognize the loss in the immediately following year; the taxpayer may not have sufficient passive activity income to use all or any of the suspended PAL's in that year. In such case, the unused suspended PAL's are again disallowed and will be similarly treated as a deduction in the next (third) year, and so on. See H. Conf. Rept. 99-841 (Vol. II), supra, 1986-3 C.B. (Vol. 4) at 137; S. Rept. 99- 313, supra, 1986-3 C.B. (Vol. 3) at 722 (where it is specified that suspended PAL's are "carried forward indefinitely").

Petitioner further points out that it is only using the suspended PAL's allocated to the properties which were sold, and not those allocated to other activities that St. Charles conducted. Petitioner goes on to argue that the losses at issue stem entirely from the operation of section 469(g)(1)(A), see supra p. 5, not from section 469(a) and (b); that is, they consist solely of excess PAL's that "shall be treated as a loss which is not from a passive activity." This, petitioner argues, is another reason why the losses which respondent disallowed are not carryovers and therefore section 1371(b) is inapplicable.

The application of section 469(g)(1)(A), however, turns on the meaning of the parenthetical phrase "determined after the application of subsection (b)" which appears twice therein, once with respect to the disposed activity and then with respect to all other passive activities. There is no way to determine the amount of excess PAL's to be treated as nonpassive losses without the application of section 469(b). Indeed, a principal function of section 469(g) is to take into account the suspended PAL's created by section 469(a) and (b). Although the excess PAL's are no longer treated as PAL's, they are derived from suspended PAL's.

In our view, a precondition to the applicability of the parenthetical language in section 469(g)(1)(A) is that the suspended PAL's be available under section 469(b). Our previous analysis indicates that section 1371(b) makes the PAL's unavailable in the year at issue and therefore precludes the application of section 469(b) and consequently section 469(g)(1)(A).

Petitioner further argues that section 469(f)(2) provides specifically for the situation at issue herein. That section provides:

If a taxpayer ceases for any taxable year to be a closely held C corporation * * *, this section shall continue to apply to losses and credits to which this section applied for any preceding taxable year in the same manner as if such taxpayer continued to be a closely held C corporation * * *.

Respondent responds that the legislative history of section 469(f)(2) indicates that this section was meant to apply to closely held C corporations that become "regular" C corporations, not to those that become S corporations.

While the legislative history discusses a closely held C corporation that, due to change in stock ownership, is no longer closely held, it does so as an example of the situation that arises "when a corporation * * * subject to the passive loss rule ceases to be subject to the passive loss rule because it ceases to meet the definition of an entity subject to the rule." S. Rept. 99-313, supra, 1986-3 C.B. (Vol. 3) at 728. Under these circumstances and given the broad statutory language, we think that section 469(f)(2) applies to St. Charles, which ceased to be a closely held C corporation by virtue of its subchapter S election.

Section 469(f) ensures that once a taxpayer has suspended PAL's, the taxpayer's use of the suspended PAL's continues to be subject to section 469. Thus, section 469(f)(1) provides that, where the activity is no longer passive with respect to the taxpayer, the unused PAL's are to be used to offset income from that activity, and any remaining PAL's shall be treated as arising from a passive activity. Section 469(f)(2) provides that PAL's shall continue to be treated as such where the taxpayer is no longer a closely held C corporation (and otherwise would not be subject to section 469). Thus, the passive nature of St. Charles' PAL's are preserved.

Petitioner argues that section 469(f)(2) requires St. Charles to use the suspended PAL's and that, if it is not permitted to use them against the gains from the disposition of the disposed passive activities, it will be denied the use of the PAL's forever. Petitioner seeks to buttress this position by arguing that section 469(b) allows those PAL's disallowed under section 469(a) to be used in subsequent years and that, if section 1371(b)(1) disallows the PAL's, section 469 does not apply because there is no other basis for allowing their subsequent use. Respondent argues that since St. Charles is the same taxpayer, albeit subject to a different taxing regime, section 1371(b)(1) merely prevents it from using the PAL's during the "new regime" but does not preclude their preservation for use by St. Charles when that "new regime" ends and St. Charles becomes a taxpayer subject to section 469, as a closely held C corporation.

We think petitioner's position [**31] as to the dire consequence of applying section 1371(b) is unfounded in that it ignores the pattern reflected by section 1371(b) in its entirety, which provides:

(b) No Carryover Between C Year and S Year.—

(1) From C year to S year.—No carryforward, and no carryback, arising for a taxable year for which a corporation is a C corporation may be carried to a taxable year for which such corporation is an S corporation.

(2) No carryover from S year.—No carryforward, and no carryback, shall arise at the corporate level for a taxable year for which a corporation is an S corporation.

(3) Treatment of S year as elapsed year.—Nothing in paragraphs (1) and (2) shall prevent treating a taxable year for which a corporation is an S corporation as a taxable year for purposes of determining the number of taxable years to which an item may be carried back or carried forward.

The clear import of section 1371 is that a change in the taxing regime applicable to a taxpayer as it moves from being an S corporation to a C corporation or vice versa should not be an occasion for permitting prior losses of one taxpayer from inuring to the benefit of another taxpayer. Thus, the losses of a C corporation should not inure to the benefit of its shareholders, thereby giving them an opportunity to utilize a deduction which would not otherwise have been available to them. Sec. 1371(b)(1). Similarly, losses of an S corporation, which pass through, i.e., inure to the benefit of, its shareholders should not be taken away from them for tax purposes in order to offset income of their corporation which has forgone its S status. Sec. 1371(b)(2). To round out the picture, section 1371(b)(3) makes it clear that the losses remain available for future use although the clock will continue to tick for the purpose of computing the period of availability. Consequently, the application of section 1371(b)(1) to preclude St. Charles from using its PAL's during the year before does not extend to destroying their availability. See *Amorient, Inc. v. Commissioner,* 103 T.C. 161, 167 (1994). In this connection, we think it significant that, unlike NOL's, PAL's may be carried over indefinitely. See S. Rept. 99-313, supra, 1986-3 C.B. (Vol. 3) at 722. Under section 469(b), contrary to petitioner's contention of permanent loss, they remain available for potential use in subsequent years if and when St. Charles relinquishes its S status.

In sum, we are satisfied that PAL's are losses within the meaning of section 1371. Not only is the word "carryforward" in that section unqualified, but PAL's are in effect NOL's albeit computed separately for a particular activity and thus should not be treated any differently than NOL's to which section 1371 unquestionably applies.

Taking into account the language of the statute and the legislative history, including the objective of Congress in enacting sections 469(b) and 1371(b)(1), we conclude that St. Charles is precluded from carrying forward its suspended PAL's to the taxable year before us. We emphasize that, as our analysis has revealed, there is no conflict between sections 469(b) and 1371(b)(1) with the result that our preclusion of use in 1991 is grounded on the unavailability of the PAL's during that year and their continued availability for future use.

In keeping with the foregoing, respondent's motion for partial summary judgment is granted, and petitioner's motion is denied.

Distributions from a Subchapter S corporation of appreciated property, either as a liquidating or nonliquidating distribution, are treated as recognition events at the corporate level in order to prevent shareholders from receiving a stepped-up basis in the distributed property without having that gain taxed. Such distributions, for federal tax purposes, are treated as though the corporation sold the appreciated assets to the shareholders at their fair market values.

Electing to be treated as a Subchapter S corporation may have certain advantages. If the shares become worthless, the shareholder may be entitled to a deduction under section 165(g) of the IRC. Subchapter S status can provide a method of splitting income from a family business to family members who are in a lower tax bracket. Because Subchapter S corporations are basically taxed like a partnership, they avoid the two-tiered level of taxation of C corporations, while still providing the shareholders limited personal liability, an attribute they would not have if the business were organized as a general partnership. However, it must be noted that because LLCs offer similar types of advantages without the attendant requisite formalities of corporations, it is possible that Subchapter S corporations may become outdated.

Exercise

Discuss the advantages and disadvantages of electing to be taxed as a Subchapter S corporation.

Form 1120S

All corporations that have elected to be taxed as a Subchapter S corporation must file Form 1120S.

Practical tip

The Subchapter S election is made by completing and filing Form 2553 with the IRS.

Once the election to be taxed as a Subchapter S corporation is made, it stays in effect until it is terminated in one of the following ways.

1. The election is revoked with the consent of the shareholders of at least 50% of the outstanding shares.

2. The election will be automatically revoked if the corporation no longer meets the definitional requirements under section 1361(b) of the code.

3. The election will be automatically terminated if the corporation has accumulated earnings and profits and has derived more than 25% of its gross receipts from passive investment income for each of three consecutive tax years.

Practical tip

If the termination was made automatically, the corporation may challenge that termination. Regs. Sec. 1.1362-4 specifies the requirements for obtaining inadvertent termination relief.

Form 1120S generally follows the format used for C corporations and for partnerships. It would beleaguer the point to repeat all of the information already provided with respect to the method of completing those forms and, therefore, for this section of the text only those items that are specific to Subchapter S corporations will be discussed. Review Exhibit 5.2.

Note that a Subchapter S corporation may not use the cash method of accounting if it qualifies as a tax shelter under section 448(d)(3) of the IRC. As a general rule, Subchapter S corporations are usually required to use the accrual method of accounting for sales and purchases of inventory items; however, the corporation should use the method that most truly reflects its income flow.

Practical tip

Security dealers operating as a Subchapter S corporation must use the "mark-to-market" method of accounting detailed in section 475 of the code. Because this is a specific type of Subchapter S corporation, it is beyond the scope of this textbook to discuss its peculiarities in detail, and the practitioner is directed to that section of the IRC.

As mentioned, there is a limitation imposed on loss deductions permitted for passive activities. However, these limitations apply to the shareholder, not the corporation. As with partnership returns, the Subchapter S corporation must report income and losses for each activity separately. As with partnership returns discussed in the previous chapter, activities also may be grouped for reporting purposes. The tax practitioner should review the grouping theories discussed in Chapter 4.

Certain reporting problems may arise if one or more of the Subchapter S corporation is a partner in a general partnership. For instructions relating to this specific type of situation, the instructional booklet that accompanies Form 1120S will prove extremely useful.

One major distinction between Form 1120 and Form 1120S is that the first section concerning income is far simpler on Form 1120S. For Subchapter S corporations, this section does not require listing income from dividends, interest, rents, royalties, or capital gains. These items of income are reported on Schedules K and K-1 as an attachment to Form 1120S, which reflects the shareholders' portion of income, credit, and deductions from these passive activities, in the same manner such activities are reported by general partnerships.

In the deduction section of Form 1120S, charitable contributions are not included for the same reason they are not included on the partnership return, because the individual shareholders take their proportionate share of this item on their own individual income tax return. Further, Form 1120S permits the corporation to take a deduction in this section for advertising expenses and pension, profit sharing, and other employee benefit programs—items that appear elsewhere on Form 1120.

The final section of the main portion of Form 1120S provides a line to include any taxes due on net passive income, which further requires an attachment if any such tax is due. Also, the Subchapter S corporation is not entitled to a credit for taxes paid on undistributed capital gains, a credit allowed C corporations.

One major difference between Form 1120S and 1120 is that the former includes a schedule to indicate the shareholders' shares of income, credits, and deductions (Schedule K) because the Subchapter S corporation is not considered to be a taxable entity but merely a conduit to the shareholders, in the same fashion as a general partnership detailed in the last chapter. Form 1120S must be signed by an officer of the corporation, just like a C corporation's return.

The Subchapter S income tax return, similar to the Subchapter S corporation itself, is a hybrid of both a general partnership and a regular business corporation.

Ethical Concerns

The corporate format is typically used in order to provide its owners with limited personal liability. However, simply creating a corporation, or an LLC, does not necessarily relieve the owner of all individual obligations. If the corporation is not treated as a separate legal entity, but used by the shareholder as yet another personal bank account, he or she may be held personally liable for the corporate debts. Further, if the shareholder self-deals (takes personal financial advantage from the operation of the entity, separate from salary or dividends), he or she will also be personally liable.

CHAPTER REVIEW

Certain advantages can result from operating a business as a corporation. First, a tax savings may result because the corporate tax rate may be less than the individual tax rate of its shareholders. Second, the corporation is able to defer payment of some taxes because of the nonrecognition rules applicable to certain business transfers under section 351 of the IRC. Third, because the corporation is a separate legal entity, it provides its owners with limited personal liability. Note that these same advantages apply to limited liability companies that elect corporate tax treatment.

C corporations are required to file Form 1120 or 1120-A to reflect all of their income, deductions, and taxes due. Similar to partnership returns, these forms require the corporation to attach a balance sheet to substantiate the items that appear on the main body of the return.

S corporations, those domestic corporations having no more than 75 shareholders, may elect to be taxed either as a partnership or as a corporation. If it elects to be taxed as a pass-through entity, it files Form 1120S which acts as an informational return; each individual shareholder, like general partners, remain personally liable for any taxes that may be due, even though as shareholders they retain limited liability for the other debts of the corporation.

Two main areas should be addressed by the tax professional with respect to corporate income taxation. The first deals with dividends, which are distributions the entity makes to its shareholders. Nonliquidating dividends are deemed to be ordinary income to the stockholder and are immediately recognized if the distribution is of cash or property. Share dividends are not recognized at the time of distribution, but rather are used to adjust the shareholder's basis in the stock to determine gain or loss at the time of eventual sale or exchange of the shares. Liquidating distributions reflect changes in the shareholder's basis in the stock, and therefore are treated as capital gains or losses.

The second area of concern deals with corporate reorganizations. When a corporation reorganizes under section 368 of the IRC it will not recognize any gain or loss resulting from the reorganization at the time of the restructuring. However, to protect itself, the corporation should obtain a private ruling letter from IRS to determine whether IRS will view the restructuring as falling within the purview of section 368 prior to effectuating all of the changes to avoid being taxed at the time of the reorganization.

Corporations and limited liability companies are two of the most important business formats in current use and the tax law professional should be cognizant of the federal tax implications of these two types of business entities.

KEY TERMS

"A" reorganization
accumulated earnings tax
"B" reorganization
basic accounting equation
binding commitment test
boot
business purpose test
"C" reorganization
capital
closely held corporation

consolidation
corporation
"D" reorganization
divisive transaction
double taxation
"E" reorganization
earnings and profits (E&P)
end result test
excess net passive income
"F" reorganization

FIFO
Form 1120
Form 1120-A
Form 1120S
holding company
income statement
intercorporate dividend
LIFO
merger
mutual interdependence test
net operating loss (NOL)
nondivisive transfer
nonliquidating dividend
nonrealization
nonrecognition
parent-subsidiary relationship
personal holding company

personal services corporation
qualified small business
qualified taxpayer
redemption
Schedule PH
simplified production method
simplified resale method
small corporation
spin-off
split-up
step transaction doctrine
Subchapter C
Subchapter S corporation
substance test
stock split
target corporation or company
tax shelter

CHAPTER 6

Estate and Gift Taxation

Introduction

One of the primary administrative responsibilities of the personal representative of a decedent's estate is the preparation of all tax returns incident to the winding up of the deceased's affairs. It is the duty of the executor or administrator to see that all applicable forms are filed and that any tax due is paid out of the estate property. If the personal representative fails to file or to make timely payments of taxes due, he or she is held personally liable for any interest or penalty assessed thereon, and, if he or she has distributed estate assets prior to paying the taxes, thereby leaving insufficient funds in the estate to meet the tax liability, then the personal representative must pay the taxes from his or her own funds.

In many instances the lawyer or law firm who prepared the decedent's will is either named as the personal representative in the will or is retained by the personal representative to assist in the administration of the estate. For this reason the legal professional, especially one involved in a small firm practice, should be conversant with current estate tax law.

This chapter will focus exclusively on the preparation of the federal estate tax return, **Form 706** (Exhibit 6.1), the primary tax return for which the estate is responsible. This form requires the categorization of all of the assets and expenditures of the estate, as well as all potential tax credits for which the estate may be entitled. Form

Form 706
Primary tax return for which the estate is responsible

254 Chapter Six

Form 706
(Rev. August 2002)
Department of the Treasury
Internal Revenue Service

United States Estate (and Generation-Skipping Transfer) Tax Return

Estate of a citizen or resident of the United States (see separate instructions).
To be filed for decedents dying after December 31, 2001, and before January 1, 2003.
For Paperwork Reduction Act Notice, see the separate instructions.

OMB No. 1545-0015

Part 1—Decedent and Executor

1a	Decedent's first name and middle initial (and maiden name, if any)	1b Decedent's last name
		2 Decedent's Social Security No.
3a	Legal residence (domicile) at time of death (county, state, and ZIP code, or foreign country)	3b Year domicile established 4 Date of birth 5 Date of death
6a	Name of executor (see page 3 of the instructions)	6b Executor's address (number and street including apartment or suite no. or rural route; city, town, or post office; state; and ZIP code)
6c	Executor's social security number (see page 3 of the instructions)	
7a	Name and location of court where will was probated or estate administered	7b Case number
8	If decedent died testate, check here ▶ ☐ and attach a certified copy of the will. 9 If Form 4768 is attached, check here ▶ ☐	
10	If Schedule R-1 is attached, check here ▶ ☐	

Part 2—Tax Computation

1	Total gross estate less exclusion (from Part 5, Recapitulation, page 3, item 12)	1
2	Total allowable deductions (from Part 5, Recapitulation, page 3, item 23)	2
3	Taxable estate (subtract line 2 from line 1)	3
4	Adjusted taxable gifts (total taxable gifts (within the meaning of section 2503) made by the decedent after December 31, 1976, other than gifts that are includible in decedent's gross estate (section 2001(b))	4
5	Add lines 3 and 4	5
6	Tentative tax on the amount on line 5 from Table A on page 4 of the instructions	6
7	Total gift tax payable with respect to gifts made by the decedent after December 31, 1976. Include gift taxes by the decedent's spouse for such spouse's share of split gifts (section 2513) only if the decedent was the donor of these gifts and they are includible in the decedent's gross estate (see instructions)	7
8	Gross estate tax (subtract line 7 from line 6)	8
9	Maximum unified credit (applicable credit amount) against estate tax	9
10	Adjustment to unified credit (applicable credit amount). (This adjustment may not exceed $6,000. See page 5 of the instructions.)	10
11	Allowable unified credit (applicable credit amount) (subtract line 10 from line 9)	11
12	Subtract line 11 from line 8 (but do not enter less than zero)	12
13	Credit for state death taxes (cannot exceed line 12). **Attach credit evidence** (see instructions). Figure the credit by using the amount on line 3 less $60,000. See Table B in the instructions. Enter the amount here from Table B ▶ .... x .75 .... ▶	13
14	Subtract line 13 from line 12	14
15	Credit for Federal gift taxes on pre-1977 gifts (section 2012) (attach computation)	15
16	Credit for foreign death taxes (from Schedule(s) P). (Attach Form(s) 706-CE.)	16
17	Credit for tax on prior transfers (from Schedule Q)	17
18	Total (add lines 15, 16, and 17)	18
19	Net estate tax (subtract line 18 from line 14)	19
20	Generation-skipping transfer taxes (from Schedule R, Part 2, line 10)	20
21	Total transfer taxes (add lines 19 and 20)	21
22	Prior payments. Explain in an attached statement	22
23	United States Treasury bonds redeemed in payment of estate tax	23
24	Total (add lines 22 and 23)	24
25	Balance due (or overpayment) (subtract line 24 from line 21)	25

Under penalties of perjury, I declare that I have examined this return, including accompanying schedules and statements, and to the best of my knowledge and belief, it is true, correct, and complete. Declaration of preparer other than the executor is based on all information of which preparer has any knowledge.

Signature(s) of executor(s)   Date

Signature of preparer other than executor   Address (and ZIP code)   Date

Cat. No. 20548R

Exhibit 6.1 Form 706

Form 706 (Rev. 8-02)

Estate of:

Part 3—Elections by the Executor

Please check the "Yes" or "No" box for each question. (See instructions beginning on page 6.)

		Yes	No
1	Do you elect alternate valuation?		
2	Do you elect special use valuation? If "Yes," you must complete and attach Schedule A-1.		▨
3	Do you elect to pay the taxes in installments as described in section 6166? If "Yes," you must attach the additional information described on page 9 of the instructions.		▨
4	Do you elect to postpone the part of the taxes attributable to a reversionary or remainder interest as described in section 6163?		

Part 4—General Information
(Note: *Please attach the necessary supplemental documents. You must attach the death certificate.*)
(See instructions on page 10.)

Authorization to receive confidential tax information under Regs. sec. 601.504(b)(2)(i); to act as the estate's representative before the IRS; and to make written or oral presentations on behalf of the estate if return prepared by an attorney, accountant, or enrolled agent for the executor:

Name of representative (print or type)	State	Address (number, street, and room or suite no., city, state, and ZIP code)

I declare that I am the ☐ attorney/ ☐ certified public accountant/ ☐ enrolled agent (you must check the applicable box) for the executor and prepared this return for the executor. I am not under suspension or disbarment from practice before the Internal Revenue Service and am qualified to practice in the state shown above.

Signature	CAF number	Date	Telephone number

1 Death certificate number and issuing authority (attach a copy of the death certificate to this return).

2 Decedent's business or occupation. If retired, check here ▶ ☐ and state decedent's former business or occupation.

3 Marital status of the decedent at time of death:
☐ Married
☐ Widow or widower—Name, SSN, and date of death of deceased spouse ▶
☐ Single
☐ Legally separated
☐ Divorced—Date divorce decree became final ▶

4a Surviving spouse's name	4b Social security number	4c Amount received (see page 10 of the instructions)

5 Individuals (other than the surviving spouse), trusts, or other estates who receive benefits from the estate (do not include charitable beneficiaries shown in Schedule O) (see instructions). For Privacy Act Notice (applicable to individual beneficiaries only), see the Instructions for Form 1040.

Name of individual, trust, or estate receiving $5,000 or more	Identifying number	Relationship to decedent	Amount (see instructions)

All unascertainable beneficiaries and those who receive less than $5,000 . . . . ▶

Total . . . .

Please check the "Yes" or "No" box for each question.

		Yes	No
6	Does the gross estate contain any section 2044 property (qualified terminable interest property (QTIP) from a prior gift or estate) (see page 10 of the instructions)?		

(continued on next page)

Exhibit 6.1 (Continued)

256 Chapter Six

Form 706 (Rev. 8-02)

Part 4—General Information (continued)

Please check the "Yes" or "No" box for each question.   Yes | No

7a	Have Federal gift tax returns ever been filed?	
	If "Yes," please attach copies of the returns, if available, and furnish the following information:	
7b	Period(s) covered 7c Internal Revenue office(s) where filed	

If you answer "Yes" to any of questions 8–16, you must attach additional information as described in the instructions.

8a	Was there any insurance on the decedent's life that is not included on the return as part of the gross estate?	
b	Did the decedent own any insurance on the life of another that is not included in the gross estate?	
9	Did the decedent at the time of death own any property as a joint tenant with right of survivorship in which **(a)** one or more of the other joint tenants was someone other than the decedent's spouse, and **(b)** less than the full value of the property is included on the return as part of the gross estate? If "Yes," you must complete and attach Schedule E	
10	Did the decedent, at the time of death, own any interest in a partnership or unincorporated business or any stock in an inactive or closely held corporation?	
11	Did the decedent make any transfer described in section 2035, 2036, 2037, or 2038 (see the instructions for Schedule G beginning on page 12 of the separate instructions)? If "Yes," you must complete and attach Schedule G	
12	Were there in existence at the time of the decedent's death:	
a	Any trusts created by the decedent during his or her lifetime?	
b	Any trusts not created by the decedent under which the decedent possessed any power, beneficial interest, or trusteeship?	
13	Did the decedent ever possess, exercise, or release any general power of appointment? If "Yes," you must complete and attach Schedule H	
14	Was the marital deduction computed under the transitional rule of Public Law 97-34, section 403(e)(3) (Economic Recovery Tax Act of 1981)?	
	If "Yes," attach a separate computation of the marital deduction, enter the amount on item 20 of the Recapitulation, and note on item 20 "computation attached."	
15	Was the decedent, immediately before death, receiving an annuity described in the "General" paragraph of the instructions for Schedule I? If "Yes," you must complete and attach Schedule I	
16	Was the decedent ever the beneficiary of a trust for which a deduction was claimed by the estate of a pre-deceased spouse under section 2056(b)(7) and which is not reported on this return? If "Yes," attach an explanation.	

Part 5—Recapitulation

Item number	Gross estate		Alternate value	Value at date of death
1	Schedule A—Real Estate	1		
2	Schedule B—Stocks and Bonds	2		
3	Schedule C—Mortgages, Notes, and Cash	3		
4	Schedule D—Insurance on the Decedent's Life (attach Form(s) 712) . .	4		
5	Schedule E—Jointly Owned Property (attach Form(s) 712 for life insurance) .	5		
6	Schedule F—Other Miscellaneous Property (attach Form(s) 712 for life insurance)	6		
7	Schedule G—Transfers During Decedent's Life (att. Form(s) 712 for life insurance)	7		
8	Schedule H—Powers of Appointment	8		
9	Schedule I—Annuities	9		
10	Total gross estate (add items 1 through 9).	10		
11	Schedule U—Qualified Conservation Easement Exclusion	11		
12	Total gross estate less exclusion (subtract item 11 from item 10). Enter here and on line 1 of Part 2—Tax Computation	12		

Item number	Deductions		Amount
13	Schedule J—Funeral Expenses and Expenses Incurred in Administering Property Subject to Claims . . .	13	
14	Schedule K—Debts of the Decedent	14	
15	Schedule K—Mortgages and Liens	15	
16	Total of items 13 through 15	16	
17	Allowable amount of deductions from item 16 (see the instructions for item 17 of the Recapitulation) .	17	
18	Schedule L—Net Losses During Administration	18	
19	Schedule L—Expenses Incurred in Administering Property Not Subject to Claims	19	
20	Schedule M—Bequests, etc., to Surviving Spouse	20	
21	Schedule O—Charitable, Public, and Similar Gifts and Bequests	21	
22	Schedule T—Qualified Family-Owned Business Interest Deduction	22	
23	Total allowable deductions (add items 17 through 22). Enter here and on line 2 of the Tax Computation	23	

Page 3

Exhibit 6.1 (Continued)

Form 706 (Rev. 8-02)

Estate of:

SCHEDULE A—Real Estate

- *For jointly owned property that must be disclosed on Schedule E, see the instructions on the reverse side of Schedule E.*
- *Real estate that is part of a sole proprietorship should be shown on Schedule F.*
- *Real estate that is included in the gross estate under section 2035, 2036, 2037, or 2038 should be shown on Schedule G.*
- *Real estate that is included in the gross estate under section 2041 should be shown on Schedule H.*
- *If you elect section 2032A valuation, you must complete Schedule A and Schedule A-1.*

Item number	Description	Alternate valuation date	Alternate value	Value at date of death
1				

Total from continuation schedules or additional sheets attached to this schedule . . .

TOTAL. (Also enter on Part 5, Recapitulation, page 3, at item 1.) . . . .

(If more space is needed, attach the continuation schedule from the end of this package or additional sheets of the same size.)
(See the instructions on the reverse side.)

Schedule A—Page 4

Exhibit 6.1 (Continued)

Form 706 (Rev. 8-02)

Instructions for Schedule A—Real Estate

If the total gross estate contains any real estate, you must complete Schedule A and file it with the return. On Schedule A list real estate the decedent owned or had contracted to purchase. Number each parcel in the left-hand column.

Describe the real estate in enough detail so that the IRS can easily locate it for inspection and valuation. For each parcel of real estate, report the area and, if the parcel is improved, describe the improvements. For city or town property, report the street and number, ward, subdivision, block and lot, etc. For rural property, report the township, range, landmarks, etc.

If any item of real estate is subject to a mortgage for which the decedent's estate is liable; that is, if the indebtedness may be charged against other property of the estate that is not subject to that mortgage, or if the decedent was personally liable for that mortgage, you must report the full value of the property in the value column. Enter the amount of the mortgage under "Description" on this schedule. The unpaid amount of the mortgage may be deducted on Schedule K.

If the decedent's estate is NOT liable for the amount of the mortgage, report only the value of the equity of redemption (or value of the property less the indebtedness) in the value column as part of the gross estate. Do not enter any amount less than zero. Do not deduct the amount of indebtedness on Schedule K.

Also list on Schedule A real property the decedent contracted to purchase. Report the full value of the property and not the equity in the value column. Deduct the unpaid part of the purchase price on Schedule K.

Report the value of real estate without reducing it for homestead or other exemption, or the value of dower, curtesy, or a statutory estate created instead of dower or curtesy.

Explain how the reported values were determined and attach copies of any appraisals.

Schedule A Examples

In this example, alternate valuation is not adopted; the date of death is January 1, 2002.

Item number	Description	Alternate valuation date	Alternate value	Value at date of death
1	House and lot, 1921 William Street NW, Washington, DC (lot 6, square 481). Rent of $2,700 due at end of each quarter, February 1, May 1, August 1, and November 1. Value based on appraisal, copy of which is attached			$108,000
	Rent due on item 1 for quarter ending November 1, 2001, but not collected at date of death			2,700
	Rent accrued on item 1 for November and December 2001			1,800
2	House and lot, 304 Jefferson Street, Alexandria, VA (lot 18, square 40). Rent of $600 payable monthly. Value based on appraisal, copy of which is attached			96,000
	Rent due on item 2 for December 2001, but not collected at date of death . . .			600

In this example, alternate valuation is adopted; the date of death is January 1, 2002.

Item number	Description	Alternate valuation date	Alternate value	Value at date of death
1	House and lot, 1921 William Street NW, Washington, DC (lot 6, square 481). Rent of $2,700 due at end of each quarter, February 1, May 1, August 1, and November 1. Value based on appraisal, copy of which is attached. Not disposed of within 6 months following death	7/1/02	90,000	$108,000
	Rent due on item 1 for quarter ending November 1, 2001, but not collected until February 1, 2002	2/1/02	2,700	2,700
	Rent accrued on item 1 for November and December 2001, collected on February 1, 2002	2/1/02	1,800	1,800
2	House and lot, 304 Jefferson Street, Alexandria, VA (lot 18, square 40). Rent of $600 payable monthly. Value based on appraisal, copy of which is attached. Property exchanged for farm on May 1, 2002	5/1/02	90,000	96,000
	Rent due on item 2 for December 2001, but not collected until February 1, 2002 .	2/1/02	600	600

Schedule A—Page 5

Exhibit 6.1 (Continued)

Estate and Gift Taxation 259

Form 706 (Rev. 8-02)

Instructions for Schedule A-1. Section 2032A Valuation

The election to value certain farm and closely held business property at its special use value is made by checking "Yes" to line 2 of Part 3, Elections by the Executor, Form 706. Schedule A-1 is used to report the additional information that must be submitted to support this election. In order to make a valid election, you must complete Schedule A-1 and attach all of the required statements and appraisals.

For definitions and additional information concerning special use valuation, see section 2032A and the related regulations.

Part 1. Type of Election

Estate and GST Tax Elections. If you elect special use valuation for the estate tax, you must also elect special use valuation for the GST tax and vice versa.

You must value each specific property interest at the same value for GST tax purposes that you value it at for estate tax purposes.

Protective Election. To make the protective election described in the separate instructions for line 2 of Part 3, Elections by the Executor, you must check this box, enter the decedent's name and social security number in the spaces provided at the top of Schedule A-1, and complete line 1 and column A of lines 3 and 4 of Part 2. For purposes of the protective election, list on line 3 all of the real property that passes to the qualified heirs even though some of the property will be shown on line 2 when the additional notice of election is subsequently filed. You need not complete columns B–D of lines 3 and 4. You need not complete any other line entries on Schedule A-1. Completing Schedule A-1 as described above constitutes a Notice of Protective Election as described in Regulations section 20.2032A-8(b).

Part 2. Notice of Election

Line 10. Because the special use valuation election creates a potential tax liability for the recapture tax of section 2032A(c), you must list each person who receives an interest in the specially valued property on Schedule A-1. If there are more than eight persons who receive interests, use an additional sheet that follows the format of line 10. In the columns "Fair market value" and "Special use value," you should enter the total respective values of all the specially valued property interests received by each person.

GST Tax Savings

To compute the additional GST tax due upon disposition (or cessation of qualified use) of the property, each "skip person" (as defined in the instructions to Schedule R) who receives an interest in the specially valued property must know the total GST tax savings on all of the interests in specially valued property received. This GST tax savings is the difference between the total GST tax that was imposed on all of the interests in specially valued property received by the skip person valued at their special use value and the total GST tax that would have been imposed on the same interests received by the skip person had they been valued at their fair market value.

Because the GST tax depends on the executor's allocation of the GST exemption and the grandchild exclusion, the skip person who receives the interests is unable to compute this GST tax savings. Therefore, for each skip person who receives an interest in specially valued property, you must attach worksheets showing the total GST tax savings attributable to all of that person's interests in specially valued property.

How To Compute the GST Tax Savings. Before computing each skip person's GST tax savings, you must complete Schedules R and R-1 for the entire estate (using the special use values).

For each skip person, you must complete two Schedules R (Parts 2 and 3 only) as worksheets, one showing the interests in specially valued property received by the skip person at their special use value and one showing the same interests at their fair market value.

If the skip person received interests in specially valued property that were shown on Schedule R-1, show these interests on the Schedule R, Parts 2 and 3 worksheets, as appropriate. Do not use Schedule R-1 as a worksheet.

Completing the Special Use Value Worksheets. On lines 2–4 and 6, enter -0-.

Completing the Fair Market Value Worksheets. Lines 2 and 3, fixed taxes and other charges. If valuing the interests at their fair market value (instead of special use value) causes any of these taxes and charges to increase, enter the increased amount (only) on these lines and attach an explanation of the increase. Otherwise, enter -0-.

Line 6—GST exemption. If you completed line 10 of Schedule R, Part 1, enter on line 6 the amount shown for the skip person on the *line 10 special use allocation schedule* you attached to Schedule R. If you did not complete line 10 of Schedule R, Part 1, enter -0- on line 6.

Total GST Tax Savings. For each skip person, subtract the tax amount on line 10, Part 2 of the special use value worksheet from the tax amount on line 10, Part 2 of the fair market value worksheet. This difference is the skip person's total GST tax savings.

Part 3. Agreement to Special Valuation Under Section 2032A

The agreement to special valuation by persons with an interest in property is required under section 2032A(a)(1)(B) and (d)(2) and must be signed by all parties who have any interest in the property being valued based on its qualified use as of the date of the decedent's death.

An interest in property is an interest that, as of the date of the decedent's death, can be asserted under applicable local law so as to affect the disposition of the specially valued property by the estate. Any person who at the decedent's death has any such interest in the property, whether present or future, or vested or contingent, must enter into the agreement. Included are owners of remainder and executory interests; the holders of general or special powers of appointment; beneficiaries of a gift over in default of exercise of any such power; joint tenants and holders of similar undivided interests when the decedent held only a joint or undivided interest in the property or when only an undivided interest is specially valued; and trustees of trusts and representatives of other entities holding title to, or holding any interests in the property. An heir who has the power under local law to caveat (challenge) a will and thereby affect disposition of the property is not, however, considered to be a person with an interest in property under section 2032A solely by reason of that right. Likewise, creditors of an estate are not such persons solely by reason of their status as creditors.

If any person required to enter into the agreement either desires that an agent act for him or her or cannot legally bind himself or herself due to infancy or other incompetency, or due to death before the election under section 2032A is timely exercised, a representative authorized by local law to bind the person in an agreement of this nature may sign the agreement on his or her behalf.

The Internal Revenue Service will contact the agent designated in the agreement on all matters relating to continued qualification under section 2032A of the specially valued real property and on all matters relating to the special lien arising under section 6324B. It is the duty of the agent as attorney-in-fact for the parties with interests in the specially valued property to furnish the IRS with any requested information and to notify the IRS of any disposition or cessation of qualified use of any part of the property.

Schedule A-1—Page 6

Exhibit 6.1 (Continued)

260 Chapter Six

Form 706 (Rev. 8-02)

Checklist for Section 2032A Election. *If you are going to make the special use valuation election on Schedule A-1, please use this checklist to ensure that you are providing everything necessary to make a valid election.*

To have a valid special use valuation election under section 2032A, you must file, in addition to the Federal estate tax return, **(a)** a notice of election (Schedule A-1, Part 2), and **(b)** a fully executed agreement (Schedule A-1, Part 3). You must include certain information in the notice of election. To ensure that the notice of election includes all of the information required for a valid election, use the following checklist. The checklist is for your use only. Do not file it with the return.

1. Does the notice of election include the decedent's name and social security number as they appear on the estate tax return?

2. Does the notice of election include the relevant qualified use of the property to be specially valued?

3. Does the notice of election describe the items of real property shown on the estate tax return that are to be specially valued and identify the property by the Form 706 schedule and item number?

4. Does the notice of election include the fair market value of the real property to be specially valued and also include its value based on the qualified use (determined without the adjustments provided in section 2032A(b)(3)(B))?

5. Does the notice of election include the adjusted value (as defined in section 2032A(b)(3)(B)) of **(a)** all real property that both passes from the decedent and is used in a qualified use, without regard to whether it is to be specially valued, and **(b)** all real property to be specially valued?

6. Does the notice of election include **(a)** the items of personal property shown on the estate tax return that pass from the decedent to a qualified heir and that are used in qualified use and **(b)** the total value of such personal property adjusted under section 2032A(b)(3)(B)?

7. Does the notice of election include the adjusted value of the gross estate? (See section 2032A(b)(3)(A).)

8. Does the notice of election include the method used to determine the special use value?

9. Does the notice of election include copies of written appraisals of the fair market value of the real property?

10. Does the notice of election include a statement that the decedent and/or a member of his or her family has owned all of the specially valued property for at least 5 years of the 8 years immediately preceding the date of the decedent's death?

11. Does the notice of election include a statement as to whether there were any periods during the 8-year period preceding the decedent's date of death during which the decedent or a member of his or her family did not **(a)** own the property to be specially valued, **(b)** use it in a qualified use, or **(c)** materially participate in the operation of the farm or other business? (See section 2032A(e)(6).)

12. Does the notice of election include, for each item of specially valued property, the name of every person taking an interest in that item of specially valued property and the following information about each such person: **(a)** the person's address, **(b)** the person's taxpayer identification number, **(c)** the person's relationship to the decedent, and **(d)** the value of the property interest passing to that person based on both fair market value and qualified use?

13. Does the notice of election include affidavits describing the activities constituting material participation and the identity of the material participants?

14. Does the notice of election include a legal description of each item of specially valued property?

(In the case of an election made for qualified woodlands, the information included in the notice of election must include the reason for entitlement to the woodlands election.)

Any election made under section 2032A will not be valid unless a properly executed agreement (Schedule A-1, Part 3) is filed with the estate tax return. To ensure that the agreement satisfies the requirements for a valid election, use the following checklist.

1. Has the agreement been signed by each and every qualified heir having an interest in the property being specially valued?

2. Has every qualified heir expressed consent to personal liability under section 2032A(c) in the event of an early disposition or early cessation of qualified use?

3. Is the agreement that is actually signed by the qualified heirs in a form that is binding on all of the qualified heirs having an interest in the specially valued property?

4. Does the agreement designate an agent to act for the parties to the agreement in all dealings with the IRS on matters arising under section 2032A?

5. Has the agreement been signed by the designated agent and does it give the address of the agent?

Page 7

Exhibit 6.1 (Continued)

Form 706 (Rev. 8-02)

Estate of: | **Decedent's Social Security Number**

SCHEDULE A-1—Section 2032A Valuation

Part 1. Type of Election (Before making an election, see the checklist on page 7.):
- ☐ **Protective election (Regulations section 20.2032A-8(b)).** Complete Part 2, line 1, and column A of lines 3 and 4. (See instructions.)
- ☐ **Regular election.** Complete all of Part 2 (including line 11, if applicable) and Part 3. (See instructions.)

Before completing Schedule A-1, see the checklist on page 7 for the information and documents that must be included to make a valid election.

The election is not valid unless the agreement (i.e., Part 3—Agreement to Special Valuation Under Section 2032A)—
- Is signed by each and every qualified heir with an interest in the specially valued property, and
- Is attached to this return when it is filed.

Part 2. Notice of Election (Regulations section 20.2032A-8(a)(3))
Note: *All real property entered on lines 2 and 3 must also be entered on Schedules A, E, F, G, or H, as applicable.*

1 Qualified use—check one ▶ ☐ Farm used for farming, or
   ▶ ☐ Trade or business other than farming
2 Real property used in a qualified use, passing to qualified heirs, and to be specially valued on this Form 706.

A Schedule and item number from Form 706	B Full value (without section 2032A(b)(3)(B) adjustment)	C Adjusted value (with section 2032A(b)(3)(B) adjustment)	D Value based on qualified use (without section 2032A(b)(3)(B) adjustment)

Totals . . . .

Attach a legal description of all property listed on line 2.
Attach copies of appraisals showing the column B values for all property listed on line 2.

3 Real property used in a qualified use, passing to qualified heirs, but not specially valued on this Form 706.

A Schedule and item number from Form 706	B Full value (without section 2032A(b)(3)(B) adjustment)	C Adjusted value (with section 2032A(b)(3)(B) adjustment)	D Value based on qualified use (without section 2032A(b)(3)(B) adjustment)

Totals . . . .
If you checked "Regular election," you must attach copies of appraisals showing the column B values for all property listed on line 3.

(continued on next page)   Schedule A-1—Page 8

Exhibit 6.1 (Continued)

Form 706 (Rev. 8-02)

4 Personal property used in a qualified use and passing to qualified heirs.

A Schedule and item number from Form 706	B Adjusted value (with section 2032A(b)(3)(B) adjustment)	A (continued) Schedule and item number from Form 706	B (continued) Adjusted value (with section 2032A(b)(3)(B) adjustment)
		"Subtotal" from Col. B, below left	
Subtotal		Total adjusted value . . .	

5 Enter the value of the total gross estate as adjusted under section 2032A(b)(3)(A). ▶

6 Attach a description of the method used to determine the special value based on qualified use.

7 Did the decedent and/or a member of his or her family own all property listed on line 2 for at least 5 of the 8 years immediately preceding the date of the decedent's death? . . . . ☐ Yes ☐ No

8 Were there any periods during the 8-year period preceding the date of the decedent's death during which the decedent or a member of his or her family: | Yes | No |

  a Did not own the property listed on line 2 above? . . . .
  b Did not use the property listed on line 2 above in a qualified use? . . . .
  c Did not materially participate in the operation of the farm or other business within the meaning of section 2032A(e)(6)? . . . .

If "Yes" to any of the above, you must attach a statement listing the periods. If applicable, describe whether the exceptions of sections 2032A(b)(4) or (5) are met.

9 Attach affidavits describing the activities constituting material participation and the identity and relationship to the decedent of the material participants.

10 Persons holding interests. Enter the requested information for each party who received any interest in the specially valued property. (Each of the qualified heirs receiving an interest in the property must sign the agreement, and the agreement must be filed with this return.)

	Name	Address
A		
B		
C		
D		
E		
F		
G		
H		

	Identifying number	Relationship to decedent	Fair market value	Special use value
A				
B				
C				
D				
E				
F				
G				
H				

You must attach a computation of the GST tax savings attributable to direct skips for each person listed above who is a skip person. (See instructions.)

11 Woodlands election. Check here ▶ ☐ if you wish to make a woodlands election as described in section 2032A(e)(13). Enter the Schedule and item numbers from Form 706 of the property for which you are making this election ▶ . . . .
You must attach a statement explaining why you are entitled to make this election. The IRS may issue regulations that require more information to substantiate this election. You will be notified by the IRS if you must supply further information.

Schedule A-1—Page 9

Exhibit 6.1 (Continued)

Form 706 (Rev. 8-02)

Part 3. Agreement to Special Valuation Under Section 2032A

Estate of:	Date of Death	Decedent's Social Security Number

There cannot be a valid election unless:
- The agreement is executed by each and every one of the qualified heirs, and
- The agreement is included with the estate tax return when the estate tax return is filed.

We (list all qualified heirs and other persons having an interest in the property required to sign this agreement)

_____,

being all the qualified heirs and _____

_____,

being all other parties having interests in the property which is qualified real property and which is valued under section 2032A of the Internal Revenue Code, do hereby approve of the election made by _____,
Executor/Administrator of the estate of _____
pursuant to section 2032A to value said property on the basis of the qualified use to which the property is devoted and do hereby enter into this agreement pursuant to section 2032A(d).

The undersigned agree and consent to the application of subsection (c) of section 2032A of the Code with respect to all the property described on line 2 of Part 2 of Schedule A-1 of Form 706, attached to this agreement. More specifically, the undersigned heirs expressly agree and consent to personal liability under subsection (c) of 2032A for the additional estate and GST taxes imposed by that subsection with respect to their respective interests in the above-described property in the event of certain early dispositions of the property or early cessation of the qualified use of the property. It is understood that if a qualified heir disposes of any interest in qualified real property to any member of his or her family, such member may thereafter be treated as the qualified heir with respect to such interest upon filing a Form 706-A and a new agreement.

The undersigned interested parties who are not qualified heirs consent to the collection of any additional estate and GST taxes imposed under section 2032A(c) of the Code from the specially valued property.

If there is a disposition of any interest which passes, or has passed to him or her, or if there is a cessation of the qualified use of any specially valued property which passes or passed to him or her, each of the undersigned heirs agrees to file a **Form 706-A,** United States Additional Estate Tax Return, and pay any additional estate and GST taxes due within 6 months of the disposition or cessation.

It is understood by all interested parties that this agreement is a condition precedent to the election of special use valuation under section 2032A of the Code and must be executed by every interested party even though that person may not have received the estate (or GST) tax benefits or be in possession of such property.

Each of the undersigned understands that by making this election, a lien will be created and recorded pursuant to section 6324B of the Code on the property referred to in this agreement for the adjusted tax differences with respect to the estate as defined in section 2032A(c)(2)(C).

As the interested parties, the undersigned designate the following individual as their agent for all dealings with the Internal Revenue Service concerning the continued qualification of the specially valued property under section 2032A of the Code and on all issues regarding the special lien under section 6324B. The agent is authorized to act for the parties with respect to all dealings with the Service on matters affecting the qualified real property described earlier. This authority includes the following:

- To receive confidential information on all matters relating to continued qualification under section 2032A of the specially valued real property and on all matters relating to the special lien arising under section 6324B.
- To furnish the Internal Revenue Service with any requested information concerning the property.
- To notify the Internal Revenue Service of any disposition or cessation of qualified use of any part of the property.
- To receive, but not to endorse and collect, checks in payment of any refund of Internal Revenue taxes, penalties, or interest.
- To execute waivers (including offers of waivers) of restrictions on assessment or collection of deficiencies in tax and waivers of notice of disallowance of a claim for credit or refund.
- To execute closing agreements under section 7121.

(continued on next page)

Schedule A-1— Page 10

Exhibit 6.1 (Continued)

Form 706 (Rev. 8-02)

Part 3. Agreement to Special Valuation Under Section 2032A *(Continued)*

Estate of:	Date of Death	Decedent's Social Security Number

• Other acts (specify) ▶ _____

By signing this agreement, the agent agrees to provide the Internal Revenue Service with any requested information concerning this property and to notify the Internal Revenue Service of any disposition or cessation of the qualified use of any part of this property.

Name of Agent	Signature	Address

The property to which this agreement relates is listed in Form 706, United States Estate (and Generation-Skipping Transfer) Tax Return, and in the Notice of Election, along with its fair market value according to section 2031 of the Code and its special use value according to section 2032A. The name, address, social security number, and interest (including the value) of each of the undersigned in this property are as set forth in the attached Notice of Election.

IN WITNESS WHEREOF, the undersigned have hereunto set their hands at _____ ,

this _____ day of _____ .

SIGNATURES OF EACH OF THE QUALIFIED HEIRS:

Signature of qualified heir	Signature of qualified heir
Signature of qualified heir	Signature of qualified heir
Signature of qualified heir	Signature of qualified heir
Signature of qualified heir	Signature of qualified heir
Signature of qualified heir	Signature of qualified heir
Signature of qualified heir	Signature of qualified heir

Signatures of other interested parties

Signatures of other interested parties

Schedule A-1—Page 11

Exhibit 6.1 (Continued)

Form 706 (Rev. 8-02)

Estate of:

SCHEDULE B—Stocks and Bonds

(For jointly owned property that must be disclosed on Schedule E, see the instructions for Schedule E.)

Item number	Description including face amount of bonds or number of shares and par value where needed for identification. Give 9-digit CUSIP number. / CUSIP number	Unit value	Alternate valuation date	Alternate value	Value at date of death
1					
	Total from continuation schedules (or additional sheets) attached to this schedule . . .				
	TOTAL. (Also enter on Part 5, Recapitulation, page 3, at item 2.)				

(If more space is needed, attach the continuation schedule from the end of this package or additional sheets of the same size.)
(The instructions to Schedule B are in the separate instructions.)

Schedule B—Page 12

Exhibit 6.1 (Continued)

Form 706 (Rev. 8-02)

Estate of:

SCHEDULE C—Mortgages, Notes, and Cash
(For jointly owned property that must be disclosed on Schedule E, see the instructions for Schedule E.)

Item number	Description	Alternate valuation date	Alternate value	Value at date of death
1				

Total from continuation schedules (or additional sheets) attached to this schedule . . .

TOTAL. (Also enter on Part 5, Recapitulation, page 3, at item 3.) . . . .

(If more space is needed, attach the continuation schedule from the end of this package or additional sheets of the same size.)
(See the instructions on the reverse side.)

Schedule C—Page 13

Exhibit 6.1 (Continued)

Form 706 (Rev. 8-02)

Instructions for Schedule C—Mortgages, Notes, and Cash

Complete Schedule C and file it with your return if the total gross estate contains any:

- mortgages,
- notes, or
- cash.

List on Schedule C:

- Mortgages and notes payable **to the decedent** at the time of death.
- Cash the decedent had at the date of death.

Do not list on Schedule C:

- Mortgages and notes payable **by the decedent.** (If these are deductible, list them on Schedule K.)

List the items on Schedule C in the following order:

- mortgages,
- promissory notes,
- contracts by decedent to sell land,
- cash in possession, and
- cash in banks, savings and loan associations, and other types of financial organizations.

What to enter in the "Description" column:

For mortgages, list:

- face value,
- unpaid balance,
- date of mortgage,
- date of maturity,
- name of maker,
- property mortgaged,
- interest dates, and
- interest rate.

Example to enter in "Description" column:

"Bond and mortgage of $50,000, unpaid balance: $24,000; dated: January 1, 1983; John Doe to Richard Roe; premises: 22 Clinton Street, Newark, NJ; due: January 1, 2002; interest payable at 10% a year--January 1 and July 1."

For promissory notes, list:

- in the same way as mortgages.

For contracts by the decedent to sell land, list:

- name of purchaser,
- contract date,
- property description,
- sale price,
- initial payment,
- amounts of installment payment,
- unpaid balance of principal, and
- interest rate.

For cash in possession, list:

- such cash separately from bank deposits.

For cash in banks, savings and loan associations, and other types of financial organizations, list:

- name and address of each financial organization,
- amount in each account,
- serial or account number,
- nature of account--checking, savings, time deposit, etc., and
- unpaid interest accrued from date of last interest payment to the date of death.

Important: If you obtain statements from the financial organizations, keep them for IRS inspection.

Schedule C—Page 14

Exhibit 6.1 (Continued)

Form 706 (Rev. 8-02)

Estate of:

SCHEDULE D—Insurance on the Decedent's Life

You must list **all** policies on the life of the decedent and attach a Form 712 for each policy.

Item number	Description	Alternate valuation date	Alternate value	Value at date of death
1				

Total from continuation schedules (or additional sheets) attached to this schedule . .

TOTAL. (Also enter on Part 5, Recapitulation, page 3, at item 4.). . . . .

(If more space is needed, attach the continuation schedule from the end of this package or additional sheets of the same size.)
(See the instructions on the reverse side.)

Schedule D—Page 15

Exhibit 6.1 (Continued)

Form 706 (Rev. 8-02)

Instructions for Schedule D—Insurance on the Decedent's Life

If you are required to file Form 706 and there was any insurance on the decedent's life, whether or not included in the gross estate, you must complete Schedule D and file it with the return.

Insurance you must include on Schedule D. Under section 2042 you must include in the gross estate:

- Insurance on the decedent's life receivable by or for the benefit of the estate; and
- Insurance on the decedent's life receivable by beneficiaries other than the estate, as described below.

The term "insurance" refers to life insurance of every description, including death benefits paid by fraternal beneficiary societies operating under the lodge system, and death benefits paid under no-fault automobile insurance policies if the no-fault insurer was unconditionally bound to pay the benefit in the event of the insured's death.

Insurance in favor of the estate. Include on Schedule D the full amount of the proceeds of insurance on the life of the decedent receivable by the executor or otherwise payable to or for the benefit of the estate. Insurance in favor of the estate includes insurance used to pay the estate tax, and any other taxes, debts, or charges that are enforceable against the estate. The manner in which the policy is drawn is immaterial as long as there is an obligation, legally binding on the beneficiary, to use the proceeds to pay taxes, debts, or charges. You must include the full amount even though the premiums or other consideration may have been paid by a person other than the decedent.

Insurance receivable by beneficiaries other than the estate. Include on Schedule D the proceeds of all insurance on the life of the decedent not receivable by or for the benefit of the decedent's estate if the decedent possessed at death any of the incidents of ownership, exercisable either alone or in conjunction with any person.

Incidents of ownership in a policy include:

- The right of the insured or estate to its economic benefits;
- The power to change the beneficiary;
- The power to surrender or cancel the policy;
- The power to assign the policy or to revoke an assignment;
- The power to pledge the policy for a loan;
- The power to obtain from the insurer a loan against the surrender value of the policy;
- A reversionary interest if the value of the reversionary interest was more than 5% of the value of the policy immediately before the decedent died. (An interest in an insurance policy is considered a reversionary interest if, for example, the proceeds become payable to the insured's estate or payable as the insured directs if the beneficiary dies before the insured.)

Life insurance not includible in the gross estate under section 2042 may be includible under some other section of the Code. For example, a life insurance policy could be transferred by the decedent in such a way that it would be includible in the gross estate under section 2036, 2037, or 2038. (See the instructions to Schedule G for a description of these sections.)

Completing the Schedule

You must list every policy of insurance on the life of the decedent, whether or not it is included in the gross estate.

Under "Description" list:

- Name of the insurance company and
- Number of the policy.

For every policy of life insurance listed on the schedule, you must request a statement on **Form 712**, Life Insurance Statement, from the company that issued the policy. Attach the Form 712 to the back of Schedule D.

If the policy proceeds are paid in one sum, enter the net proceeds received (from Form 712, line 24) in the value (and alternate value) columns of Schedule D. If the policy proceeds are not paid in one sum, enter the value of the proceeds as of the date of the decedent's death (from Form 712, line 25).

If part or all of the policy proceeds are not included in the gross estate, you must explain why they were not included.

Schedule D—Page 16

Exhibit 6.1 (Continued)

Form 706 (Rev. 8-02)

Estate of:

SCHEDULE E—Jointly Owned Property

(If you elect section 2032A valuation, you must complete Schedule E and Schedule A-1.)

PART 1.—Qualified Joint Interests—Interests Held by the Decedent and His or Her Spouse as the Only Joint Tenants (Section 2040(b)(2))

Item number	Description For securities, give CUSIP number.	Alternate valuation date	Alternate value	Value at date of death

	Total from continuation schedules (or additional sheets) attached to this schedule		
1a	Totals	**1a**	
1b	Amounts included in gross estate (one-half of line **1a**)	**1b**	

PART 2.—All Other Joint Interests

2a State the name and address of each surviving co-tenant. If there are more than three surviving co-tenants, list the additional co-tenants on an attached sheet.

	Name	Address (number and street, city, state, and ZIP code)
A.		
B.		
C.		

Item number	Enter letter for co-tenant	Description (including alternate valuation date if any) For securities, give CUSIP number.	Percentage includible	Includible alternate value	Includible value at date of death

	Total from continuation schedules (or additional sheets) attached to this schedule		
2b	Total other joint interests	**2b**	
3	**Total includible joint interests** (add lines 1b and 2b). Also enter on Part 5, Recapitulation, page 3, at item 5	**3**	

(If more space is needed, attach the continuation schedule from the end of this package or additional sheets of the same size.) (See the instructions on the reverse side.)

Schedule E—Page 17

Exhibit 6.1 (Continued)

Form 706 (Rev. 8-02)

Instructions for Schedule E—Jointly Owned Property

If you are required to file Form 706, you must complete Schedule E and file it with the return if the decedent owned any joint property at the time of death, whether or not the decedent's interest is includible in the gross estate.

Enter on this schedule all property of whatever kind or character, whether real estate, personal property, or bank accounts, in which the decedent held at the time of death an interest either as a joint tenant with right of survivorship or as a tenant by the entirety.

Do not list on this schedule property that the decedent held as a tenant in common, but report the value of the interest on Schedule A if real estate, or on the appropriate schedule if personal property. Similarly, community property held by the decedent and spouse should be reported on the appropriate Schedules A through I. The decedent's interest in a partnership should not be entered on this schedule unless the partnership interest itself is jointly owned. Solely owned partnership interests should be reported on Schedule F, "Other Miscellaneous Property."

Part 1—Qualified joint interests held by decedent and spouse. Under section 2040(b)(2), a joint interest is a qualified joint interest if the decedent and the surviving spouse held the interest as:

- Tenants by the entirety, or
- Joint tenants with right of survivorship if the decedent and the decedent's spouse are the only joint tenants.

Interests that meet either of the two requirements above should be entered in Part 1. Joint interests that do not meet either of the two requirements above should be entered in Part 2.

Under "Description," describe the property as required in the instructions for Schedules A, B, C, and F for the type of property involved. For example, jointly held stocks and bonds should be described using the rules given in the instructions to Schedule B.

Under "Alternate value" and "Value at date of death," enter the full value of the property.

Note: *You cannot claim the special treatment under section 2040(b) for property held jointly by a decedent and a surviving spouse who is not a U.S. citizen. You must report these joint interests on Part 2 of Schedule E, not Part 1.*

Part 2—Other joint interests. All joint interests that were not entered in Part 1 must be entered in Part 2.

For each item of property, enter the appropriate letter A, B, C, etc., from line 2a to indicate the name and address of the surviving co-tenant.

Under "Description," describe the property as required in the instructions for Schedules A, B, C, and F for the type of property involved.

In the "Percentage includible" column, enter the percentage of the total value of the property that you intend to include in the gross estate.

Generally, you must include the full value of the jointly owned property in the gross estate. However, the full value should not be included if you can show that a part of the property originally belonged to the other tenant or tenants and was never received or acquired by the other tenant or tenants from the decedent for less than adequate and full consideration in money or money's worth, or unless you can show that any part of the property was acquired with consideration originally belonging to the surviving joint tenant or tenants. In this case, you may exclude from the value of the property an amount proportionate to the consideration furnished by the other tenant or tenants. Relinquishing or promising to relinquish dower, curtesy, or statutory estate created instead of dower or curtesy, or other marital rights in the decedent's property or estate is not consideration in money or money's worth. See the Schedule A instructions for the value to show for real property that is subject to a mortgage.

If the property was acquired by the decedent and another person or persons by gift, bequest, devise, or inheritance as joint tenants, and their interests are not otherwise specified by law, include only that part of the value of the property that is figured by dividing the full value of the property by the number of joint tenants.

If you believe that less than the full value of the entire property is includible in the gross estate for tax purposes, you must establish the right to include the smaller value by attaching proof of the extent, origin, and nature of the decedent's interest and the interest(s) of the decedent's co-tenant or co-tenants.

In the "Includible alternate value" and "Includible value at date of death" columns, you should enter only the values that you believe are includible in the gross estate.

Schedule E—Page 18

Exhibit 6.1 (Continued)

Form 706 (Rev. 8-02)

Estate of:

SCHEDULE F—Other Miscellaneous Property Not Reportable Under Any Other Schedule
(For jointly owned property that must be disclosed on Schedule E, see the instructions for Schedule E.)
(If you elect section 2032A valuation, you must complete Schedule F and Schedule A-1.)

		Yes	No
1	Did the decedent at the time of death own any articles of artistic or collectible value in excess of $3,000 or any collections whose artistic or collectible value combined at date of death exceeded $10,000? . . . . If "Yes," submit full details on this schedule and attach appraisals.		
2	Has the decedent's estate, spouse, or any other person, received (or will receive) any bonus or award as a result of the decedent's employment or death? . . . . If "Yes," submit full details on this schedule.		
3	Did the decedent at the time of death have, or have access to, a safe deposit box? . . . . If "Yes," state location, and if held in joint names of decedent and another, state name and relationship of joint depositor. If any of the contents of the safe deposit box are omitted from the schedules in this return, explain fully why omitted.		

Item number	Description For securities, give CUSIP number.	Alternate valuation date	Alternate value	Value at date of death
1				
	Total from continuation schedules (or additional sheets) attached to this schedule . .			
	TOTAL. (Also enter on Part 5, Recapitulation, page 3, at item 6.)			

(If more space is needed, attach the continuation schedule from the end of this package or additional sheets of the same size.)
(See the instructions on the reverse side.)

Schedule F—Page 19

Exhibit 6.1 (Continued)

Form 706 (Rev. 8-02)

Instructions for Schedule F—Other Miscellaneous Property

You must complete Schedule F and file it with the return.

On Schedule F list all items that must be included in the gross estate that are not reported on any other schedule, including:

- Debts due the decedent (other than notes and mortgages included on Schedule C)
- Interests in business
- Insurance on the life of another (obtain and attach **Form 712,** Life Insurance Statement, for each policy)

Note for single premium or paid-up policies: *In certain situations, for example where the surrender value of the policy exceeds its replacement cost, the true economic value of the policy will be greater than the amount shown on line 59 of Form 712. In these situations, you should report the full economic value of the policy on Schedule F. See Rev. Rul. 78-137, 1978-1 C.B. 280 for details.*

- Section 2044 property (see **Decedent Who Was a Surviving Spouse** below)
- Claims (including the value of the decedent's interest in a claim for refund of income taxes or the amount of the refund actually received)
- Rights
- Royalties
- Leaseholds
- Judgments
- Reversionary or remainder interests
- Shares in trust funds (attach a copy of the trust instrument)
- Household goods and personal effects, including wearing apparel
- Farm products and growing crops
- Livestock
- Farm machinery
- Automobiles

If the decedent owned any interest in a partnership or unincorporated business, attach a statement of assets and liabilities for the valuation date and for the 5 years before the valuation date. Also attach statements of the net earnings for the same 5 years.

You must account for goodwill in the valuation. In general, furnish the same information and follow the methods used to value close corporations. See the instructions for Schedule B.

All partnership interests should be reported on Schedule F unless the partnership interest, itself, is jointly owned. Jointly owned partnership interests should be reported on Schedule E.

If real estate is owned by the sole proprietorship, it should be reported on Schedule F and not on Schedule A. Describe the real estate with the same detail required for Schedule A.

Line 1. If the decedent owned at the date of death articles with artistic or intrinsic value (e.g., jewelry, furs, silverware, books, statuary, vases, oriental rugs, coin or stamp collections), check the "Yes" box on line 1 and provide full details. If any one article is valued at more than $3,000, or any collection of similar articles is valued at more than $10,000, attach an appraisal by an expert under oath and the required statement regarding the appraiser's qualifications (see Regulations section 20.2031-6(b)).

Decedent Who Was a Surviving Spouse

If the decedent was a surviving spouse, he or she may have received qualified terminable interest property (QTIP) from the predeceased spouse for which the marital deduction was elected either on the predeceased spouse's estate tax return or on a gift tax return, Form 709. The election was available for gifts made and decedents dying after December 31, 1981. List such property on Schedule F.

If this election was made and the surviving spouse retained his or her interest in the QTIP property at death, the full value of the QTIP property is includible in his or her estate, even though the qualifying income interest terminated at death. It is valued as of the date of the surviving spouse's death, or alternate valuation date, if applicable. Do not reduce the value by any annual exclusion that may have applied to the transfer creating the interest.

The value of such property included in the surviving spouse's gross estate is treated as passing from the surviving spouse. It therefore qualifies for the charitable and marital deductions on the surviving spouse's estate tax return if it meets the other requirements for those deductions.

For additional details, see Regulations section 20.2044-1.

Schedule F—Page 20

Exhibit 6.1 (Continued)

Form 706 (Rev. 8-02)

Estate of:

SCHEDULE G—Transfers During Decedent's Life
(If you elect section 2032A valuation, you must complete Schedule G and Schedule A-1.)

Item number	Description For securities, give CUSIP number.	Alternate valuation date	Alternate value	Value at date of death
A.	Gift tax paid by the decedent or the estate for all gifts made by the decedent or his or her spouse within 3 years before the decedent's death (section 2035(b))	x x x x x		
B.	Transfers includible under section 2035(a), 2036, 2037, or 2038:			
1				
	Total from continuation schedules (or additional sheets) attached to this schedule . .			
	TOTAL. (Also enter on Part 5, Recapitulation, page 3, at item 7.).			

SCHEDULE H—Powers of Appointment
(Include "5 and 5 lapsing" powers (section 2041(b)(2)) held by the decedent.)
(If you elect section 2032A valuation, you must complete Schedule H and Schedule A-1.)

Item number	Description	Alternate valuation date	Alternate value	Value at date of death
1				
	Total from continuation schedules (or additional sheets) attached to this schedule . .			
	TOTAL. (Also enter on Part 5, Recapitulation, page 3, at item 8.).			

(If more space is needed, attach the continuation schedule from the end of this package or additional sheets of the same size.)
(The instructions to Schedules G and H are in the separate instructions.)

Schedules G and H—Page 21

Exhibit 6.1 (Continued)

Form 706 (Rev. 8-02)

Estate of:

SCHEDULE I—Annuities

Note: *Generally, no exclusion is allowed for the estates of decedents dying after December 31, 1984 (see page 14 of the instructions).*

A Are you excluding from the decedent's gross estate the value of a lump-sum distribution described in section 2039(f)(2) (as in effect before its repeal by the Deficit Reduction Act of 1984)?
If "Yes," you must attach the information required by the instructions.

Yes	No

Item number	Description Show the entire value of the annuity before any exclusions.	Alternate valuation date	Includible alternate value	Includible value at date of death
1				

Total from continuation schedules (or additional sheets) attached to this schedule . .

TOTAL. (Also enter on Part 5, Recapitulation, page 3, at item 9.) . . . .

(If more space is needed, attach the continuation schedule from the end of this package or additional sheets of the same size.)

Schedule I—Page 22   (The instructions to Schedule I are in the separate instructions.)

Exhibit 6.1 (Continued)

Form 706 (Rev. 8-02)

Estate of:

SCHEDULE J—Funeral Expenses and Expenses Incurred in Administering Property Subject to Claims

Note: *Do not list on this schedule expenses of administering property not subject to claims. For those expenses, see the instructions for Schedule L.*

If executors' commissions, attorney fees, etc., are claimed and allowed as a deduction for estate tax purposes, they are not allowable as a deduction in computing the taxable income of the estate for Federal income tax purposes. They are allowable as an income tax deduction on Form 1041 if a waiver is filed to waive the deduction on Form 706 (see the Form 1041 instructions).

Item number	Description	Expense amount	Total amount
1	**A. Funeral expenses:**		
	Total funeral expenses . . . . ▶		....
	B. Administration expenses:		
	1 Executors' commissions—amount estimated/agreed upon/paid. (Strike out the words that do not apply.)		....
	2 Attorney fees—amount estimated/agreed upon/paid. (Strike out the words that do not apply.) . .		....
	3 Accountant fees—amount estimated/agreed upon/paid. (Strike out the words that do not apply.).		....
	4 Miscellaneous expenses:	Expense amount	
	Total miscellaneous expenses from continuation schedules (or additional sheets) attached to this schedule		
	Total miscellaneous expenses . . . . ▶		....
	TOTAL. (Also enter on Part 5, Recapitulation, page 3, at item 13.) . . . . ▶		....

(If more space is needed, attach the continuation schedule from the end of this package or additional sheets of the same size.) (See the instructions on the reverse side.)

Schedule J—Page 23

Exhibit 6.1 (Continued)

Form 706 (Rev. 8-02)

Instructions for Schedule J—Funeral Expenses and Expenses Incurred in Administering Property Subject to Claims

General. You must complete and file Schedule J if you claim a deduction on item 13 of Part 5, Recapitulation.

On Schedule J, itemize funeral expenses and expenses incurred in administering property subject to claims. List the names and addresses of persons to whom the expenses are payable and describe the nature of the expense. **Do not list expenses incurred in administering property not subject to claims on this schedule. List them on Schedule L instead.**

The deduction is limited to the amount paid for these expenses that is allowable under local law but may not exceed:

1. The value of property subject to claims included in the gross estate, plus

2. The amount paid out of property included in the gross estate but not subject to claims. This amount must actually be paid by the due date of the estate tax return.

The applicable local law under which the estate is being administered determines which property is and is not subject to claims. If under local law a particular property interest included in the gross estate would bear the burden for the payment of the expenses, then the property is considered property subject to claims.

Unlike certain claims against the estate for debts of the decedent (see the instructions for Schedule K in the separate instructions), you cannot deduct expenses incurred in administering property subject to claims on both the estate tax return and the estate's income tax return. If you choose to deduct them on the estate tax return, you cannot deduct them on a Form 1041 filed for the estate. Funeral expenses are only deductible on the estate tax return.

Funeral Expenses. Itemize funeral expenses on line A. Deduct from the expenses any amounts that were reimbursed, such as death benefits payable by the Social Security Administration and the Veterans Administration.

Executors' Commissions. When you file the return, you may deduct commissions that have actually been paid to you or that you expect will be paid. You may not deduct commissions if none will be collected. If the amount of the commissions has not been fixed by decree of the proper court, the deduction will be allowed on the final examination of the return, provided that:

- The Estate and Gift Tax Territory Manager is reasonably satisfied that the commissions claimed will be paid;
- The amount entered as a deduction is within the amount allowable by the laws of the jurisdiction where the estate is being administered;
- It is in accordance with the usually accepted practice in that jurisdiction for estates of similar size and character.

If you have not been paid the commissions claimed at the time of the final examination of the return, you must support the amount you deducted with an affidavit or statement signed under the penalties of perjury that the amount has been agreed upon and will be paid.

You may not deduct a bequest or devise made to you instead of commissions. If, however, the decedent fixed by will the compensation payable to you for services to be rendered in the administration of the estate, you may deduct this amount to the extent it is not more than the compensation allowable by the local law or practice.

Do not deduct on this schedule amounts paid as trustees' commissions whether received by you acting in the capacity of a trustee or by a separate trustee. If such amounts were paid in administering property not subject to claims, deduct them on Schedule L.

Note: *Executors' commissions are taxable income to the executors. Therefore, be sure to include them as income on your individual income tax return.*

Attorney Fees. Enter the amount of attorney fees that have actually been paid or that you reasonably expect to be paid. If on the final examination of the return the fees claimed have not been awarded by the proper court and paid, the deduction will be allowed provided the Estate and Gift Tax Territory Manager is reasonably satisfied that the amount claimed will be paid and that it does not exceed a reasonable payment for the services performed, taking into account the size and character of the estate and the local law and practice. If the fees claimed have not been paid at the time of final examination of the return, the amount deducted must be supported by an affidavit, or statement signed under the penalties of perjury, by the executor or the attorney stating that the amount has been agreed upon and will be paid.

Do not deduct attorney fees incidental to litigation incurred by the beneficiaries. These expenses are charged against the beneficiaries personally and are not administration expenses authorized by the Code.

Interest Expense. Interest expenses incurred after the decedent's death are generally allowed as a deduction if they are reasonable, necessary to the administration of the estate, and allowable under local law.

Interest incurred as the result of a Federal estate tax deficiency is a deductible administrative expense. Penalties are not deductible even if they are allowable under local law.

Note: *If you elect to pay the tax in installments under section 6166, you may **not** deduct the interest payable on the installments.*

Miscellaneous Expenses. Miscellaneous administration expenses necessarily incurred in preserving and distributing the estate are deductible. These expenses include appraiser's and accountant's fees, certain court costs, and costs of storing or maintaining assets of the estate.

The expenses of selling assets are deductible only if the sale is necessary to pay the decedent's debts, the expenses of administration, or taxes, or to preserve the estate or carry out distribution.

Schedule J—Page 24

Exhibit 6.1 (Continued)

Chapter Six

Form 706 (Rev. 8-02)

Estate of:

SCHEDULE K—Debts of the Decedent, and Mortgages and Liens

Item number	Debts of the Decedent—Creditor and nature of claim, and allowable death taxes	Amount unpaid to date	Amount in contest	Amount claimed as a deduction
1				

Total from continuation schedules (or additional sheets) attached to this schedule . . . .

TOTAL. (Also enter on Part 5, Recapitulation, page 3, at item 14.) . . . .

Item number	Mortgages and Liens—Description	Amount
1		

Total from continuation schedules (or additional sheets) attached to this schedule . . . .

TOTAL. (Also enter on Part 5, Recapitulation, page 3, at item 15.) . . . .

(If more space is needed, attach the continuation schedule from the end of this package or additional sheets of the same size.)
(The instructions to Schedule K are in the separate instructions.)

Schedule K—Page 25

Exhibit 6.1 (Continued)

Form 706 (Rev. 8-02)

Estate of:

SCHEDULE L—Net Losses During Administration and Expenses Incurred in Administering Property Not Subject to Claims

Item number	Net losses during administration (Note: *Do not deduct losses claimed on a Federal income tax return.*)	Amount
1		
	Total from continuation schedules (or additional sheets) attached to this schedule	
	TOTAL. (Also enter on Part 5, Recapitulation, page 3, at item 18.)	

Item number	Expenses incurred in administering property not subject to claims (Indicate whether estimated, agreed upon, or paid.)	Amount
1		
	Total from continuation schedules (or additional sheets) attached to this schedule	
	TOTAL. (Also enter on Part 5, Recapitulation, page 3, at item 19.)	

(If more space is needed, attach the continuation schedule from the end of this package or additional sheets of the same size.)

Schedule L—Page 26   (The instructions to Schedule L are in the separate instructions.)

Exhibit 6.1 (Continued)

Form 706 (Rev. 8-02)

Estate of:

SCHEDULE M—Bequests, etc., to Surviving Spouse

Election To Deduct Qualified Terminable Interest Property Under Section 2056(b)(7). If a trust (or other property) meets the requirements of qualified terminable interest property under section 2056(b)(7), and

    a. The trust or other property is listed on Schedule M, and
    b. The value of the trust (or other property) is entered in whole or in part as a deduction on Schedule M,

then unless the executor specifically identifies the trust (all or a fractional portion or percentage) or other property to be excluded from the election, the executor shall be deemed to have made an election to have such trust (or other property) treated as qualified terminable interest property under section 2056(b)(7).

If less than the entire value of the trust (or other property) that the executor has included in the gross estate is entered as a deduction on Schedule M, the executor shall be considered to have made an election only as to a fraction of the trust (or other property). The numerator of this fraction is equal to the amount of the trust (or other property) deducted on Schedule M. The denominator is equal to the total value of the trust (or other property).

Election To Deduct Qualified Domestic Trust Property Under Section 2056A. If a trust meets the requirements of a qualified domestic trust under section 2056A(a) and this return is filed no later than 1 year after the time prescribed by law (including extensions) for filing the return, and

    a. The entire value of a trust or trust property is listed on Schedule M, and
    b. The entire value of the trust or trust property is entered as a deduction on Schedule M,

then unless the executor specifically identifies the trust to be excluded from the election, the executor shall be deemed to have made an election to have the entire trust treated as qualified domestic trust property.

		Yes	No
1	Did any property pass to the surviving spouse as a result of a qualified disclaimer? If "Yes," attach a copy of the written disclaimer required by section 2518(b).		
2a	In what country was the surviving spouse born? _____		
b	What is the surviving spouse's date of birth? _____		
c	Is the surviving spouse a U.S. citizen?		
d	If the surviving spouse is a naturalized citizen, when did the surviving spouse acquire citizenship? _____		
e	If the surviving spouse is not a U.S. citizen, of what country is the surviving spouse a citizen? _____		
3	**Election Out of QTIP Treatment of Annuities**—Do you elect under section 2056(b)(7)(C)(ii) **not** to treat as qualified terminable interest property any joint and survivor annuities that are included in the gross estate and would otherwise be treated as qualified terminable interest property under section 2056(b)(7)(C)? (see instructions)		

Item number	Description of property interests passing to surviving spouse	Amount
1		

	Total from continuation schedules (or additional sheets) attached to this schedule		
4	**Total** amount of property interests listed on Schedule M	4	
5a	Federal estate taxes payable out of property interests listed on Schedule M	5a	
b	Other death taxes payable out of property interests listed on Schedule M	5b	
c	Federal and state GST taxes payable out of property interests listed on Schedule M	5c	
d	Add items 5a, b, and c	5d	
6	Net amount of property interests listed on Schedule M (subtract 5d from 4). Also enter on Part 5, Recapitulation, page 3, at item 20	6	

(If more space is needed, attach the continuation schedule from the end of this package or additional sheets of the same size.)
(See the instructions on the reverse side.)

Schedule M—Page 27

Exhibit 6.1 (Continued)

Form 706 (Rev. 8-02)

Examples of Listing of Property Interests on Schedule M

Item number	Description of property interests passing to surviving spouse	Amount
1	One-half the value of a house and lot, 256 South West Street, held by decedent and surviving spouse as joint tenants with right of survivorship under deed dated July 15, 1957 (Schedule E, Part I, item 1)	$132,500
2	Proceeds of Gibraltar Life Insurance Company policy No. 104729, payable in one sum to surviving spouse (Schedule D, item 3)	200,000
3	Cash bequest under Paragraph Six of will	100,000

Instructions for Schedule M—Bequests, etc., to Surviving Spouse (Marital Deduction)

General

You must complete Schedule M and file it with the return if you claim a deduction on item 20 of Part 5, Recapitulation.

The marital deduction is authorized by section 2056 for certain property interests that pass from the decedent to the surviving spouse. You may claim the deduction only for property interests that are included in the decedent's gross estate (Schedules A through I).

Note: *The marital deduction is generally not allowed if the surviving spouse is **not** a U.S. citizen. The marital deduction is allowed for property passing to such a surviving spouse in a "qualified domestic trust" or if such property is transferred or irrevocably assigned to such a trust before the estate tax return is filed. The executor must elect qualified domestic trust status on this return. See the instructions that follow, on pages 29–30, for details on the election.*

Property Interests That You May List on Schedule M

Generally, you may list on Schedule M all property interests that pass from the decedent to the surviving spouse and are included in the gross estate. However, you should not list any "Nondeductible terminable interests" (described below) on Schedule M unless you are making a QTIP election. The property for which you make this election must be included on Schedule M. See "Qualified terminable interest property" on the following page.

For the rules on common disaster and survival for a limited period, see section 2056(b)(3).

You may list on Schedule M only those interests that the surviving spouse takes:

1. As the decedent's legatee, devisee, heir, or donee;

2. As the decedent's surviving tenant by the entirety or joint tenant;

3. As an appointee under the decedent's exercise of a power or as a taker in default at the decedent's nonexercise of a power;

4. As a beneficiary of insurance on the decedent's life;

5. As the surviving spouse taking under dower or curtesy (or similar statutory interest); and

6. As a transferee of a transfer made by the decedent at any time.

Property Interests That You May Not List on Schedule M

You should not list on Schedule M:

1. The value of any property that does not pass from the decedent to the surviving spouse;

2. Property interests that are not included in the decedent's gross estate;

3. The full value of a property interest for which a deduction was claimed on Schedules J through L. The value of the property interest should be reduced by the deductions claimed with respect to it;

4. The full value of a property interest that passes to the surviving spouse subject to a mortgage or other encumbrance or an obligation of the surviving spouse. Include on Schedule M only the net value of the interest after reducing it by the amount of the mortgage or other debt;

5. Nondeductible terminable interests (described below);

6. Any property interest disclaimed by the surviving spouse.

Terminable Interests

Certain interests in property passing from a decedent to a surviving spouse are referred to as *terminable interests.* These are interests that will terminate or fail after the passage of time, or on the occurrence or nonoccurrence of some contingency. Examples are: life estates, annuities, estates for terms of years, and patents.

The ownership of a bond, note, or other contractual obligation, which when discharged would not have the effect of an annuity for life or for a term, is not considered a terminable interest.

Nondeductible terminable interests.

A terminable interest is *nondeductible,* and should not be entered on Schedule M (unless you are making a QTIP election) if:

1. Another interest in the same property passed from the decedent to some other person for less than adequate and full consideration in money or money's worth; and

2. By reason of its passing, the other person or that person's heirs may enjoy part of the property after the termination of the surviving spouse's interest.

This rule applies even though the interest that passes from the decedent to a person other than the surviving spouse is not included in the gross estate, and regardless of when the interest passes. The rule also applies regardless of whether the surviving spouse's interest and the other person's interest pass from the decedent at the same time.

Property interests that are considered to pass to a person other than the surviving spouse are any property interest that: **(a)** passes under a decedent's will or intestacy; **(b)** was transferred by a decedent during life; or **(c)** is held by or passed on to any person as a decedent's joint tenant, as appointee under a decedent's exercise of a power, as taker in default at a decedent's release or nonexercise of a power, or as a beneficiary of insurance on the decedent's life.

For example, a decedent devised real property to his wife for life, with remainder to his children. The life interest that passed to the wife does not qualify for the marital deduction because it will terminate at her death and the children will thereafter possess or enjoy the property.

However, if the decedent purchased a joint and survivor annuity for himself and his wife who survived him, the value of the survivor's annuity, to the extent that it is included in the gross estate, qualifies for the marital deduction because even though the interest will terminate on the wife's death, no one else will possess or enjoy any part of the property.

The marital deduction is not allowed for an interest that the decedent directed the executor or a trustee to convert, after death, into a terminable interest for the surviving spouse. The marital deduction is not allowed for such an interest even if there was no interest

Page 28

Exhibit 6.1 (Continued)

Form 706 (Rev. 8-02)

in the property passing to another person and even if the terminable interest would otherwise have been deductible under the exceptions described below for life estate and life insurance and annuity payments with powers of appointment. For more information, see Regulations sections 20.2056(b)-1(f) and 20.2056(b)-1(g), Example (7).

If any property interest passing from the decedent to the surviving spouse may be paid or otherwise satisfied out of any of a group of assets, the value of the property interest is, for the entry on Schedule M, reduced by the value of any asset or assets that, if passing from the decedent to the surviving spouse, would be nondeductible terminable interests. Examples of property interests that may be paid or otherwise satisfied out of any of a group of assets are a bequest of the residue of the decedent's estate, or of a share of the residue, and a cash legacy payable out of the general estate.

Example: A decedent bequeathed $100,000 to the surviving spouse. The general estate includes a term for years (valued at $10,000 in determining the value of the gross estate) in an office building, which interest was retained by the decedent under a deed of the building by gift to a son. Accordingly, the value of the specific bequest entered on Schedule M is $90,000.

Life Estate With Power of Appointment in the Surviving Spouse. A property interest, whether or not in trust, will be treated as passing to the surviving spouse, and will not be treated as a nondeductible terminable interest if: **(a)** the surviving spouse is entitled for life to all of the income from the entire interest; **(b)** the income is payable annually or at more frequent intervals; **(c)** the surviving spouse has the power, exercisable in favor of the surviving spouse or the estate of the surviving spouse, to appoint the entire interest; **(d)** the power is exercisable by the surviving spouse alone and (whether exercisable by will or during life) is exercisable by the surviving spouse in all events; and **(e)** no part of the entire interest is subject to a power in any other person to appoint any part to any person other than the surviving spouse (or the surviving spouse's legal representative if the surviving spouse is disabled. See Rev. Rul. 85-35, 1985-1 C.B. 328). If these five conditions are satisfied only for a specific portion of the entire interest, see the section 2056(b) regulations to determine the amount of the marital deduction.

Life Insurance, Endowment, or Annuity Payments, With Power of Appointment in Surviving Spouse. A property interest consisting of the entire proceeds under a life insurance, endowment, or annuity contract is treated as passing from the decedent to the surviving spouse, and will not be treated as a nondeductible terminable interest if: **(a)** the surviving spouse is entitled to receive the proceeds in installments, or is entitled to interest on them, with all amounts payable during the life of the spouse, payable only to the surviving spouse; **(b)** the installment or interest payments are payable annually, or more frequently, beginning not later than 13 months after the decedent's death; **(c)** the surviving spouse has the power, exercisable in favor of the surviving spouse or of the estate of the surviving spouse, to appoint all amounts payable under the contract; **(d)** the power is exercisable by the surviving spouse alone and (whether exercisable by will or during life) is exercisable by the surviving spouse in all events; and **(e)** no part of the amount payable under the contract is subject to a power in any other person to appoint any part to any person other than the surviving spouse. If these five conditions are satisfied only for a specific portion of the proceeds, see the section 2056(b) regulations to determine the amount of the marital deduction.

Charitable Remainder Trusts. An interest in a charitable remainder trust will **not** be treated as a nondeductible terminable interest if:

1. The interest in the trust passes from the decedent to the surviving spouse; and

2. The surviving spouse is the only beneficiary of the trust other than charitable organizations described in section 170(c).

A "charitable remainder trust" is either a charitable remainder annuity trust or a charitable remainder unitrust. (See section 664 for descriptions of these trusts.)

Election To Deduct Qualified Terminable Interests (QTIP)

You may elect to claim a marital deduction for qualified terminable interest property or property interests. You make the QTIP election simply by listing the qualified terminable interest property on Schedule M and deducting its value. You are presumed to have made the QTIP election if you list the property and deduct its value on Schedule M. If you make this election, the surviving spouse's gross estate will include the value of the "qualified terminable interest property." See the instructions for line 6 of Part 4, General Information, for more details. **The election is irrevocable.**

If you file a Form 706 in which you do not make this election, you may not file an amended return to make the election unless you file the amended return on or before the due date for filing the original Form 706.

The effect of the election is that the property (interest) will be treated as passing to the surviving spouse and will not be treated as a nondeductible terminable interest. All of the other marital deduction requirements must still be satisfied before you may make this election. For example, you may not make this election for property or property interests that are not included in the decedent's gross estate.

Qualified terminable interest property is property **(a)** that passes from the decedent, and **(b)** in which the surviving spouse has a qualifying income interest for life.

The surviving spouse has a *qualifying income interest for life* if the surviving spouse is entitled to all of the income from the property payable annually or at more frequent intervals, or has a usufruct interest for life in the property, and during the surviving spouse's lifetime no person has a power to appoint any part of the property to any person other than the surviving spouse. An annuity is treated as an income interest regardless of whether the property from which the annuity is payable can be separately identified.

Amendments to Regulations sections 20.2044-1, 20.2056(b)-7 and 20.2056(b)-10 clarify that an interest in property is eligible for QTIP treatment if the income interest is contingent upon the executor's election even if that portion of the property for which no election is made will pass to or for the benefit of beneficiaries other than the surviving spouse.

The QTIP election may be made for all or any part of qualified terminable interest property. A partial election must relate to a fractional or percentile share of the property so that the elective part will reflect its proportionate share of the increase or decline in the whole of the property when applying sections 2044 or 2519. Thus, if the interest of the surviving spouse in a trust (or other property in which the spouse has a qualified life estate) is qualified terminable interest property, you may make an election for a part of the trust (or other property) only if the election relates to a defined fraction or percentage of the entire trust (or other property). The fraction or percentage may be defined by means of a formula.

Qualified Domestic Trust Election (QDOT)

The marital deduction is allowed for transfers to a surviving spouse who is not a U.S. citizen only if the property passes to the surviving spouse in a "qualified domestic trust" (QDOT) or if

Page 29

Exhibit 6.1 (Continued)

Form 706 (Rev. 8-02)

such property is transferred or irrevocably assigned to a QDOT before the decedent's estate tax return is filed.

A QDOT is any trust:

1. That requires at least one trustee to be either an individual who is a citizen of the United States or a domestic corporation;

2. That requires that no distribution of corpus from the trust can be made unless such a trustee has the right to withhold from the distribution the tax imposed on the QDOT;

3. That meets the requirements of any applicable regulations; and

4. For which the executor has made an election on the estate tax return of the decedent.

Note: *For trusts created by an instrument executed before November 5, 1990, paragraphs 1 and 2 above will be treated as met if the trust instrument requires that all trustees be individuals who are citizens of the United States or domestic corporations.*

You make the QDOT election simply by listing the qualified domestic trust or the **entire value** of the trust property on Schedule M and deducting its value. You are presumed to have made the QDOT election if you list the trust or trust property and deduct its value on Schedule M. **Once made, the election is irrevocable.**

If an election is made to deduct qualified domestic trust property under section 2056A(d), the following information should be provided for each qualified domestic trust on an attachment to this schedule:

1. The name and address of every trustee;

2. A description of each transfer passing from the decedent that is the source of the property to be placed in trust; and

3. The employer identification number (EIN) for the trust.

The election must be made for an entire QDOT trust. In listing a trust for which you are making a QDOT election, unless you specifically identify the trust as not subject to the election, the election will be considered made for the entire trust.

The determination of whether a trust qualifies as a QDOT will be made as of the date the decedent's Form 706 is filed. If, however, judicial proceedings are brought before the Form 706's due date (including extensions) to have the trust revised to meet the QDOT requirements, then the determination will not be made until the court-ordered changes to the trust are made.

Line 1

If property passes to the surviving spouse as the result of a qualified disclaimer, check "Yes" and attach a copy of the written disclaimer required by section 2518(b).

Line 3

Section 2056(b)(7) creates an automatic QTIP election for certain joint and survivor annuities that are includible in the estate under section 2039. To qualify, only the surviving spouse can have the right to receive payments before the death of the surviving spouse.

The executor can elect out of QTIP treatment, however, by checking the "Yes" box on line 3. Once made, the election is irrevocable. If there is more than one such joint and survivor annuity, you are not required to make the election for all of them.

If you make the election out of QTIP treatment by checking "Yes" on line 3, you cannot deduct the amount of the annuity on Schedule M. If you do not make the election out, you must list the joint and survivor annuities on Schedule M.

Listing Property Interests on Schedule M

List each property interest included in the gross estate that passes from the decedent to the surviving spouse and for which a marital deduction is claimed. This includes otherwise nondeductible terminable interest property for which you are making a QTIP election. Number each item in sequence and describe each item in detail. Describe the instrument (including any clause or paragraph number) or provision of law under which each item passed to the surviving spouse. If possible, show where each item appears (number and schedule) on Schedules A through I.

In listing otherwise nondeductible property for which you are making a QTIP election, unless you specifically identify a fractional portion of the trust or other property as not subject to the election, the election will be considered made for all of the trust or other property.

Enter the value of each interest before taking into account the Federal estate tax or any other death tax. The valuation dates used in determining the value of the gross estate apply also on Schedule M.

If Schedule M includes a bequest of the residue or a part of the residue of the decedent's estate, attach a copy of the computation showing how the value of the residue was determined. Include a statement showing:

• The value of all property that is included in the decedent's gross estate (Schedules A through I) but is not a part of the decedent's probate estate, such as lifetime transfers, jointly owned property that passed to the survivor on decedent's death, and the insurance payable to specific beneficiaries.

• The values of all specific and general legacies or devises, with reference to the applicable clause or paragraph of the decedent's will or codicil. (If legacies are made to each member of a class; for example, $1,000 to each of decedent's employees, only the number in each class and the total value of property received by them need be furnished.)

• The date of birth of all persons, the length of whose lives may affect the value of the residuary interest passing to the surviving spouse.

• Any other important information such as that relating to any claim to any part of the estate not arising under the will.

Lines 5a, b, and c—The total of the values listed on Schedule M must be reduced by the amount of the Federal estate tax, the Federal GST tax, and the amount of state or other death and GST taxes paid out of the property interest involved. If you enter an amount for state or other death or GST taxes on lines 5b or 5c, identify the taxes and attach your computation of them.

Attachments. If you list property interests passing by the decedent's will on Schedule M, attach a certified copy of the order admitting the will to probate. If, when you file the return, the court of probate jurisdiction has entered any decree interpreting the will or any of its provisions affecting any of the interests listed on Schedule M, or has entered any order of distribution, attach a copy of the decree or order. In addition, the IRS may request other evidence to support the marital deduction claimed.

Page 30

Exhibit 6.1 (Continued)

284 Chapter Six

Form 706 (Rev. 8-02)

Estate of:

SCHEDULE O—Charitable, Public, and Similar Gifts and Bequests

		Yes	No
1a	If the transfer was made by will, has any action been instituted to have interpreted or to contest the will or any of its provisions affecting the charitable deductions claimed in this schedule? . . . . If "Yes," full details must be submitted with this schedule.		
b	According to the information and belief of the person or persons filing this return, is any such action planned? If "Yes," full details must be submitted with this schedule.		
2	Did any property pass to charity as the result of a qualified disclaimer? . . . . If "Yes," attach a copy of the written disclaimer required by section 2518(b).		

Item number	Name and address of beneficiary	Character of institution	Amount
1			

Total from continuation schedules (or additional sheets) attached to this schedule . . . .

3 Total		**3**
4a Federal estate tax payable out of property interests listed above	**4a**	
b Other death taxes payable out of property interests listed above	**4b**	
c Federal and state GST taxes payable out of property interests listed above	**4c**	
d Add items 4a, b, and c		**4d**
5 Net value of property interests listed above (subtract 4d from 3). Also enter on Part 5, Recapitulation, page 3, at item 21		**5**

(If more space is needed, attach the continuation schedule from the end of this package or additional sheets of the same size.)
(The instructions to Schedule O are in the separate instructions.)

Schedule O—Page 31

Exhibit 6.1 (Continued)

Form 706 (Rev. 8-02)

Estate of:

SCHEDULE P—Credit for Foreign Death Taxes

List all foreign countries to which death taxes have been paid and for which a credit is claimed on this return.

If a credit is claimed for death taxes paid to more than one foreign country, compute the credit for taxes paid to one country on this sheet and attach a separate copy of Schedule P for each of the other countries.

The credit computed on this sheet is for the _____
(Name of death tax or taxes)

_____ imposed in _____
(Name of country)

Credit is computed under the _____
(Insert title of treaty or "statute")

Citizenship (nationality) of decedent at time of death

(All amounts and values must be entered in United States money.)

1 Total of estate, inheritance, legacy, and succession taxes imposed in the country named above attributable to property situated in that country, subjected to these taxes, and included in the gross estate (as defined by statute)	1
2 Value of the gross estate (adjusted, if necessary, according to the instructions for item 2)	2
3 Value of property situated in that country, subjected to death taxes imposed in that country, and included in the gross estate (adjusted, if necessary, according to the instructions for item 3)	3
4 Tax imposed by section 2001 reduced by the total credits claimed under sections 2010, 2011, and 2012 (see instructions).	4
5 Amount of Federal estate tax attributable to property specified at item 3. (Divide item 3 by item 2 and multiply the result by item 4.)	5
6 Credit for death taxes imposed in the country named above (the smaller of item 1 or item 5). Also enter on line 16 of Part 2, Tax Computation	6

SCHEDULE Q—Credit for Tax on Prior Transfers

Part 1—Transferor Information

	Name of transferor	Social security number	IRS office where estate tax return was filed	Date of death
A				
B				
C				

Check here ▶ ☐ if section 2013(f) (special valuation of farm, etc., real property) adjustments to the computation of the credit were made (see page 19 of the instructions).

Part 2—Computation of Credit (see instructions beginning on page 19)

Item	Transferor A	Transferor B	Transferor C	Total A, B, & C
1 Transferee's tax as apportioned (from worksheet, (line 7 ÷ line 8) × line 35 for each column)				
2 Transferor's tax (from each column of worksheet, line 20)				
3 Maximum amount before percentage requirement (for each column, enter amount from line 1 or 2, whichever is smaller)				
4 Percentage allowed (each column) (see instructions)	%	%	%	
5 Credit allowable (line 3 × line 4 for each column)				
6 TOTAL credit allowable (add columns A, B, and C of line 5). Enter here and on line 17 of Part 2, Tax Computation				

Schedules P and Q—Page 32   (The instructions to Schedules P and Q are in the separate instructions.)

Exhibit 6.1 (Continued)

Form 706 (Rev. 8-02)

SCHEDULE R—Generation-Skipping Transfer Tax

Note: *To avoid application of the deemed allocation rules, Form 706 and Schedule R should be filed to allocate the GST exemption to trusts that may later have taxable terminations or distributions under section 2612 even if the form is not required to be filed to report estate or GST tax.*

The GST tax is imposed on taxable transfers of interests in property located **outside the United States** *as well as property located inside the United States.*

See instructions beginning on page 20.

Part 1—GST Exemption Reconciliation (Section 2631) and Section 2652(a)(3) (Special QTIP) Election

You no longer need to check a box to make a section 2652(a)(3) (special QTIP) election. If you list qualifying property in Part 1, line 9, below, you will be considered to have made this election. See page 22 of the separate instructions for details.

1 Maximum allowable GST exemption . . . . | 1 |
2 Total GST exemption allocated by the decedent against decedent's lifetime transfers . . . . | 2 |
3 Total GST exemption allocated by the executor, using Form 709, against decedent's lifetime transfers . . . . | 3 |
4 GST exemption allocated on line 6 of Schedule R, Part 2 . . . . | 4 |
5 GST exemption allocated on line 6 of Schedule R, Part 3 . . . . | 5 |
6 Total GST exemption allocated on line 4 of Schedule(s) R-1 . . . . | 6 |
7 Total GST exemption allocated to intervivos transfers and direct skips (add lines 2–6) . . . | 7 |
8 GST exemption available to allocate to trusts and section 2032A interests (subtract line 7 from line 1) . . . . | 8 |
9 Allocation of GST exemption to trusts (as defined for GST tax purposes):

A Name of trust	B Trust's EIN (if any)	C GST exemption allocated on lines 2–6, above (see instructions)	D Additional GST exemption allocated (see instructions)	E Trust's inclusion ratio (optional—see instructions)

9D Total. May not exceed line 8, above . . . . | 9D |

10 GST exemption allocated to section 2032A interests received by individual beneficiaries (subtract line 9D from line 8). You must attach special use allocation schedule (see instructions) . . . | 10 |

(The instructions to Schedule R are in the separate instructions.)

Schedule R—Page 33

Exhibit 6.1 (Continued)

Estate and Gift Taxation

Form 706 (Rev. 8-02)

Estate of:

Part 2—Direct Skips Where the Property Interests Transferred Bear the GST Tax on the Direct Skips

Name of skip person	Description of property interest transferred	Estate tax value

1. Total estate tax values of all property interests listed above . . . . | 1 |
2. Estate taxes, state death taxes, and other charges borne by the property interests listed above . | 2 |
3. GST taxes borne by the property interests listed above but imposed on direct skips other than those shown on this Part 2 (see instructions) . . . . | 3 |
4. Total fixed taxes and other charges (add lines 2 and 3) . . . . | 4 |
5. Total tentative maximum direct skips (subtract line 4 from line 1) . . . . | 5 |
6. GST exemption allocated . . . . | 6 |
7. Subtract line 6 from line 5 . . . . | 7 |
8. GST tax due (divide line 7 by 3.0) . . . . | 8 |
9. Enter the amount from line 8 of Schedule R, Part 3 . . . . | 9 |
10. **Total GST taxes payable by the estate** (add lines 8 and 9). Enter here and on line 20 of Part 2—Tax Computation, on page 1 . . . . | 10 |

Schedule R—Page 34

Exhibit 6.1 (Continued)

Form 706 (Rev. 8-02)

Estate of:

Part 3—Direct Skips Where the Property Interests Transferred Do Not Bear the GST Tax on the Direct Skips

Name of skip person	Description of property interest transferred	Estate tax value

1. Total estate tax values of all property interests listed above **1**
2. Estate taxes, state death taxes, and other charges borne by the property interests listed above . **2**
3. GST taxes borne by the property interests listed above but imposed on direct skips other than those shown on this Part 3 (see instructions) **3**
4. Total fixed taxes and other charges (add lines 2 and 3). **4**
5. Total tentative maximum direct skips (subtract line 4 from line 1) **5**
6. GST exemption allocated **6**
7. Subtract line 6 from line 5 . . . . **7**
8. GST tax due (multiply line 7 by .50). Enter here and on Schedule R, Part 2, line 9 . . . . . **8**

Schedule R—Page 35

Exhibit 6.1 (Continued)

Estate and Gift Taxation 289

SCHEDULE R-1
(Form 706)
(Rev. August 2002)
Department of the Treasury
Internal Revenue Service

Generation-Skipping Transfer Tax
Direct Skips From a Trust
Payment Voucher

OMB No. 1545-0015

Executor: File one copy with Form 706 and send two copies to the fiduciary. Do not pay the tax shown. See the **separate instructions.**
Fiduciary: See instructions on the following page. Pay the tax shown on line 6.

Name of trust		Trust's EIN
Name and title of fiduciary	Name of decedent	
Address of fiduciary (number and street)	Decedent's SSN	Service Center where Form 706 was filed
City, state, and ZIP code	Name of executor	
Address of executor (number and street)	City, state, and ZIP code	
Date of decedent's death	Filing due date of Schedule R, Form 706 (with extensions)	

Part 1—Computation of the GST Tax on the Direct Skip

Description of property interests subject to the direct skip	Estate tax value

1	Total estate tax value of all property interests listed above	1
2	Estate taxes, state death taxes, and other charges borne by the property interests listed above	2
3	Tentative maximum direct skip from trust (subtract line 2 from line 1)	3
4	GST exemption allocated	4
5	Subtract line 4 from line 3	5
6	**GST tax due from fiduciary** (divide line 5 by 3.0) **(See instructions if property will not bear the GST tax.)**	6

Under penalties of perjury, I declare that I have examined this return, including accompanying schedules and statements, and to the best of my knowledge and belief, it is true, correct, and complete.

Signature(s) of executor(s) _____ Date _____

_____ Date _____

Signature of fiduciary or officer representing fiduciary _____ Date _____

Schedule R-1 (Form 706)—Page 36

Exhibit 6.1 (Continued)

290 Chapter Six

Form 706 (Rev. 8-02)

Instructions for the Trustee

Introduction Schedule R-1 (Form 706) serves as a payment voucher for the Generation-Skipping Transfer (GST) tax imposed on a direct skip from a trust, which you, the trustee of the trust, must pay. The executor completes the Schedule R-1 (Form 706) and gives you 2 copies. File one copy and keep one for your records.

How to pay You can pay by check or money order.
- Make it payable to the "United States Treasury."
- Make the check or money order for the amount on line 6 of Schedule R-1.
- Write "GST Tax" and the trust's EIN on the check or money order.

Signature You must sign the Schedule R-1 in the space provided.

What to mail Mail your check or money order and the copy of Schedule R-1 that you signed.

Where to mail Mail to the Service Center shown on Schedule R-1.

When to pay The GST tax is due and payable 9 months after the decedent's date of death (shown on the Schedule R-1). You will owe interest on any GST tax not paid by that date.

Automatic extension You have an automatic extension of time to file Schedule R-1 and pay the GST tax. The automatic extension allows you to file and pay by 2 months after the due date (with extensions) for filing the decedent's Schedule R (shown on the Schedule R-1).
  If you pay the GST tax under the automatic extension, you will be charged interest (but no penalties).

Additional information For more information, see Code section 2603(a)(2) and the instructions for Form 706, United States Estate (and Generation-Skipping Transfer) Tax Return.

Schedule R-1 (Form 706)—Page 37

Exhibit 6.1 (Continued)

Form 706 (Rev. 8-02)

Estate of:

SCHEDULE T—Qualified Family-Owned Business Interest Deduction

For details on the deduction, including trades and businesses that do not qualify, see page 23 of the separate Instructions for Form 706.

Part 1—Election

Note: *The executor is deemed to have made the election under section 2057 if he or she files Schedule T and deducts any qualifying business interests from the gross estate.*

Part 2—General Qualifications

1. Did the decedent and/or a member of the decedent's family own the business interests listed on line 5 of this schedule for at least 5 of the 8 years immediately preceding the date of the decedent's death? . ☐ Yes ☐ No

2. Were there any periods during the 8-year period preceding the date of the decedent's death during which the decedent or a member of his or her family: | Yes | No |

   a Did not own the business interests listed on this schedule? . . . .

   b Did not materially participate, within the meaning of section 2032A(e)(6), in the operation of the business to which such interests relate?. . . . .

   If "Yes" to either of the above, you must attach a statement listing the periods. If applicable, describe whether the exceptions of sections 2032A(b)(4) or (5) are met.

   Attach affidavits describing the activities constituting material participation and the identity and relationship to the decedent of the material participants.

3. Check the applicable box(es). The qualified family-owned business interest(s) is:
   ☐ An interest as a proprietor in a trade or business carried on as a proprietorship.
   ☐ An interest in an entity, at least 50% of which is owned (directly or indirectly) by the decedent and members of the decedent's family.
   ☐ An interest in an entity, at least 70% of which is owned (directly or indirectly) by members of 2 families and at least 30% of which is owned (directly or indirectly) by the decedent and members of the decedent's family.
   ☐ An interest in an entity, at least 90% of which is owned (directly or indirectly) by members of 3 families and at least 30% of which is owned (directly or indirectly) by the decedent and members of the decedent's family.

4. **Persons holding interests.** Enter the requested information for each party who received any interest in the family-owned business. If any qualified heir is not a U.S. citizen, see the line 4 instructions on page 24 of the separate instructions. **(Each of the qualified heirs receiving an interest in the business must sign the agreement that begins on the following page 40, and the agreement must be filed with this return.)**

	Name	Address
A		
B		
C		
D		
E		
F		
G		
H		

	Identifying number	Relationship to decedent	Value of interest
A			
B			
C			
D			
E			
F			
G			
H			

Schedule T (Form 706)—Page 38

Exhibit 6.1 (Continued)

Form 706 (Rev. 8-02)

Part 3—Adjusted Value of Qualified Family-Owned Business Interests

5 Qualified family-owned business interests reported on this return.
   Note: *All property listed on line 5 must also be entered on Schedules A, B, C, E, F, G, or H, as applicable.*

A Schedule and item number from Form 706	B Description of business interest and principal place of business	C Reported value

6 **Total** reported value . . . .
7 Amount of claims or mortgages deductible under section 2053(a)(3) or (4) (see separate instructions). . . . .
8a Enter the amount of any indebtedness on qualified residence of the decedent (see separate instructions) . . . .
 b Enter the amount of any indebtedness used for educational or medical expenses (see separate instructions) .
 c Enter the amount of any indebtedness other than that listed on line 8a or 8b, but do not enter more than $10,000 (see separate instructions) . . . .
 d Total (add lines 8a through 8c). . . . .
9 Subtract line 8d from line 7 . . . .
10 Adjusted value of qualified family-owned business interests (subtract line 9 from line 6) . .

Part 4—Qualifying Estate

11 Includible gifts of qualified family-owned business interests (see separate instructions):

 a Amount of gifts taken into account under section 2001(b)(1)(B) .
 b Amount of such gifts excluded under section 2503(b) . . . .
 c Add lines 11a and 11b . . . .
12 Add lines 10 and 11c. . . . .
13 Adjusted gross estate (see separate instructions):
 a Amount of gross estate . . . . .
 b Enter the amount from line 7 . . .
 c Subtract line 13b from line 13a . .
 d Enter the amount from line 11c . .
 e Enter the amount of transfers, if any, to the decedent's spouse (see inst.)
 f Enter the amount of other gifts (see inst.)
 g Add the amounts on lines 13d, 13e, and 13f . . . .
 h Enter any amounts from line 13g that are otherwise includible in the gross estate . . . .
 i Subtract line 13h from line 13g . . . .
 j Adjusted gross estate (add lines 13c and 13i). . . . .
14 Enter one-half of the amount on line 13j . . . .
   Note: *If line 12 does not exceed line 14, stop here; the estate does not qualify for the deduction. Otherwise, complete line 15.*
15 Net value of qualified family-owned business interests you elect to deduct (line 10 reduced by any marital or other deductions)—**DO NOT** enter more than $675,000—(see instructions) (attach schedule)—enter here and on Part 5, Recapitulation, page 3, at item 22 . . . . .

Schedule T—Page 39

Exhibit 6.1 (Continued)

Estate and Gift Taxation 293

Form 706 (Rev. 8-02)

Part 5—Agreement to Family-Owned Business Interest Deduction Under Section 2057

| Estate of: | Date of Death | Decedent's Social Security Number |

There cannot be a valid election unless:
- The agreement is executed by each and every one of the qualified heirs, and
- The agreement is included with the estate tax return when the estate tax return is filed.

We (list all qualified heirs and other persons having an interest in the business required to sign this agreement) _____

_____,

being all the qualified heirs and _____

_____,

being all other parties having interests in the business(es) which are deducted under section 2057 of the Internal Revenue Code, do hereby approve of the election made by _____

Executor/Administrator of the estate of _____,

pursuant to section 2057 to deduct said interests from the gross estate and do hereby enter into this agreement pursuant to section 2057(h).

The undersigned agree and consent to the application of subsection (f) of section 2057 of the Code with respect to all the qualified family-owned business interests deducted on Schedule T of Form 706, attached to this agreement. More specifically, the undersigned heirs expressly agree and consent to personal liability under subsection (c) of 2032A (as made applicable by section 2057(i)(3)(F) of the Code) for the additional estate tax imposed by that subsection with respect to their respective interests in the above-described business interests in the event of certain early dispositions of the interests or the occurrence of any of the disqualifying acts described in section 2057(f)(1) of the Code. It is understood that if a qualified heir disposes of any deducted interest to any member of his or her family, such member may thereafter be treated as the qualified heir with respect to such interest upon filing a new agreement and any other form required by the Internal Revenue Service.

The undersigned interested parties who are not qualified heirs consent to the collection of any additional estate tax imposed under section 2057(f) of the Code from the deducted interests.

If there is a disposition of any interest which passes or has passed to him or her, each of the undersigned heirs agrees to file the appropriate form and pay any additional estate tax due within 6 months of the disposition or other disqualifying act.

It is understood by all interested parties that this agreement is a condition precedent to the election of the qualified family-owned business deduction under section 2057 of the Code and must be executed by every interested party even though that person may not have received the estate tax benefits or be in possession of such property.

Each of the undersigned understands that by making this election, a lien will be created and recorded pursuant to section 6324B of the Code on the interests referred to in this agreement for the applicable percentage of the adjusted tax differences with respect to the estate as defined in section 2057(f)(2)(C).

As the interested parties, the undersigned designate the following individual as their agent for all dealings with the Internal Revenue Service concerning the continued qualification of the deducted property under section 2057 of the Code and on all issues regarding the special lien under section 6324B. The agent is authorized to act for all the parties with respect to all dealings with the Service on matters affecting the qualified interests described earlier. This authority includes the following:

- To receive confidential information on all matters relating to continued qualification under section 2057 of the deducted interests and on all matters relating to the special lien arising under section 6324B.
- To furnish the Service with any requested information concerning the interests.
- To notify the Service of any disposition or other disqualifying events specified in section 2057(f)(1) of the Code.
- To receive, but not to endorse and collect, checks in payment of any refund of Internal Revenue taxes, penalties, or interest.
- To execute waivers (including offers of waivers) of restrictions on assessment or collection of deficiencies in tax and waivers of notice of disallowance of a claim for credit or refund.
- To execute closing agreements under section 7121.

(continued on next page)

Schedule T, Part 5—Page 40

Exhibit 6.1 (Continued)

Form 706 (Rev. 8-02)

Part 5. Agreement to Family-Owned Business Interest Deduction Under Section 2057 (continued)

Estate of:	Date of Death	Decedent's Social Security Number

● Other acts (specify) ▶ _____

By signing this agreement, the agent agrees to provide the Internal Revenue Service with any requested information concerning the qualified business interests and to notify the Internal Revenue Service of any disposition or other disqualifying events with regard to said interests.

Name of Agent	Signature	Address

The interests to which this agreement relates are listed in Form 706, United States Estate (and Generation-Skipping Transfer) Tax Return, along with their fair market value according to section 2031 (or, if applicable, section 2032A) of the Code. The name, address, social security number, and interest (including the value) of each of the undersigned in this business(es) are as set forth in the attached Schedule T.

IN WITNESS WHEREOF, the undersigned have hereunto set their hands at _____ ,

this _____ day of _____ .

SIGNATURES OF EACH OF THE QUALIFIED HEIRS:

Signature of qualified heir	Signature of qualified heir
Signature of qualified heir	Signature of qualified heir
Signature of qualified heir	Signature of qualified heir
Signature of qualified heir	Signature of qualified heir
Signature of qualified heir	Signature of qualified heir
Signature of qualified heir	Signature of qualified heir

Signature(s) of other interested parties

Signature(s) of other interested parties

Schedule T, Part 5—Page 41

Exhibit 6.1 (Continued)

Form 706 (Rev. 8-02)

Estate of:

SCHEDULE U. Qualified Conservation Easement Exclusion

Part 1—Election

Note: *The executor is deemed to have made the election under section 2031(c)(6) if he or she files Schedule U and excludes any qualifying conservation easements from the gross estate.*

Part 2—General Qualifications

1. Describe the land subject to the qualified conservation easement (see separate instructions) _____

2. Did the decedent or a member of the decedent's family own the land described above during the 3-year period ending on the date of the decedent's death? . . . . ☐ Yes ☐ No

3. Describe the conservation easement with regard to which the exclusion is being claimed (see separate instructions).

Part 3—Computation of Exclusion

4. Estate tax value of the land subject to the qualified conservation easement (see separate instructions) 4
5. Date of death value of any easements granted prior to decedent's death and included on line 10 below (see instructions) 5
6. Add lines 4 and 5 6
7. Value of retained development rights on the land (see instructions) 7
8. Subtract line 7 from line 6 8
9. Multiply line 8 by 30% (.30) 9
10. Value of qualified conservation easement for which the exclusion is being claimed (see instructions) 10

    Note: *If line 10 is less than line 9, continue with line 11. If line 10 is equal to or more than line 9, skip lines 11 through 13, enter ".40" on line 14, and complete the schedule.*

11. Divide line 10 by line 8. Figure to 3 decimal places (e.g., .123) . 11

    If line 11 is equal to or less than .100, stop here; the estate does not qualify for the conservation easement exclusion.

12. Subtract line 11 from .300. Enter the answer in hundredths by rounding any thousandths up to the next higher hundredth (i.e., .030 = .03; but .031 = .04). 12
13. Multiply line 12 by 2 13
14. Subtract line 13 from .40 14
15. Deduction under section 2055(f) for the conservation easement (see separate instructions) 15
16. Amount of indebtedness on the land (see separate instructions) 16
17. Total reductions in value (add lines 7, 15, and 16) 17
18. Net value of land (subtract line 17 from line 4) 18
19. Multiply line 18 by line 14 19
20. Enter the smaller of line 19 or the exclusion limitation (see instructions). Also enter this amount on item 11, Part 5, Recapitulation, Page 3. 20

Schedule U—Page 42

Exhibit 6.1 (Continued)

Form 706 (Rev. 8-02)

(Make copies of this schedule before completing it if you will need more than one schedule.)

Estate of:

CONTINUATION SCHEDULE

Continuation of Schedule _____
(Enter letter of schedule you are continuing.)

Item number	Description For securities, give CUSIP number.	Unit value (Sch. B, E, or G only)	Alternate valuation date	Alternate value	Value at date of death or amount deductible

TOTAL. (Carry forward to main schedule.) . . . .

See the instructions on the reverse side.

Continuation Schedule—Page 43

Exhibit 6.1 (Continued)

Estate and Gift Taxation 297

Form 706 (Rev. 8-02)

Instructions for Continuation Schedule

When you need to list more assets or deductions than you have room for on one of the main schedules, use the Continuation Schedule on page 43. It provides a uniform format for listing additional assets from Schedules A through I and additional deductions from Schedules J, K, L, M, and O.

Please keep the following points in mind:

- Use a separate Continuation Schedule for each main schedule you are continuing. Do not combine assets or deductions from different schedules on one Continuation Schedule.
- Make copies of the blank schedule before completing it if you expect to need more than one.
- Use as many Continuation Schedules as needed to list all the assets or deductions.
- Enter the letter of the schedule you are continuing in the space at the top of the Continuation Schedule.
- Use the *Unit value* column only if continuing Schedule B, E, or G. For all other schedules, use this space to continue the description.
- Carry the total from the Continuation Schedules forward to the appropriate line on the main schedule.

If continuing	Report	Where on Continuation Schedule
Schedule E, Pt. 2	*Percentage includible*	Alternate valuation date
Schedule K	*Amount unpaid to date*	Alternate valuation date
Schedule K	*Amount in contest*	Alternate value
Schedules J, L, M	*Description of deduction continuation*	Alternate valuation date **and** Alternate value
Schedule O	*Character of institution*	Alternate valuation date **and** Alternate value
Schedule O	*Amount of each deduction*	Amount deductible

Continuation Schedule—Page 44

Exhibit 6.1 (Continued)

Form 706 (Rev. 8-02)

Internal Revenue Service
Cincinnati, OH 45999

Contact Person:
Badge Number:
Telephone:
(Not Toll Free)

- **Date:**

Estate Tax Closing Document
(Not a bill for tax due)

Executor or POA name
- Address:
- Address:
- City, State, and ZIP:

Estate Name:
Social Security Number:
Date of Death:

We have determined the following:

- NET ESTATE TAX: $
- STATE DEATH TAX CREDIT: $
- GENERATION-SKIPPING TAX: $

These figures do not include any interest or penalties that may be charged.

Please keep this document in your permanent records. You may need it to complete administration of the estate, such as: close probate proceedings, transfer title to property, and settle state taxes. Keep it with your cancelled check(s) to show that you have met the estate tax obligation. **Proof of payment in the amount shown above releases you of personal liability (IRC 2204). If the time for payment is extended under section 6161, 6163 or 6166, personal liability is not released until full payment has been received.**

We will not reopen this return unless you notify us of changes to the return, or there is evidence of misrepresentation of a material fact, a clearly defined substantial error based upon an established Service position or a serious administrative omission. (See IRC 7121).

- Signature of Authorized Official   Title   Date
- c.c. Power of Attorney

Exhibit 6.1 (Continued)

Form 706 (Rev. 8-02)

Instructions for Estate Tax Closing Document

We are providing a copy of an Estate Tax Closing Document for your convenience. Completing it should facilitate the processing of the estate tax return.

Complete the entries for Executor or POA name and address, the Estate Name, the decedent's Social Security Number, and the Date of Death, and file the Document with Form 706.

Printed on recycled paper

*U.S. Government Printing Office: 2002—715-015/27023

Exhibit 6.1 (Continued)

706 must be filed nine months from the date of death of the decedent. If the personal representative anticipates a problem in filing within this time frame, because of a potential will contest or difficulty in locating assets or defending claims, Form 4768, Application for Extension of Time to File U.S. Estate Tax Return, may be filed. Form 4768 should be filed as soon as possible so that the Internal Revenue Service may rule on the application prior to the filing date for the Form 706, although an extension will be granted automatically for six months. Furthermore, the personal representative must file Form SS-4, Application for Employer I.D. Number, on behalf of the estate. As a taxable entity the estate must have its own taxpayer identification number.

Form 706: United States Estate and Generation-Skipping Transfer Tax Return

Form 706 is divided into five main sections. Part 1 requires general information about the decedent, such as name, address, date of death, and name of the personal representative. Part 2 is a compilation of the total tax due. This section of the return is dependent on the 20 schedules that are attached to the form. Part 3 concerns certain tax elections. The primary election decision that must be made concerns the date on which the decedent's assets are to be valued. IRS permits all of the assets (except cash) to be valued either at the date of death or exactly six months from the date of death, whichever results in a lower valuation [IRC sec. 2032(a).] This election is known as the **alternate valuation,** and valuing estate property is one of the most important determinations made by the personal representative. It is important to bear in mind that *all* of the assets must be valued on the date chosen—assets may not be divided up so as to value some at the date of death and some six months later. This election is only made if it will reduce the taxable estate.

alternate valuation
Election to value an estate at date of death or six months later

Part 4 asks for general information about the estate, including a copy of the death certificate and court authority of the personal representative, as well as the names, addresses, social security numbers, and amounts received by all beneficiaries of the estate. Part 5 is merely a recapitulation of the totals appearing on the attached schedules.

Many times people attempt to decrease the value of their estates by transferring property to family members while they are alive. Although this may prove excellent estate planning, in certain instances, IRS will look through some of these transactions and still include the value of the transferred property as part of the decedent's estate. In *Estate of Musgrove v. U.S.*, 33 Fed. Cl. 657 (1995), the court held that intrafamily loans may still be included as part of the deceased family member's estate.

Form 706 need only be filed if the value of the gross taxable estate exceeds the amount that will pass tax free pursuant to the **Unified Tax Credit** (IRC sec. 2012). The Unified Tax Credit permits a taxpayer to make tax-free transfers during his or her life, and then reduce the amount of the estate tax due on death by the amount so transferred while he or she was alive.

Pursuant to the **Economic Growth and Tax Reconciliation Act of 2001,** the amount of an estate that may pass tax free is $1.5 million in 2004, $2 million in 2006, and $3.5 million in 2009. In 2010, pursuant to this act, there will be no estate tax imposed on any estate. The avowed purpose behind the enactment of this statute was to do away with all taxation of estates, regardless of the value. However, because of a sunset provision of the statute, unless it is reenacted by Congress, on January 1, 2011, the amount of a person's estate that may pass tax free will revert to the amounts in effect prior to June 2001. Further, the federal lifetime gift tax exemption is $1 million.

The Internal Revenue Service imposes a tax on property transferred by gift, either inter vivos or testamentary. A donor may transfer, tax free, up to $11,000 worth of property each year per donee. Gifts above this amount, except for gifts to spouses, to charities, or for tuition or medical care, must be reported to the IRS on Form 709. No tax is due on these gifts until the total amount exceeds the maximum size of an estate that may pass tax free because of this Unified Tax Credit. The amount of such estates is increasing each year until year 2009, after which the future of the Unified Tax Credit is uncertain. When the donor dies, the gifts reported on Form 709 are deducted from the dollar exemption permitted for the year of death. This tax exclusion means that a person may transfer much of his or her estate while alive. Note that the amount of the gift exclusion is doubled if the gift is made jointly by husbands and wives.

Unified Tax Credit
Tax law permitting a taxpayer to make tax-free transfers during life

Economic Growth and Tax Reconciliation Act of 2001
Law that increased the value of an estate that may pass tax free

Exercise

How would you be able to document and prove that the value of an item transferred does not exceed $11,000? Would a bill of sale for the item when purchased 10 years ago be sufficient? Why?

Even if the gross estate exceeds this amount, taxes still may not be due if the net estate (assets minus liabilities) falls below the tax-free limit.

Practical tip

The federal Form 706 should be prepared prior to any potential state estate tax returns because most state forms follow the 706. Because some states impose estate taxes on estates valued *below* the federal Unified Tax Credit amount, even though no federal return need be filed, or federal estate taxes paid, state forms and taxes also may still be required. Each jurisdiction must be individually analyzed.

Exercise

Should the income generated by an asset valued by the alternative method of valuation be included as part of the value? Read *Johnston v. United States,* 779 F.2d 1123 (5th Cir, 1986).

Assets

The first nine schedules that are attached to Form 706 concern the assets of the estate. The personal representative must not only marshal the assets, but also prove the value of the assets to satisfy IRS. Each schedule will be presented in turn.

Schedule A—Real Estate

Schedule A—Real Estate [IRC sec. 2032] identifies all real property owned by the decedent either individually or as a tenant in common. The property must be valued at the fair market value of the property, not the decedent's basis, evidenced by recent sales of adjacent property, tax assessments, or appraisals by experts in the field. The value of the property must include all mortgages for which the decedent was personally liable. The value of this mortgage is later deducted on Schedule K. If the deceased was not personally liable for the loan repayment, the value of the outstanding loan may be deducted on Schedule A.

The federal government imposes a tax lien on all real estate owned by a decedent as soon as it is informed of the decedent's death, and the lien will only be removed once the Form 706 has been filed and any tax due thereon is paid, or the personal representative demonstrates to IRS that no return need be filed. Before title to the property can be transferred, the personal representative must receive a release from the government. For the purpose of this lien, IRS also includes any cooperative shares the decedent owned.

Example

Part of the property of an estate includes a parcel of real estate valued at $200,000. The decedent had a mortgage on the land of $50,000, for which she was personally responsible. For the purposes of Schedule A, a value of $200,000, the $50,000 mortgage is deducted on Schedule K.

Schedule B—Stocks and Bonds

Stocks and bonds that are publicly traded are valued for estate tax purposes at the mean trading average on the date chosen for valuation (date of death or six months later). Proof of the trading price is evidenced by the *New York Times* or *Wall Street Journal.* If the individual died on the weekend or on a holiday, the mean trading averages of the trading days surrounding the date of death are determined, and the value for estate tax purposes is the average of these two values.

If the decedent dies after the record date for payment of a stock dividend but before the payment date, the value of the dividend is included in the value of the stock, but the dividend itself is considered income to the beneficiary of that security. This is known as **income in respect of a decedent (IRD)** (IRC sec. 1022). The beneficiary is responsible for income tax on that dividend, but may deduct any estate tax paid on the IRD.

income in respect of a decedent (IRD)
Income a beneficiary derives from property that is inherited

Example

The decedent died on February 5, owning several shares of stock in a publicly traded corporation. The corporation declared a dividend on January 31, but distribution will not take place until February 15. The value of the dividend is both part of the value of the estate and income to the beneficiary of those shares.

Bonds are valued in the same manner as stocks, and interest accruing on the bond is prorated over the period from the last payment date until the date of death. All interest includable in this period is attributable to the estate.

Closely held stock, those shares that are not publicly traded, have no readily ascertainable value, and IRS is usually very suspicious of valuations placed on these shares. As a general rule, if the shareholders had a shareholders' agreement with a buy-sell provision (a clause requiring the company to repurchase the shares at a price established by the condition expressed in the contract itself), IRS may accept the price computed by reference to the agreement for the purpose of Schedule B—Stocks and Bonds (IRC sec. 2031). However, if there is no shareholders' agreement, it will be necessary to get an independent appraisal for the value of these closely held securities. Because these valuations are carefully scrutinized by the IRS, it may behoove the estate to get several appraisals and use an average price for this stock.

Shares in cooperative residences are included on this schedule of Form 706, not Schedule A—Real Estate. The value placed on these shares is deemed to be the fair market value of the shares as reflected by recent sales of the stock. Include evidence of the recent sales as an attachment to Schedule B.

Series E government savings bonds are valued at their redemption rate on the date of death, and money market accounts held by brokerage firms (also included on this schedule) are valued by the brokerage house, which must provide the personal representative with a letter indicating the value of the account on the date of death.

Treasury bills and other types of government securities are traded on the open market and are valued in the same manner as stocks and bonds indicated previously.

Exercise

When valuing stock, may the personal representative deduct transfer and brokerage fees? For one court's opinion read *Gillespie v. United States*, 23 F.3d 36 (2d Cir. 1994).

Schedule C—Mortgages, Notes, and Cash

Schedule C—Mortgages, Notes, and Cash (IRC sec. 2033) includes the value of all notes for which the decedent was the creditor or promissee. Mortgages and notes are valued at the **discount rate,** the amount someone would pay to become the assignee of the creditor even though the note is not due until sometime in the future. Banks and financial institutions will issue letters indicating the discount rate of all notes held by the deceased.

discount rate
Amount someone would pay today for a promissory note payable in the future

Bank savings and checking accounts must be valued on the date of death, and the depository institution will issue letters indicating the value in the accounts as of that date.

Example

A man dies holding a promissory note for $100,000, due and payable in three years. For purposes of estate taxation, this note may be valued at only $85,000, the value someone would be willing to pay for the note and have to wait three years to receive the face value.

Exercise

Go to your local bank to obtain the documents it uses to provide a discount rate.

Schedule D—Insurance on the Decedent's Life

Although the face value of the policy passes directly to the named beneficiary, that value may also be included as part of the decedent's estate if the decedent retained any incident of ownership over the policy within three years of death. An **incident of ownership** includes the following rights:

1. Naming the estate as the beneficiary
2. Retaining the right to change the beneficiary
3. Having the right to surrender or cancel the policy
4. Having the right to assign the policy
5. Having the right to pledge the policy
6. Having the right to borrow against the policy

incident of ownership Rights retained by an insured that prevent life insurance proceeds from passing tax free

Under these circumstances, because the decedent retained control over the policy and its proceeds, it is deemed to be taxable as part of the estate.

Exercise

Obtain a copy of a life insurance policy and determine whether the insured retains any incidents of ownership under its provisions.

Example

A decedent was the insured under a life insurance policy. As part of the terms of the policy the decedent had the right to cash it in. This would constitute an incident of ownership, and therefore the face value of the policy would appear on his estate tax return.

In addition to the foregoing, the value of the policy is included on the Schedule D—Insurance on the Decedent's Life (IRC sec. 2042) if the decedent transferred the life insurance policy within three years of death or had a life insurance policy as part of his or her employment benefit package and the employer changed the policy within three years of the decedent's death. The rationale for this is that the employer's ability to change the policy acts as an assignment by the employee to the employer, and is therefore considered to be a retained incident of ownership. The values of these policies are determined by the insurance company itself. The tax preparer must get Form 712 from the company that gives the value that is placed on the policy for Schedule D.

Schedule E—Jointly Owned Property

All property that was jointly held by the deceased and another, both real and personal, is included on Schedule E—Jointly Owned Property (IRC sec. 2040). The full value of the property must be included unless the personal representative can prove that the surviving joint tenants participated in the acquisition of the property, in which case the value will be apportioned.

If the surviving joint tenant is the decedent's spouse, only half of the value is included on this schedule.

The following case indicates how the court can harmonize two apparently conflicting statutes to arrive at an equitable tax policy.

TAX LAW & POLICY

GALLENSTEIN V. UNITED STATES OF AMERICA
975 F.2D 286 6TH CIR. 1992)

The United States District Court for the Eastern District of Kentucky found for the taxpayer in a tax refund action against the United States. The government argued that *26 U.S.C.S. § 2040,* as amended, required including only 50 percent of the value of certain farm property in the taxpayer's deceased husband's estate.

The taxpayer filed an action against the United States in a tax refund dispute. The district court found for the taxpayer and interpreted *26 U.S.C.S. § 2040* as requiring 100 percent of the farm property to be included in her deceased husband's estate. With 100 percent inclusion, the taxpayer received a stepped-up basis for the entire property; and consequently, no taxable gain from the sale. On appeal, the government argued that pursuant to § 2040, as amended, the taxpayer could be taxed on the gain realized in the 50 percent not included in her husband's estate. Consequently, the taxpayer could be taxed on the gain realized on the 50 percent not included in the husband's estate. The court held that there was no express or implied repeal of § 2040. The court held that both the taxpayer's and the government's interpretations were capable of coexistence, and therefore it was the duty of the court to regard each as effective. The court found that *26 U.S.C.S. § 2040*(b)(1), which applied to a qualified joint interest created after 1976, and *26 U.S.C.S. § 2040*(b)(2), which redefined a qualified joint interest for estates of decedents dying after 1981, worked in harmony.

Affirmed.

Schedule F—Other Miscellaneous Property

All property that is not otherwise included on another attachment must appear on Schedule F—Other Miscellaneous Property (IRC sec. 2033). The tax preparer must be able to substantiate the values for this property by attaching such proof to the schedule. These valuations may be documented by sales receipts, appraisals, insurance records, and so forth.

Exercise

Prepare a tickler that can be used to catalogue and marshal all assets of an estate. This tickler can be used when originally creating an estate plan for the client.

In the following case the Internal Revenue Service, and appellee/cross-appellant estate sought review of the decision from the United States Tax Court, which determined that the estate could offset intrayear overpayments and liabilities but could not offset interyear overpayments and liabilities. This exemplifies some other types of property that might be included in an estate tax return.

TAX LAW & POLICY

ESTATE OF EDWARD P. BENDER V. COMMISSIONER OF INTERNAL REVENUE (827 F.2D 884 3D CIR. 1987)

An estate tax return was filed, which reflected prior gross tax overpayments as assets of the estate and the gross outstanding tax liabilities as debts. The Internal Revenue Service issued a notice of deficiency and determined that the gross overpayments had to be netted with the gross taxes owed so as to leave only a gross debt to the estate. The estate challenged the deficiency notice in the tax court, which determined that overpayments and liabilities within the same year were required to be netted but overpayments and liabilities of different years were not. Both parties challenged the decision and the court affirmed in part and reversed in part. The court concluded that the IRS had discretion, pursuant to *26 U.S.C.S. § 6402*(a), as to whether to net out overpayments and liabilities within different years and its determination to net the estate liabilities and overpayments was proper. Under *26 U.S.C.S. § 2031*(a), the mere possibility of a refund was not sufficient to qualify as an estate asset. Accordingly, the testator's net tax overpayments for individual years never attained the status of independent assets for estate tax purposes.

The court affirmed the decision that required the estate to offset its intrayear tax overpayments and liabilities. The court reversed the decision that did not require the estate to offset its interyear overpayments and liabilities and held that gross overpayments were not an estate asset because offsets could be required in different years and the mere expectancy of a refund was not an asset for tax purposes.

Schedule G—Transfers During Decedent's Life

All property other than incidental gifts that the decedent transferred without consideration within three years of death (and for which no gift tax was reported) must be included as part of the decedents' taxable estate in Schedule G—Transfers During Decedent's Life (IRC secs. 2035 and 2038). This also includes all property the decedent transferred to an inter vivos trust within the period.

In *Estate of Slater v. Commissioner of Internal Revenue,* 93 T.C. 513 (1989), the court looked at the history of this section, as discussed in the following case.

TAX LAW & POLICY

Before being amended by the Tax Reform Act of 1976, Pub. L. 94-455, 90 Stat. 1520, section 2035(a) required the inclusion in a decedent's gross estate of the value (at date of death) of all property which he had gratuitously transferred "in contemplation of death" within three years of his death. Gratuitous transfers were treated as having been made in contemplation of death "unless shown to the contrary." This was changed by the Tax Reform Act of 1976, which brought into the gross estate under section 2035 all gratuitous transfers (except generally those qualifying for the annual gift tax exclusion) made within three years of decedent's death.

The Economic Recovery Tax Act of 1981 (ERTA), Pub. L. 97-34, 95 Stat. 172, again amended section 2035 by providing that only certain types of gratuitous transfers are included in the gross estate if made within three years of decedent's death, namely, transfers described in sections 2036, 2037, or 2038, or those which consist of insurance on the life of decedent. Section 2035 was amended to provide generally that all other transfers made by a person dying after December 31, 1981, are not included in his gross estate. However, ERTA also added section 2035(d)(3), which states in relevant part the following:

SEC. 2035(d). Decedents Dying After 1981.—

> (1) In general.—Except as otherwise provided in this subsection, subsection (a) [including gifts made within three years in a decedent's gross estate] shall not apply to the estate of a decedent dying after December 31, 1981.
> * * * *
> (3) 3-year rule retained for certain purposes.—Paragraph (1) shall not apply for purposes of—
> * * * *
> (B) section 2032A (relating to special valuation of certain farm, etc., real property) * * *

Schedule H—Powers of Appointment

All property over which the decedent held an unexercised general power of appointment is includable as part of the decedent's estate, as listed in Schedule H—Powers of Appointment [IRC sec. 2036(a)].

The term **power of appointment** need not be used to create such a power. In *Quie v. U.S.,* 1990 U.S. Dist. LEXIS 884 (D. Minn.), the federal court held that property given to a beneficiary to use "in any way she may deem proper" created a general power of appointment and thus was includable in the beneficiary's estate.

power of appointment
Legal ability to name a beneficiary

If the deceased possessed a general power of appointment wherein he or she could have exercised the power either in his or her own favor or in the favor of his or her estate or creditors, then the value of the property incident to the power is included as part of that estate. On the other hand, if the power was a special power of appointment, wherein the deceased could only exercise the power in favor of other named persons, the property is not considered part of the estate.

Example

In his father's will, a man was given a house for his lifetime and was instructed to pass title to the house to one of his children upon his death. The property would not be included in the man's estate because the power of appointment could only be exercised on his death.

Exercise

The Restatement Second of Property defines several different types of powers of appointment. Read the Restatement to determine which would create a taxable asset of an estate.

Schedule I—Annuities

If the decedent was an annuitant of a policy that provided for the survivor's annuity payments, the actuarial value of the policy with respect to the deceased is included as an asset of the annuitant's estate in Schedule I—Annuities (IRC sec. 2038). The company issuing the policy will provide documentation to prove the actuarial value of the policy to the decedent.

As an example, in *Levin v. Commissioner of Internal Revenue, 90 T.C. 723 (1988),* the petitioner filed an action against the respondent alleging that the respondent improperly determined a deficiency in the petitioner's federal estate tax and the petitioner's gift tax for a prior year.

The respondent contended that the decedent made an inter vivos transfer or gift to his spouse of a postmortem annuity that was payable by a corporation that he controlled, under its officers' surviving spouse plan. Petitioner asserted that the commuted value of the annuity was not includable in the decedent's gross estate pursuant to either *I.R.C. § 2035* or *§ 2038,* and that the annuity did not constitute an inter vivos gift by the decedent to his spouse subject to gift taxation under § 2511. The court awarded a judgment in favor of the respondent. The court held that the annuity was includable in the decedent's gross estate under § 2038 because the corporation was contractually obligated to pay the postmortem annuity benefits to the decedent's widow because the annuity was procured by consideration furnished by the decedent. Additionally, the decedent retained the power to alter, amend, revoke, or terminate the transfer during his life. The court held that § 2511 was inapplicable because the annuity was not a completed gift during the decedent's lifetime.

The court awarded a judgment in favor of the respondent in the petitioner's action that alleged the respondent improperly determined a deficiency in the petitioner's federal estate tax and the petitioner's gift tax for a prior year.

Exercise

Contact an insurance company to obtain a copy of an annuity insurance contract and analyze its provisions to determine its tax consequences for the insured and his estate.

Deductions

The next eight schedules provide for deductions from the gross estate. If the total value of the first nine schedules (the gross taxable estate) is less than the Unified Tax Credit amount, Form 706 need not be filed and no other schedule need be completed. If the total of the first nine schedules exceeds the Unified Tax Credit limit, then the following schedules must be prepared to determine the net taxable estate.

Schedule J–Funeral and Administrative Expenses

All reasonable expenses associated with the funeral service and burial, cremation, or other disposition of the decedent's body may be included in Schedule J—Funeral and Administrative Expenses [Regs. sec. 20.2053-3(a)1(d)] as a deduction from the taxable estate. These expenses are also permitted to be deducted from Form 1041. This item cannot appear on both tax returns. The tax planner or accountant will decide on which form to take the deduction, depending on the most favorable tax consequences.

Other administrative expenses, such as legal fees and court filing fees, are included on this schedule as deductions. Take careful note, however, that the fee for the attorney must be for legal matters in order to be deductible from the estate, not for acting as the personal representative. Accounting fees are also deductible on the federal return, but may not be deductible on individual state estate returns. Each jurisdiction must be checked for the state deductibility of this item.

Also included on this schedule are any expenses incurred in keeping the estate intact during the administration, such as paying insurance on the property, rent, utility payments, and fees for the safe deposit box.

In *Estate of Millikin v. Commissioner,* 125 F. 3d 339 (6th Cir. 1997), the court enumerated a two-pronged test for determining deductibility of administrative expenses:

> The structure of 26 U.S.C. § 2053(a) compels a two-part test for deductibility of expenses under that statute. First, an expense must be one of the four types of expenses specifically enumerated in the statute. If an expense qualifies as one of those four types, it must further be "allowable by the laws of the jurisdiction . . . under which the estate is being administered." 26 U.S.C. § 2053(a). We agree with the Commissioner that the phrase "administration expenses" is neither self-defining nor unambiguous. Moreover we find that the Treasury Regulation's construction of that phrase to include only those expenses "actually and necessarily[] incurred in the administration of the decedent's estate; that is, in the collection of assets, payment of debts, and distribution of property to the persons entitled to

it," 26 C.F.R. § 20.2053-3(a), is a permissible construction of the statute. We are therefore bound by that construction.

Schedule K—Debts of the Decedent

All monies owed by the decedent are deductible from the gross taxable estate; however, such evidence of indebtedness must be proven and the debt must actually be discharged from the estate funds.

Because the estate is responsible for paying the reasonable debts of the decedent, and those debts diminish the value of the estate, they are deductible on Schedule K—Debts of the Decedent [Regs. sec. 20.2053-1(b)(3)]. The schedule divides the debts into those that are secured and those that are unsecured. The **secured debts** include all mortgages and liens, and any other debts to which the decedent pledged estate property as collateral. The **unsecured debts** are real estate taxes owed, general bills and credit card payments, the cost of the last illness, and other miscellaneous expenses—that is, all amounts owed by the decedent at the date of death. Remember, however, that the mortgages that are included on this schedule are only those for which the decedent was personally liable (Schedule A).

secured debt
Obligation guaranteed by collateral

unsecured debt
Obligation that is not guaranteed

Exercise

Would an oral promise to pay made by the deceased be considered a deductible debt? Read *United States v. Mitchell*, 74 F.2d 571 (7th Cir. 1934).

Schedule L—Net Losses During Administration [IRC sec. 2054]

TAX LAW & POLICY

26 U.S.C. SEC. 2054 LOSSES

For purposes of the tax imposed by section 2001, the value of the taxable estate shall be determined by deducting from the value of the gross estate losses incurred during the settlement of estates arising from fires, storms, shipwrecks, or other casualties, or from theft, when such losses are not compensated for by insurance or otherwise.

26 CFR 20.2054-1

§ 20.2054-1 Deduction for losses from casualties or theft.

A deduction is allowed for losses incurred during the settlement of the estate arising from fires, storms, shipwrecks, or other casualties, or from theft, if the losses are not compensated for by insurance or otherwise. If the loss is partly compensated for, the excess of the loss over the compensation may be deducted. Losses which are not of the nature described are not deductible. In order to be deductible a loss must occur during the settlement of the estate. If a loss with respect to an asset occurs after its distribution to the distributee it may not be deducted. Notwithstanding the foregoing, no deduction is allowed under this section if the estate has waived its right to take such a deduction pursuant to the provisions of section 642(g) in order to permit its allowance for income tax purposes. See further § 1.642(g)-1.

Schedule M—Bequests to Surviving Spouse

All property inherited by a surviving spouse constitutes a **marital deduction** and is subtracted from the gross taxable estate in Schedule M—Bequests to Surviving Spouse [IRC sec. 2056(a)]. This is true regardless of whether the spouse inherited the property by will, by intestate succession, or by exercising a right of election. The only caveat is that the spouse must inherit the property outright or receive a qualified terminable interest in the property.

marital deduction Doctrine that permits a surviving spouse to inherit an unlimited amount of property tax free

Example

A woman dies without a valid will, survived by her husband and three children. The portion of the estate that passes to the widower according to the state's intestate succession law passes tax free as a marital deduction.

Exercise

How does the concept of a QTIP trust tally with the tax concept that the surviving spouse must inherit the property outright? Find the statute that permitted QTIP trusts.

Schedule N—Qualified ESOP Sales

This schedule has been abolished.

Schedule O—Charitable, Public, and Similar Gifts and Bequests [IRC sec. 2055(a)(2)]

IRS permits an unlimited deduction for all gifts made to qualified charitable organizations. Two problems, however, may arise with respect to this schedule.

1. The organization must qualify under IRS rules to receive tax deductible contributions (see IRS Publication 78).

2. If the property given is not cash, its value must be proved to IRS. This usually requires the personal representative to acquire an appraisal by an expert in the field.

In *Mellon Bank, N.A. v. United States of America,* 762 F.2d 283 (3d Cir. 1985), the federal government challenged the decision of the United States District Court for the Western District of Pennsylvania, which determined that a bequest to a nonprofit cemetery was deductible for estate tax purposes as a bequest to an organization operating exclusively for charitable purposes under *26 U.S.C.S. § 2055*(a)(2).

An individual died and his will provided that the residue of his estate was to be distributed to a nonprofit cemetery. Appellee estate executors filed an estate tax return claiming a charitable deduction for the amount distributed to the cemetery. The Internal Revenue Service disallowed the deduction. Appellees filed an action seeking a refund. The district court granted appellees summary judgment. On appeal, the court reversed. The court held that a cemetery was not a corporation organized and operated exclusively for charitable purposes within the meaning of *26 U.S.C.S. § 2055*(a)(2). The court noted that *26 U.S.C.S. § 170*(c)(5) provided for a deduction for income tax purposes of contributions to cemeteries, but there was no corollary provision for estate tax purposes. The court directed the district court to enter judgment for appellant federal government.

Schedule T—Qualified Family Owned Business Interest Deduction

This deduction was first introduced in 1998. In order to be able to take advantage of this deduction, there are many requirements that must be met by the estate, which includes both a family ownership of the enterprise and the material participation in the operation of the business by the deceased or a member of the deceased's family. This deduction has been repealed for the estates of persons dying after the year 2003.

Schedule U—Qualified Conservation Easement Exclusion

This deduction is a fairly recent addition to Form 706, and has limited application for most estates. The purpose of the deduction is provide an incentive to allocate real property for conservation. To qualify for this deduction, the property must have been owned by the decedent for at least three years prior to the creation of the easement, and the property, for persons dying in 2003 or thereafter, must be valued for at least $500,000. This is a voluntary election to create the easement.

Credits

After the deductions schedules have been totaled, the result is subtracted from the gross taxable estate to determine the net taxable estate. If the resulting number is beneath the Unified Tax Credit no estate tax is due. If the resulting number is above that amount, the estate tax is calculated on the amount over the Unified Tax Credit.

If a tax is due, the estate may be allowed certain tax credits. A **tax credit** reduces the dollar amount of taxes due.

tax credit Reduction in the amount of tax owed

Schedule P—Credit for Foreign Death Taxes Paid

If the deceased owned property overseas and the estate paid an estate tax to the foreign government on the value of that property, IRS permits a credit for such taxes paid using Schedule P—Credit for Foreign Taxes Paid [IRC sec. 2031(a)].

TAX LAW & POLICY

REV. RUL. 90-101
1990 IRB LEXIS 496; 1990-49 I.R.B. 8

Estate tax: unified credit. Rev. Rul. 81-303, 1981-2 C.B. 255, which held that the term "specific exemption" referred to in the estate tax convention between the U.S. and Switzerland may not be construed to include the section 2010 unified credit, is revoked.

Rev. Rul. 81-303, 1981-2 C.B. 255, held that the term "specific exemption" referred to in Article III of the United States–Switzerland Estate and Inheritance Tax Convention, 1957-1 C.B. 657, may not be construed to include the section 2010 unified credit added to the Code by the Tax Reform Act of 1976. Under the ruling, the U.S. estate of a Swiss resident (who is not a U.S. citizen) dying after December 31, 1976, would be entitled to only the smaller exemption allowed under section 2102(c)(1) of the Code.

Section 5032 of the Technical and Miscellaneous Revenue Act of 1988 (TAMRA), P.L. 100-647, 1988-3 C.B. 329, amended section 2102(c)(3) of the Code to include the following:

(A) Coordination with treaties.—To the extent required under any treaty obligation of the United States, the credit allowed under this subsection shall be equal to the amount which bears the same ratio to $192,800 as the value of the part of the decedent's gross estate which at the time of his death is situated in the United States bears to the value of his entire gross estate wherever situated.

This amendment follows the decisions in *Mudry v. United States,* 11 Cl. Ct. 207 (1986) and *Estate of Burghardt v. Commissioner,* 80 T.C. 705 (1983), aff'd., 734 F.2d 3 (3rd Cir. 1984). H. Rep. No. 100-795, 100th Cong., 2d Sess. 594 (July 26, 1988). The amendment applies to estates of decedents dying after November 10, 1988. TAMRA, section 5032(d). Accordingly, Rev. Rul. 81-303 does not apply to estates of decedents dying after November 10, 1988. Furthermore, the Internal Revenue Service will follow *Mudry* and *Burghardt* for decedents dying prior to the effective date of section 5032 of TAMRA.

The estate tax conventions between the United States and Australia, Finland, Greece, Italy, Japan, and Norway contain provisions substantially similar to Article III of the Swiss Convention. This revenue ruling is equally applicable to those conventions.

Schedule Q—Credit for Tax on Prior Transfers

If the decedent's estate includes property that the decedent received as the result of being the beneficiary of someone else's estate within 10 years before the decedent's death, there is a federal estate tax credit for the estate taxes paid on such property by the other estate. The credit is given on a sliding scale depending on how long before the deceased's death the property was inherited. The credit for such taxes paid is as follows:

When Acquired before Death	Credit for Taxes Paid
Less than 2 years	100%
Between 3 and 4 years	80%
Between 5 and 6 years	60%
Between 7 and 8 years	40%
Between 9 and 10 years	20%

To take advantage of this credit, the legal professional must discover how the decedent acquired the property subject to the estate tax and whether it was previously taxed, and then document the payment of those previous taxes.

When property included in an estate is derived from a prior transfer from another estate, § 2013(a) and (b) allows the recipient estate a credit for estate tax paid on the property by the donor estate. Section 2013(c), however, limits the credit to the amount by which the transferred property increases the estate tax liability of the recipient estate. In a case where there is but one transferor, the 2013(b) credit (called the "first limitation" in Treasury Reg. § 20.2013) and the 2013(c) limitation on credit (called the "second limitation" in Treasury Reg. § 20.2013) is easy to compute—it is the lesser of these two figures that is the actual credit available to the decedent's estate.

Schedule R—Generation-Skipping Transfer Tax

Probably the most complex area of tax law concerned with trusts and estates deals with generation-skipping transfers. A **generation skipping transfer** is a transfer of property into a trust or otherwise in which the beneficiaries or transferees are two or more generations removed from the transferor. An example would be a trust established to benefit the creator's children and grandchildren—the grandchildren are two generations removed from the creator. Most trusts are established to provide income for future generations, but a tax consequence of these trusts is that, as a separate legal entity, the trust exists for several generations and the government loses revenue from potential estate taxes that would be due as each generation died.

To recapture this "lost" revenue, the generation-skipping transfer tax was established in the 1980s by the U.S. Congress. The tax is complex and is subject to a variety of its own rules and regulations that are far too complicated for the purposes of this textbook. The legal professional, however, should bear in mind a few of the general rules when called upon to draft a trust in which the beneficiaries are several generations removed from the creator. Some tax may be due when a beneficiary of such a trust dies, and that tax consequence appears in Schedule R—Generation Skipping Transfer Tax (IRC sec. 2601 et seq.).

Basic rules to remember are as follows:

1. There is a $1 million exclusion for gifts benefiting the creator's grandchildren.

2. There must be two or more generations of beneficiaries in the trust for the rules to apply.

3. The tax's purpose is to tax the property as beneficiaries of each succeeding generation benefits from the trust.

generation-skipping transfer Transfer of property into a trust or otherwise in which the beneficiaries or transferees are two or more generations removed from the transferor

4. The generation-skipping transfer tax can be avoided if the creator pays a gift tax when the trust is created.

5. The tax on the corpus is due as each generation succeeds to the benefits.

6. The trustee is liable for payment of the taxes.

7. All taxes are computed on actuarial tables representing the generation's expected interest in the trust.

8. For the purposes of the imposition of the tax, anyone with a power of appointment is considered a beneficiary of the trust.

9. The tax is imposed only once per generation.

10. The tax may be imposed even if the beneficiaries are not related to the creator if the trust exists for multiple generations.

This complex area of tax law is more appropriate for financial professionals or persons involved with fiduciary accounting on a regular basis. The legal professional should be aware of the potential tax consequences of these transfers and obtain guidance from a financial professional.

Schedule S—Increased Estate Tax Due to Excess Retirement Accumulations

Taxpayer Relief Act of 1997
Federal statute that repealed the increased estate tax due to excess retirement accumulations

The excise tax on both excess distributions and excess retirement accumulations was repealed by the **Taxpayer Relief Act of 1997** (PL 105-34, August 5) effective for excess distributions received on or after January 1, 1997, and for the estates of decedents dying on or after January 1, 1997.

Excess distributions are the aggregate amount of retirement distributions made with respect to an individual during a calendar year in excess of the greater of $150,000 or of the statutory amount of $112,500 (indexed at the same time and in the same manner as the dollar limitation on annual benefits under defined benefit (DB) plans. In the case of lump sum distributions, the amounts were five times higher [former IRC sec. 4980A(c)].

Practical tip

To facilitate the marshaling of assets and distributing of an estate, purchase an accordion folder with alphabetical division. Use each division to indicate the 706 schedules, and use the additional divisions for the will, letters testamentary, and so forth. In this fashion all estate material will be easily organized.

Ethical Concerns

The law office that prepares a client's will may often be appointed as the executor of the estate, which entitles the firm to an additional fee that is statutorily established. Current ethical standards require the firm to alert the client to this additional fee before including his or her name as the executor under the will. Because the estate also may become involved in litigation, query whether it is ethical for the firm, as executor, to retain itself, for additional fees, to represent the estate in legal representation.

CHAPTER REVIEW

One of the primary responsibilities of a legal professional with respect to estate taxation is the preparation of the various tax forms the personal representative is required to file on behalf of the decedent and the estate. Although most legal professionals are not expected to perform the computations (which is the function of the estate accountant), the legal professional is expected to have all of the assets and expenditures of the estate appropriately grouped and recorded. It is from these records maintained by the legal professional that the tax returns are prepared.

For the purpose of Form 706, it is necessary to catalog assets according to the schedules attached to the return and to maintain records of expenditures and taxes paid on behalf of the estate. The legal professional must also acquire proof of the value of the estate assets, either by reference to external documents, certified appraisals, or documents prepared by the tax professional hired to handle the more complicated tax matters of the estate.

The following chart may help in organizing the items for the estate return.

Item	Schedule
Assets	
Annuities, if payments are made to a survivor	I
Brokerage accounts	B
Co-op shares	B
Debts owed to decedent	C
Gifts to minors	G
Insurance on decedent's life	D
Jointly held property	E
Miscellaneous property	F
Mortgages	A & K
Power of appointment	H
Real estate individually held	A
Savings bonds	B
Stocks and bonds publicly traded	B
Transfers within 3 years of death	G
Treasury bills	B
Deductions	
Bequests to surviving spouse	J
Charitable bequests	O
Debts owed by decedent	K
ESOPs	N
Funeral and administrative expenses	J
Losses to estate during administration	L
Qualified family owned business interest deduction	T
Qualified conservation easement exclusion	U
Tax Credits	
Foreign death taxes paid	P
Generation-skipping transfers	R
Property acquired within 10 years of death from an earlier estate	Q

The same records maintained to prepare federal Form 706 are also used to complete any state estate tax returns that may be required to be filed.

Key Terms

alternate valuation

discount rate

Economic Growth and Tax Reconciliation Act of 2001

Form 706

generation-skipping transfer

incident of ownership

income in respect of a decedent (IRD)

marital deduction

power of appointment

secured debt

tax credit

Taxpayer Relief Act of 1997

Unified Tax Credit

unsecured debt

CHAPTER 7

Fiduciary Income Taxes

Introduction

fiduciary
A person who, by law, is held to be in a position of trust with respect to another

A **fiduciary** is a person who, by law, is held to be in a position of trust with respect to another. For the purposes of fiduciary income taxation, all executors and administrators of a decedent's estate, all trustees of a trust, either inter vivos or testamentary, and all trustees of estates in bankruptcy are required to file income tax returns. This is so because the estate and/or the trust is deemed to be a separate legal entity from the person who receives the financial benefit of that entity, and consequently is required to report all of its income separately and pay any taxes due thereon.

Not all estates and trusts are required to file federal income tax returns (IRC sec. 6012). Under present federal tax law, only estates or trusts that generate at least $600 in annual income or that have as a beneficiary a nonresident alien, regardless of the amount of annual income, are required to file income tax returns. The federal return that must be used to file fiduciary taxes is **Form 1041,** the U.S. Tax Return for Estates and Trusts (see Exhibit 7.1). This return must be signed by the appropriate fiduciary, and each beneficiary of the estate or trust must receive a form K-1 (Form 1041) for the beneficiary's personal income tax obligation. Take note that, pursuant to the **Tax Relief Act of 2001,** the government provides some relief for victims of terrorist attacks with regard to reporting income.

Form 1041
Federal fiduciary income tax return

Tax Relief Act of 2001
Tax relief for victims of terrorist attacks

Fiduciary Income Taxes

Form 1041 — Department of the Treasury—Internal Revenue Service
U.S. Income Tax Return for Estates and Trusts — 2002
OMB No. 1545-0092

For calendar year 2002 or fiscal year beginning _____, 2002, and ending _____, 20 ___

A Type of entity (see instr.):
- ☐ Decedent's estate
- ☐ Simple trust
- ☐ Complex trust
- ☐ Qualified disability trust
- ☐ ESBT (S portion only)
- ☐ Grantor type trust
- ☐ Bankruptcy estate–Ch. 7
- ☐ Bankruptcy estate–Ch. 11
- ☐ Pooled income fund

Name of estate or trust (If a grantor type trust, see page 11 of the instructions.)

Name and title of fiduciary

Number, street, and room or suite no. (If a P.O. box, see page 11 of the instructions.)

City or town, state, and ZIP code

C Employer identification number

D Date entity created

E Nonexempt charitable and split-interest trusts, check applicable boxes (see page 12 of the instructions):
- ☐ Described in section 4947(a)(1)
- ☐ Not a private foundation
- ☐ Described in section 4947(a)(2)

B Number of Schedules K-1 attached (see instructions) ▶

F Check applicable boxes:
- ☐ Initial return ☐ Final return ☐ Amended return
- ☐ Change in fiduciary's name ☐ Change in fiduciary's address

G Pooled mortgage account (see page 13 of the instructions):
- ☐ Bought ☐ Sold Date:

Income

1	Interest income	1
2	Ordinary dividends	2
3	Business income or (loss) (attach Schedule C or C-EZ (Form 1040))	3
4	Capital gain or (loss) (attach Schedule D (Form 1041))	4
5	Rents, royalties, partnerships, other estates and trusts, etc. (attach Schedule E (Form 1040))	5
6	Farm income or (loss) (attach Schedule F (Form 1040))	6
7	Ordinary gain or (loss) (attach Form 4797)	7
8	Other income. List type and amount _____	8
9	**Total income.** Combine lines 1 through 8 ▶	9

Deductions

10	Interest. Check if Form 4952 is attached ▶ ☐	10
11	Taxes	11
12	Fiduciary fees	12
13	Charitable deduction (from Schedule A, line 7)	13
14	Attorney, accountant, and return preparer fees	14
15a	Other deductions **not** subject to the 2% floor (attach schedule)	15a
b	Allowable miscellaneous itemized deductions subject to the 2% floor	15b
16	**Total.** Add lines 10 through 15b	16
17	Adjusted total income or (loss). Subtract line 16 from line 9. Enter here and on Schedule B, line 1 ▶	17
18	Income distribution deduction (from Schedule B, line 15) (attach Schedules K-1 (Form 1041))	18
19	Estate tax deduction (including certain generation-skipping taxes) (attach computation)	19
20	Exemption	20
21	**Total deductions.** Add lines 18 through 20 ▶	21
22	Taxable income. Subtract line 21 from line 17. If a loss, see page 17 of the instructions	22
23	Total tax (from Schedule G, line 7)	23

Tax and Payments

24	**Payments: a** 2002 estimated tax payments and amount applied from 2001 return	24a
b	Estimated tax payments allocated to beneficiaries (from Form 1041-T)	24b
c	Subtract line 24b from line 24a	24c
d	Tax paid with extension of time to file: ☐ Form 2758 ☐ Form 8736 ☐ Form 8800	24d
e	Federal income tax withheld. If any is from Form(s) 1099, check ▶ ☐	24e
	Other payments: **f** Form 2439 _____; **g** Form 4136 _____; Total ▶	24h
25	**Total payments.** Add lines 24c through 24e, and 24h ▶	25
26	Estimated tax penalty (see page 18 of the instructions)	26
27	Tax due. If line 25 is smaller than the total of lines 23 and 26, enter amount owed	27
28	Overpayment. If line 25 is larger than the total of lines 23 and 26, enter amount overpaid	28
29	Amount of line 28 to be: **a** Credited to 2003 estimated tax ▶ _____; **b** Refunded ▶	29

Sign Here
Under penalties of perjury, I declare that I have examined this return, including accompanying schedules and statements, and to the best of my knowledge and belief, it is true, correct, and complete. Declaration of preparer (other than taxpayer) is based on all information of which preparer has any knowledge.

Signature of fiduciary or officer representing fiduciary — Date — EIN of fiduciary if a financial institution

May the IRS discuss this return with the preparer shown below (see instr.)? ☐ Yes ☐ No

Paid Preparer's Use Only
- Preparer's signature
- Date
- Check if self-employed ☐
- Preparer's SSN or PTIN
- Firm's name (or yours if self-employed), address, and ZIP code
- EIN
- Phone no. ( )

For Paperwork Reduction Act Notice, see the separate instructions. Cat. No. 11370H Form **1041** (2002)

Exhibit 7.1 Form 1041

Form 1041 (2002) Page **2**

Schedule A — Charitable Deduction. Do not complete for a simple trust or a pooled income fund.

1	Amounts paid or permanently set aside for charitable purposes from gross income (see page 19)	1
2	Tax-exempt income allocable to charitable contributions (see page 19 of the instructions)	2
3	Subtract line 2 from line 1	3
4	Capital gains for the tax year allocated to corpus and paid or permanently set aside for charitable purposes	4
5	Add lines 3 and 4	5
6	Section 1202 exclusion allocable to capital gains paid or permanently set aside for charitable purposes (see page 19 of the instructions)	6
7	**Charitable deduction.** Subtract line 6 from line 5. Enter here and on page 1, line 13	7

Schedule B — Income Distribution Deduction

1	Adjusted total income (see page 19 of the instructions)	1
2	Adjusted tax-exempt interest	2
3	Total net gain from Schedule D (Form 1041), line 16, column (1) (see page 20 of the instructions)	3
4	Enter amount from Schedule A, line 4 (reduced by any allocable section 1202 exclusion)	4
5	Capital gains for the tax year included on Schedule A, line 1 (see page 20 of the instructions)	5
6	Enter any gain from page 1, line 4, as a negative number. If page 1, line 4, is a loss, enter the loss as a positive number	6
7	**Distributable net income (DNI).** Combine lines 1 through 6. If zero or less, enter -0-	7
8	If a complex trust, enter accounting income for the tax year as determined under the governing instrument and applicable local law	8
9	Income required to be distributed currently	9
10	Other amounts paid, credited, or otherwise required to be distributed	10
11	Total distributions. Add lines 9 and 10. If greater than line 8, see page 20 of the instructions	11
12	Enter the amount of tax-exempt income included on line 11	12
13	Tentative income distribution deduction. Subtract line 12 from line 11	13
14	Tentative income distribution deduction. Subtract line 2 from line 7. If zero or less, enter -0-	14
15	**Income distribution deduction.** Enter the smaller of line 13 or line 14 here and on page 1, line 18	15

Schedule G — Tax Computation (see page 21 of the instructions)

1	Tax: a ☐ Tax rate schedule or ☐ Schedule D (Form 1041)	1a
	b Tax on lump-sum distributions (attach Form 4972)	1b
	c Alternative minimum tax (from Schedule I, line 56)	1c
	d **Total.** Add lines 1a through 1c	1d
2a	Foreign tax credit (attach Form 1116)	2a
b	Other nonbusiness credits (attach schedule)	2b
c	General business credit. Enter here and check which forms are attached: ☐ Form 3800 ☐ Forms (specify) ▶	2c
d	Credit for prior year minimum tax (attach Form 8801)	2d
3	**Total credits.** Add lines 2a through 2d	3
4	Subtract line 3 from line 1d. If zero or less, enter -0-	4
5	Recapture taxes. Check if from: ☐ Form 4255 ☐ Form 8611	5
6	Household employment taxes. Attach Schedule H (Form 1040)	6
7	**Total tax.** Add lines 4 through 6. Enter here and on page 1, line 23	7

Other Information

		Yes	No
1	Did the estate or trust receive tax-exempt income? If "Yes," attach a computation of the allocation of expenses. Enter the amount of tax-exempt interest income and exempt-interest dividends ▶ $		
2	Did the estate or trust receive all or any part of the earnings (salary, wages, and other compensation) of any individual by reason of a contract assignment or similar arrangement?		
3	At any time during calendar year 2002, did the estate or trust have an interest in or a signature or other authority over a bank, securities, or other financial account in a foreign country? See page 22 of the instructions for exceptions and filing requirements for Form TD F 90-22.1. If "Yes," enter the name of the foreign country ▶		
4	During the tax year, did the estate or trust receive a distribution from, or was it the grantor of, or transferor to, a foreign trust? If "Yes," the estate or trust may have to file Form 3520. See page 22 of the instructions		
5	Did the estate or trust receive, or pay, any qualified residence interest on seller-provided financing? If "Yes," see page 22 for required attachment		
6	If this is an estate or a complex trust making the section 663(b) election, check here (see page 23) ▶ ☐		
7	To make a section 643(e)(3) election, attach Schedule D (Form 1041), and check here (see page 23) ▶ ☐		
8	If the decedent's estate has been open for more than 2 years, attach an explanation for the delay in closing the estate, and check here ▶ ☐		
9	Are any present or future trust beneficiaries skip persons? See page 23 of the instructions		

Form **1041** (2002)

Exhibit 7.1 (Continued)

Fiduciary Income Taxes **325**

Form 1041 (2002) Page **3**

Schedule I   Alternative Minimum Tax (see pages 23 through 29 of the instructions)

Part I—Estate's or Trust's Share of Alternative Minimum Taxable Income

1	Adjusted total income or (loss) (from page 1, line 17)	1	
2	Interest	2	
3	Taxes	3	
4	Miscellaneous itemized deductions (from page 1, line 15b)	4	
5	Refund of taxes	5	( )
6	Depletion (difference between regular tax and AMT)	6	
7	Net operating loss deduction. Enter as a positive amount	7	
8	Interest from specified private activity bonds exempt from the regular tax	8	
9	Qualified small business stock (42% of gain excluded under section 1202)	9	
10	Exercise of incentive stock options (excess of AMT income over regular tax income)	10	
11	Other estates and trusts (amount from Schedule K-1 (Form 1041), line 9)	11	
12	Electing large partnerships (amount from Schedule K-1 (Form 1065-B), box 6)	12	
13	Disposition of property (difference between AMT and regular tax gain or loss)	13	
14	Depreciation on assets placed in service after 1986 (difference between regular tax and AMT)	14	
15	Passive activities (difference between AMT and regular tax income or loss)	15	
16	Loss limitations (difference between AMT and regular tax income or loss)	16	
17	Circulation costs (difference between regular tax and AMT)	17	
18	Long-term contracts (difference between AMT and regular tax income)	18	
19	Mining costs (difference between regular tax and AMT)	19	
20	Research and experimental costs (difference between regular tax and AMT)	20	
21	Income from certain installment sales before January 1, 1987	21	( )
22	Intangible drilling costs preference	22	
23	Other adjustments, including income-based related adjustments	23	
24	Alternative tax net operating loss deduction	24	( )
25	Adjusted alternative minimum taxable income. Combine lines 1 through 24	25	

Note: *Complete Part II below before going to line 26.*

26	Income distribution deduction from line 44 below	26	
27	Estate tax deduction (from page 1, line 19)	27	
28	Add lines 26 and 27	28	
29	Estate's or trust's share of alternative minimum taxable income. Subtract line 28 from line 25	29	

If line 29 is:

- $22,500 or less, stop here and enter -0- on Schedule G, line 1c. The estate or trust is not liable for the alternative minimum tax.
- Over $22,500, but less than $165,000, go to line 45.
- $165,000 or more, enter the amount from line 29 on line 51 and go to line 52.

Part II—Income Distribution Deduction on a Minimum Tax Basis

30	Adjusted alternative minimum taxable income (see page 27 of the instructions)	30	
31	Adjusted tax-exempt interest (other than amounts included on line 8)	31	
32	Total net gain from Schedule D (Form 1041), line 16, column (1). If a loss, enter -0-	32	
33	Capital gains for the tax year allocated to corpus and paid or permanently set aside for charitable purposes (from Schedule A, line 4)	33	
34	Capital gains paid or permanently set aside for charitable purposes from gross income (see page 28 of the instructions)	34	
35	Capital gains computed on a minimum tax basis included on line 25	35	( )
36	Capital losses computed on a minimum tax basis included on line 25. Enter as a positive amount	36	
37	Distributable net alternative minimum taxable income (DNAMTI). Combine lines 30 through 36. If zero or less, enter -0-	37	
38	Income required to be distributed currently (from Schedule B, line 9)	38	
39	Other amounts paid, credited, or otherwise required to be distributed (from Schedule B, line 10)	39	
40	Total distributions. Add lines 38 and 39	40	
41	Tax-exempt income included on line 40 (other than amounts included on line 8)	41	
42	Tentative income distribution deduction on a minimum tax basis. Subtract line 41 from line 40	42	
43	Tentative income distribution deduction on a minimum tax basis. Subtract line 31 from line 37. If zero or less, enter -0-	43	
44	**Income distribution deduction on a minimum tax basis.** Enter the smaller of line 42 or line 43. Enter here and on line 26	44	

Form **1041** (2002)

Exhibit 7.1 (Continued)

Form 1041 (2002) Page **4**

Part III—Alternative Minimum Tax

45	Exemption amount	45	$22,500 00
46	Enter the amount from line 29	46	
47	Phase-out of exemption amount	47	$75,000 00
48	Subtract line 47 from line 46. If zero or less, enter -0-	48	
49	Multiply line 48 by 25% (.25)	49	
50	Subtract line 49 from line 45. If zero or less, enter -0-	50	
51	Subtract line 50 from line 46	51	
52	Go to Part IV of Schedule I to figure line 52 if the estate or trust has a gain on lines 15a and 16 of column (2) of Schedule D (Form 1041) (as refigured for the AMT, if necessary). Otherwise, if line 51 is—		
	• $175,000 or less, multiply line 51 by 26% (.26).		
	• Over $175,000, multiply line 51 by 28% (.28) and subtract $3,500 from the result	52	
53	Alternative minimum foreign tax credit (see page 28 of the instructions)	53	
54	Tentative minimum tax. Subtract line 53 from line 52	54	
55	Enter the tax from Schedule G, line 1a (minus any foreign tax credit from Schedule G, line 2a) .	55	
56	**Alternative minimum tax.** Subtract line 55 from line 54. If zero or less, enter -0-. Enter here and on Schedule G, line 1c	56	

Part IV—Line 52 Computation Using Maximum Capital Gains Rates

*Caution: If the estate or trust **did not** complete Part V of Schedule D (Form 1041), see page 29 of the instructions before completing this part.*

57	Enter the amount from line 51	57	
58	Enter the amount from Schedule D (Form 1041), line 21, or line 9 of the Schedule D Tax Worksheet, whichever applies (as refigured for AMT, if necessary)	58	
59	Enter the amount from Schedule D (Form 1041), line 15d, column (2) (as refigured for AMT, if necessary)	59	
60	If you did not complete a Schedule D Tax Worksheet for the regular tax or the AMT, enter the amount from line 58. Otherwise, add lines 58 and 59 and enter the **smaller** of that result or the amount from line 4 of the Schedule D Tax Worksheet (as refigured for the AMT, if necessary).	60	
61	Subtract line 60 from line 57. If zero or less, enter -0-	61	
62	If line 61 is $175,000 or less, multiply line 61 by 26% (.26). Otherwise, multiply line 61 by 28% (.28) and subtract $3,500 from the result . . . . ▶	62	
63	Enter the amount from Schedule D (Form 1041), line 26, or line 16 of the Schedule D Tax Worksheet (as figured for the regular tax)	63	
64	Enter the **smallest** of line 57, line 58, or line 63	64	
65	Enter the estate's or trust's allocable portion of qualified 5-year gain, if any, from Schedule D (Form 1041) line 15c, column (2) (as refigured for the AMT, if necessary)	65	
66	Enter the smaller of line 64 or line 65	66	
67	Multiply line 66 by 8% (.08) . . . . ▶	67	
68	Subtract line 66 from line 64	68	
69	Multiply line 68 by 10% (.10) . . . . ▶	69	
70	Enter the **smaller** of line 57 or line 58	70	
71	Enter the amount from line 64	71	
72	Subtract line 71 from line 70. If zero or less, enter -0-	72	
73	Multiply line 72 by 20% (.20) . . . . ▶	73	
74	Enter the amount from line 57	74	
75	Add lines 61, 64, and 72	75	
76	Subtract line 75 from line 74	76	
77	Multiply line 76 by 25% (.25) . . . . ▶	77	
78	Add lines 62, 67, 69, 73, and 77	78	
79	If line 57 is $175,000 or less, multiply line 57 by 26% (.26). Otherwise, multiply line 57 by 28% (.28) and subtract $3,500 from the result	79	
80	Enter the **smaller** of line 78 or line 79 here and on line 52 . . . . ▶	80	

Form **1041** (2002)

Exhibit 7.1 (Continued)

SCHEDULE D
(Form 1041)
Department of the Treasury
Internal Revenue Service

Capital Gains and Losses

▶ Attach to Form 1041 (or Form 5227). See the separate instructions for Form 1041 (or Form 5227).

OMB No. 1545-0092

2002

Name of estate or trust | Employer identification number

Note: *Form 5227 filers need to complete* **only** *Parts I and II.*

Part I — Short-Term Capital Gains and Losses—Assets Held One Year or Less

(a) Description of property (Example, 100 shares 7% preferred of "Z" Co.)	(b) Date acquired (mo., day, yr.)	(c) Date sold (mo., day, yr.)	(d) Sales price	(e) Cost or other basis (see page 31)	(f) Gain or (Loss) (col. (d) less col. (e))
1					

2. Short-term capital gain or (loss) from Forms 4684, 6252, 6781, and 8824 . . . | 2 |
3. Net short-term gain or (loss) from partnerships, S corporations, and other estates or trusts . . . . | 3 |
4. Short-term capital loss carryover. Enter the amount, if any, from line 9 of the 2001 Capital Loss Carryover Worksheet . . . . | 4 ( )
5. **Net short-term gain or (loss).** Combine lines 1 through 4 in column (f). Enter here and on line 14 below . . . . ▶ | 5 |

Part II — Long-Term Capital Gains and Losses—Assets Held More Than One Year

(a) Description of property (Example, 100 shares 7% preferred of "Z" Co.)	(b) Date acquired (mo., day, yr.)	(c) Date sold (mo., day, yr.)	(d) Sales price	(e) Cost or other basis (see page 31)	(f) Gain or (Loss) (col. (d) less col. (e))	(g) 28% Rate Gain or (Loss) *(see instr. below)
6						

7. Long-term capital gain or (loss) from Forms 2439, 4684, 6252, 6781, and 8824 . | 7 |
8. Net long-term gain or (loss) from partnerships, S corporations, and other estates or trusts . | 8 |
9. Capital gain distributions . . . . | 9 |
10. Gain from Form 4797, Part I . . . . | 10 |
11. Long-term capital loss carryover. Enter in both columns (f) and (g) the amount, if any, from line 14, of the 2001 Capital Loss Carryover Worksheet . . . . | 11 ( )( )
12. Combine lines 6 through 11 in column (g) . . . . | 12 |
13. **Net long-term gain or (loss).** Combine lines 6 through 11 in column (f). Enter here and on line 15 below . . . . ▶ | 13 |

*28% rate gain or loss includes all "collectibles gains and losses" (as defined on page 31 of the instructions) and up to 50% of the eligible gain on qualified small business stock (see page 30 of the instructions).

Part III — Summary of Parts I and II

	(1) Beneficiaries' (see page 32)	(2) Estate's or trust's	(3) Total
14 Net short-term gain or (loss) (from line 5 above) . . .	14		
15 Net long-term gain or (loss):			
a Total for year (from line 13 above)	15a		
b 28% rate gain or (loss) (from line 12 above)	15b		
c Qualified 5-year gain	15c		
d Unrecaptured section 1250 gain (see line 17 of the worksheet on page 33)	15d		
16 **Total net gain or (loss).** Combine lines 14 and 15a . . ▶	16		

Note: *If line 16, column (3), is a net gain, enter the gain on Form 1041, line 4. If lines 15a and 16, column (2), are net gains, go to Part V, and* **do not** *complete Part IV. If line 16, column (3), is a net loss, complete Part IV and the* **Capital Loss Carryover Worksheet,** *as necessary.*

For Paperwork Reduction Act Notice, see the Instructions for Form 1041.   Cat. No. 11376V   Schedule D (Form 1041) 2002

Exhibit 7.1 (Continued)

Schedule D (Form 1041) 2002

Part IV Capital Loss Limitation

17 Enter here and enter as a (loss) on Form 1041, line 4, the **smaller** of:
   a The loss on line 16, column (3) **or**
   b $3,000 . . . . 17 (   )

If the loss on line 16, column (3), is more than $3,000, **or** if Form 1041, page 1, line 22, is a loss, complete the **Capital Loss Carryover Worksheet** on page 34 of the instructions to determine your capital loss carryover.

Part V Tax Computation Using Maximum Capital Gains Rates (Complete this part **only** if both lines 15a and 16 in column (2) are gains, and Form 1041, line 22 is more than zero.)

Note: If line 15b, column (2) or line 15d, column (2) is more than zero, complete the worksheet on page 35 of the instructions to figure the amount to enter on lines 20 and 38 below and skip all other lines below. Otherwise, go to line 18.

18 Enter taxable income from Form 1041, line 22 18
19 Enter the **smaller** of line 15a or 16 in column (2)   19
20 If the estate or trust is filing Form 4952, enter the amount from line 4e; otherwise, enter -0- ▶ 20
21 Subtract line 20 from line 19. If zero or less, enter -0- 21
22 Subtract line 21 from line 18. If zero or less, enter -0- 22
23 Figure the tax on the amount on line 22. Use the 2002 Tax Rate Schedule on page 21 of the instructions 23
24 Enter the **smaller** of the amount on line 18 or $1,850 24

If line 24 is greater than line 22, go to line 25. Otherwise, skip lines 25 through 31 and go to line 32.

25 Enter the amount from line 22 25
26 Subtract line 25 from line 24. If zero or less, enter -0- and go to line 32 26
27 Enter the estate's or trust's allocable portion of qualified 5-year gain, if any, from line 15c, column (2) 27
28 Enter the **smaller** of line 26 or line 27 28
29 Multiply line 28 by 8% (.08) 29
30 Subtract line 28 from line 26 30
31 Multiply line 30 by 10% (.10) 31

If the amounts on lines 21 and 26 are the same, skip lines 32 through 35 and go to line 36.

32 Enter the **smaller** of line 18 or line 21 32
33 Enter the amount, if any, from line 26 33
34 Subtract line 33 from line 32 34
35 Multiply line 34 by 20% (.20) 35

36 Add lines 23, 29, 31, and 35 36
37 Figure the tax on the amount on line 18. Use the 2002 Tax Rate Schedule on page 21 of the instructions 37
38 **Tax on all taxable income (including capital gains).** Enter the **smaller** of line 36 or line 37 here and on line 1a of Schedule G, Form 1041 38

Schedule D (Form 1041) 2002

Exhibit 7.1 (Continued)

SCHEDULE K-1
(Form 1041)
Department of the Treasury
Internal Revenue Service

Beneficiary's Share of Income, Deductions, Credits, etc.
for the calendar year 2002, or fiscal year
beginning ...., 2002, ending ...., 20 ....
▶ Complete a separate Schedule K-1 for each beneficiary.

OMB No. 1545-0092

2002

Name of trust or decedent's estate

☐ Amended K-1
☐ Final K-1

Beneficiary's identifying number ▶

Estate's or trust's EIN ▶

Beneficiary's name, address, and ZIP code

Fiduciary's name, address, and ZIP code

	(a) Allocable share item		(b) Amount	(c) Calendar year 2002 Form 1040 filers enter the amounts in column (b) on:
1	Interest	1		Schedule B, Part I, line 1
2	Ordinary dividends	2		Schedule B, Part II, line 5
3	Net short-term capital gain	3		Schedule D, line 5
4	Net long-term capital gain: **a** Total for year	4a		Schedule D, line 12, column (f)
b	28% rate gain	4b		Schedule D, line 12, column (g)
c	Qualified 5-year gain	4c		Line 5 of the worksheet for Schedule D, line 29
d	Unrecaptured section 1250 gain	4d		Line 11 of the worksheet for Schedule D, line 19
5a	Annuities, royalties, and other nonpassive income before directly apportioned deductions	5a		Schedule E, Part III, column (f)
b	Depreciation	5b		⎫ Include on the applicable line of the
c	Depletion	5c		⎬ appropriate tax form
d	Amortization	5d		⎭
6a	Trade or business, rental real estate, and other rental income before directly apportioned deductions (see instructions)	6a		Schedule E, Part III
b	Depreciation	6b		⎫ Include on the applicable line of the
c	Depletion	6c		⎬ appropriate tax form
d	Amortization	6d		⎭
7	Income for minimum tax purposes	7		
8	Income for regular tax purposes (add lines 1, 2, 3, 4a, 5a, and 6a)	8		
9	Adjustment for minimum tax purposes (subtract line 8 from line 7)	9		Form 6251, line 14
10	Estate tax deduction (including certain generation-skipping transfer taxes)	10		Schedule A, line 27
11	Foreign taxes	11		Form 1040, line 45 or Schedule A, line 8
12	Adjustments and tax preference items (itemize):			
a	Accelerated depreciation	12a		⎫ Include on the applicable
b	Depletion	12b		⎬ line of Form 6251
c	Amortization	12c		⎭
d	Exclusion items	12d		2003 Form 8801
13	Deductions in the final year of trust or decedent's estate:			
a	Excess deductions on termination (see instructions)	13a		Schedule A, line 22
b	Short-term capital loss carryover	13b	( )	Schedule D, line 5
c	Long-term capital loss carryover	13c	( )	Schedule D, line 12, columns (f) and (g)
d	Net operating loss (NOL) carryover for regular tax purposes	13d	( )	Form 1040, line 21
e	NOL carryover for minimum tax purposes	13e		See the instructions for Form 6251, line 27
f		13f		⎫ Include on the applicable line
g		13g		⎭ of the appropriate tax form
14	Other (itemize):			
a	Payments of estimated taxes credited to you	14a		Form 1040, line 63
b	Tax-exempt interest	14b		Form 1040, line 8b
c		14c		⎫
d		14d		⎪
e		14e		⎬ Include on the applicable line
f		14f		⎪ of the appropriate tax form
g		14g		⎭
h		14h		

For Paperwork Reduction Act Notice, see the Instructions for Form 1041.   Cat. No. 11380D   Schedule K-1 (Form 1041) 2002

Exhibit 7.1 (Continued)

Instructions for Beneficiary Filing Form 1040

Note: *The fiduciary's instructions for completing Schedule K-1 are in the Instructions for Form 1041.*

General Instructions

Purpose of Form

The fiduciary of a trust or decedent's estate uses Schedule K-1 to report your share of the trust's or estate's income, credits, deductions, etc. **Keep it for your records. Do not file it with your tax return.** A copy has been filed with the IRS.

Inconsistent Treatment of Items

Generally, you must report items shown on your Schedule K-1 (and any attached schedules) the same way that the estate or trust treated the items on its return.

If the treatment on your original or amended return is inconsistent with the estate's or trust's treatment, or if the estate or trust was required to but has not filed a return, you must file **Form 8082,** Notice of Inconsistent Treatment or Administrative Adjustment Request (AAR), with your original or amended return to identify and explain any inconsistency (or to note that an estate or trust return has not been filed).

If you are required to file Form 8082 but fail to do so, you may be subject to the accuracy-related penalty. This penalty is in addition to any tax that results from making your amount or treatment of the item consistent with that shown on the estate's or trust's return. Any deficiency that results from making the amounts consistent may be assessed immediately.

Errors

If you believe the fiduciary has made an error on your Schedule K-1, notify the fiduciary and ask for an amended or a corrected Schedule K-1. **Do not** change any items on your copy. Be sure that the fiduciary sends a copy of the amended Schedule K-1 to the IRS. **If you are unable to reach an agreement with the fiduciary regarding the inconsistency, you must file Form 8082.**

Tax Shelters

If you receive a copy of **Form 8271,** Investor Reporting of Tax Shelter Registration Number, see the Instructions for Form 8271 to determine your reporting requirements.

Beneficiaries of Generation-Skipping Trusts

If you received **Form 706-GS(D-1),** Notification of Distribution From a Generation-Skipping Trust, and paid a generation-skipping transfer (GST) tax on **Form 706-GS(D),** Generation-Skipping Transfer Tax Return for Distributions, you can deduct the GST tax paid on income distributions on Schedule A (Form 1040), line 8. To figure the deduction, see the Instructions for Form 706-GS(D).

Specific Instructions

Lines 3 and 4

If there is an attachment to this Schedule K-1 reporting a disposition of a passive activity, see the Instructions for **Form 8582,** Passive Activity Loss Limitations, for information on the treatment of dispositions of interests in a passive activity.

Lines 6b through 6d

The deductions on lines 6b through 6d may be subject to the passive loss limitations of Internal Revenue Code section 469, which generally limits deductions from passive activities to the income from those activities. The rules for applying these limitations to beneficiaries have not yet been issued. For more details, see **Pub. 925,** Passive Activity and At-Risk Rules.

Line 12d

If you pay alternative minimum tax in 2002, the amount on line 12d will help you figure any minimum tax credit for 2003. See the 2003 **Form 8801,** Credit for Prior Year Minimum Tax—Individuals, Estates, and Trusts, for more information.

Line 14a

To figure any underpayment and penalty on **Form 2210,** Underpayment of Estimated Tax by Individuals, Estates, and Trusts, treat the amount entered on line 14a as an estimated tax payment made on January 15, 2003.

Lines 14c through 14h

The amount of gross farming and fishing income is included on line 6a. This income is also separately stated on line 14 to help you determine if you are subject to a penalty for underpayment of estimated tax. Report the amount of gross farming and fishing income on Schedule E (Form 1040), line 41.

Exhibit 7.1 (Continued)

Form 1041 is divided into four main parts: Part I reflects general information about the entity, indicating income, deductions, and amount of taxes owed. This section also includes various subsections that are used to compute the information needed to determine the entity's tax liability. Part II provides for income deductions for distributions on a minimum tax basis, which will be discussed in detail later in the chapter. Part III provides for computation of an alternative minimum tax, similar to the individual income tax discussed in Chapter 2. Part IV computes any taxes due using the maximum capital gains rates.

As with the previous chapter, this chapter will analyze the tax obligation of the trust or estate by referencing the Form 1041 as provided in Exhibit 7.1. The legal professional may obtain copies of all current federal tax forms either in person at an IRS office, by telephone at 1-800-TAXFORM, or over the Internet at <http://www.irs.gov>, and all forms are available on CD-ROM (either <http://www.irs.gov/cdorders> or 1-1877-CDFORMS).

Form 1041: Part I, Estate's Share of Alternative Minimum Taxable Income

General

The opening section of Form 1041 requires general information about the entity whose tax liability is being reported and the person filing the return. Each trust or estate must obtain its own taxpayer identification number from the Internal Revenue Service (Form SS-4), and that identifying number must be used as a reference on all correspondence with the IRS, including on all returns filed. The taxation of an estate or testamentary trust commences with the date of death of the taxpayer.

Income

Questions 1 through 9 refer to the income generated by the entity during the reporting period. Trusts and estates, like individuals, may report transactions on a cash or accrual basis; however, unless suitable reasons can be presented to IRS, almost all taxpayers are required to report income on a cash basis. The **accrual** method of reporting income mandates that income be reported when billed regardless of when it may be received, and is generally only permitted for business taxpayers. With the cash method, income is reported when actually received. Further, although in theory taxpayers may

accrual
Method of reporting income when billed regardless of receipt

file income tax returns either on a calendar or fiscal reporting cycle, IRS generally requires taxpayers to file on a calendar basis unless a sufficient justification can be presented as to why a fiscal reporting period is more truly reflective of the taxpayer's cash flow than the calendar method. Note that once the method of reporting income is selected it cannot be easily changed.

Exercise

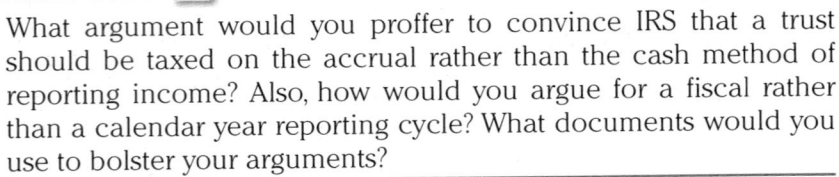

What argument would you proffer to convince IRS that a trust should be taxed on the accrual rather than the cash method of reporting income? Also, how would you argue for a fiscal rather than a calendar year reporting cycle? What documents would you use to bolster your arguments?

In computing income, either for an estate or a testamentary trust, the fiduciary must take into account all items of income that are deemed to be income in respect of a decedent. As discussed in Chapter 6, income in respect of a decedent (IRC sec. 1022) is that which the decedent was entitled to receive but was not included on the decedent's final personal income tax return. Such items of income may include:

- Lump sum distributions from an IRA
- Interest on a savings bond
- Corporate dividend distributions
- Deferred sales payments

This income is reflected on Form 1041 in the same way that it would be reported on the decedent's individual return, either as ordinary income, interest and dividend income, or capital gains, depending on its source. Income in respect of a decedent was discussed in Chapter 6 with respect to the federal estate tax return.

The following revenue ruling discusses the IRS position with respect to income in respect of a decedent.

TAX LAW & POLICY

REV. RUL. 78-32 *1978-1 C.B. 198; 1978 IRB LEXIS 555*

Income in respect of decedent; sale of real property completed by executor. The gain realized from a sale of real property that was completed by the executor of a cash basis decedent who, prior to death, had entered into a binding executory contract for sale of the property and had substantially fulfilled the prerequisites to consummation of the sale is income in respect of a decedent under section 691(a) of the Code.

Advice has been requested whether, under the circumstances described below, the gain realized from the sale of real property is income in respect of a decedent within the meaning of section 691(a) of the Internal Revenue Code of 1954.

In June 1971, A, who used the cash receipts and disbursements method of accounting, acquired a tract of land for 50x dollars. On January 1, 1976, A signed a binding executory contract agreeing to sell the land to B for 70x dollars. The closing was scheduled for March 15, 1976. A died on February 5, 1976, after substantial fulfillment of the prerequisites to consummation of the sale. The remaining obligations to be performed were ministerial. A's executor completed the sale pursuant to the contract and transferred title and possession of the land to B on March 15, 1976.

Section 691(a) of the Code provides, in part, that the amount of all items of gross income in respect of a decedent that are not properly includible in respect of the taxable period in which falls the date of death or a prior period shall be included in the gross income, for the taxable year when received, of: (1) the estate of the decedent, if the right to receive the amount is acquired by the decedent's estate from the decedent; (2) the person who, by reason of the death of the decedent, acquires the right to receive the amount, if the right to receive the amount is not acquired by the decedent's estate from the decedent; or (3) the person who acquires from the decedent the right to receive the amount by bequest, devise, or inheritance, if the amount is received after a distribution by the decedent's estate of such right.

Section 1.691(a)–1(b) of the Income Tax Regulations provides, in general, that the term "income in respect of a decedent" refers to those amounts to which a decedent was entitled as gross income, but which were not properly includible in computing taxable income for the taxable year ending with the date of death or for a previous taxable year under the method of accounting employed by the decedent. Specifically, section 1.691(a)–1(b)(3) of the regulations provides that the term "income in respect of a decedent" includes income to which the decedent had a contingent claim at the time of death.

Based on section 1.691(a)–1(b) of the regulations, the United States Court of Appeals for the Fifth Circuit, in *Trust Company of Georgia v. Ross,* 392 F.2d 694 (5th Cir. 1967), cert. denied, 393 U.S. 830, adopted the "entitlement test" for purposes of determining whether income from the disposition of property owned by a decedent is taxable as income in respect of a decedent. Under this test, such income is to be included in the gross income of the recipient under section 691 of the Code if the decedent was entitled to the income at the date of death. Applying this standard to the facts before it, the court in Trust Company of Georgia held that, because the decedent was entitled to the proceeds of a sale of stock under an executory contract binding at the time of death, the gain realized on the proceeds of the contract was income in respect of a decedent. See also *Keck v. Commissioner,* 415 F.2d 531 (6th Cir. 1969), rev'g 49 T.C. 313 (1968).

In the instant case, A entered into a binding contract prior to death. At the time of death, A had substantially fulfilled all of the substantive prerequisites to consummation of the sale and was unconditionally entitled to the proceeds of the sale at the time of death. Accordingly, the gain realized from the sale of A's real property is income in respect of a decedent within the meaning of section 691(a) of the Code.

Exercise

Use Lexis or Westlaw to locate a decision discussing the taxation of a grantor trust. Use the Internet to locate a sample that you can use as a format for creating a *grantor trust.*

grantor trust
Trust in which creator retains certain ownership interests

It is also important to note that if the entity whose income is being reported is a grantor trust, no direct amount appears on the Form 1041. In this instance only the first section of the 1041 is completed and all of the calculations are reported on form K-1, which is given to the grantor-beneficiary. A **grantor trust** (IRC sec. 671) is one in which the grantor retains certain incidents of ownership so as to make the grantor, rather than the trust or the beneficiary, liable for the taxes on the trust's income. If the trust was created after March 1, 1986, the grantor is treated as the owner of the trust profit if the grantor retained a reversionary interest in either the income or the corpus of the trust if, at the time the trust was created, such interest exceeded 5% of the total value of the corpus. A trust is also treated as a grantor trust if such interest was retained by the spouse of the grantor.

If the trust is considered to be a grantor trust, the trustee must either give all persons who generated any income for the trust the name and tax identification number of the grantor or may receive the income from the trust and then file a Form 1099 showing the trust as the payor and the grantor as the payee of that income. Either method of reporting the income in these circumstances is permissible.

The following is included as a quick reference for the tax law professional with respect to the reporting requirements for grantor trusts.

TAX LAW & POLICY

GRANTOR TRUST REPORTING REQUIREMENTS
59 FR 37450

DATE: Friday, July 22, 1994

PART 1-INCOME TAXES

Paragraph 1. The authority citation for part 1 continues to read in part as follows:

Authority: *26 U.S.C. 7805* * * *

Par. 2. Section 1.671-4 is revised to read as follows:

§ 1.671-4—Method of reporting.

(a) *Portion of trust treated as owned by the grantor or another person.* Except as otherwise provided in paragraph (b) of this section, items of income, deduction, and credit attributable to any portion of a trust which, under the provisions of subpart E (section 671 and following), part I, subchapter J, chapter 1 of the Internal Revenue Code, is treated as owned by the grantor or another person are not reported by the trust on Form 1041, but are shown on a separate statement to be attached to that form.

(b) *A trust all of which is treated as owned by one or more grantors or other persons.* In the case of a trust all of which is treated as owned by one or more grantors or other persons, the trustee has the option of reporting by one of the methods described in this paragraph (b) rather than by the method described in paragraph (a) of this section. However, if the trustee reports by one of the methods described in this paragraph (b) for a taxable year of the trust, the trustee must continue to report by that method until the first taxable year that the trust is no longer a trust described in this paragraph (b).

(1) *A trust all of which is treated as owned by one grantor or by one other person*—(i) *In general.* In the case of a trust all of which is treated as owned by one grantor or one other person, the trustee reporting under this paragraph must—

(A) Furnish the name and taxpayer identification number (TIN) of the grantor or other person treated as the owner of the trust, and the address of the trust, to all payors of income and proceeds during the taxable year, and comply with the additional requirements described in paragraph (b)(1)(ii) of this section; or

(B) Furnish the name, TIN, and address of the trust to all payors of income and proceeds during the taxable year, and comply with the additional requirements described in paragraph (b)(1)(iii) of this section.

(ii) *Additional obligations of the trustee when name and TIN of the grantor or other person and the address of the trust are furnished to payors.* (A) Unless the grantor or other person treated as the owner of the trust is the trustee or a co-trustee of the trust, the trustee must furnish the grantor or other person with a statement that—

(1) Shows all items of income, deduction, and credit of the trust for the taxable year;

(2) Identifies the payor of each item of income;

(3) Provides the grantor or other person with the information necessary to take the items into account in computing the grantor's or other person's taxable income; and

(4) States that all items of income or gross proceeds that the payors reported to the Internal Revenue Service on Form 1099 have been included on the statement.

(B) The trustee, however, is not required to file any type of return with the Internal Revenue Service reporting those payments.

(iii) *Additional obligations of the trustee when name, TIN, and address of the trust are furnished to payors*—(A) *Obligation to file Forms 1099.* The trustee reporting under this paragraph must file with the Internal Revenue Service the appropriate Forms 1099, reporting the income or gross proceeds paid to the trust during the taxable year, and showing the trust as the payor and the grantor or other person as the payee. The trustee has the same obligations for filing the appropriate Forms 1099 as would a payor making reportable payments directly to the grantor or other person, except that the trustee must report each type of income in the aggregate, and each item of gross proceeds separately.

(B) *Obligation to furnish statement. (1)* Unless the grantor or other person treated as the owner of the trust is the trustee or a co-trustee of the trust, the trustee reporting under this paragraph must also furnish the grantor or other person with a statement that—

(i) shows all items of income, deduction, and credit of the trust for the taxable year;

(ii) provides the grantor or other person with the information necessary to take the items into account in computing the grantor's or other person's taxable income; and

(iii) states that all items of income or gross proceeds that the trustee is required to report to the Internal Revenue Service on Form 1099 have been included on the statement.

(2) By furnishing the statement, the trustee is treated as having satisfied any obligation to furnish statements to recipients with respect to the Forms 1099 filed by the trustee.

(iv) *Examples.* The following examples illustrate the provisions of this paragraph (b)(1).

Example 1. G creates an irrevocable trust which provides that the ordinary income is to be payable to him for life and that on his death the corpus shall be distributed to B, an unrelated person. Except for the right to receive income,

G retains no right or power which would cause him to be treated as an owner under sections 671 through 677. Under the applicable local law, capital gains must be added to corpus. Since G has a right to receive income, he is treated as an owner of a portion of the trust under section 677. The tax consequences of any items of capital gain of the trust are governed by the provisions of subparts A, B, C, and D (section 641 and following), part I, subchapter J, chapter 1 of the Internal Revenue Code. Because not all of the trust is treated as owned by the grantor, the trustee may not report by the methods described in paragraph (b)(1) of this section.

. . .

(2) *A trust all of which is treated as owned by two or more grantors or other persons*—(i) *In general.* In the case of a trust all of which is treated as owned by two or more grantors or other persons, the trustee reporting under this paragraph must furnish the name, TIN, and address of the trust to all payors of income and proceeds during the taxable year, and comply with the additional requirements described in paragraph (b)(2)(ii) of this section.

(ii) *Additional obligations of trustee*—(A) *Obligation to file Forms 1099.* The trustee must file with the Internal Revenue Service the appropriate Forms 1099, reporting the income or gross proceeds paid to the trust during the taxable year attributable to the portion of the trust treated as owned by each grantor or other person, and showing the trust as the payor and each grantor or other person as a payee. The trustee has the same obligations for filing the appropriate Forms 1099 as would a payor making reportable payments directly to the grantor or other person, except that the trustee must report each type of income in the aggregate, and each item of gross proceeds separately.

(B) *Obligation to furnish statement. (1)* The trustee must also furnish to each grantor or other person a statement that—

(i) Shows all items of income, deduction, and credit of the trust for the taxable year attributable to the portion of the trust treated as owned by the grantor or other person;

(ii) Provides the grantor or other person with the information necessary to take the items into account in computing the grantor's or other person's taxable income; and

(iii) States that all items of income or gross proceeds that the trustee is required to report to the Internal Revenue Service on Form 1099 have been included on the statement.

(2) By furnishing the statement, the trustee is treated as having satisfied any obligation to furnish statements to recipients with respect to the Forms 1099 filed by the trustee.

(3) *Common Trust Funds.* This paragraph (b) does not apply to a common trust fund as defined in section 584.

(4) *Trusts with foreign situs or assets.* This paragraph (b) does not apply to a trust if its situs or any of its assets are located outside the United States.

(c) *Due date for Forms 1099 required to be filed by trustee.* The due date otherwise in effect for filing Forms 1099 applies in the case of any Forms 1099 required to be filed with the Internal Revenue Service by a trustee pursuant to paragraph (b) of this section.

(d) *Due date and other requirements with respect to statement required to be furnished by trustee.* The due date for the statement required to be furnished by a trustee to the grantor or other person pursuant to paragraph (b) of this section is the date specified in section 6034A(a). The trustee must maintain in its records a copy of the statement furnished to the grantor or other person for a period of three years from the due date for furnishing such statement specified in this paragraph.

(e) *Application to brokers and customers.* For purposes of this section, a broker within the meaning of section 6045 is considered a payor, and a customer within the meaning of section 6045 is considered a payee.

(f) *Effective date and transition rule*-(1) *In general.* The trustee of a trust any portion of which is treated as owned by the grantor or another person must report pursuant to this section for taxable years beginning on or after the first day of the first calendar year after the date of publication of the final regulations in the **Federal Register.** However, if the trustee has filed a Form 1041 for any taxable year ending before that date (and has not filed a final Form 1041 pursuant to § 1.671-4(b)(3) in the 26 CFR part 1 edition revised as of April 1, 1994), or files a Form 1041 for any taxable year thereafter, the trustee must file a final Form 1041 for the taxable year which ends after the date of publication of the final regulations in the **Federal Register** and which immediately precedes the first taxable year for which the trustee reports pursuant to paragraph (b) (1) or (2) of this section, on the front of which form the trustee must write: "Pursuant to § 1.671-4(f), this is the final Form 1041 for this grantor trust.".

(2) *Transition rule.* For taxable years beginning prior to the first day of the first calendar year following the date of publication of the final regulations in the **Federal Register,** the Internal Revenue Service will not challenge the manner of reporting of

(i) A trustee of a trust all of which is treated as owned by one or more grantors or other persons who did not report in accordance with 1.671-4(a) (26 CFR part 1 revised as of April 1, 1994) as in effect for taxable years beginning prior to the first day of the first calendar year following the date of publication of the final regulations in the **Federal Register,** but did report in a manner substantially similar to one of the reporting methods described in paragraph (b) of this section; or

(ii) A trustee of two or more trusts all of which are treated as owned by grantors or other persons who filed a single Form 1041 for all of the trusts, rather than a separate Form 1041 for each trust, provided that the items of income, deduction, and credit of each trust were shown on a statement attached to the single Form 1041.

(g) *Cross-references.* For special rules relating to backup withholding requirements, see section 3406 and the regulations thereunder. For rules relating to employer identification numbers, and to the obligation of a payor of income or proceeds to the trust to furnish to the payee a statement to recipients with respect to the information return filed by the payor, see § 301.6109-1(a)(2) of this chapter.

Par. 3. Section 1.6012-3 is amended by revising paragraph (a)(9) to read as follows:

§ 1.6012-3—Returns by fiduciaries.

(a) * * *

(9) *A trust any portion of which is treated as owned by the grantor or another person pursuant to section 671 and following.* In the case of a trust any part of which is treated as owned by the grantor or another person under the provisions of subpart E (section 671 and following) part I, subchapter J, chapter 1 of the Internal Revenue Code, see § 1.671-4.

* * * * *

PART 301—PROCEDURE AND ADMINISTRATION

Par. 4. The authority citation for part 301 continues to read in part as follows:

Authority: *26 U.S.C. 7805* * * *

Par. 5. Section 301.6109-1 is amended by revising paragraph (a)(2) to read as follows:

§ 301.6109-1—Identifying numbers.

(a) * * *

(2) *A trust all of which is treated as owned by the grantor or another person pursuant to section 671 and following*—(i) *Obtaining an employer identification number.*

If the trustee furnishes the name and taxpayer identification number of the grantor or other person and the address of the trust to all payors pursuant to § 1.671- 4(b)(1)(i)(A) of this chapter, the trustee need not obtain an employer identification number for the trust until the first taxable year of the trust in which the trust is no longer described in § 1.671-4(b) of this chapter. If the trustee furnishes the name, taxpayer identification number, and address of the trust to all payors pursuant to § 1.671-4 (b)(1)(i)(B) or (b)(2)(i) of this chapter, and the trustee has not already obtained a taxpayer identification number for the trust, the trustee must obtain an employer identification number for the trust as provided in paragraph (d)(2) of this section.

(ii) *Obligations of persons who make payments of income or proceeds to certain trusts.* Any payors of income or proceeds that are required to file an information return with respect to payments of income or proceeds to a trust must show the name and taxpayer identification number that the trustee has furnished to the payor on the return. Regardless of whether the trustee furnishes to the payor the name and taxpayer identification number of the grantor or other person, or the name and taxpayer identification number of the trust, the payor must furnish a statement to recipients to the trustee of the trust, rather than to the grantor or other person. Under these circumstances, the payor is considered to have satisfied any obligation to show the name and taxpayer identification number of the payee on the information return and to furnish to the person whose taxpayer identification number is required to be shown on the form a statement to recipients.

* * * * *

Form 1041 must also be filed for all individuals who have applied for protection under the bankruptcy laws.

The sources of income of the trust or estate are divided into eight separate categories (note that these categories parrot the same categories discussed in Chapter 2 with respect to individual income taxation, and, therefore, specific case exhibits have not been repeated):

> *Line 1: Interest Income* [IRC sec. 61(a)(4)]. Interest income includes all interest payments received by the estate or trust from bank accounts, notes, loans, mortgages, bills, and interest from a Real Estate Mortgage Investment Conduit (REMIC). Basically, it is the same interest income that an individual would report (Chapter 2).

Exercise

The law with respect to creating REMICs is fairly complicated and beyond the scope of this textbook. However, to expand on the text material, locate a law review article on the subject using Lexis or Westlaw.

> *Line 2: Ordinary Dividends* (IRC sec. 61). Dividends represent a shareholder's profit on investment in a business entity. All such items of income are reported on the Form 1041.
>
> *Line 3: Business Income or Loss* (IRC secs. 61 and 162). This line is used to report all income from the operation of a business enterprise operated by the trust or estate as a sole proprietorship or partnership. To determine this amount, the fiduciary should use the Schedule C discussed in Chapter 3 and the partnership returns discussed in Chapter 4.
>
> *Line 4: Capital Gains (or Losses)* (IRC sec. 1222). The number appearing on this line is derived from the Schedule D of this form (see the discussion later in the chapter).

Line 5: Rents, Royalties, Partnerships, other Estates and Trusts (IRC sec. 543). The amount of this income is derived from the Schedule E of Form 1040 which was discussed in Chapter 2.

Line 6: Farm Income (IRC sec. 471 et seq.). If the trust or estate operates a farming operation as part of its assets, the fiduciary must include the Schedule F from the Form 1040 to report all such income and expenses, and to determine whether there is a gain or loss for the reporting period.

Line 7: Ordinary Gains (or Losses) (IRC sec. 1221). This item reflects the gains or losses emanating from the sale of business property or other asset that is not held as a capital asset. The fiduciary must use Form 4797, which has been previously discussed in this text, to indicate this item.

Line 8: Other Income (IRC sec. 61). All other income of the trust or estate that does not appear on one of the earlier lines must be included here. Examples would be income in respect of a decedent and distributions from annuity and retirement plans that are treated as ordinary income.

Line 9 totals all of the above items to calculate the entity's total income for the reporting period.

Deductions

As with all taxpayers, an estate or trust is entitled to subtract from its total income certain deductions that have the effect of reducing its total tax liability. The trust or estate may take a deduction for depreciation, depletion, and amortization, but only to the extent that such items are not apportioned to the beneficiaries. Therefore, if all such items are assigned to the beneficiary's share of the income, the trust or estate is not permitted to deduct that amount from its own income because that would cause those items to be deducted twice (the trust or estate and the beneficiary).

If the trust or estate is involved in any passive investment activity it may only deduct losses attributable to such passive activities to the extent of income so derived. In other words, losses from passive investments may not be carried over or used to reduce the amount of other sourced income. Generally, passive investment income is income derived from any source in which the investor does not take an active part in management, except for gas and oil investments, which are afforded special tax treatment, and portfolio income.

Exercise

Locate the section of the Internal Revenue Code that deals with passive investment income, using the library or the Internet.

Line 10: Interest (IRC sec. 163). Any interest the trust or estate pays for money it borrowed may be deducted, unless the funds so borrowed are used to generate tax exempt income, such as borrowing money to purchase tax exempt municipal bonds. Personal interest payments also are not deductible. The items of interest that are permitted to be included on this line are:

A. Investment interest
B. Mortgage interest
C. Interest on unpaid estate taxes

Line 11: Taxes (IRC sec. 2053). The fiduciary may deduct state and local income taxes and real property taxes imposed on any generation-skipping transfer.

Line 12: Fiduciary Fees (IRC sec. 2053). Fees charged by the fiduciary are deductible, either here or on the Form 706 (for estates). The taxpayer must attach a statement that the item was not charged on the estate tax return.

Line 13: Charitable Deductions. This amount is derived from Schedule A, discussed later in the chapter.

Line 14: Attorney, Accountant, and Return Preparer Fees. This item should be self-explanatory; however, the fiduciary should attach all bills and receipts for such services to evidence the amount declared.

Line 15: Other Deductions not Subject to the 2% Floor. The 2% floor refers to 2% of the entity's adjusted gross income. This line is divided into two parts; part a is for deductions not subject to the 2% floor, which includes such items as casualty and theft losses and net operating losses, and part b provides for deductions for certain items that exceed 2% of the adjusted gross income of the estate or trust, and includes such items as expenses for the production or collection of income, insurance, cost of a safe deposit box, and so forth.

In *Scott v. United States of America,* 186 F. Supp. 2d 664 (E.D. Va. 2002), plaintiffs, trustees, and trust's income beneficiaries brought a tax refund action against the government after the Internal Revenue Service assessed a deficiency related to the full deduction of financial advisor fees when computing federal income taxes. The parties filed cross-motions for summary judgment.

The plaintiffs contended that they were entitled to deduct the full amount of fees paid to financial advisors from trust income for federal income tax purposes under *26 U.S.C.S. § 67*(e). The IRS asserted that the fees were subject to the 2% limitation provided in § 67(a), (b), because the miscellaneous deductions were deductible only to the extent they exceed 2% of the trust's adjusted gross income. The court granted summary judgment for the IRS and denied summary judgment for the plaintiffs, because the plaintiffs could not show that the trustees were required to seek investment advice in order to fulfill the fiduciary duties imposed by law. The court found that under state law the trustees had absolute immunity from claims that they did not follow the "prudent investor" rule in managing trust assets, provided that they invested in statutorily approved investments. Therefore, plaintiffs could not show that the financial advisors' fees had to be incurred to fulfill the trustees' duties. They were not entitled to the full deduction under § 67(e), because they could not show that the fees would not have been incurred but for the fact that property was held in trust. The court granted the government's motion for summary judgment and denied the plaintiff's motion for a tax refund.

To determine the adjusted gross income, subtract lines 12, 14, and 15 from line 9.

Line 16: Total. The is the total of lines 10 through 15b.

Line 17: Adjusted Total Income (or Loss). Subtract line 16 from line 9.

Line 18: Income Distribution Deduction. A trust or estate may deduct the amount of its income that it distributes to the beneficiaries. To calculate this amount, the fiduciary must prepare Schedule B of this form (see later in the chapter) and attach the K-1 to the return.

Exercise

Read *Union Trust Co. of Indianapolis v. Commissioner*, 111 F.2d 60 (7th Cir. 1940), for a discussion of including payments from an estate on Form 1041.

344 Chapter Seven

Line 19: Estate Tax Deduction (IRC sec. 691). This line permits a deduction for taxes paid by an estate on income in respect of a decedent, provided that such income appeared on the Form 706 and an estate tax was paid. In such instance the fiduciary may deduct the proportion of the estate tax that was attributable to the IRD. Also, a deduction is allowed for the generation-skipping transfer tax that was paid as a result of a taxable termination of a generation.

Exercise

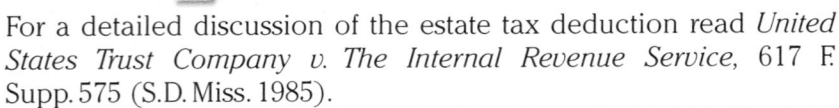

For a detailed discussion of the estate tax deduction read *United States Trust Company v. The Internal Revenue Service*, 617 F. Supp. 575 (S.D. Miss. 1985).

qualified disability trust
Trust to pay for care of a disabled person that qualifies for a $2900 exemption

Line 20: Exemptions. An estate is allowed a $600 exemption, and a trust that is required to distribute all of its income may take a $300 deduction. Further, a trust that is considered a **qualified disability trust** (IRC sec. 642) is permitted an exemption of $2900 if the trust's adjusted gross income does not exceed $132,950. If such trust's adjusted gross income exceeds $132,950, but does not exceed $255,450, the exemption is zero. All other trusts are allowed an exemption of $100.

Line 21: Total Deductions. This line is the total of lines 10 through 20.

Taxes and Payments

The remainder of the introductory section concerns taxes and payments and is purely mathematical.

Schedules

The remaining introductory sections concern the schedules that may have to be included as part of the calculations of the above amounts. There are five schedules appended to Form 1041.

Schedule A: Charitable Deduction [IRC sec. 624(c)]

Estates and trusts are permitted to deduct from their gross taxable income any income that is used or dispensed for a charitable purpose. If the income is paid to a charitable organization, the purpose for which the organization is formed must conform to the provisions of section 170(c) of the Internal Revenue Code. If the taxable entity is a trust, the trust must file Form 1041-A in addition to completing

Schedule A on Form 1041. Further, certain trusts must attach a separate document if claiming the deduction rather than using the Schedule A. The trusts that must attach such separate documents are:

- Nonexempt charitable trusts
- Trusts with unrelated business income
- Income funds

For all items of income used for charitable purposes, the taxpaying entity must subtract tax exempt income used for such charitable purposes. From this amount, any capital gain on property set aside for charitable purposes must be added. If a portion of such income was attributable to the sale or exchange of small business stock, the amount that was excluded under section 1202 of the IRC must be determined and subtracted from the above total. The result represents the charitable deduction that the trust or estate may take subtracted from its taxable income appearing on line 13 (see previous discussion).

Schedule B: Income Distribution Deduction (IRC sec. 661)

Basically, a trust or estate may deduct from its gross taxable income all distributions it makes to beneficiaries during the tax year in question. If the tax entity is an estate or a complex trust, distributions to beneficiaries made within 65 days following the close of the tax year may also be included as a deduction on this schedule.

If the trust or estate must make distributions to multiple beneficiaries, the fiduciary is required to compute the amount of income attributable to each such beneficiary pursuant to a concept called the **separate share rule,** if each share is selectively different. If such is the case, separate shares must be calculated to indicate the proportion of income distributed to each such beneficiary.

If the total amount of all the distributions to the beneficiaries exceeds the income, meaning that the fiduciary is **invading the corpus,** the fiduciary must file a separate attachment, Schedule J.

The results of these calculations appear in Part I on line 18 (see above). Remember that the beneficiaries who receive such distributions must receive a Form K-1 for their own income tax returns (Chapter 2). The total amount of these income distributions to beneficiaries is called the **distributable net income (DNI).** The DNI establishes the ceiling on the amount of distributions that will be taxed to the beneficiaries as income.

In *Casco Bank and Trust Co. v. United States of America,* 406 F. Supp. 247 (C. Maine 1975), a refund of $15,519 in federal income taxes plus statutory interest was claimed having alleged to have been

separate share rule
Attributing the share to each beneficiary of a trust when the interests are different

invading the corpus
Using the trust property as well as its income

distributable net income (DNI)
Distributions of trust income to its beneficiaries

erroneously assessed to and paid by plaintiff trustee under the will of the decedent for the years 1966, 1967, and 1968. The case was before the court on cross-motions for summary judgment by defendant government and the trustee.

The distributions of corpus from the estate to the trust for each year exceeded the estate's distributable net income. The trustee, following the instructions of the will, held these assets as principal and distributed no portion of them to the income beneficiaries. The trust then claimed an *I.R.C. § 642(c)* (1954) deduction as gross income permanently set aside for charitable purposes. The government's assertion was that the deduction for each year was properly disallowed because it was not for an amount of the gross income of the trust. The court granted the trustee's motion for summary judgment because both prerequisites to the § 642(c) deduction were met. Section 662(a)(2) required an estate beneficiary to include in gross income any amounts paid to the beneficiary for the taxable year up to the amount of the distributable net income of the estate, even though the amount distributed to the beneficiary was corpus under local state fiduciary accounting law. The permanent allocation of the assets to charitable purposes was pursuant to the terms of the governing instrument. The court held that the trust properly claimed a deduction under § 642(c) for 1966, 1967, and 1968.

The court denied the government's motion for summary judgment, granted the trustee's motion for summary judgment, and entered judgment for the trustee against the government in the amount of $15,519, plus statutory interest and costs.

Schedule G: Tax Computation The purpose of this schedule is both to determine the amount of taxes due from the trust or estate and to ascertain whether the trust or estate is entitled to any tax credits. As discussed in Chapter 6, a tax credit reduces the amount of taxes owed as compared to a tax deduction that reduces the amount of income on which the tax is assessed.

Exercise

Tax credits and tax deductions have been discussed throughout this textbook. How would you explain the difference between them to a client? How would you take them into consideration in creating a tax plan?

The tax rates are adjusted periodically by the government, and current rates will appear on the instructions that accompany the Form 1041. For the purposes of this textbook, however, several tax credits should be pointed out.

Foreign tax credit [IRC sec. 2053]. Similar to the tax credit permitted on Form 706 (Chapter 6), the Form 1041 permits the fiduciary to take a credit for any foreign income taxes paid on the income reported on the form.

Exercise

For the most part, the determination as to whether a given foreign tax qualifies for the tax credit is dependent on the nature of that foreign tax. In many instances, the United States has entered into tax treaties with foreign nations, and those treaties specify the nature of the foreign tax. Use the library or the Internet to locate the current tax treaties in force.

General business credit. If the trust or estate is claiming a business credit, such credit cannot have been attributable to the distributions made to the beneficiaries. The types of business credits permitted include the following:

- Investment credit (Form 3468)
- Welfare-to-work credit (Form 8861)
- Alcohol used as fuel (Form 6478)
- Low-income housing credit (Form 8586)
- Oil recovery credit (Form 8830)
- Disabled workers credit (Form 8826)
- Indian employment credit (Form 8845)

Other non-business credits. The trust or estate may also take as a tax credit income used to produce fuel from a nonconventional source or for the production of an electric vehicle.

The trust or estate must add back as a credit recapture taxes if the entity took a depreciation credit prior to the termination of the recapture period. The trust or estate may also claim a credit for employment taxes paid for household employees who were paid wages of at least $1300. For this purpose, the fiduciary must file Schedule H from the Form 1040.

Schedule I: Alternative Minimum Tax [IRC sec. 55]

This schedule need only be completed for the following entities.

1. If the trust or estate completed Schedule B, Income Distribution Deduction

2. If the estate's or trust's share of the alternative minimum taxable income exceeds $23,500

3. If the trust or estate claims a credit on Schedule G, Tax Computations

In *Charles H. Ungerman, Jr. Revocable Trust v. Commissioner,* 89 T.C. 1131 (1987), the government determined a deficiency in the petitioner's fiduciary income tax after disallowing a deduction claimed by the petitioner for an interest expense incurred and paid by the petitioner on the unpaid balance of a federal estate tax liability that was deferred under *I.R.C. § 6166*. The petitioner challenged the respondent's determination.

In a notice of deficiency to the petitioner, the government determined that interest claimed as a deduction by the petitioner on its fiduciary tax return under *I.R.C. § 212* was deductible only as interest under *I.R.C. § 163*. Therefore, according to the respondent, the claimed deduction was not allowable under *I.R.C. § 212* because it was specifically allowable under *I.R.C. § 163*. The effect of the determination was to subject the petitioner to the alternative minimum tax imposed by *I.R.C. § 55*. The court entered a decision in favor of the respondent. The court held that because *I.R.C. § 162* and *I.R.C. § 163* were of equal dignity and transparently not inconsistent with each other, it necessarily followed that *I.R.C. § 212* and *I.R.C. § 163* were of equal dignity and not inconsistent with each other. Therefore, the interest expense was allowable as a deduction under *I.R.C. § 212* because it satisfied the tests for deductibility under that section, even though it also was allowable as a deduction under *I.R.C. § 163*. The court held for the petitioner.

Just as for individuals (Chapter 2), a trust or estate may be permitted to pay an alternative minimum tax (AMT). To determine the AMT, the fiduciary must start with the amount appearing on line 17 of Form 1041, and from that amount make adjustments based on the following:

- Add back any net operating loss from line 15a
- Interest
- Taxes
- Depreciation of property placed in service after 1986
- Research expenses
- Mining exploration and development costs
- Long-term contracts entered into after February 28, 1987

- Amortization of pollution control facilities
- Installment sales that occurred after August 16, 1986
- Adjusted gain or loss on income-producing property
- Tax shelter farm activities
- Passive investment income
- Tax exempt interest
- Depletion and depreciation
- Certain loss limitations

These amounts are then totaled. From this adjusted amount the fiduciary deducts any alternative tax net operating loss deductions, and then the fiduciary may deduct income distribution deductions from Part II of Form 1041 and any estate tax deductions from line 19. If the total does not exceed $22,500, no tax is due; if the total is greater than $22,500, the fiduciary must continue to Part III to determine the amount of the alternative minimum tax. Caveat: All of the actual computations should be completed by a person qualified to make such computations.

Form 1041: Part II, Income Distribution Deduction on a Minimum Tax Basis

If the fiduciary is utilizing the provisions of the alternative minimum tax, he or she must complete Part II to determine the amount of the income that is deducted based on the calculations appearing in Part I. Recall that for the alternative minimum tax determination, certain items of deductions are added back to the adjusted income to calculate the minimum tax. This means that distributions to the beneficiaries may compute as a different percentage of the total income than would appear if the fiduciary did not use the alternative minimum tax method. Basically, Part II simply requires recomputation based on a figure that appears earlier on the Form 1041, and is more appropriately left to the financial professional.

Form 1041: Part III, Alternative Minimum Tax

If the estate or trust has an adjusted income appearing on line 12 of Schedule I greater than $22,500, the fiduciary should complete Part III of Form 1041. From the amount appearing on line 12 of Schedule I, the fiduciary may deduct $75,000, and this amount is multiplied by

25%. The result is then subtracted from $22,500. The amount left after these subtractions is then further subtracted from the amount appearing on line 12 of Schedule I. Unless the trust or estate has a capital gain, the amount of the alternative minimum tax is 26% of the total if it does not exceed $175,000, or 28% if the amount does exceed $175,000 (an additional $3500 is subtracted from this multiplication). Certain tax credits from Schedule G are permitted, and the end number is the alternative minimum tax.

The trust or estate must file Schedule D if it has any capital gain during the tax period.

Exercise

Using USCS or USCA read the annotations discussing the alternative minimum tax.

Schedule D: Capital Gains and Losses This schedule is used to report gains and losses from the sale or exchange of capital assets by an estate or trust. These gains and losses are then separated into long-term and short-term gains and losses in the same fashion that they may appear on the individual income tax return, Form 1040 (Chapter 2). Note, however, that for assets held on January 1, 2001, the fiduciary may elect to treat these assets as being sold and then reacquired on the same date so as to make the asset eligible for a reduced capital gains tax rate in its future transfer (18% as opposed to 20%). Any gain on this "deemed" sale must be recognized; losses are not recognized.

Form 1041: Part IV

Part IV of Form 1041 is not to be used if any gain or loss appears in the calculations for the alternative minimum tax or if the amount on line 22 of Form 1041 is zero or less. Otherwise, the amount appearing on Schedule D or Schedule I may be used for these computations, which, once again, are purely mathematical.

Schedule J: Accumulated Distributions for Certain Complex Trusts This schedule is only to be completed in the following instances.

1. The taxable entity is a domestic complex trust that had previously been treated as a foreign trust.
2. The taxable entity is a domestic trust that was created prior to February 1, 1984.

An **accumulated distribution** is defined as the excess amount paid, calculated, or required to be distributed over and above the distributable net income. In other words, for this schedule to apply, the distributions from the trust must exceed its income.

accumulated distribution
Excess amount paid, calculated, or required to be distributed over and above the distributable net income

Schedule K-1   Schedule K-1 (Form 1041) is an informational document sent to the beneficiary of a trust or estate to inform the beneficiary of the allocation of the trust or estate income, deductions and depreciation attributable to that beneficiary's share. The K-1 is not filed with the beneficiary's own individual income tax return, but its information is used so that the beneficiary may properly report such items on his or her own Form 1040. Remember that if the beneficiary is receiving the distribution as a gift, the distribution may be excluded from the beneficiary's taxable income.

Exercise

Read *Cheek v. Commissioner*, T.C. Memo 1987-84, for a discussion of income shifting versus a gift for the purposes of Form 1041.

Ethical Concerns

Although tax lawyers and tax law legal assistants often prepare tax forms for clients, if they are not qualified, either by experience or education, to perform financial calculations, it may be considered an ethical violation for them to do such work as part of their legal representation. The Canons of Ethics require all legal professionals to be qualified in the work they perform.

CHAPTER REVIEW

All fiduciaries of estates, trusts, and estates in bankruptcy are required to file Form 1041 if the entity's income exceeds $600 or it has a nonresident alien beneficiary. In many respects this form follows the provisions of the individual income tax return, Form 1040, but is geared to reflect income and expenditures for tax entities that transfer their income to others.

Form 1041 is divided into four main parts. The first part requires basic information regarding the income and deductions of the entity during the tax year. The remaining parts are used to compute income distributions on a minimum tax basis, an alternative minimum tax basis, or the maximum capital gains rates, depending on the amount and source of the entity's income.

As with the other federal tax forms discussed in this textbook, the legal professional is responsible for gathering all of the information regarding income, deductions, and credits, and provide legal justification for the classification of those items. The actual calculations should be left to an accountant or professional tax preparer unless the legal professional is qualified in that area. For the most part, Form 1041 follows the same general principles discussed in the earlier chapters, depending on the source of the item under scrutiny.

KEY TERMS

accrual	grantor trust
accumulated distribution	invading the corpus
distributable net income (DNI)	qualified disability trust
fiduciary	separate share rule
Form 1041	Tax Relief Act of 2001

APPENDIX A

Tax-Related Web Sites

<http://www.irs.gov>
   Official site for the Internal Revenue Service, free access to all IRS forms

<http://www.lexis.com>
   Computer-assisted legal research site that affords subscribers all statutes, cases, and governmental publications concerning tax law

<http://www.westlaw.com>
   Computer-assisted legal research site that affords subscribers all statutes, cases, and governmental publications concerning tax law

<http://www.loislaw.com>
   Computer-assisted legal research site that provides limited tax research materials

<http://www.lexisone.com>
   Free legal Web site that has case law and other materials available

<http://www.firstgov.gov>
   A clearinghouse site for a wide variety of information for all branches of the federal government

<http://http://thomas.loc.gov>
   Library of Congress site, one of the best sources of information on the status of bills pending in Congress and for copies of enacted legislation

<http://www.my.yahoo.com>
   A portal site for press releases

<http://www.findlaw.com>
   A useful first-step site in finding appropriate links for a particular question

GLOSSARY

30-day Letter Document giving a taxpayer 30 days in which to challenge an IRS determination internally

"A" reorganization Corporate restructuring by a merger or consolidation

accelerated depreciation Method of depreciating an item whereby most of the depreciation is taken during the first few years of the item's useful life rather than over the entire useful life

accrual Method of accounting whereby income is reported when billed, not when paid

accumulated distribution Excess amount paid over and above the distributable net income

accumulated earnings tax Tax imposed on undistributed operational profits

acquiescences or **nonacquiescences** Printed decisions of IRS as to whether it will follow or not follow a tax court ruling

advance rent Rent paid for future use of the premises or property

aggregate approach Treating a partnership as a conglomeration of individual partners

alimony or **maintenance** Payments made to a former spouse deemed to be income to the recipient spouse and a deduction from the income of the payor spouse

allocation cost recovery system (ACRS) Statutorily determined period of useful life pursuant to the Economic Recovery Tax Act

alternative minimum tax (AMT) Minimum tax for which a taxpayer would be liable

alternative valuation Valuing the assets in an estate either on the date of death or six months from the date of death

American Federal Tax Reports (AFTR) Unofficial reporter for tax court decisions

annuity A form of insurance in which, for a premium paid, the insured is guaranteed certain payments for life starting at a specified age. These payments are income to the recipient for the amount over the return of the premium payments

assets Items of value owned or over which an entity has control and the right of assignment

athletic facility An employee fringe benefit if maintained for workers by the employer

at risk rule Method of determining the allocation of distributions based on the distributee partner's degree of financial risk for the partnership obligations

audit IRS examination of a taxpayer's return

"B" reorganization Corporate restructuring by an exchange

bad debt Expense permitted for business debts that cannot be collected

balance sheet Document representing the basic accounting equation

barter An exchange of goods or services without money changing hands

base amount Amount of income above which IRS taxes social security benefits

basic accounting equation Assets = Liabilities + Equity

basis Original value of property in the hands of a taxpayer, sometimes reflecting the original cost plus improvements to the property

bill Proposed legislation

binding commitment test IRS will not recognize gain if the restructuring can be shown to bind the parties

boot Cash and other property given along with stock when a person invests in a corporation

business purpose test IRS will not recognize gain if the restructuring furthers a legitimate corporate purpose

"C" reorganization Corporate restructuring by an exchange that creates a holding company

cancelled debt Forgiveness of a loan that is considered income to the debtor

capital Account representing the investors' contributions to the corporation

capital asset All property held by a taxpayer not used in the regular course of business

capital gain or loss Increase or decrease in value of a capital asset to the holder when the asset is transferred

carried forward Ability to continue to deduct a loss in tax years after the year in which the loss was realized

charitable gift Gift to a nonprofit organization made with no expectation of benefit to the donor

child and dependant care credit Tax credit for expenses incurred in caring for a qualifying child or incapacitated person

child care credit Tax credit limited to $55 to pay for the care of a child

Circular 230 IRS rules with respect to the responsibilities of tax preparers

closely held corporation A corporation owned by a limited number of shareholders and whose shares are not publically traded

Code of Federal Regulations (CFR) Official publication of government agency rules

codification Placement of laws in a sequential and logical order

conference committee Congressional committee that resolves differences between the House and Senate versions of a bill

consolidation Two or more corporations pool their resources and transfer them to a new entity; the original entities cease to exist

conversion table Method of indicating how laws that appear in one publication can be found in another publication

corporation A legal entity separate and distinct from its shareholder-owners

correspondence audit IRS audit by exchange of letters

cost of goods sold (COGS) Cost of a business's inventory used to determine the profit realized from the sale of the product

credit Amount used to reduce the amount of tax imposed

credit for the elderly and disabled One of the tax credits permitted to a taxpayer to reduce the amount of taxes owed

current distribution Distribution of current income, profit, and losses

"D" reorganization Corporate restructuring that creates a spin-off or a split-up

deduction Item used to reduce amount of taxable income

de minimus **rule** An item of little or inconsequential value

dependent A person for whom the taxpayer provides over half of his or her support

depletion Form of depreciation for natural resources

depreciation Paper expense for the loss in value of a good due to the passage of time and wear and tear

direct tax A tax that is levied directly against the person who is obligated to pay it

discount rate Amount someone would pay today for a promissory note payable in the future

distributable net income Trust income paid to beneficiaries

distributive share Portion of a distribution allocated to each partner

dividend A shareholder's return on investment

divisive transaction Reorganization that creates a spin-off or split-up

double taxation Theory that corporate income is taxed twice, once at the corporate level and then at the shareholder level

"E" reorganization Corporate restructuring that changes the capital account of the corporation

Glossary

earned income credit Tax credit for low-income taxpayers on income derived from wages, salaries, tips, and self-employment

earnings and profits (E&P) Net income derived from the operations of a business

Economic Growth and Tax Reconciliation Act of 2001 Federal statute that increased the amount of an estate that can pass tax free

Economic Recovery Tax Act of 1981 (ERTA) Federal statute that, among other things, created ACRS

education credit One of two types of tax credits permitted for educational expenses paid

enactment Legislative process to create a law

end result test IRS will not recognize gains of a restructure if the end result of the process furthers a corporate purpose

equity Portion of the balance sheet that reflects the owners' contributions and profit or loss from business operations

examination IRS audit

excessive net passive income Income derived from passive activities after expenses have been deducted

exemption Reduction in gross income permitted for every taxpayer and for each of the taxpayer's dependents

exemption for dependents Rule permitting a taxpayer to exclude from income a specified amount for each of the taxpayer's dependents

"F" reorganization Corporate restructuring resulting in a change in the format of the entity

Federal Reporter Official publication for decisions of the U.S. Court of Appeals

Federal Supplement Official reporter for federal district court decisions

Federal Tax Citator Publication that updates tax cases

fiduciary A person who, by law, is held to be in a position of trust with respect to another

Field examination IRS audit in which an IRS agent goes to the taxpayer

FIFO First in, first out; method of valuing inventory sold

fixed expenses Overhead

foreign tax Tax paid to a country other than the United States

Form 706 Federal estate tax return

Form 872 Document used to grant IRS an extension of the statutory period to assess a deficiency

Form 879 Document used to waive the 90-day letter

Form 1040 Basic federal income tax return

Form 1040X Document used to amend an individual income tax return

Form 1040EZ Simplified federal individual income tax return

Form 1041 Federal fiduciary income tax return

Form 1065 Federal tax form for partnerships

Form 1120 Income tax return filed by C corporations

Form 1120-A Simplified federal income tax return for C corporations

Form 1120S Federal income tax return for S corporations

fringe benefits Financial benefits in addition to wages and salaries afforded employees

general partnership An association of two or more persons engaged in business for profit as co-owners

general rule Method of determining the nontaxable amount of annuity payments

generation-skipping transfer Transfer of property to persons two or more generations removed from the transferor

Government Printing Office Official publisher of federal legislation

grantor trust Trust in which the creator retains certain incidents of ownership

gross income All income from whatever source derived

gross receipts All revenue generated from the sale of goods and services

head of household Filing status

holding company A company whose income is derived solely from investments in other entities

hope credit Education credit permitted for students during their first two years of college

hot assets Assets that are immediately convertible to cash

House Ways and Means Committee House of Representatives committee that oversees tax legislation

incident of ownership Retaining certain rights which make the proceeds of a life insurance policy deemed to be part of the deceased insured's gross estate

income in respect of a decedent (IRD) Income vested in a decedent but paid after decedent's death, attributable to both the estate and the beneficiary

income shifting Attempt to have earned income attributed to someone other than the income earner

income statement Document prepared along with the balance sheet to indicate sales and expenses incurred in operating the business

indirect tax A tax that is levied against a person who may pass the burden on to another

inside basis Value of the partnership

intercorporate dividend Dividend paid by one corporation to an interconnected corporation

interest Income derived from letting another use one's money

Internal Revenue Code (IRC) of 1939 First codification of the U.S. tax laws

Internal Revenue Service (IRS) Agency that oversees taxes

Internal Revenue Service Restructure and Reform Act of 1998 Federal statute designed to curb IRS abuses

invading the corpus Using trust property in addition to trust income

investment Source of passive income

investment interest Income from a passive activity

item Any figure used to express income, deduction, credit, or nontaxable event

itemized deductions Detailing the amount of expenses incurred by a taxpayer so as to adjust the taxpayer's gross income

Keogh plan Retirement plan for self-employed individuals

liabilities Debt portion of the balance sheet

lifetime learning credit Education credit not limited to the first two years of college

LIFO Last in, first out; method of valuing inventory sold

like kind exchange Transfer of similar items that does not result in a taxable event

limited liability company (LLC) An unincorporated association whose owners have limited personal liability and which may be taxed either as a partnership or a corporation

limited partnership An association of two or more persons as co-owners of a business for profit, with one or more general partners and one or more limited partners

liquidating distribution Distribution made at the termination of a partner's interest in the partnership

long-term capital gain or loss Increase or decrease realized from the sale of a capital asset held over one year

married filing jointly Filing status permitted for persons who are legally married on the last day of the tax year

married filing separately Filing status permitted for persons who are legally married but who wish to have each spouse's tax liability computed individually

marital deduction All property passing to a surviving spouse passes tax free

memorandum decision Tax court decision based merely on factual determinations

merger One corporation absorbs another corporation; the one absorbed ceases its individual existence

mutual interdependence test IRS will not recognize a gain in a restructuring if the entities are mutually dependent

net operating loss (NOL) Loss occasioned by the operation of the business

net passive income Gross income from passive activities less incident expenses

net precontribution gain Gain a partner would recognize if all of his or her contributions made within seven years of the distribution in question were distributed to another partner

net sales Gross receipts less returns and allowances

90-day letter Document giving a taxpayer 90 days in which to file suit in the tax court

nondivisive transfer Transfer of assets that is similar to a "C" reorganization

nonrealization Gain recognized but no funds produced thereby

Nonrecognition Gain or loss not accounted for tax purposes

Nontaxable event Transfer of property that does not result in an immediate tax consequence

Notes of Decisions Section of USCA containing synopses of judicial decision

office audit IRS examination in which the taxpayer goes to an IRS office

operating agreement

partnership Partnership formed with a formal partnership agreement

ordering rules Method of determining distributions

outside basis Value of a partner's interest in the partnership

parent-subsidiary relationship One corporation owning a controlling block of stock in another corporation

passive investment Income derived from investments for which the taxpayer does not perform any services

personal exemption Specified amount of income not subject to taxation

personal holding company Corporation that has no more than five shareholders and at least 60% of its income is derived from passive sources

personal services corporation Company that only provides services, such as law or accounting

pocket part Stapled update to legal publications

points Charges imposed when acquiring a mortgage

power of appointment Legal ability to name a beneficiary

private ruling letters IRS decisions that only affect specific taxpayers

progressive tax rate Percentage of income taxed increases as the income increases

publically traded partnership Partnership whose shares may be acquired by anyone

Public Law Bills that are enacted into law

qualified disability trust Trust established to pay for the needs of a person who is disabled and qualifies for an income tax exemption of $2900 per year

qualified employee discount Permitting an employee to purchase the employer's goods at a reduced price which may or may not be considered a taxable benefit

qualified small business Business that meets the definition of IRC sec. 448

qualified taxpayer Individual who completes Schedule A

qualified widow(er) with dependent child Filing status

qualifying child Requirement for taking the child and dependent care tax credit

quantify Allocating a dollar value to an item

quantity discount Price reduction permitted because of the amount of goods purchased

receivables Account indicating sales made but not yet paid for

redemption Process by which a corporation repurchases its own shares

regulations (Regs.) Agency interpretation of tax laws

rental income Money received from leasing property

returns and allowances Reduction in gross sales due to goods being returned or discounted

revenue Sales

revenue procedure (Rev. Proc.) IRS dictate of procedural requirements

revenue ruling (Rev. Rul.) IRS published decision having the force of case law

royalty Payment

Schedule C Attachment to Form 1040 for sole proprietorships
Schedule PH Attachment for personal holding company
Schedules A&B Attachments to Form 1040
secured debt Financial obligation that guarantees the creditor a minimum amount of property will be available to satisfy the debt
security deposit Funds left with a lessor by the lessee that must be returned at the termination of the lease if the lessee has completely fulfilled his or her rental obligations
Senate Finance Committee Congressional committee that deals with tax legislation
separate share rule Trust distributions must be allocated to each beneficiary
short-term capital gain or loss Increase or decrease in the value of an item occasioned by the sale of a capital asset held for less than one year
significant participation passive activity Activity in which a partner is engaged more than 100 days per year
simplified production method Certain costs are required to be capitalized rather than expensed
simplified resale method Allocation of costs to determine COGS
simplified rule Method of determining nontaxable portion of an annuity payment
single Filing status
slip law Published by the GPO when a bill becomes a law
small corporation Corporation that meets the definition of IRC sec. 55
small tax case procedure Expedited procedure for controversy involving less than $50,000
sole proprietor Owner of a sole proprietorship
sole proprietorship Business owned and managed by just one person
special trial judge Person who presides over small tax cases

spin-off A corporation distributes to its shareholders stock in one of its controlled companies
split-up Shareholders of a corporation relinquish their shares to acquire shares of a newly created corporation
sponsor Person who proposes a new law
standard deduction Deduction permitted to adjust gross income for persons who do not itemize deductions
Standard Federal Tax Reporter Loose-leaf service
step transaction doctrine IRS will not recognize gain if multiple transactions can be viewed as a whole
stock split Method of restructuring capital whereby the same dollar amount represents a different number of shares than it did prior to the split
straight line depreciation Depreciation allocated evenly over the entire useful life of the good
Subchapter K Section of the Internal Revenue Code dealing with partnerships
Subchapter S corporation Domestic corporation that has only one class of stock, no more than 75 shareholders, and no shareholder is a nonresident alien
substance test IRS will not recognize gain if the substance of the transaction, rather than its form, does not warrant recognition
Supreme Court Reports Publication for decisions of the U.S. Supreme Court
Supreme Court Reports, Lawyers' Edition Publication for decisions of the U.S. Supreme Court
target company Company taken over as part of a merger
taxable income Income from whatever source derived
tax court Federal court that handles tax matters
Tax Court Reports Publication for decisions of the tax court

tax credit Reduction in the amount of tax owed

tax deficiency IRS determination that a taxpayer has failed to pay the correct tax

Tax Notes Publication that updates tax decisions

Tax Reform Act of 1969 Federal statute that made the tax court an Article I court

Tax Reform Act of 1976 Federal law that revised tax law and procedure

Tax Relief Act of 1997 Federal statute that repealed the increased estate tax on excess retirement accumulations

Tax Relief Act of 2001 Federal statute that granted certain tax relief to victims of terrorist attacks

tax shelter Business formed primarily to provide tax benefits to its owners

Taxpayer Bill of Rights Acts of 1988 and 1996 Federal statutes that granted taxpayers certain rights vis-a-vis IRS

taxpayer identification number Number issued by IRS to identify a taxpayer, similar to a social security number

Termination Dissolution of a business

uncollectibles Billings that will never be paid

Unified Tax Credit Combining the estate tax credit and the gift tax exemption

United States Code (USC) Codification of all U.S. laws

United States Code Annotated (USCA) Annotated version of the U.S. Code

United States Code Congressional and Administrative News (USCCAN) Monthly publication that includes texts of laws

United States Code Service Annotated version of the U.S. Code

United Stated Code Service (USCS), Advance Pamphlet Monthly publication of laws that were passed with a conversion table

United States Law Weekly Weekly publication that publishes laws it deems significant

United States Reports Official publication for decisions of the U.S. Supreme Court

United States Statutes at Large Bound publication containing all slip laws enacted during a congressional session

United States Tax Cases Unofficial publication of tax court decisions

United States Tax Court Official name of the tax court

United States Tax Reporter Loose-leaf service

unsecured debt Obligation that does not guarantee the creditor any specific property will be available to satisfy the debt

useful life Period of time for which an item has a perceived value

Westlaw Computer-assisted legal research program

working capital Cash on hand used to operate a business

working condition fringe benefit A financial benefit derived as an adjunct to wages for employees

INDEX

A

Accelerated depreciation, 115
Accident and health insurance benefits, 53
Accountants as income tax preparers, 1–2, 27
Accounting principles in partnership taxation, 170–74
Accrual, 331
Accumulated distribution, 351
Accumulated earnings tax, 192
Acquiescences or nonacquiescences, 14–16
ACRS. *See* Allocation cost recovery system
Adams v. Commissioner, 79
Adjustments to income (Schedules A&B), 66–75
  alternative minimum tax, 75–80
  casualty and theft losses, 73–74
  charitable gifts, 73
  health insurance premiums of self-employed, 67
  interest, 70–72
  itemized deductions, 67
  job and miscellaneous expenses, 74–75
  medical and dental expenses, 67
  Schedules A&B (Form 1040), 68–69
  standard deduction, 66
  taxes, 67, 70
  See also Credits; Individual income taxation
Administrative action as source of tax law, 8–17
Adoption credit, 93
Advance rent, 49
Advertising expenses, 112
AFTR. *See* American Federal Tax Reports
Aggregate approach, 154
Allocation cost recovery system (ACRS), 116
Allocation of distributions in partnership taxation, 181–86
Allocation of income, 54–56

Alterman Foods, Inc. v. United States, 140
Alternate valuation, 300
Alternative minimum tax (AMT), 75–80, 348
American Federal Tax Reports (AFTR), 19
Amorient, Inc. v. Commissioner, 247
AMT. *See* Alternative minimum tax
Annuities, 50
Apportionment, 3
Appreciated property, 227
Arrowsmith v. Commissioner, 15
Artwork, 227
Assets in partnership taxation, 168
At risk rule, 173
Athletic facilities, 43
Audits, 20

B

Bad debts, 112–14
Badaracco v. Commissioner, 80
Balance sheet, 168
Balance sheet and income statement in corporate income taxation, 199–206
Barter exchanges, 43, 53, 99
Base amount in social security benefits, 51
Basic accounting equation, 199
Basis in the stock, 46
Bell Lines, Inc. v. United States, 60
Berthold v. Commissioner, 140
Betson v. Commissioner, 133
Bills (in proposed legislation), 4
Binding commitment test, 191
Black v. Commissioner, 79
Bob Jones Univ. v. United States, 79
Boot, 202
Braunfeld v. Brown, 79
Briggs v. Commissioner, 59
Brown v. Commissioner, 15
Browne v. Thorn, 64
Bulova Watch Co. v. United States, 244
Burlington N. R.R. Co. v. Oklahoma Tax Commn., 77–78
Burnet v. Harmel, 65
Business as hobby, 148
Business expenses versus personal expenses, 148

Business gifts, 142
Business interest (Schedule C), 72
Business purpose test, 190

C

C corporations, 170
Calvert Anesthesia Associates v. Commissioner, 78
Campbell v. Commissioner, 162
Cancelled debts, 53, 105
Capital, 202
Capital assets, 62, 63–66
Capital gains or losses, 62
Car expenses, 114
Carbine v. Commissioner, 123
Carlton v. United States, 59
Carried forward capital losses, 62
Casco Bank and Trust Co. v. United States of America, 345–46
Cash, 206–7
Casualty and theft losses, 73–74
CFR. *See* Code of Federal Regulations
Charitable contributions, 227
Charitable gifts, 73
Charles H. Ungerman, Jr. Revocable Trust v. Commissioner, 348
Child care credit, 80–81, 84–86
Chism v. Commissioner, 139
Christine v. Commissioner, 79
Circular 230, 26, 27
Clayton v. Commissioner, 104
Closely held corporations, 100–105, 209
Code of Federal Regulations (CFR), 7, 8
Codification, 3–4
COGS. *See* Cost of goods sold
Cohan v. Commissioner, 120
Columbia Rope Co. v. Commissioner, 140, 141
Commissioner v. Heininger, 123
Commissioner v. Lundy, 80
Commissioner v. Soliman, 121
Commissioner v. Tellier, 123
Commissions and fees, 114
Computer-assisted legal research programs, 7, 20
Comstock v. Group of Investors, 65
Conference committee, 5

363

Index

Consolidation, 217
Conversion table, 7
Corporate income taxation, 189–252
  accumulated earnings tax, 192
  balance sheet and income statement, 199–206
    assets, 201–202
    basic accounting equation, 199
    boot, 202
    capital, 202
    equity, 202
    income statement, 202–203
    liabilities, 202
  binding commitment test, 191
  business purpose test, 190
  closely held corporations, 209
  corporation defined, 189, 192
  dividends, 206–14
    cash, 208–9
    earnings and profits (E&P), 206
    intercorporate dividends, 212–13
    liquidating dividends, 206
    nonliquidating dividends, 206
    property, 209
    redemption, 213–16
    Rev. Rul. 85-14, 214–16
    shares of stock, 210
  double taxation, 189
  end result test, 191
  ethical concerns, 250
  Form 1120 (C corporations), 192, 193–96, 219–29
    deductions, 225–28
    Form 1120-A, 219–24
    Form 1120-W, 223
    Form 4466, 223
    income, 223–25
    personal services corporation, 223
    Schedule C, 228
    Schedule PH, 223
    taxes and payments, 228–29
  Form 1120 schedules, 229–36
    Schedule A, cost of goods sold, 229–34
    Schedule C, dividends and special deductions, 234
    Schedule E, compensation of officers, 235
    Schedule J, tax computation, 235–36
    Schedule K, other information, 236

Schedule L, balance sheet, 236
Schedule M-1, reconciliation, 236
Schedule M-2, analysis of unappropriated retained earnings, 236
Form 1120S (S corporations), 192, 197–98, 248–50
Form 2553, 248
  Regs. Sec. 1.1362–4, 248
mutual interdependence test, 191
nonrealization, 190
nonrecognition, 190
personal holding companies, 201
reorganizations, 216–19
  "A" reorganizations, 216–17
  "B" reorganizations, 217
  "C" reorganizations, 217–18
  "D" reorganizations, 218–19
  "E" reorganizations, 219
  "F" reorganizations, 219
small corporations, 192
step transaction doctrine, 190
Subchapter C, 190
Subchapter S corporations, 192, 236–47
substance test, 190
tax shelters, 191
Corporation defined, 189, 192
Correspondence audits, 20
Cost of goods sold (COGS), 109
Court awards, 52
Court of federal claims, 19
Credits, 75–93
  adoption credit, 93
  child and dependent care credit, 80–81
  child care, 81, 84–86
  defined, 80
  earned income credit, 89, 93
  education credit, 86–92
  elderly and disabled, 81, 82–83
  employer taxes for household help, 81
  foreign tax credit, 93
  hope credit, 86–92
  lifetime learning credit, 86–92
  See also Adjustments to income (Schedules A&B)
Crowley v. Commissioner, 206
Cumulative Bulletin (C.B.), *Internal Revenue Bulletin,* 10–11
Current distribution in partnership taxation, 178

D

Davis v. Commissioner, 45
Dawkins v. Commissioner, 121
De minimus rule, 38, 42
Deductions, 38
  itemized, 67
  partnership taxation, 171–72
  standard, 66
Dependent care credit, 80–81
Dependents, 37
Depletion, 114
Depreciation, 115
Deputy v. du Pont, 120, 123, 133
Diamond v. Commissioner, 162
Diedrich v. Commissioner, 53–54
Dietrick v. Commissioner of Internal Revenue, 127–42
DiLeo v. Commissioner, 104
Dinardo v. Commissioner, 133, 134
Direct taxes, 2
Disabled credit, 81, 82–83
Discount rate, 304
Distributable net income (DNI), 345
Distributions in partnerships, 178–86
Distributive share in partnership taxation, 155
Dividends, 46, 47–49
  corporate income taxation, 206–14
Divisive transactions, 218
DNI. *See* Distributable net income
Dodd v. Commissioner, 133, 136
Double taxation, 189

E

Earlene T. Barker v. Commissioner of Internal Revenue, 60, 61
Earned income credit, 89, 93
Earnings and profits (E&P), 206
Economic Growth and Tax Reconciliation Act of 2001, 301
  See also Estate and gift taxation
Economic Recovery Tax Act of 1981 (ERTA), 116
Educational expenses, 74
Elderly and disabled credit, 81, 82–83
Electronic filing (Form 1524), 164
Eligible students, 86
Employee benefit programs, 116
Employee discounts, 42

Index 365

Employer taxes for household help, 81
Enactment process, 4–5
End result test, 191
Enoch v. Commissioner, 48
Entertainment expenses, 74
Equity, 202
   partnership taxation, 168
ERTA. *See* Economic Recovery Tax Act of 1981 (ERTA)
Estate and gift taxation, 253–321
   assets, 302–10
      Schedule A—Real Estate, 302
      Schedule B—Stocks and Bonds, 303–4
      Schedule C—Mortgages, Notes, and Cash, 304
      Schedule D—Insurance on the Decedent's Life, 305–6
      Schedule E—Jointly Owned Property, 306
      Schedule F—Other Miscellaneous Property, 307–8
      Schedule G—Transfers During Decedent's Life, 308
      Schedule H—Powers of Appointment, 309
      Schedule I—Annuities, 310
   chart for organizing items for the estate return, 319–20
   credits, 315–19
      Schedule P—Credit for Foreign Death Taxes Paid, 315–16
      Schedule Q—Credit for Tax on Prior Transfers, 316–17
      Schedule R—Generation-Skipping Transfer Tax, 317–18
      Schedule S—Increased Estate Tax, 318–19
   deductions, 310–15
      Schedule J—Funeral and Administrative Expenses, 311–12
      Schedule K—Debts of the Decedent, 312
      Schedule L—Net Losses During Administration, 312–13
      Schedule M—Bequests to Surviving Spouse, 313
      Schedule N (has been abolished), 313
      Schedule O—Charitable, Public, and Similar Gifts and Bequests, 314
      Schedule T—Qualified Family Owned Business Interest Deduction, 314
      Schedule U—Qualified Conservation Easement Exclusion, 315
   ethical concerns, 319
   Form 706, 253–99, 319
   overview, 300–302
   personal representative of decedent's estate, 253, 319
Estate of Burghardt v. Commissioner, 316
Estate of Cowser v. Commissioner, 79
Estate of Edward P. Bender v. Commissioner of Internal Revenue, 307–8
Estate of Milliken v. Commissioner, 311-12
Estate of Owen v. Commissioner, 78
Estate of Slater v. Commissioner of Internal Revenue, 308
Estate taxes, 67
Examinations, 20
Excess net passive income, 238
Exclusion for partnership accounting rules, 169–70
Exemptions, 37
Exemptions for dependents, 37
Expenses for business use of your home (Form 8829), 118, 119
Expenses in sole proprietorship taxation, 109–47

F

Federal Bulk Carriers, Inc. v. Commissioner, 15
Federal income taxation, 33
Federal Reporter, 19
Federal Supplement, 19
Federal Tax Citator, 20
Federal tax forms, obtaining copies of, 331
Fiduciary income taxes, 322–52
   defined, 322
   ethical concerns, 351
   Form 1041: Part I, 331–49
      deductions, 341–44
      general, 331
      Grantor Trust Reporting Requirements, 335–40
      income, 331–41
      schedules, 344–49
         Schedule A—Charitable Deduction, 344–45
         Schedule B—Income Distribution Deduction, 345–46
         Schedule G—Tax Computation, 346–47
         Schedule I—Alternative Minimum Tax, 347–49
      taxes and payments, 344
   Form 1041: Part II, 349
   Form 1041: Part III, 349–50
      Schedule D—Capital Gains and Losses, 350
   Form 1041: Part IV, 350–51
      Schedule J—Accumulated Distributions, 350–51
      Schedule K-1, 351
   Form 1041 (sample form), 322–31
Field examinations, 20, 21
FIFO, 224
Financial calculations, performing, 351
Financial Documents and Accounting for Legal Professionals (Helewitz), 168
Fixed expenses, 109
Foreign income taxation, 67, 70
Foreign tax credit, 93
Form 706, 253–99, 319
Form 872, 21, 22–23
Form 879, 21
Form 1040, 30–37
Form 1040, Schedule C, 96, 97–98
Form 1040, Schedules A&B, 68–69
Form 1040EZ, 37–39
Form 1040X, 21, 24–25, 26
Form 1041 (sample form), 322–31
   See also Fiduciary income taxes
Form 1065, 164–69
Form 1065 (Schedule K), 167
Form 1065 (Schedules L, M-1, M-2), 168
Form 1065-B, Schedule K-1, 155, 156–61
Form 1099, 334
Form 1120 (C corporations), 192, 193–96, 217–29
Form 1120 schedules, 229–36
Form 1120-A, 217–24
Form 1120-W, 223

Form 1120S (S corporations), 192, 197–98, 248–50
Form 1524 (electronic filing), 164
Form 2553, 248
Form 4466, 223
Form 8829 (expenses for business use of your home), 118, 119
Fraudulent claims, 21, 27
Frederick v. Commissioner, 240
Fringe benefits, 41
    working conditions, 42

G

Gains and losses, 56–66
Gallenstein v. United States of America, 306
Geiger v. Commissioner, 123
General partnerships, 150, 150–51
General rule in annuities, 50
Generation-skipping transfer, 317–18
Generation-skipping transfer tax return, 300
    See also Estate and gift taxation
Geographic placement of assets for tax planning, 3
Gift taxation. *See* Estate and gift taxation
Gifts, 53, 74
    business, 142
    charitable, 73
Gould v. Commissioner, 133
Government Printing Office (GPO), 4
GPO. *See* Government Printing Office
Graff v. Commissioner, 79
Grantor trust, 334
Grantor Trust Reporting Requirements, 335–40
Gross income, 30, 38
Gross profit, 106
Gross receipts, 99, 106–8

H

Hagaman v. Commissioner, 206
Head of household category, 34–35, 35–37
Health insurance benefits, 53
Health insurance premiums of self-employed, 67
Helewitz, Jeffrey A., *Financial Documents and Accounting for Legal Professionals*, 168

Heller & Son, Inc. v. Commissioner, 133
Helvering v. Winmill, 66
Hobby, business as, 148
Holding companies, 218, 223
Home sales, 66
Hood v. Commissioner, 147
Hope credit, 86–92
Hort v. Commissioner, 65
Hot assets, 181
House Ways and Means Committee, 4
Household help employer taxes, 81
Hradesky v. Commissioner, 102, 120
Huntsberry v. Commissioner, 78

I

In re: Freedom Newspapers, Inc., 14–16
Inadvertent termination relief, 248
Incident of ownership, 305
Income, 38
    from sole proprietorship versus closely held corporation, 100–105
    in sole proprietorship taxation, 99–109
    See also Sources of individual income
Income allocation, 54–56
Income in respect of a decedent (IRD), 303
Income not subject to federal income taxation, 53–54
Income or loss, partnership, 174–78
Income shifting, 54–56
    and partnerships, 186
Income statement in corporate income taxation, 202–203
Income tax preparers, 1–2, 27
Indirect taxes, 2
Individual income taxation, 30–95
    allocation of income, 54–56
    categories of taxpayers, 33–37
    ethical concerns, 93
    exemptions, 37
    Form 1040, 30–37
    Form 1040EZ, 37–39
    gains and losses, 56–66
    progressive income tax rate, 33
    See also Adjustments to income (Schedules A&B); Sources of individual income
INDOPCO, Inc. v. Commissioner, 123
Inside basis, 155

Insurance, 117
Inter vivos gifts, 53
Intercorporate dividends, 211–13
Interest, 45–46, 70–72, 117
Interest and dividends for accounts, 105
Internal Revenue Bulletin, Cumulative Bulletin (C.B.), 10–11
Internal Revenue Code (IRC) of 1939, 3–4
Internal Revenue Code (IRC) of 1986, 4
Internal Revenue Service (IRS), 6, 8
    abuse of power, 20
    negotiation with, 26
Internal Revenue Service Restructure and Reform Act of 1998, 20
Invading the corpus, 345
Investing partnership, 169–70
Investment interest, 72
IRC SEC. 1231, property used in the trade or business and involuntary conversions, 174–77
IRD. *See* Income in respect of a decedent
IRS. *See* Internal Revenue Service
Itemized deductions, 67
Items on tax form, 30

J

Jackson v. Commissioner, 207
Jean v. Kresser, 182
Jenkins v. Commissioner, 137, 138
Job and miscellaneous expenses, 74–75
Judicial decisions as sources of tax law, 17–20

K

Kaltreider v. Commissioner, 102
Keck v. Commissioner, 334
Keel v. Commissioner, 45
Keene v. Commissioner of Internal Revenue, 18
Keogh plans, 50
Kieselbach v. Commissioner, 65
Kinch v. Commissioner, 211–12
King v. Commissioner, 126–27
Klaassen v. Commissioner of Internal Revenue, 76–80
Knight v. Commissioner, 37, 40

Index 367

L

Lare v. Commissioner, 102
Larson v. Commissioner, 152
Leboeuf v. Commissioner of Internal Revenue, 100–105
Legal and professional services, 117
Legal professionals, qualifications of, 351
Legal research programs, 7, 20
Legal tax practice, 1
Lerch v. Commissioner, 123
Leroy Jewelry Co. v. Commissioner, 48
Levin v. Commissioner of Internal Revenue, 310
Liabilities in partnership taxation, 168
License fees, 75
Life expectancies of natural resources, 114
Life insurance policy proceeds, 53
Lifetime learning credit, 86–92
LIFO, 224
Like kind exchanges, 56–62
Limited liability company (LLC), 151, 154, 186, 250
Limited partnerships, 150–51
Liquidating distribution, 180–81
Liquidating dividends, 208
LLC. See Limited liability company
Local income taxation, 3, 33, 67
Loftin & Woodard, Inc. v. United States, 206
Lohrke v. Commissioner, 133, 134, 135, 136, 137, 138
Long-term capital gains or losses, 62
Losses, 56–66
Lucas v. Earl, 55

M

Maerki v. Commissioner of Internal Revenue, 142–46
Marital deduction, 313
"Market-to-market" method of accounting, 249
Married filing jointly category, 34
Married filing separately category, 34
Maxwell v. United States of America, 57–62
Mayhew v. Commissioner of Internal Revenue, 113–14
Meals and lodging expenses, 74
Medical and dental expenses, 67

Mellon Bank, N.A. v. United States of America, 314
Memorandum decisions, 18
Mergers, 217
Montano v. Commissioner of Internal Revenue, 106–8
Montgomery v. United States, 51–52
Mortgage loan interest (Form 1098), 17, 71–72
Moving expenses, 43, 75
Murdry v. United States, 316
Mutual interdependence test, 191

N

Nasser v. United States, 139
Net operating loss (NOL), 227, 228
Net passive income, 165
Net precontribution gain, 179
Net sales, 106
New Colonial Ice Co. v. Helvering, 79, 111
Ninety-day letters, 21
No-additional-cost services, 42
No-change letters, 21
NOL. See Net operating loss
Nondiscriminatory treatment, 42
Nondivisive transfers, 218–19
Nonliquidating dividends, 208
Nonrealization, 190
Nonrecognition, 190
Nontaxable events, 62
Norfolk S. Corp. v. Commissioner, 241
Notes of Decisions, 7–8

O

Office audits, 20
Office expenses, 117
Okin v. Commissioner, 78, 79
Operating agreement partnership, 169
Operating expenses, 109
Ordering rules, 172
Ordinary and necessary expenses, 109
Orrisch v. Commissioner of Internal Revenue, 181–86
Outside basis, 155, 171, 172

P

Paralegal's services as a sole proprietorship, 109–12
Parent-subsidiary relationship, 217
Partnership taxation, 150–88
  accounting principles, 170–74
  aggregate approach, 154
  allocation of distributions, 181–86
  assets, 168
  at risk rule, 173
  balance sheet, 168
  classification of partnerships, 150–54
  current distribution, 178
  deductions, 171–72
  distributive share, 155
  equity, 168
  ethical concerns, 186
  exclusion for partnership accounting rules, 169–70
  Form 1065, 164–69
  Form 1065 (Schedule K), 167
  Form 1065 (Schedules L, M-1, M-2), 168
  Form 1065-B, Schedule K-1, 155, 156–61
  general partnerships, 150–51
  hot assets, 181
  inside basis, 155
  investing partnership, 169–70
  IRC SEC. 1231, property used in the trade or business and involuntary conversions, 174–77
  liabilities, 168
  limited liability company (LLC), 151, 154, 186
  limited partnerships, 150–51
  liquidating distribution, 180–81
  net passive income, 165
  net precontribution gain, 179
  operating agreement partnership, 169
  ordering rules, 172
  outside basis, 155, 171, 172
  partnership distributions, 178–86
  partnership income or loss, 174–78
  passive loss limitation, 173
  Publication 538 (accounting rules for partnerships), 174
  Publication 946 (depreciation methods), 178
  publicly traded partnership, 164
  Rev. Proc. 93-27, 161–63
  Rev. Rul. 88-76 (partnership classification), 151–54
  Rev. Rul. 94-4, 172–73
  significant participation passive activities, 165

Subchapter K, 154
    substantial economic effect, 163
    tax accounting for, 169–74
    termination of a partnership, 186
    unrealized receivables, 179
Passive investments, 45
Passive loss limitation, 173
Pelayo-Zabalza v. Commissioner of Internal Revenue, 35–37
Pension and profit sharing plans, 117
Pension income exclusion, 47–49
Pension plans, 227
Pepper v. Commissioner, 133
Personal exemptions, 37
Personal expenses versus business expenses, 148
Personal holding companies, 201
Personal property taxes, 67
Personal representative of decedent's estate, 253, 319
Personal services corporation, 223
Petition for certiorari, 19
Petty v. Commissioner of Internal Revenue, 122–26
Pierce v. Commissioner, 140
Pittman v. Commissioner of Internal Revenue, 203–8
Pocket part, 7, 8
Points, 70
Poole v. Commissioner, 80–81
Portillo v. Commissioner, 207
Power of appointment, 309
Private ruling letters, 16–17
Profit sharing plans, 227
Progressive income tax rate, 33
Property, 209
Property gifts, 73
Public Laws, 5
Publication 538 (accounting rules for partnerships), 174
Publication 946 (depreciation methods), 178
Publicly traded partnership, 164
Pusateri v. Commissioner of Internal Revenue, 110–12

Q

Qualified disability trust, 344
Qualified small business, 230
Qualified taxpayer, 229
Qualified widow(er) with dependent child category, 35
Qualifying child, 93
Quantify, 38
Quantity discounts, 106
Quie v. U.S., 309

R

Rankin v. Commissioner, 102
Rath v. Commissioner, 77
Real Estate Mortgage Investment Conduit (REMIC), 340
Real estate taxes, 67
Receivables, 112
Redemption, 213–16
Regs. Sec. 1.1362–4, 248
Regulations (Regs), 8–10
REMIC. *See* Real Estate Mortgage Investment Conduit
Rent, 117, 118
Rental income, 49–50, 105
Rents, 99
Reorganizations in corporate income taxation, 216–19
Repairs and maintenance, 122
Retirement plans, 50–52
Returns and allowances, 106–8
Rev. Proc. 93–27, 161–63
Rev. Rul. 85–14, 214–16
Rev. Rul. 88–76 (partnership classification), 151–54
Rev. Rul. 94–4, 172–73
Revenue, 99, 105
Revenue procedures (Rev. Procs.), 12–14
Revenue rulings (Rev. Ruls.), 10–11
Rosenberg v. Commissioner, 240, 242
Royalties, 53
Ruth v. United States, 205

S

St. Charles Investment Co. v. Commissioner, 238–47
St. John v. United States, 162
Salaries, 41–45
Sale of a home, 66
Sale of the business's product, 99
Schaefer v. Commissioner, 240
Schedule C, 96, 97–98, 142–46
Schedules A&B (Form 1040), adjustments to income, 68–69
Scott v. United States of America, 342
Scrap value, 115
Secured debt, 312
Securities Exchange Act of 1934, 225
Security dealers, 249
Security deposits, 49
Self-dealing by shareholders, 250
Self-employed
    health insurance premiums of, 67
    Petty v. Commissioner of Internal Revenue, 122–26

Senate Finance Committee, 4
Separate share rule, 345
Shareholder self-dealing, 250
Shares of stock, 210
Shepherds, 20
Short-term capital gains or losses, 62
Significant participation passive activities, 165
Simon v. Commissioner, 116
Simplified production method, 233
Simplified resale method, 233
Simplified rule in annuities, 50
Single category, 33–34
Sirrine Bldg. No. 1 v. Commissioner, 102
Sixteenth Amendment, United States Constitution, 3
Slip laws, 6
Small corporations, 192
Small tax case procedure, 26
Smith v. Commissioner, 102, 182
Smith v. Commissioner of Internal Revenue, 47–49
Snow v. Commissioner, 133
Social security benefits, 51
Sole proprietor, 96
Sole proprietorship taxation, 96–149
    advertising, 112
    bad debts, 112–14
    car expenses, 114
    commissions and fees, 114
    defined, 96
    depletion, 114
    depreciation, 115
    employee benefit programs, 116
    ethical concerns, 148
    expenses, 109–47
    expenses for business use of your home (Form 8829), 118, 119
    income, 99–109
    insurance, 117
    interest, 117
    legal and professional services, 117
    office expenses, 117
    other expenses, 142
    pension and profit sharing plans, 117
    rent, 117, 118
    repairs and maintenance, 122
    Schedule C, 96, 97–98, 142–46
    supplies, 126
    tax advantages in, 99
    taxes and licenses, 126

Index **369**

taxpayer identification number, 96
travel, meals, and entertainment, 126–27
utilities, 127
wages, 127
Sources of individual income, 38–54
  accident and health insurance benefits, 53
  alimony or maintenance payments, 52
  athletic facilities, 43
  barter exchanges, 43, 53
  basis in the stock, 46
  cancelled debts, 53
  court awards, 52
  de minimus rule, 38, 42
  deductions, 38
  fringe benefits, 41
  gifts, 53
  gross income, 38
  income not subject to federal income taxation, 53–54
  interest and dividends, 45–49
  life insurance policy proceeds, 53
  no-additional-cost services, 42
  nondiscriminatory treatment, 42
  passive investments, 45
  qualified employee discounts, 42
  qualified moving expenses, 43
  qualified transportation, 42
  quantify, 38
  rental income, 49–50
  retirement plans, 50–52
  royalties, 53
  taxable income, 38
  wages and salaries, 41–45
  working conditions fringe benefit, 42
  See also Individual income taxation
Sources of tax law, 1–29
  administrative action, 8–17
  judicial decisions, 17–20
  statutes, 6–8
  See also Tax law
Special trial judge, 26
Spin-offs, 218
Split-ups, 218
Sponsors of proposed legislation, 4
Standard deduction, 66
Standard Federal Tax Reporter, 20
Starker v. United States, 60
State estate tax returns, 302
State income taxation, 3, 33, 67

Statutes as sources of tax law, 6–8
Step transaction doctrine, 190
Stock shares, 210
Stock splits, 219
Straight line depreciation, 115
Student loan interest, 70
Subchapter C, 190
Subchapter K, 154
Subchapter S corporations, 192, 236–47
Substance test, 190
Substantial economic effect, 163
Supplies, 126
Supreme Court Reports, 19
Supreme Court Reports, Lawyers' Edition, 19
Swain v. United States, 59

T

Target corporation or company, 217
Tax accounting for partnership taxation, 169–74
Tax advantages in sole proprietorship taxation, 99
Tax Court Reports, 18
Tax courts, 17
Tax credits, 315
Tax deficiencies, 17
Tax law
  ethical concerns, 27
  general proceedings, 20–26
  genesis of, 2–5
  See also Sources of tax law
Tax Notes, 20
Tax planning, geographic placement of assets, 3
Tax Reform Act of 1969, 17
Tax Reform Act of 1976, 16, 308
Tax Relief Act of 2001, 322
Tax shelters, 191
  and partnerships, 186–87
Taxable income, 38
Taxes and licenses, 126
Taxes in adjustments to income (Schedules A&B), 67, 70
Tax-free transfers during life, 301
  See also Estate and gift taxation
Taxpayer Bill of Rights Acts of 1988 and 1996, 20
Taxpayer categories, 33–37
Taxpayer identification number, 96
Taxpayer Relief Act of 1997, 318
Termination of a partnership, 186
Terrorist attacks, Tax Relief Act of 2001, 322

Testamentary gifts, 53
Theft losses, 73–74
Thirty-day letters, 21
Tokarski v. Commissioner, 123
Total tax liability, 3
Trade journals, 142
Transportation, 42
Travel expenses, 74
Travel, meals, and entertainment, 126–27
Trust Company of Georgia v. Ross, 333

U

Uncollectibles, 112
Unified Tax Credit, 301, 302
  See also Estate and gift taxation
Union dues, 75
United States Code (USC), 7
United States Code Annotated (USCA), 7
United States Code Congressional and Administrative News (USCCAN), 6
United States Code Service (USCS), 8
United States Code Service (USCS), *Advance Pamphlet,* 6–7
United States Congress
  Internal Revenue Code (IRC) of 1939, 3
  Internal Revenue Code (IRC) of 1986, 4
  power to tax, 3
United States Constitution
  and power to tax, 2
  Sixteenth Amendment, 3
United States Law Weekly, 6
United States Reports, 19
United States Statutes at Large, 7
United States Tax Cases (USTC), 19
United States Tax Court, 17–18
United States Tax Reporter, 20
United States Treasury Department, 5, 8
United States v. American Trucking Associations, Inc., 77
United States v. New York Coffee & Sugar Exchange, 64
Unrealized receivables in partnership taxation, 179
Unsecured debt, 312
USC. *See United States Code*
USCA. *See United States Code Annotated*

USCCAN. *See United States Code Congressional and Administrative News*
USCS. *See United States Code Service*
Useful life, 115
USTC. *See United States Tax Cases*
Utilities, 127

V

Vanicek v. Commissioner, 120
Vimar Seguros Y. Reaseguros, S.A. v. M/V Sky Reefer, 244

W

Wages, 127
Wages and salaries, 41–45
Wallach v. United States, 79
Waring v. Commissioner, 102
Web sites, 353
Weimerskirch v. Commissioner, 207
Welch v. Helvering, 48, 111, 120, 133, 135, 139, 142
Westlaw, 7
Whipple v. Commissioner, 133
Williams v. Commissioner of Internal Revenue, 119
Williams v. United States, 120
Working capital, 106
Working conditions fringe benefit, 42
Wyly v. United States, 79

Y

Young & Rubicam, Inc. v. United States, 140, 141